Second Edition

The Controller's Function

THE WORK OF THE MANAGERIAL ACCOUNTANT

Janice M. Roehl-Anderson
Steven M. Bragg

JOHN WILEY & SONS, INC.

New York • Chichester • Weinheim • Brisbane • Singapore • Toronto

Library of Congress Cataloging-in-Publication Data:

Roehl-Anderson, Janice M.
  The controller's function: the work of the managerial accountant/Janice M. Roehl-Anderson, Steven M. Bragg.—2nd ed.
      p. cm.
    Includes index.
    ISBN 0-471-38307-4 (pbk.)
    1. Managerial accounting. 2. Controllership. 3. Auditing. 4. Budget in business.
  I. Bragg, Steven M. II. Title.
  HF5657.4. R63 2000
  658.15′11—dc21   00-036654

CONTENTS

PREFACE

This revised edition of *The Controller's Function* is a complete operations reference manual for the corporate controller. Within these pages the reader will find a comprehensive discussion of how to manage all major aspects of the controller's job, including strategic and annual planning, financial reporting, and managing all aspects of the accounting department, as well as peripheral issues such as the fast close, electronic data interchange, best practices, software selection and implementation, and financial analysis—and much, much more.

This book was written in response to the growing realization that the controller is no longer being called upon just to process accounting transactions and issue financial statements, which are tasks requiring detailed technical knowledge, but no considerable management or analysis skill. Instead, the modern controller must exhibit additional mastery of a multitude of management skills, so that the accounting department runs in an efficient and effective manner, offers a detailed analysis of financial statement results, along with recommendations for improvements, monitors the activities of other departments, and perhaps even the management of the computer systems in a smaller organization. This book gives considerable attention to the most recent advances in all these new areas of responsibility, so that the controller will be fully capable of installing and using them to improve his or her company's level of competitive advantage. Included in our coverage of these advances are the use of electronic spreadsheets for financial analysis, client-server computing applications, target costing, disaster recovery planning, activity-based costing, outsourcing, and management in an explosive growth environment.

In addition to these more advanced categories, the book also includes such "bread and butter" topics as cash management, internal control systems and fraud prevention, accounts receivable collections, inventory valuation, budgeting, taxes, insurance, and capital budgeting. By combining basic and advanced accounting management topics in one volume, the reader has access to the complete reference for mastering the controller's function.

Englewood, Colorado
July, 2000

Acknowledgments

With the rapidly changing business environment, it is essential that the material contained in this revision be accurate, up-to-date, and relevant. Accordingly, in addition to the chapters written and revised by the co-authors, these contributing authors, listed alphabetically, wrote the chapters indicated:

Alan R. Arnold, Manager
IT Management Consulting Group
Ernst & Young, Irvine, California
   Chapter 25, Systems Performance Management

E. Edward Bassett III, Senior Systems Security Engineer
Denver Technological Laboratories, Denver
   Chapter 23, Information Security Systems

Sandra Borchardt, Senior Manager
Ernst & Young LLP, Boston
   Chapter 26, Software Package Integration

Sarah Moulton-Reger, Principal
IBM Consulting Group, Denver
   Chapter 24, Project Risk Management
   Chapter 29, Change Management

Atanas Povov, Manager
Randall E. Jacops, Partner
Deloitte Consulting, Detroit, Michigan
   Chapter 27, Shared Services Today and Tomorrow

Jan Roehl-Anderson would like to thank God for His unending blessings. Additionally, thanks should be given to Fritz Anderson for his patience and moral support.

A special note of thanks to our editor, Sheck Cho, for not only suggesting the original edition, but for also suggesting a revised and enlarged version.

About the Authors

Janice M. Roehl-Anderson, MBA, is a partner with Deloitte Consulting LLC, with over 17 years of consulting experience. She specializes in information systems security; financial and cost accounting system analysis, design, selection, and implementation; long-range information system planning; and information management review/audits. She has also worked for US West and has successfully completed the CPA exam.

Steven M. Bragg, CPA, CMA, CIA, CDP, CSP, CPM, CPIM, has been the Chief Financial Officer or Controller of four companies, as well as a consulting manager at Ernst & Young. He received a master's degree in finance from Bentley College and an MBA from Babson College. He has also written *Just-in-Time Accounting, Advanced Accounting Systems, Outsourcing, Accounting Best Practices,* and *Managing Explosive Corporate Growth,* and has co-authored *Controllership* and *The Controller's Function.* Mr. Bragg resides in Englewood, Colorado.

1

THE CONTROLLER'S JOB

Today's corporation operates in an increasingly complex environment, where there are far too many activities for a chief executive officer (CEO) to keep track of. To an increasing degree, this monitoring function falls upon the shoulders of the controller, who must keep the CEO apprised of the performance of all departments, product sales, costs, and profits, control issues in a variety of transaction processing systems, and the impact of new government taxes and other regulations on the conduct of the business. Thus, the controller can reasonably be compared to the ship's navigator, who warns the captain of current or foreseeable problems in the shoals of the business environment that lie ahead and on all sides. In this chapter, we explore the main functions of the controller, how they have changed over time, what kind of background a controller should have, and the role of ethics in the conduct of the job.

HISTORY OF THE CONTROLLER'S FUNCTION

The controller was originally nothing more than a bookkeeper. This person's role was to accurately record all transactions passing through the accounting department, which were primarily related to the payment of suppliers, the billing of customers, or the handling of cash. The controller was also required to issue periodic financial statements, which were just that—no supporting footnotes, executive summaries, or other types of analysis were expected or required. The traditional career path leading to this position was through the clerical ranks, so that the person in the controller's job was intimately familiar with how to manage the transaction flow, and could be relied upon to keep the same old systems running forever.

The function changed with the advent of computers, since accounting was one of the first company departments to adopt automation. The controller was now required to have more than a passing knowledge of computer systems, including how to select, install, and operate them. The controller even became the manager of the management information systems (MIS) department for many smaller companies, since the accounting department was the main beneficiary of computers. This was also a distinctly different job requirement, which led to the hiring of more college-level people into the position. By doing so, many companies sidestepped the traditional advancement method that no longer yielded controllers with a die-hard attitude toward maintaining the old accounting systems. Instead, we now saw controllers who were willing to modify their systems to make the best use of the new computer software, which brought about some improvements in departmental efficiency.

In the 1970s and 1980s, CEOs became more concerned with the efficiency of *all* company departments, including the accounting function. Supported by the efforts of many consulting gurus, such as Michael Hammer (author of *Reengineering the Corporation*), increasing pressure came to bear on controllers to find new ways to run their departments in order to wring out all possible inefficiencies. This trend forced out many old-line controllers who were uncomfortable with new systems, but brought in a new breed of heavily educated controllers, many of them with advanced educations and consulting experience, who streamlined many transactional systems and began to reach outside of the accounting department to other areas of the company to provide a profit center and other specialized forms of financial analysis.

In the 1990s, and probably well into the new millennium, the focus has progressed along the same trend line we saw established in the last two decades, which is for the controller to manage the accounting department's costs and efficiencies as tightly as possible, while also using a great deal of process and financial analysis skill to assist all parts of the corporation in many ways. Over the course of one century, the controller's function has risen from one of senior clerk to one of the most advanced, highly educated, and useful positions in the entire corporate structure.

MAIN JOB FUNCTIONS

The controller has a number of distinct job functions. The first four are ones that can be ascribed to any manager in any department. The last two are more specialized, and do not refer to management skill. They are as follows:

- *Planning.* The controller is responsible for determining who does the work, what work is to be done, and the timing of work completion in the accounting department, especially in regard to the timely processing of transactions and the issuance of accurate financial statements. This also extends to the budget, where the controller guides the budgeting process through other departments.
- *Organizing.* The controller is responsible for obtaining and keeping the services of experienced and well-trained accounting personnel; this is by far the

most important organizational task. This also involves obtaining sufficient floor space, office equipment, and computer hardware and software to complete all assigned work.

- *Directing.* The controller is responsible for ensuring that all employees in the department work together in an orderly manner to achieve the controller's plans.
- *Measuring.* The controller is responsible for measuring the performance of all key aspects of the department to ensure that performance matches or exceeds standards, and that errors are caught and corrected.
- *Financial analysis.* The controller is responsible for the review, interpretation, and generation of recommendations related to corporate financial performance. This requires excellent communication skills (both written and oral), so that the controller's information is properly and effectively conveyed to the other members of the management team.
- *Process analysis.* The controller is responsible for periodically reviewing and evaluating the performance of each major process that is involved in the completion of transactions, with the dual (and sometimes conflicting) objectives of maintaining tight financial controls over processes while also running them in a cost-effective and efficient manner.

The successful controller in years past would only be concerned with the first four of the above job functions, but the recent expansion of the controller's job description calls for the addition of the last two items.

JOB DESCRIPTION

The controller has one of the most complex job descriptions of all company managers, because there are so many functional areas for which he or she is responsible. In this section, we list a detailed job description that is sorted by general category in alphabetical order. The controller's responsibilities are as follows:

Auditing

- The scheduling and management of periodic internal audits, as well as the preparation of resulting audit reports and the communication of findings and recommendations to management and the Board of Directors.
- The preparation of work papers for the external auditors, and the rendering of any additional assistance needed by them to complete the annual audit.

Budgeting

- The coordination of the annual budgeting process, including maintenance of the company budget, and the transfer of final budget information into the financial statements.

Cost Accounting

- The coordination of periodic physical inventory counts.
- The periodic analysis and allocation of costs based on activity-based costing pools and allocation methods.
- The continual cost review of products currently under development, using the principles of target costing.
- The periodic compilation and evaluation of inventory costs.

Financial Analysis

- The periodic comparison of actual to budgeted results, and the communication of variances to management, along with recommendations for improvement.
- The continuing review of revenue and expense trends, and the communication of adverse trend results to management, along with recommendations for improvement.
- The periodic compilation of business cycle forecasting statistics, and the communication of this information to management, along with predictions related to the impact on company operations.
- The periodic calculation of a standard set of ratios for corporate financial performance, and the formulation of management recommendations based on the results.

Financial Statements

- The preparation of all periodic financial statements, as well as their accompanying footnotes.
- The preparation of an interpretive analysis of the financial statements.
- The preparation and distribution of recurring and one-time management reports.

Fixed Assets

- The annual audit of fixed assets to ensure that all recorded assets are present.
- The periodic recording of fixed assets in the financial records, and their proper recording under the correct asset categories and depreciation methods.
- The proper analysis of all capital expenditure requests.

Policies and Procedures

- The creation and maintenance of all policies and procedures related to the control of company assets and the proper completion of financial transactions.

- The training of department personnel in the use of accounting policies and procedures.
- The modification of existing policies and procedures to match the requirements of government regulations.

Process Analysis

- The periodic review of all processes involving financial analysis, to see if they can be completed with better controls, lower costs, or greater speed.

Recordkeeping

- The proper indexing, storage, and retrieval of all accounting documents.
- The orderly planning for and scheduling of document destruction, in accordance with the corporate document retention policy.

Tax Preparation

- The timely preparation and filing of tax returns, as well as the supervision of all matters relating to corporate taxation, such as conducting an effective tax management program, and both providing and enforcing policies and procedures related to the compliance of all corporate personnel with applicable government tax laws.

Transaction Processing

- The timely completion of all accounting transactions at the intervals and in the manner specified in the accounting policies and procedures manual.
- The proper completion of all transactions authorized by the Board of Directors or in accordance with the terms of all authorized contracts.
- The proper approval of those transactions requiring them, in accordance with company policy.

The above list may appear overwhelming, but just because the controller is responsible for them all does not mean that this person must actually do each one. Instead, the controller is mostly involved in the six job functions noted in the preceding section that are primarily concerned with managing the work of other people and ensuring that they complete the tasks noted in the bulk of the above job description. In particular, a controller can rely on the services of assistant controllers who are responsible for smaller portions of the accounting department.

JOB QUALIFICATIONS

To be fully qualified to undertake the job description noted in the last section, the controller should have a number of qualifications, which we outline in this section. Though not all controllers will possess these skills, it is most important to have those related to transaction processing and the production of accurate financial statements, for these two areas remain the core of the accounting function. The key job qualifications are as follows:

- *Analysis of information.* The controller must be sufficiently comfortable with financial information to readily understand the meaning of a variety of ratios and trends, and what they portend for a company.
- *Communication ability.* A key component of the controller's function is compiling information and communicating it to management. If the compiling part of the job goes well, but management does not understand its implications, then the controller must improve his or her communication skills in order to better impart financial information to the management team.
- *Company and industry knowledge.* No accounting system is completely "plain vanilla," because the companies and industries in which it operates have a sufficient number of quirks to require some variation from the typical accounting system. Accordingly, the controller must have a good knowledge of both company and industry operations in order to know how they impact the operations of the accounting department.
- *Management skill.* The controller will presumably have a staff, and if so will have considerable control over the productivity of that group. Accordingly, the controller must have an excellent knowledge of the planning, organizational, directing, and measurement functions needed to manage the accounting department.
- *Provision of timely and cost-effective services.* The controller must run the accounting department as though it were a profit center, so that the most efficient methods are used to complete each task, and the attention of the department is focused squarely on the most urgent tasks.
- *Technical knowledge.* To create an accurate financial statement, especially one for a publicly held company, requires a considerable knowledge of accounting rules and regulations. Accordingly, a controller should be thoroughly versed in all Generally Accepted Accounting Principles (GAAP).

ORGANIZATIONAL STRUCTURE OF THE ACCOUNTING DEPARTMENT

The controller does not operate alone, having to complete all the tasks outlined through the last few sections. On the contrary, there may be quite a large accounting staff that completes the bulk of the work. In this section, we review the structure of the typical accounting department, and the tasks completed by each part of it.

The controller is usually helped by one or more assistant controllers who are assigned different sets of tasks. For example, one may be in charge of the more technically difficult general ledger, tax reporting, financial analysis, cost accounting, and financial reporting tasks, while another covers the major transactions, which are accounts payable, accounts receivable, payroll, and cash application. For smaller organizations, there may also be managers for the human resources and MIS functions who are at the assistant controller level, and who also report to the controller. Below these managers there are a number of sub-categories, staffed either by clerks or degreed accountants, who are responsible for specific tasks. These sub-categories are as follows:

- *Cost accounting.* This position is filled by a degreed accountant who conducts job or process costing and verifies the inventory valuation.
- *Financial analysis.* This position is filled by a degreed accountant who compiles both standard and special-request analysis reports.
- *Financial reporting.* This position is filled by either a degreed accountant or a senior-level bookkeeper who prepares the financial statements and accompanying footnotes, as well as other periodic reports for public consumption if the company is publicly held.
- *General ledger accounting.* Frequently combined with the financial reporting function, this is staffed by similar personnel, and is involved with the review and recording of journal entries and summary entries for subsidiary journals.
- *Payroll processing.* This position is filled by clerks who calculate pay levels and hours worked, and generate payments to employees.
- *Tax form preparation and filing.* This position is filled by a degreed accountant, frequently with tax experience in a public accounting background, who completes and files all government tax forms.
- *Transaction processing.* This position is filled by clerks (usually comprising the bulk of all department headcount) who process all accounts payable, accounts receivable, and cash application transactions in accordance with rigidly defined procedures.

In a smaller company, the controller may also inherit all the finance and office management functions, which means that some of the staff will be responsible for analyzing and monitoring customer credit, investing funds, supervising risk management, monitoring the phone system, and arranging for the repair of office equipment. Conversely, a larger company will not only separate these added functions, but may also move the financial analysis function under the control of the chief financial officer. Thus, the exact layout of the accounting department will depend to a large extent on the size of the company and the presence of other managers.

There can be several levels of controller within a company. The corporate controller is located at the corporate headquarters, while each division may have its own controller. There will likely be plant controllers at each location, as well.

In most organizations, the controller reports directly to the most senior on-site executive. For example, the plant controller reports to the plant manager, the division controller reports to the division manager, and the corporate controller reports to the chief financial officer or president. All three levels of controllership noted here have many of the same functional responsibilities that the corporate controller has on a company-wide basis.

The corporate controller must decide if accounting operations through all company locations are to be centralized, decentralized, or occupy a position somewhere in between. Many controllers favor centralization, because they can more tightly manage the function and have fewer worries about accounting control issues arising at some far-off company location. However, not all aspects of the accounting function are so amenable to centralization. Here are some of the reasons why decentralization should at least be considered as an option:

- The local organization and retention of accounting information avoids some excuses for inactivity or poor performance because "the report was late" or "the report was wrong."
- The information sent to a central location is frequently duplicated at the local site, so that the duplication can be avoided by processing it locally.
- The information can be more rapidly processed locally because there is less transit time involved. However, in this day of digital data transmission, most information can be sent to a central location with hardly any delay.
- The widespread distribution of accounting responsibility in the field allows a company to more quickly train promising accounting managers and evaluate them for promotion.
- The presence of a local accountant can assist in the rapid investigation and resolution of problems that would be impossible from a central location.

Offsetting these arguments in favor of decentralization are a number of factors in favor of centralization. The primary reasoning behind the bulk of the pro-centralization approach is that the efficient use of employees to complete a high volume of transactions will keep accounting costs down to a bare minimum. The reasons are as follows:

- The accounting staff can be shifted between tasks to meet peak workloads.
- The use of centralized transaction processing may have a sufficient amount of volume to justify the use of expensive computer hardware and software that will considerably improve efficiency, though it would be cost-prohibitive for a smaller division to use.
- The use of a centralized staff may allow for the added expense of a tailored training program for accountants that will increase their efficiency, but which would be too expensive to create for the smaller numbers of accountants at a single division location.

- The use of a centralized operation may allow for the hiring of more experienced (and expensive) accounting personnel who can do a better job of managing the department.

Thus, the controller has countervailing arguments for using either approach to organizing the department. If a company has a highly diversified group of divisions, then their transactions, chart of accounts, and processes may differ so wildly from each other that it makes no sense to centralize the accounting department. However, a company with "cookie cutter" divisions that are essentially identical in their operating characteristics may be ideal for accounting centralization. In many cases, though, the correct method is to opt for a slightly more expensive middle ground, using a centralized transaction processing organization, but also paying for a small local staff that can process exception transactions, investigate variance problems on behalf of the central organization, and also be a training ground for junior accounting managers from the central accounting office.

ETHICS

The controller is in the uniquely difficult position of having a significant impact on the level of ethics practiced throughout a company. If the controller tends to wink at monetary indiscretions or alter the timing or amount of accruals or other transactions in order to influence reported financial results, then this attitude will gradually percolate down through the organization, until management suddenly finds that the entire company is rife with ethical problems of all kinds. The alternative approach is for the controller to adopt a methodical and rigorous approach to ethical problems, as is outlined in this section.

The first step by the controller is to convince the management team, and the president in particular, that the company must adopt a written ethical standard and force the rest of the organization to adhere to it through regular audits. Once the code of ethics and all related standards of conduct are complete, the management team as a whole must present them to employees, and continue to reiterate, both by example and communication, that these principles are a significant foundation underlying all company operations.

Using these preliminary guidelines, the controller can then expand the concept and promulgate a series of additional guidelines in specific areas related to accounting. Some of them are as follows:

- Attaining annual business plan objectives
- Compliance with SEC and other securities laws and regulations
- Employee discrimination
- Gifts and payments of money for no return consideration
- Leave for military or other federal service

- Meals and entertainment expense reporting
- Period-end accounting adjustments
- Political contributions
- Preservation of assets
- Restrictive trade practices
- Use of the company car
- Workplace safety

Only by adhering closely to these ethical guidelines, and clearly communicating to the accounting staff that they are the corporate law, will the controller alter the mindset of the company as a whole (and the accounting department in particular) in the direction of using the highest possible ethical standards.

2

INTERNAL CONTROL

Perhaps the most important function of the controller is to create and maintain the corporate financial control system. This involves documenting the existing control structure, eliminating redundant controls, and adding new controls to cover potential risks arising out of new business situations. In order to properly assess risks, the controller must have a firm grasp of the general types of fraud and how to prevent them. This knowledge should extend to legally required controls over assets, such as those listed in Foreign Corrupt Practices Act. This chapter provides an overview of all these topics.

MANAGEMENT CONCERN

Business managers have an interest in earning a profit. By implication, therefore, the business person has a corollary interest in the practices or procedures, including controls, used to teach the goal of the enterprise.

The focus of attention on business policies and procedures has been heightened by the publicity given white-collar crime, such as issuance of fraudulent financial statements and acts of bribery and kickbacks. All of these matters are addressed in this chapter primarily as they relate to the work of corporate financial officers, especially the controller.

BASIC ELEMENTS

Many policies and procedures have been established to achieve the specific objectives of an organization. This set of procedures is called the internal control structure. Technically, appropriate control procedures apply to every function, to every activity of the enterprise. The emphasis in this chapter is on those controls relevant to a proper recording of transactions (income, expenses, assets, liabilities, and net worth), and the proper reporting thereof, together with safeguarding the assets of the business. The applicable control objectives, discussed later in this chapter, are a basic concern of the controller.

The controller should be aware of the various types of controls that must be interlinked to create a control system that adequately safeguards the company assets: accounting controls, administrative controls, and primary operational controls.

Accounting controls are defined as the plan of organization and all methods and procedures that are concerned with the safeguarding of assets and the reliability of the financial records. They generally include such controls as the systems of authorization and approval; separation of duties concerned with record-keeping and accounting reports from those concerned with operations or asset custody; physical controls over assets; and internal auditing. It was these controls with which historically the independent accountant was primarily concerned.

Administrative controls comprise the plan of organization and all methods and procedures that relate to operational efficiency and adherence to managerial policies, and that usually are only indirectly concerned with the financial records. Included would be such controls as statistical analyses, time and motion studies, performance reports, employee training programs, and quality control.

Primary operational control concerns the establishment of policy and basic guidelines by which an enterprise will be directed as a means of achieving the business objectives.

Given the recent broadening of the traditional definition of controls; and the various statements on the subject, it facilitates discussion if the internal control structure of an entity is divided in four parts:

- Control environment
- External factors
- Accounting systems
- Control procedures

Control Environment

A company's control environment is the corporate atmosphere in which the accounting (and other) controls exist and in which the financial statements are prepared. It reflects management's commitment to an effective system of internal control. The control segment has recently been given increased importance in general analysis of controls. It represents the collective effort of many factors, including:

- *Management philosophy and operating style*—This factor concerns "the tone at the top" and includes a broad range of topics that influence the control environment, including:

— Emphasis on meeting profit goals, targets, or budgets.

— Basic attitude about risk taking.

— Attitude about the need for controls.

— Attitude about the importance and sanctity of the financial statements, both internal and published.

- *Organization structure*—How is the organizing, planning, directing, and controlling of operations handled? On a decentralized basis? Does strong central control exist? Does one or do a few individuals dominate the company?

- *Functioning of the board of directors and the board committees*—Does the board exert influence or largely follow the dictates of the CEO? Does it examine or discuss important policies and procedures? Does an audit committee composed of outside directors exist? Does it oversee accounting policies and procedures, including controls? Does it meet independently with the outside auditors, and with internal auditors?

- *Methods of assigning authority and responsibility*—Are policy matters such as ethical standards, conflicts of interest, and competitive response discussed?

- *Management control methods*—This category involves the heart of operational control—how management delegates authority to others and effectively supervises all company activities—and includes:

— The planning system, both short and long term.

— The measurement system, comparing actual with planned performance, and communication of the results to appropriate individuals.

— The methods of taking timely and corrective action to bring actual performance at least to budgeted levels.

— The methods of developing procedures, modifying systems, and monitoring systems and procedures.

- *The existence and effectiveness of an internal audit function*—Included in the audit function are the proper authority, organization structure and status, properly qualified personnel, and adequate resources.

- *Personnel policies and procedures*—This category includes policies and procedures for hiring, training, evaluating, promoting, and compensating personnel so that a proper and adequate corps of employees is available and permitted to carry out their assigned responsibilities.

- *Influence of external factors*—While external influences are largely outside the control of an organization, how management monitors and deals with outside influences such as legislative and regulatory bodies, international events, economic trends, and how it complies with the requirements, is germane to accomplishing the company's objectives.

How management copes with these factors reveals the overall attitude of the board of directors and top management concerning ethics and the significance of proper controls. Anyone searching for fraud could use the above control elements to narrow the search area; for example, if a department had a poor attitude toward controls, then an auditor might consider that department to be a high risk area.

Controllers, as chief accounting officers, should understand how these various factors actually operate in their areas of responsibility; that is to say, it is one thing to have written policies and procedures, but another to know that they are followed. Management may give lip service to certain policies, but act in ways that condone departures from the standard. In the control environment the controller's attention should be on the same matters that would warrant examination by an independent auditor.

As the internal control structure becomes more widely discussed among management members, many operating managers regard the matter as primarily a financial or accounting concern and not theirs. Since many evaluations have been made by either internal auditors or independent accountants, managers sense no direct tie-in to corporate governance and the achievement of the corporate objectives, such as profitability, growth, and adherence to ethical standards. What is needed, and what is occurring in many companies, is the education of operating management about their role in the control system.

One company, in an effort to educate all department managers, held a series of one-day seminars for the professional and management staff of the organization. In these meetings, the business objectives for each department were stated by the departmental vice president and supplemented by group discussion. The "control mechanisms," or actions required to accomplish each department's objectives, were reviewed for their effectiveness. The relationship of the elements of internal control to the attainment of departmental objectives was appraised.

While the elements may differ by organization, these are the control segments covered by the example company above as meaningful to its operating management:[1]

- Organization controls: Personnel standards, a plan of organization, and the corporate culture
- System development and change controls
- Authorization and reporting controls; planning and budgeting; accountability
- Accounting system controls
- Safeguarding controls: Protection of assets and avoidance of unintentional risks
- Management supervisory controls: Supervision and management information
- Documentation controls: Formal policies and procedures; systems documentation

The objective of the approach was to involve all of management in the educational process and make use of the control system of the company to attain departmental objectives.

External Factors

Another aspect of the control environment now receiving greater recognition is the influence of external factors. These outside influences, as previously stated, are largely beyond the control of a business; but how management deals with them may be relevant to how it attains its objectives. Until recently, external factors received scant attention in the evaluation of control systems. The Auditing Standards Board (ASB), in an internal control risk assessment pronouncement, stated that there are various "external influences that affect an entity's operations and practices, such as examinations by bank regulatory agencies."[2]

When external factors are mentioned, often it is legislatures and regulatory bodies and their laws or pronouncements that first come to mind. In a report prepared for the Treadway Commission relating to fraudulent financial reporting, its authors stated that "The scope of internal auditing responsibilities for examining and evaluating control should extend to every point affected by the organization—even to certain external entities."[3]

The report grouped the external entities into these three general classes: regulators, customers, and suppliers. Our concern here is with significant suppliers and customers.

Consider, first, the recent rise in just-in-time (JIT) manufacturing. A successful JIT system depends on a close buyer-vendor relationship, with a limited number of dependable suppliers who will deliver materials on time. Moreover, a supplier will deliver in smaller lot sizes, using statistical quality control to maintain a high quality, defect-free product, and thus reduce or avoid the cost of inspecting the incoming units. In effect, the input inspection is transferred to the supplier organization, and an important control point is moved to an external location. When such a transfer happens, the internal auditors of the manufacturer, in conjunction with the purchasing and manufacturing staff, must at least consider the need to review the adequacy and effectiveness of the external inspection system.

Similarly, with the expansion of electronic data interchange (EDI) between large suppliers, as well as between suppliers and large customers, the concept of external control becomes relevant. If, for example, certain predetermined conditions automatically trigger large buy or sell orders, some of the traditional control mechanisms disappear, and new concerns must be addressed. Thus, between a manufacturer and a large retailer, who has the authority to structure a transaction, place it in the electronic envelope, send it, and receive the message? Under such circumstances, transaction control becomes the responsibility of the seller–buyer partnership and not that of a single party.

There are now many circumstances where new technologies are making it desirable to examine external control points. Sometimes this examination may be part of a JIT agreement. In other instances, no legal agreement may exist, but the buying and selling parties establish close working relationships that facilitate internal auditor access to selected external control points.

The Accounting System

Another element of the internal control structure is the accounting system. The proper direction of the accounting system is one of the principal responsibilities of the controller. An effective accounting system encompasses those principles, methods, and procedures, as well as those records, that will:

- Identify properly and record all valid transactions.
- Describe the transactions on a timely basis and in sufficient detail to permit proper classification of transactions for financial reporting.
- Determine the time period in which the transactions occurred so as to permit recording in the proper accounting period.
- Measure the value of the transaction in a manner that permits recording of the proper monetary value in the financial statements.
- Permit proper presentation of the transactions and related required disclosures in the financial statements.

The Control Procedures

Control procedures are also a part of the internal control structure. In most companies, the executive responsible for adequate control procedures is the controller. Accordingly, the procedural elements generally regarded as essential to a proper control system are discussed in some detail later in this chapter. Suffice it to state here that the procedures include adequate segregation of duties, adequate records, and proper procedures for authorization of transactions.

Appraising the Control System

With the apparent rise in inappropriate activity by some businesspersons, such as issuance of fraudulent financial statements, kickbacks, and bribery, the adequacy of the control systems takes on increased importance. Yet such a determination usually cannot be done quickly or easily. An analytical and detailed approach probably is desirable. Some representative actions in the area of procedure, some essential elements in the control system, and a suggested assignment of responsibility for different phases of control are discussed in the next few sections.

There are two fundamental steps to be taken by management in evaluating internal controls. First, management must identify the principal activities, risks, and exposures in each operating component of the business and define the control objectives related to those activities. Second, they must describe, perhaps by flowcharts, and understand the various systems used to process transactions, safeguard assets, and prepare the financial reports. This information is then used to evaluate the system, giving particular attention to possible significant weaknesses, in order to ascertain that the system provides reasonable assurance that the control objective can be achieved.

Identifying the Activities, Risks, and Control Objectives

One way to identify a company's principal activities and control objectives is to separate the typical company into four basic operating components and define the control objectives of the various activities in each component. Suggested components are sales, production or service, finance, and administration. Examples of control objectives are:

- *Sales control objectives:* That correct billings are produced for shipped products or services rendered, customer credit is checked prior to approving orders, and customer returns are approved.
- *Production or service control objectives:* That minimal scrap occurs as products are created, the correct quantities of products are produced, and pilferage is kept to a minimum.
- *Finance control objectives:* That cash receipts are deposited on the day of receipt, petty cash is only issued with proper authorization, and bad debts are properly authorized before being removed from the receivables ledger.
- *Administration control objectives:* That office equipment is only purchased with the proper authorization, vacations are only taken with previous authorization, and hiring only occurs after proper authorization.

Another approach is to identify types of transactions common to most businesses. Each transaction flow is a grouping of related events, and the focus is on whether appropriate control exists over each step in the transaction through the processing system. Some suggested transaction cycles are the revenue cycle, production cycle, payments cycle, and time cycle (economic events caused by time, such as an interest accrual). In any event, whatever approach is used results in the identification of major functions and the control objectives for each.

In reviewing operations, transactions, or cycles, the possibility of loss or risk (or error in the financial statements) should be considered in an effort to minimize theft, for example, and to provide early warning of other potential loss, including:

- Loss or destruction of assets.
- Fraud or embezzlement.
- Statutory sanctions or violations.
- Excessive costs or insufficient revenues.
- Unacceptable accounting.

- Erroneous recording.
- Expropriation.

Understanding Control Systems

Accounting transactions should be clearly flow charted, so that they can be studied for possible weaknesses by the controller's staff. This review involves a businessperson's perspective of what should be done, a consideration of things that can go wrong, and a recognition of the accounts that would be affected. Any issues concerning the control of those transactions should be documented.

When reviewing the flowcharts for control weaknesses, the following five general control objectives should be kept in mind:

1. *Authorization.* Was the transaction authorized by management? This could be evidenced in a general way by establishing related policies, contract authorization limits, investment limits, standard price lists, and so on. Or, in a given situation, a specific authorization may be needed.
2. *Recording.* Transactions should be recorded in the proper account, at the proper time (proper cutoff), with the proper description. No fictitious transactions should be recorded, and erroneous material or incomplete descriptions should be avoided.
3. *Safeguarding.* Physical assets should not be under the physical custody of those responsible for related record-keeping functions. Access to the assets should be restricted to certain designated individuals.
4. *Reconciliation.* Periodic reconciliations of physical assets to records, or control accounts, should be made. Some examples are bank reconciliations, securities inventories and physical inventories of raw material, and work in process and finished goods to control accounts.
5. *Valuation.* Provision should be made for assurances that the assets are properly valued in accordance with generally accepted accounting principles—and that the adjustments are made.

ELEMENTS OF INTERNAL ACCOUNTING CONTROL

There are seven basic elements that are necessary to meet the broad objectives of good internal accounting control—objectives that include safeguarding the assets against loss arising from intentional (fraud) or unintentional errors and producing reliable financial records for internal use and for external reporting purposes. These elements are:

1. *Competent and trustworthy personnel, with clearly defined lines of authority and responsibility.* People are the most important ingredient in a control sys-

tem. If employees are competent and trustworthy, then reliable financial statements can result even though other control elements are missing. Incompetent and dishonest personnel, even given a theoretically good system of controls, will produce worthless statements. Thus, a proper evaluation of employees is paramount.

2. *Adequate separation of duties.* To prevent intentional or unintentional errors, several separations are desirable:

   a. *Separation of operating responsibility from financial record-keeping.* In those instances where an operating department maintains its own records and prepares its own financial reports, there is a temptation to biased data to report improved performance. Grouping of the financial records under a controller is desirable.

   b. *Separation of custody of the assets.* Separation of accounting from custody is done to protect the company against defalcation. Thus the separation of custody of cash from maintenance of the accounts receivable is desirable to reduce the possibility of converting cash to personal use and adjusting the customer account by a fictitious credit.

   c. *Separation of the authorization of transactions from the custody of any related assets.* For example, the person authorizing the payment of an invoice should not sign the check that pays the bill.

   d. *Separation of duties within the accounting function.* Those maintaining the general ledger should be separated from those handling the subsidiary ledger, or those handling cash journals should be separated from those handling sales journals.

3. *Proper procedures for authorization of transactions.* Authorizations may be general or specific, depending on management desires. Management may give general approval for sales to customers, given a certain credit approval. Or management may desire to approve each contract above a given amount, say $10 million.

4. *Adequate records and documents.* The documents must provide reasonable assurance that the transaction is properly recorded and that the asset is controlled. Thus purchase orders, receiving reports, and vendor invoices should exist.

5. *Proper physical control over both assets and records.* Properly controlled warehouses, safety deposit vaults, or fireproof safes are examples of physical control. Proper safeguard of records against destruction or other loss is necessary.

6. *Proper procedures for adequate record keeping.* Procedures to assure the proper recording of all transactions—such as procedure manuals—may be desirable.

7. *A staff that can provide independent verifications.* The existence of an internal audit staff, or other means of checking, may be helpful.

LEVELS OF CONTROLS

In reviewing internal controls, the greatest amount of time is usually spent in analyzing and evaluating the very detailed controls that exist. And perhaps this is the way it should be. However, given the responsibilities of the board of directors and top management, the ultimate purpose of the system is to aid in meeting the business goals and objectives. Hence the control system to be reviewed should include all levels of planning and related control. All these levels can be included in the following three groups:

1. *Strategic—Board of directors and top management, who plan and control:*
   - Organizational structure
   - Corporate goals and objectives
   - Long-range planning procedures
   - Marketing policy decision making
   - Management policy decision making
   - Financial policy decision making
2. *Tactical—Board of directors and senior management, who plan and control:*
   - Annual profit plans
   - Executive–personnel policies (inventories, replacement)
   - Capital expenditures
   - Annual research and development plan
3. *Operational, where planning and control involves:*
   - Credit approval practices
   - Treatment of uncollectible accounts
   - Billing procedure
   - Purchasing procedure
   - Salary and wage authorization
   - Pension plan performance

Consideration has to be given to which of the controls in a company should be handled at each level and, further, which should require corporate-level (as opposed to divisional) review and approval.

RESPONSIBILITY FOR PROPER INTERNAL CONTROLS

Who should be responsible for the existence of proper controls? Several groups will likely have specific responsibilities. Some suggested areas of responsibility for several management levels, and for independent public accountants, are outlined below.

- *Role of the board of directors.* The board of directors is responsible for general, non-detailed oversight and the monitoring of management. The board of directors must do the following:
  — Understand in a general way how the financial–accounting recording system works.
  — Satisfy itself, perhaps through the audit committee, that an adequate system of internal control exists.
  — Ascertain that the system is effective and sufficient to the proper safeguarding of assets, issuance of correct final reports, and compliance with federal or state regulation.
  — Determine that a carefully prepared code of ethics exists to govern the conduct of the corporate employees.
  — Assume ultimate responsibility for monitoring the compliance of management and other employees with the rules of corporate governance and for taking appropriate action for violations.
- *Role of senior corporate management.* Although the board of directors may have an oversight responsibility, it is the management of the company that must assume primary responsibility for the proper company environment and for effective systems for internal control, correct financial statements, and safeguarding of assets. It is this management group that is responsible for detailed implementation and enforcement of the systems. Senior corporate management must do the following:
  — Identify the risks inherent in the business venture and the potential for errors and irregularities.
  — Provide the proper environment, including policies, directives, and other communications, to enforce the necessary controls.
  — Direct those responsible for business decisions and those who technically must be involved to create and maintain a documented internal control system, and employ appropriate legal review of the system.
  — Assume responsibility to shareholders for the financial statements.
- *Role of financial management.* The senior financial managers have the same responsibilities for internal controls that the other senior and operating managers have. However, the financial officers, and especially the controller, have a greater responsibility for effective internal accounting controls, given their presumed professionalism and experience in the controls area. It is in the accounting area that the bulk of the checks and balances will come to bear.

  Specifically, with regard to internal accounting controls, the controller should have these obligations:
  — Know the technical requirements of a sound and adequate internal accounting control system. Install and maintain an effective system.
  — Ascertain that the system exists and operates.
  — Enforce conformance with policies and procedures.

— Assume responsibility to the CEO and senior financial management for reliability of the financial statements.

- *Role of the internal auditor.* The existence of a qualified internal audit department, certainly in a medium to large company and often in smaller firms, is an important element of the system of internal control. The internal auditor is the eyes and ears of management for ascertaining the status of the internal control system, especially the internal accounting controls. The chief internal auditor must, by his review, assure senior management (1) that an adequate system exists in each profit center; (2) that the systems are effective for the purposes intended; and (3) that any deficiencies are brought to the attention of appropriate parties for corrective actions.

- *Role of the independent auditor.* The independent auditor is not a part of the company's internal accounting control system. However, this person must evaluate the system to ascertain its reliability as a basis for rendering an opinion on the financial statements. This auditor is in a position to give the board of directors an independent and objective opinion concerning the adequacy of the internal accounting controls, taking into account the firm's experience and the systems of other companies.

Accordingly, the duties of the independent auditor may be summarized as follows:

1. Review the system of internal control to determine the degree of reliability of audit tests to be performed on financial statements, and to communicate material findings to the appropriate level of management—audit committee, senior management, and financial management.
2. Provide instructional manuals on methods and techniques for reviewing, testing, and evaluating internal controls.
3. Conduct training programs for company personnel selected to review and modify internal controls.

Aside from these responsibilities, the independent auditor, given present SEC proclivities, may be required to concur in the management representations about the adequacy of the internal accounting controls.

FRAUD

The word "fraud" is used synonymously with "defalcation," "embezzlement," and "swindle." For the purposes of this discussion, fraud is an *intentional financial misstatement or the misappropriation of funds.* Fraud is not an unintentional mistake, such as an incorrect accounting estimate, the application of a cost to an incorrect account, or a lost inventory tag during a physical count.

Common Types

Fraud is a complex subject. Different types of individuals and different activities may be involved. Some of the types of fraud are management fraud, employee fraud, computer fraud, and financial reporting fraud. The controller may be curious about commonly occurring kinds of fraud. A few of the more common kinds are listed below. This list should not be considered complete, because the types of fraud are only limited by the imagination of the perpetrator. (For an ongoing listing of fraud cases, refer to the "Round Table" department of the *Internal Auditor,* the journal of the Institute of Internal Auditors.)

- *Generate bills from nonexistent companies.* Employees can bill the company for services from a nonexistent company. This is easy if the accounts payable staff does not review services for completion or materials for receipt. The fraud is detected by auditing billing approvals. Also, the auditor can review the numerical sequence of invoices received from the supplier to see if most of the supplier's invoices are going to the company.
- *Use telephones.* Employees can use companies phone lines for personal calls. The fraud is detected by reviewing the phone bills for numbers called.
- *Pay personal bills.* Employees can have the company pay their own bills for them, or have the company pay for items that were ordered for the employees through the company. The fraud is detected by auditing bills received, and can only be prevented by rigorous approvals of all expenses.
- *Alter approved expense amounts.* Employees can alter expense reports after supervisors have approved the reports. The fraud is difficult to detect, but auditors may be able to find altered or erased numbers on those reports. This type of fraud can be prevented by routing expense reports directly to the accounts payable department after the supervisors approve them, so that the employees who originally submitted the reports do not have further access to the documents.
- *Rig bids between purchasers and suppliers.* Buyers can be influenced to accept high bids in exchange for kickbacks from suppliers. The fraud is detected by comparing winning bid amounts to market rates, and by reviewing the number of bids rejected due to spurious causes. For example, cheaper bids can be thrown out by marking the bid receipt date as being later than the posted due date (and can be audited by comparing the bidder sign-in date in the visitor log to the date posted on the bid by the purchasing department).
- *Submit multiple expense receipts.* Employees can submit credit card receipts in one month for reimbursement and then submit the actual receipt for reimbursement in a different month. The fraud is detected by comparing expense reports that were submitted over a period of several months.
- *Cancel reimbursed education.* Employees can cancel classes that have been paid for by the company and pocket the proceeds (or have the classes paid for by a second party, such as the Veteran's Administration, and keep the over-

payment). The fraud is detected by getting permission to review the college's financial records for each employee. The fraud can still occur if the company only pays on proof of completion of a class, because a second party can still pay for the class.

- *Sell company assets.* Employees can sell company assets right off the company premises and have the check made out and delivered to them. The fraud is detected by frequent reviews of fixed assets records to actual assets. Prevention can be difficult if a high-level person is the perpetrator.

While the controller has an interest in preventing any type of fraud, this chapter discusses the two kinds with which he or she should be especially concerned: management fraud and financial reporting fraud. As for the other common types, the reader is referred to the many books and articles on the subject, some of which are listed in the "Selected References" section.

Some Causes

If a controller is aware of the circumstances that encourage fraud, he may be more sensitive to signs that it has occurred. In most circumstances, and certainly when collusion is involved, there is no way to guarantee the absence of fraud. But there is reason to conclude that fraud results from a combination of pressures on the individual officer or employee and the circumstances that allow the act to occur. The conditions that lay the foundations for fraud include:

- *Poor internal controls or a poor internal control environment.*
  - Management does not punish or prosecute offenders.
  - Management does not set an example of high ethical standards.
  - Management does not stress the need for strong controls.
  - Management has not published rules governing ethical conduct.
  - Highly placed executives are seen as lavish spenders on business trips.
  - The CEO approves heavy business expenditures by his staff despite restrictive policies and procedures.
- *Existence of heavy financial pressures on individuals.*
  - Heavy personal indebtedness.
  - Socially unacceptable behavior (e.g., gambling, use of drugs or alcohol).
  - Extravagant means of living.
  - High inflation rates not accompanied by adequate adjustment in compensation.
- *Other sources of pressure.*
  - Unreasonable profit goals for the company, or for a division or subsidiary.
  - High rate of management personnel turnover.
  - Management operating and financial decisions dominated by a very aggressive individual.

- The company is part of a declining industry.
- *Contributing conditions.*
  - Inadequate hiring practices (e.g., lack of reference checks).
  - Deteriorating living environment.
  - Undesirable personal traits.
  - Unsatisfactory home life.

Note that some of the above signs are difficult to detect.

Management Override

The responsibility for an effective internal control system rests with management. Yet some of the most widely publicized cases of improper activity are those that were carried on by a limited number of business managers themselves. It is these cases that are among the most difficult to detect.

Quite often fraud committed by senior management is more subtle than the "ordinary ways." It involves management override. This condition occurs when executives with sufficient real or apparent authority cause subordinates to improperly conceal or record transactions, or cause documents to be processed outside of the established procedure. These executives are in a position to override the controls. Such actions may result in a material misstatement of financial results or condition, and/or a defrauding of the company. The controller, along with the independent accountants and internal auditors, should be alert to, or assess the risks of, such a possibility. Management override probably would not occur under normal circumstances, but the following conditions might tempt some managers:

- Management compensation is directly and substantially affected by operating results, and those results tend to be erratic.
- The management of the business unit is under extreme pressure to achieve specified earnings.
- The operating unit is in an industry experiencing a large number of business failures.
- The organization has been sold and the management will benefit from the price, which is related to operating results and financial condition.

Some of the areas where management override is more common include:

- *Reserve estimates.* Inventory reserves, reserves for doubtful accounts, tax accruals, litigation reserves, among others, may be understated in order to increase profits.
- *Depreciation allowances.* Depreciation rates on machinery and equipment might be changed.

- *Sales.* Advance sales may be billed, or shipments may be made ahead of schedule.
- *Cost of sales.* Cost of sales may be understated, thus providing higher margins (and possibly later inventory losses).
- *Deferring expenses.* Current expenses may be capitalized on one pretext or another, to be written off over a period of time.

Auditing for Fraud

Auditing for fraud, especially for small-scale fraud, is like looking for the proverbial needle in the haystack. There are several reasons why it is so difficult to find:

- *Too many transactions.* The auditor typically reviews only a small number of transactions. If fraud is only being committed with one transaction out of many, the odds of finding the fraud are slim.
- *Ineffective use of audit time.* Looking for fraud is very time-consuming. There are hundreds, if not thousands, of ways to illegally remove company assets, and tracking down all possibilities will fill the work schedule of any internal audit staff.
- *Audits have time limits.* Like all well-run projects, fraud audits have specific time boundaries; once the completion date is reached, the audit team moves on to another audit. Since fraud audits can take considerable periods of time to uncover issues, there may not be time available to detect a suspected fraud situation.
- *Trend analysis not sufficient.* Smaller cases of fraud will not be highlighted by analyzing expense levels over time, because the small surges in expense levels will not appear significant.
- *Perpetrators know the procedures.* Those who are committing frauds may not only know the procedures being circumvented, but also may be in charge of the procedures. If so, then frauds may be cleverly concealed, since the criminal parties are experts in the control procedures. The auditor, on the other hand, is not primarily trained in fraud detection, but in evaluating overall systems of controls and reporting. Thus, in terms of training or ability, the perpetrator may outclass the auditor.
- *Fraud is hard to recognize.* Fraud is difficult to detect even when you are looking at it. The perpetrator has probably taken a great deal of time to carry out the fraud, and has either eliminated or reduced all traces of the crime. For example, when conducting an audit, how many auditors will follow up on missing documentation? The reason for the missing documentation may be simple misfiling, but it may also be deliberate misplacement to cover a fraud situation.

The above points are not designed to make the auditor despair of ever uncovering a fraud; doing so is difficult, but not impossible. The problem is, what tools can you use to quickly hone in on likely fraud situations? The following suggestions may help.

- *Watch the environment.* As stated several times in this chapter, the environment is a key factor. If the management has a low regard for controls, then the attitude may rub off on their employees. If management uses the company for personal gain, then other employees may feel that it is acceptable for them to do so as well. Of course, the environment may be worse in one area; if so, then the auditor's fraud search should narrow to that area.
- *Watch the controls.* If control over an area is concentrated in one person's job, then the opportunity for fraud has been presented to that employee. The auditor should not only review such situations, but also recommend splitting responsibilities in order to remove any temptation from the employee.
- *Watch employee lifestyles.* Some perpetrators flaunt their wealth and bring their gains back to the workplace in the form of fancy automobiles or new clothes. We are not suggesting that the auditor review the parking lot each day, but an inquiring person might want to know why an accounting clerk is driving an expensive sports car.
- *Be available.* Fraud can be surprisingly well-known among employees. For the auditor to be told about such situations by employees, availability is crucial. Consequently, the successful fraud auditor is the one who talks to auditees frequently, is available at audit sites, and is known for protecting sources.

FRAUDULENT FINANCIAL REPORTING

Another area of fraud that is of particular interest for the controller is that involving fraudulent financial reporting. This has been the case for many years; the possibility of fraudulent financial reporting was a consideration in the passage of such legislation as The Securities Act of 1933, The Securities and Exchange Act of 1934, and The Foreign Corrupt Practices Act of 1977.

In October 1985 the National Commission on Fraudulent Financial Reporting (NCFFR), also known as the Treadway Commission, was formed as a private sector initiative. It focuses on publicly held companies, and was directed to examine three areas:

1. The extent to which fraudulent financial reporting undermines the integrity of financial reporting, including the environment; forces contributing to the fraudulent acts; and, among other things, the extent to which it can be detected and prevented.
2. The role of the independent public accountant in detecting fraud.
3. Those attributes of the corporate structure that may contribute to acts of fraudulent financial reporting, or to the failure to promptly detect such acts.

The Treadway Commission issued its final report in 1987. The report is quite lengthy, and should be read in its entirely. Many recommendations are to the auditing profession, business schools, and the SEC, and are not covered here. A few salient points that directly affect controllers are:

- The company must have an independent audit committee that is adequately staffed and funded to conduct thorough reviews of company operations.
- The company's annual report should include a discussion of the company's internal accounting controls, as well as activities of the company's audit committee.
- The company should publicly disclose all material accounting issues discussed with its auditors for the three years prior to a change of auditors.
- The company should require its accountants and internal auditors to study the issues surrounding fraudulent activities (i.e., indications of it, conditions leading to it) as part of their continuing professional education.
- The company, if public, should include in its annual report to stockholders a management report signed by the CEO and the chief accounting officer. It should acknowledge management's responsibilities for the financial statements and internal control, discuss how these responsibilities were fulfilled, and provide management's assessment of the effectiveness of the company's internal controls.

Suggestions for the Controller

The NCFFR has provided yardsticks by which companies, public accountants, higher education institutions, and others may measure themselves. The controller should consider the following actions:

- Study the entire NCFFR report, and especially review the 20 recommendations for the public company to evaluate the ease with which fraudulent financial reporting could occur in the controller's company. The report, *Internal Control—Integrated Framework* (commonly referred to as the "COSO Report) consists of four volumes:
  - *Executive Summary.* A top-level overview directed to the CEO, other senior executives, and the board of directors, as well as to legislators, regulators, professional organizations, and academics.
  - *Framework.* A definition of internal control and its components; provides criteria against which managements, boards of directors, and others can assess a relevant control system.
  - *Reporting to External Parties.* A guide to organizations that report publicly on internal control regarding the preparation of relevant published financial statements.
  - *Evaluation Tools.* A set of illustrations of material that could be useful in conducting an evaluation of an internal control system.

- Suggest to the CEO that all senior officers review the Treadway Commission report and consider what their responsibilities are, and where special problems could arise.
- Arrange for the internal audit department, on a timely basis, to evaluate and report on the internal controls.
- Examine and make recommendations to appropriate authority whether the actions of top management match the organization's code of conduct.
- Be certain that the accounting staff understand both the interrelationship of the financial statements and the possible impact of alternative acceptable accounting principles.
- Encourage the development of qualified professional personnel in the accounting function, as well as in internal accounting. Encourage professional development.
- Encourage objectivity by the internal auditor, and see that the position has direct access to the CEO and the Audit Committee.

Evolution of the Internal Control Concept

As judged by the Treadway Commission report and its follow-up, the report of the Committee of Sponsoring Organizations (COSO), the concept of internal control has been expanded from that contained in earlier accounting literature. In the 1930s and 1940s, internal control seemed to concentrate on accounting controls and administrative controls so as to safeguard the assets of the corporation by reducing theft as well as internal fraud. Later, attention focused on compliance with laws and regulations because certain managements became entangled in illegal payments to foreign representatives, bribery, or similar practices. Finally, in the 1980s, attention was further expanded to encompass fraudulent financial reporting. Now, according to the COSO report, a review of internal control should extend to the entire range of business activities that have to do with achieving various business objectives (such as meeting the annual business plan) and to the related tasks inherent in the process. To many, it has seemed that the review of internal controls does not sufficiently distinguish between such processes and the other aspects of the business management function. In fairness, however, it should be stated that the COSO report attempts to make clear that such management activities as establishing objectives, reaching business decisions, and carrying out management plans are activities that should be integrated with, but not made a part of, the internal control system. In today's competitive world, the existence of effective and efficient operations is germane to the survival of the business and the enhancement of shareholder value.

Revised and Enlarged Definition of Internal Control

According to the COSO report, internal control is broadly defined as a process or group of processes that are effected by an entity's board of directors, management, and other personnel and designed to provide reasonable assurance regarding the achievement of objectives in each of the following three categories:

1. Effectiveness and efficiency of operations.
2. Reliability of financial reporting.
3. Compliance with applicable laws and regulations.

Several concepts are inherent in this definition. First, internal control is not just a single event, but rather a series of actions that permeate an organization's activities. They are innate to the way a management runs the business. Internal control is intertwined with a business's operating activities and exists for fundamental reasons.

Second, the system provides only reasonable—not absolute—assurance to management and the board of directors that the specified objectives are being achieved. It cannot provide absolute assurance because systems do break down, and controls can be circumvented by the collusion of two or more individuals. Moreover, management has the ability to override the internal control system.

Third, internal control is accomplished or effected by people—whether by the board of directors, management, or other personnel. People establish the objectives and put the controls into operation. By the same token, internal controls affect the actions of the people involved, and these people may fail to understand, to communicate properly, or to perform consistently.

Fourth, internal controls are objective-oriented and exist in many categories. The three concepts just defined concern (1) the effective and efficient use of resources, including safeguarding assets or meeting the business plan; (2) the preparation of reliable published financial statements; and (3) the tracking and enforcement of compliance with applicable laws and regulations.

It will be observed that the definition of internal controls is broad, facilitating the use of subsets of internal control definitions and activities so that those concerned with special aspects (such as accounting control or budgetary control) can focus on those concerns and establish consistent subdefinitions. The system of controls in particular business units or activities of the organization can be accommodated. The definition is broad, too, because this is the manner in which top management often views the subject of controls.

Components of Internal Control

The COSO report identified a fivefold separation of the components of internal control, all of which are interrelated and all of which must exist to a sufficient degree if the internal control system is to function properly and if the business objectives are to be achieved. These components are:

- Control environment
- Risk assessment

- Control activities
- Information and communication
- Monitoring

Risk Assessment. Risk assessment is the identification and analysis of relevant risks to achieving certain stated objectives. It forms the basis for determining how risk should be managed. Thus, objective setting—which is not an internal control function—is a precondition to risk assessment, which *is* an internal control function.

Given the definition of internal control, three broad categories can be established:

1. Operations objectives, which pertain to the effectiveness and efficiency of the entity's operations. Operations objectives may range from profitability goals or objectives down to division objectives, department objectives, and even activity objectives such as processing sales orders or handling customer invoices.
2. Financial reporting objectives, which relate to the preparation of reliable published financial statements and the prevention of fraudulent public financial reporting.
3. Compliance objectives, which relate to the adherence to laws and regulations with which the entity must comply.

When the objectives are set, procedures must be established to track performance in meeting the objectives and keeping the identified risk within acceptable bounds.

As to risk assessment, when internal controls were more restricted to safeguarding assets and similar concerns, the relevant objectives seem to have had a narrower nature (such as seeing that all sales invoices were recorded in the accounts receivable), rather than the present broad management objectives (such as profit goals).

Control Activities. Control activities are the policies and procedures that help ensure that the necessary actions are taken to address the risks involved in achieving the objectives of the entity. Control activities occur throughout the entire organization—at all levels and for all activities and conditions. In addition to a top-management review of entity performance, they include a vast range of actions: reviewing unit and departmental performance, requiring certain authorizations or approvals, performing reconciliations, verifying certain conditions, segregating duties, restricting access to certain areas or assets, and so on.

Information and Communication. For management to be effective, it is essential that all relevant and pertinent information be identified, secured or captured, and communicated in a proper format and within a suitable time period so that those involved can carry out their responsibilities. Information should be relevant, timely, and accurate, and prepared in a format that is usable, comparable, and accessible. It may be financial or nonfinancial, and it may relate to some standard or objective, to internal or external operations, or to specific conditions. In short, the information to be made available should be that which facilitates decision making and related reporting.

Not only must the information itself be available, but it must also be communicated in a manner that secures attention and gets it used. It may be necessary to communicate the data to more than one individual—to higher and lower echelons; to those in charge of related functions; and to creditors, suppliers, regulatory agencies, owners, and other outside parties.

Monitoring. The final component of an effective control system consists of monitoring. This process of watching, observing, or checking the internal control system permits an assessment of the quality of the system's performance. Monitoring may be performed in an ongoing fashion by observing the findings or results of each regular, periodic review of each element—for example, each day, each month, or each quarter. Or, it may be accomplished as a separate evaluation. Whether a special evaluation is necessary will depend on the extent and nature of occurring changes, the extent of risks, the competence of the people who implement the controls, and what developments are disclosed by the ongoing monitoring. Perhaps both types of monitoring will be necessary.

Monitoring should extend, as circumstances demand, to every element of the internal control system (control environment, risk assessment, control activities, information and communication). Important deficiencies or violations should be reported to either senior management or the board of directors.

Effectiveness of Internal Control

The controller, and indeed the management of a public company or any other organization, often must ask, "How can we judge that the internal control system of our organization is effective?" Because the internal control system is defined as a threefold, objective-oriented process, the COSO report and other writings have provided the following standard:

Internal control can be judged effective in each of the three categories, respectively, if the board of directors and management have reasonable assurance that:

- They understand the extent to which the entity's operational objectives are being achieved.
- Published financial statements are being prepared reliably.
- Applicable laws and regulations are being complied with.

Conclusions regarding the effectiveness of the control system can be reached for each of the three objectives only when the five components (control environment, risk assessment, control activities, information and communication, and monitoring) are present and are functioning properly. From one organization to another, each component may function somewhat differently. Further, components may complement each other in different degrees, or may differ in how they address a particular risk. Determining whether a particular internal control system is effective is, therefore, a subjective judgment and must include a review of the components as well as the objectives. A member of management may know that risks have been evaluated, but may not realize that an important risk has been overlooked. Continuing periodic monitoring and evaluation are necessary.

In its fourth volume, *Evaluation Tools,* the COSO report contains a discussion of the effectiveness of the internal control system and includes an excellent guide to appraising the internal control system and its various components. The listings of points of focus, objectives, and risks should also prove useful. The examples are illustrative only, and not indicative of all matters that need to be considered in a particular situation.

Other topics that the COSO report addresses include responsibility for internal control by the various members of management, by external auditors, and by other interested groups reporting to external parties, and the limitations on internal control. Orders for copies of *Internal Control—Integrated Framework* are processed by the AICPA and the Institute of Management Accountants.

INTERNAL AUDITING

The controller is sometimes placed in charge of the internal auditing staff, though this normally occurs only in smaller organizations. A more typical situation is for the internal auditing director to report to the audit committee that is comprised of members of the Board of Directors. However, in those cases where the controller manages this group, it can be an excellent tool for reviewing potential control issues throughout the company. Even when the internal auditors report to the audit committee, the controller should still suggest a number of audits to that group, which they may approve.

The internal audit director usually sorts through a number of requests from the audit committee, controller, president, and other members of management, and assembles a proposed schedule of audits to conduct over the course of the upcoming year. If these are approved, the director then creates a work schedule for the various audit teams (which may be reshuffled for different audits, based on the skill levels required). After the work is completed, the audit team writes a report on its findings, which works its way back through the director and eventually to various members of management, where its findings are usually cause for systemic changes that either eliminate or mitigate any uncovered control problems. The audit teams will sometimes conduct post-audit reviews to see if subsequent system changes have resulted in better controls.

The controller can suggest a number of internal audits, with the intent of uncovering control problems. Here are a number of suggested audits that the teams can review, and which will give the controller much better information about how to resolve control issues:

- *Accounts payable.* Verify that all payments are properly authorized and supported by receiving documentation. Also verify that there are no late payment fees being paid, and that early payment discounts are taken when the discounts exceed the corporate cost of capital.
- *Accounts receivable credits.* Verify that all accounts receivable credits are properly authorized, and that bad debts are expensed to the bad debt allowance, rather than reduced with a credit to sales. Verify that customers are not taking early payment discounts and still paying at longer terms than those required by the early payment discount deal.
- *Advertising credits.* Verify that all credits issued to customers for advertising are supported by copies of advertisements, clearly showing the dates when the advertisements were run, as well as accompanying documentation for advertising fees.
- *Contracts.* Verify that there is an updated file containing all current contracts, as well as an accurate summary-level contract listing that itemizes key dates for each contract, such as termination dates, penalty clauses, and review dates.
- *Debt.* Verify that debt payments are made on time, and that no penalty payments are incurred. Also verify that the interest rates charged by lenders are in agreement with the rates listed on loan documentation, and that no additional fees are being charged.
- *Expense reports.* Verify that submitted expenses meet company guidelines for approved travel and entertainment expenses. Also verify that all expense reports have been approved in advance by department managers, and that expense reports do not include expenses for an excessively large number of time periods.
- *Fixed assets.* Verify that all capitalized assets are above the capitalization limit, and that they are being expensed at the correct rate of depreciation. Also verify that capital expenditures were properly authorized, and that a net present value analysis was conducted, reviewed, and approved for each one.
- *Freight revenue.* Verify that customers are charged the correct amounts for freight. Also verify that freight billings are reconciled against actual shipments by freight carriers.
- *Inventory.* Verify that inventory accuracy is at least 95%. Also verify that cycle counts are being completed in a timely manner, and that counters are investigating the root causes of any errors they find. Verify that customer-owned inventory is properly segregated and that it is not included in the inventory that has received a valuation. Verify that all inventory costs are properly supported by backup documentation regarding actual product costs.
- *Payroll.* Verify that all employee pay changes and bonuses have been properly authorized, and that all legal requirements for employee files, such as I–9 form verification, have been completed and are present in employee files. Also verify that all employee garnishment deductions are properly supported by legal documentation, and that the payroll staff is aware of the dates on which the garnishments are to be terminated.

- *Pricing.* Verify that customers are being charged the correct prices, based on pricing tables for quantities and dates shipped.
- *Product Invoicing.* Verify that all items shipped are invoiced, and vice versa. Also verify that all invoices are printed within one day of shipment.
- *Service invoicing.* Verify that all service invoices are billed within one day of the completion of work, or in accordance with a pre-agreed invoicing schedule, and that services billed are matched by supporting documentation.

The recommended internal audits itemized here are only the most standard ones that apply to most industries. A controller should also review specialized systems within the company that require special attention and design additional audit programs to ensure that their controls are also adequate.

FOREIGN CORRUPT PRACTICES ACT

As stated earlier in this chapter, responsible business management long has had an interest in the proper operation of internal controls. In 1977, after disclosure by the Office of the Watergate Special Prosecutor and the SEC of the use of U.S. corporate resources for domestic political contributions and for the bribery of foreign governmental officials, Congress enacted the Foreign Corrupt Practices Act. Commentary on some events indicated that some of the payments were illegal and others were questionable. A few were achieved through the use of "off-the-books" funds as well as methods that circumvented the internal accounting control systems. The effects of the Act were to set certain accounting standards for a company with publicly traded stock. Basically, the Accounting Standards Provision of the Act is the segment in which the controller should be particularly interested if his employer is subject to the law. It requires that the company keep in reasonable detail "books, records and accounts" that accurately and fairly reflect the company's transactions and disposition of assets, and maintain an adequate system of internal controls. More specifically, the Act requires that:

- The company shall maintain books that accurately show asset transactions and dispositions.
- The company shall create internal controls that will provide reasonable assurance that:
  - Transactions occur as authorized by management.
  - Transactions are recorded that permit the company to create financial statements and account for assets.
  - Management authorizes access to assets.
  - On-hand assets are periodically compared to the book records, and any variances are investigated.

While little is printed in current business publications about this section of the Act, it continues in effect, and the controller, especially of a multinational entity, should be aware of its existence and comply with its terms. The controller should keep in mind continually that financial record-keeping is not in fact separable from the internal accounting systems that generate the records, and that the operation of the entire internal control system should be consistently monitored. A minority of skillful executives might sometimes be tempted to override or bypass the system, and cause records to be created that look entirely proper to even a trained person who is not suspicious and who is not aware of the deviation from the usual routine.

ENDNOTES

1. Paul G. Makosz and Bruce W. McCuaig, Gulf Canada Resources, "Is everything under control? A new approach to corporate governance," *Financial Executive* (January/February 1990), p. 26.
2. Auditing Standards Board, "Consideration of the Internal Control Structure in a Financial Statement Audit," Sas No. 55 (AICPA, April 1988), paragraph 9.
3. Michael J. Barrett and R. N. Carolus, "Control and Internal Auditing," *The Institute of Internal Auditors Report on Fraud,* Institute of Internal Auditors (September 1986), p. 65.

3

PLANNING AND THE
STRATEGIC PLAN

This chapter discusses the various elements of the strategic plan and provides an overview of the planning process. It reviews some of the basic questions raised in the planning process and considers the elements of strategic planning, for example, constructing a mission statement, factors to consider when picking objectives and strategies, and possible ways to manage the planning process. The following two chapters examine the strategic plan by looking at the qualified long-range plan and the annual budget.

STRATEGIC PLAN OVERVIEW

Strategic planning begins with the present and extends as far into the future as useful for planning purposes. The purpose of strategic planning is to set the company guidelines and policies that serve as the basis for the next echelon of plans, the development plan and the operations plan. The strategic plan focuses on the needs, dangers, and opportunities facing the company. It identifies the key decisions that must be made and usually sets guidelines and deadlines for making them. The process guides the company in decisions about the current generation of products as well as the next and succeeding generations of products and markets. This thinking and communicating process helps assure that the plans and decisions of the various units are moving the company to the same agreed-on objectives.

The plan must contain these six elements:

1. *A statement of purpose*—Identifying the purpose of the plan gives the reader the reason for the action required. It sets forth the objective. The purpose of the strategic plan may be broad, but as the plans become more detailed so also must the reasons for proposed action become more specific.

2. *Actions to take*—The purpose of formulating a plan is to take action, and the plan must stipulate what kind of action need be taken. Again, the more detailed the purpose, the more specific must be the action—from general terms in the strategic plan to minute details in a segment of an operating plan.

3. *Resources to use*—The basic task of management is to use all resources wisely. A firm's resources include not only funds but also people, plant and equipment, technical know-how, and other proprietary knowledge. Plans must indicate which resources are needed, and whether they are on hand or must be acquired, to avoid a conflicting assignment or a less than optimal use of these resources.

4. *Goals to meet*—The goals define the level of accomplishment expected from the action taken. Goals answer the question, What is to result from the activity?

5. *Time schedules to follow*—Progress toward goals must be measured not only in degree of achievement but also in time.

6. *Assumptions made*—The important underlying conditions on which the plan depends must be made known to those who approve the recommendations. If these conditions do not come to pass, then the responsible executive must be made aware of this situation at planned checkpoints so that corrective action, including changes in plans, may be made.

Much planning is done using the most likely set of events in the assumptions. This set of events may be called the most probable scenario. Yet a company must be prepared if these events do not take place. Hence alternative plans are also necessary. Thus management must be made aware of financial results should certain possible but less likely occurrences happen. Financial management must have some sense of the maximum financing needs should events proceed differently than expected. Given these conditions, some managements prepare supplemental financial plans to give a reasonable range of possibilities. Although the emphasis may be on the most probable case, sufficient analysis should be done on the alternate scenarios so that the full financial implications are understood.

The strategic plan is usually communicated to the board of directors in summary form, and typically includes the following areas:

- Comparison to the prior year plan.
- The major planning assumptions.
- The growth strategy.
- Business goals.
- Perceived strengths, weaknesses, opportunities, problems, and threats.

- Profit plans for the existing business.
- Programs and strategies for new business development.
- Financial summaries of major factors, trends, and return on assets.

Remember to keep in mind, while reading about the "nuts and bolts" of the planning process, that it is difficult to encourage long-term thinking and planning, because most companies reward their employees based on short-term results. Thus, long-term planning will not work without long-term incentive plans. Also, strategic planning still involves largely unquantifiable factors such as experience, instinct, guesswork, and luck. Finally, beware that most long-range plans involve too much quantification of rough guesses and estimates. A good plan does not require detail down to the Nth degree!

SYSTEM OF PLANS

In this section, we discuss how the various types of plans work together. But first we define some planning terminology. A plan is a predetermined course of action. A strategic plan is the company's formal plan for achieving its objectives with policies, strategies, and detailed actions. The process of thinking ahead, of making a judgment on a course of action for which consideration has been given to the feasible alternatives, is the planning process.

An integrated planning structure has three components:

1. At the summit, or vertex, is the *strategic plan.* It seeks to outline in general terms the characteristics and objectives of the firm. As detailed later in this chapter, the plan should include a clear statement of the company's basic purpose ("Business Mission"), a set of objectives to accomplish this purpose ("Developing Long-Range Objectives"), and a detailed list of strategies needed to meet the objectives ("Developing Long-Range Strategies"). The plan should also include a statement of assumptions needed to match the goals, such as an assumed continuing increase in the national GNP or inflation rate throughout the planning period.

2. Stemming from the strategic plan is the *development plan,* which concerns itself with the development of new products, services, and markets. It works toward:

   - Establishing those conditions that foster the creation of new products and markets.
   - Gathering pertinent data to identify those fields with the highest potential return on the corporate resources. This effort also involves establishing the procedures needed to identify areas of less desirable growth.
   - Determining resource requirements and the scheduling needed to implement the program as it passes into normal operations.

The development plan includes a divestment plan for selling, merging, or shutting down parts of the business. It also includes a diversification plan for developing new products for new markets, either by internal development, merger, or acquisition.

3. Also proceeding from the strategic plan is the *operations plan* that focuses largely on the existing generation of products and existing markets. It is detailed in nature and specifies plans by individual function, which in essence becomes the annual plan.

PLANNING CYCLE

A company's planning cycle is typically an interactive process, and roughly follows this path:

- Set tentative goals and objectives.
- Analyze expected internal and external environments in which it expects to operate for the planning period.
- Make assumptions about this environment and the company's current posture.
- Conduct a market analysis to determine or confirm the most effective marketing method.
- Devise a marketing plan (taking into account the new products and markets, and status of existing markets and products) for each year of the planning cycle.
- Create a market support plan by year (sales strategy, required staff, advertising and sales promotion, and so on).
- Develop sales estimates by year, product, territory, and salesperson, based on the market support plan.
- Complete the related organization and manpower needs throughout the rest of the company, based on the sales estimate, and itemize the costs by monthly planning period.
- Develop fixed assets (facilities) plans by year of need and amount of expenditure.
- Develop the financial plan (cash, cash generation, income and financial condition, time-phased).
- Reach conclusions as to whether or not the plan is satisfactory. If not, the iterative process may begin again until an acceptable plan is developed.
- Approve the strategic plan. Once done, the appropriate sections serve as the basis for developing a detailed annual plan

An important part of the planning cycle is the *environmental analysis* since it is the foundation of the company's strategic direction. The company's environment has two aspects:

1. *The external environment.* Those influences outside the company that are or will be dominant factors in its activities. The factors can include:

   • *Economic*—The stage of the business cycle, level of general business activity, entrance of new competitors, stage in the industry cycle, and foreign exchange rates.

   • *Technical*—New products of the same type or of a different kind that serve the same need, new processes, and new capital equipment.

   • *Political*—Legislation affecting the product/activity, court decisions relating to interpretation of the laws, and administrative actions affecting the enforcement of the law.

   • *Social*—Social mores change, and what may be acceptable in one country may be unacceptable in another.

2. *The internal environment.* Those forces inside the company that will be significant forces in just how it will function. The following factors should be considered:

   • *Company strengths and weaknesses*—This involves: (a) knowing the functions and areas in which the company performs well, (b) understanding how its strengths compare with competitors', and (c) reaching conclusions on whether or not its strong points may be improved and its weaknesses overcome. Some of the indicators to examine are:
     — Product acceptability
     — Share of the market
     — Marketing posture
     — Proprietary product status
     — Manufacturing costs
     — Quality control
     — Product deliverability
     — Patent status
     — Research and development success
     — Raw material sources
     — Foreign market status
     — Plant capacity
     — Financial strength
     — Judgment and skill of the management
     — Flexibility and capacity to change

   • *The success factors*—This means knowing what particular attributes are responsible for the company's success. It may be such characteristics as good quality control, quick response time to sales orders, personality of the representatives, solid engineering, and so on.

   • *Status of each product in each market segment*—Included in this grouping might be:

— Understanding the life-cycle stage of each product (embryonic, growth, mature, declining).
— Understanding each business segment as to market share and growth rate, according to the Boston Consulting Group matrix, as either:
  * A *star*—high market share, high growth rate.
  * A *cash cow*—high market share, low growth rate, significant generator of cash.
  * A *wild cat*—low market share, high growth rate; probably a cash user until the product is more developed.
  * A *dog*—low market share, low growth; a candidate for divestment.

Those who know the market and the product must be able to reach objective decisions about each. Knowledge of the preceding internal and external factors is important in deciding on the corporate mission and the strategy needed to reach the corporate objectives.

PLANNING ROLES

The CEO is responsible to the board of directors for the strategic plans of the company; therefore, the CEO is the chief long-range planner. However, the long-range planning process must involve most members of management. Accordingly, *who* does the planning will depend on the company's circumstances. The planning could involve only the CEO; or the chief executive and his staff; or a committee, composed of representatives of each major discipline, or each major operating group; or even a separate permanent planning department that would provide leadership and coordination of the process, with adequate support from the chief line and staff officers.

Which of these options it will be hinges on several factors, including:

• *The stage of evolution of planning in the company.* If the planning is informal and sporadic, the chances are that the chief executive will be the chief planner, with limited assistance from others.
• *The attitude of the CEO.* This may determine the breadth or depth of the planning activity. Support from this source is a must for effective planning.
• *The size of the company.* Generally, the larger the company the more likely it is to make formal long-range plans.
• *The nature of the company's markets.* Military suppliers, for example, often do more planning than consumer goods manufacturers.

In general, a balanced planning group containing several disciplines is desirable; these disciplines should include marketing, engineering, finance, human resources, and research. Regardless of background, the prime requisites of the individual planner are flexibility and creativity.

The controller's role is obvious in the later stages of converting strategies into financial terms for the planning period. However, there is also work to be done in the earlier phases of strategic planning in the following areas:

- *The corporate mission.* The mission is determined based on a thorough knowledge of the company's strengths and weaknesses and a host of subjective opinions. If erroneous financial or economic assumptions are used, then the controller should disclose them and provide alternative suggestions.
- *The corporate long-range objectives.* The controller should make any analysis for long-range objectives based on financial facts or calculations.
- *Developing strategies.* The controller should conduct the financial analysis related to some of the strategies. Areas to analyze would include profit impact of alternative choices or relative to cost/effectiveness, unrealistic earnings estimates of proposed acquisitions, unduly optimistic economic assumptions, an excessive inflation rate, or cost estimates that are too low.

PLANNING TIMING AND THE PLANNING PERIOD

To achieve a sound strategic or short-term plan on a reasonably timely basis, it is desirable to prepare a calendar of events. With respect to the strategic plan, this may be issued at the time of the chief executive's announcement of the annual strategic planning effort. A sample calendar of events is outlined below. In this instance, the cycle for the strategic plan is separated from the short-range planning cycle, in order to distribute more evenly the time spent in the planning effort. The key plan dates are as follows:

May 31	Issuance of general guidelines by the CEO to division heads and other interested parties
July 31	Receipt of division plans by chief planning officer
September 30	Completion of review and analysis of division plans by corporate staff
October 31	Preparation of consolidated and corporate position
November 30	Review with top management and board of directors

Although the dates cited indicate the latest acceptable time for completion of the activity, there is in fact continuous communication between the corporate and division planners, and often the financial officer will devise alternative scenarios that are needed for the long-term financial plans.

Strategic planning is sometimes referred to as "long-range planning." But just how far ahead should a company plan? What are some of the factors to be considered in selecting the proper period for which to plan? Each business has characteristics that must be identified in determining the time period of planning. Obviously, a company should plan ahead only so far as is useful. Surveys on this subject indicate that among companies that do long-range planning, the most common period is five years, although the trend is toward a greater distance into the future.

Some of the factors that serve as a guide in selecting the proper planning time span are:

- *Lead time for product development*—This includes the length of time from the data for a new product until the design, manufacture, and distribution are completed. One company may take three months, whereas another may require several years.
- *Lifespan of the product*—The probable period before a product is considered obsolete will be a factor.
- *Market development time*—This period will vary tremendously, from several years for a complicated industrial product to perhaps only several weeks for, say, women's fashions.
- *Development time for raw materials and components*—Some extractive industries such as iron ore mining or oil drilling may require a decade of advance planning. Wood products companies may consider a period beyond the life expectancy of their present management.
- *Time for construction of physical facilities*—For many plants a minimum of two years for design and construction of a plant and its equipment is needed.
- *Payout period for capital investment*—The period over which the investment in capital equipment will be recovered must be weighed. Payoff may vary from several months in a highly speculative and profitable field (such as certain chemicals) to perhaps more than a decade (for some utilities). Thought must be given to conditions that will prevail during this payout period to focus on the probability of recovering the investment and earning an adequate return on it.

Many companies find it practical to update the strategic plan on an annual basis. In effect, one year is dropped and a new one is added. Each year, as new perceptions of the business or new opportunities or threats emerge, the new factors are studied and incorporated into the planning process and resultant plan. However, changes in the conditions should not be the excuse for revision of the plan when, over and above those changes, the operating group is not achieving its goals. The impact of the deviation and expected year-end (or other period) result can be identified without changing the plan, by quantifying the indicated final results for the year, and the departure from the budget (plan).

BUSINESS MISSION

One of the principal tasks of top management is to formulate the basic purposes of the company. This requires a great deal of thinking as to what the business is all about. It is this mission statement that serves as the guideline for strategic planning.

How should the mission statement be formulated? In smaller companies it tends to depend largely on the thinking and values of the CEO. But in larger companies it is done more effectively by consultation and exchange of ideas among the management (although the CEO still has an important voice). Why? Because any basic change in the nature of the business can have ramifications for the operating methods, the interrelationship of people, and use of skills.

There is no uniform content in mission statements, which vary from lofty statements of principle, representing the values of the CEO, to very detailed and concrete guidelines. Excess detail may be counterproductive, and vague statements may not be useful in formulating objectives and strategies. A middle ground best serves the purpose.

So, what factors are important to the survival and growth of the company? The following subjects, which can be identified and/or refined by the planning meetings, should be considered when creating a mission statement:

- Product or product line.
- Market and market share.
- Profitability on sales, assets, and/or shareholders' equity.
- Growth in sales, market share, specific product lines, earnings, earnings per share, jobs, and/or markets served.
- Research and development.
- Productivity or efficiency.
- Flexibility in R&D methods, meeting customer delivery needs, and/or responding to competitive actions.
- Company image.
- Observance of a code of conduct.
- Development of the managerial pool.

Based on a consideration of the above factors, here are three examples of company mission statements:

1. To be the predominant supplier of electronics countermeasures to the U.S. Air Force.
2. To assist our clients in achieving cost-effective employee benefit plans through the effective marketing of innovative and specially designed concepts intended to reflect the strengths of the client company.
3. To maintain a viable, growing business by designing, developing, manufacturing and marketing custom engineered products and services to meet the needs of selected utility and construction companies.

Keep in mind that the principal application of a mission statement is to serve as a guide to policy decisions, to provide direction. Accordingly, it should be quite specific, and not a lofty statement of admirable purpose. Also, careful designation may be important; that is, whether the product/service is defined in broad terms or more narrowly described. The wording of the statement can be significant. Thus, a statement that company Y is in the communication business might have quite a different impact than to specify narrower business lines, such as newspapers, television, and/or radio. And remember that the mission generally should include the scope of operations. While the mission will identify the line of business, the scope will delineate the market (e.g., U.S. rather than worldwide).

A realistic statement of purpose probably will be influenced by these three factors:

1. The basic competence and characteristics of the company (e.g., skill of the management, capital resources, operational capabilities, physical assets, geographical locations, availability of skilled personnel, raw material sources, etc.).
2. The expectations of those who have something at stake in the firm: management, shareholders, creditors, employees, suppliers, and customers. The relative weight of each group's influence will help shape the relative importance of different elements of the mission.
3. The expected future external environment (e.g., regulation, social trends, inflation rates, and the stage of the business cycle).

DEVELOPING LONG-RANGE OBJECTIVES

Once the business mission has been determined, the long-term objectives must be established. The establishment of objectives is an interactive process, closely coupled with the determination of strategies. One influences the other. In any event, experience shows that satisfactory long-term objectives must be:

- *Suitable*—An objective should support the basic purposes and missions of the company. Achieving the objective should move the enterprise in the direction of meeting its purpose.
- *Feasible*—Objectives should be achievable. It serves no useful purpose to set an unrealistic goal. Any objective should be established giving recognition to the expected environment: competitive actions, technical achievements, political feasibility, and so on.
- *Compatible*—Each objective should be compatible with the other objectives. For example, the objective for product A or strategic business unit X should be in harmony with the objectives for the overall organization.
- *Measurable*—Actual results should be measurable against planned results over a specified time span. Thus, if the objective is "to attain a sales level of $100 million by the year 2000," then attainment is readily identifiable. Objectives may be quantified in dollars, units, cost, rate, or percentage. Only when

the objective is stated in concrete terms and for specified periods of time can their attainment be measured objectively.

- *Flexible*—Objectives should not be easily changed; nor should they be immovable. When major unforeseen contingencies occur, they should be changeable to be more realistic.

- *Motivating*—Another important characteristic of a proper objective is its motivating power. An objective should not be so easily achieved that it is certain of attainment. Nor should it be too difficult to accomplish. It should be set at such a level that those to be judged by it generally agree it can be reached. This implies that those who are to meet an objective should have a voice in setting it. The management members involved should regard it as a commitment to be met with adequate effort.

In practice, most companies have only a few long-term planning objectives. In theory, however, goals or objectives could be set for every function and every department in the business. Typically, many of the objectives are financially expressed and relate to sales volume, profitability, and market share. But measures may be developed for any number of factors that need change: labor content, share of minorities in the work force, skill diversification in the engineering or research staff, labor turnover rates, productivity, R&D expenditures, and so on. Table 3–1 provides some illustrative long-term objectives for the company as a whole.

Those involved in setting company objectives should realize that major objectives are closely related to sub-objectives. Thus, the return on shareholders' equity must be supported by a proper gross margin objective and asset turnover objective, and a satisfactory leverage factor. The margin objective in turn should allow for a product mix objective, a sales volume objective, and, perhaps, a productivity increase goal.

Table 3–1: Sample Company Long-Term Objectives

Objective	Achieve by Year	
	2000	2005
Aggregate sales volume (millions)	$560	$1,200
Percent of non-U.S. sales	20%	25%
Percent of new products	15%	30%
Operating profit (% of sales)	17%	22%
Rate of return:		
On total assets	10%	12%
On net worth	19%	25%
Earnings per share	$2.50	$4.25
Price/earnings ratio	11x	15x
Labor content in products	25%	22%
Minorities as % of work force	10%	12%

Setting realistic long-term objectives is not as simple as having one executive, the CEO, or a group, dictate a figure or goal. To be sure, the process might commence with suggestions from those sources; but it is more satisfactory to have some identifiable points of reference recognizable by those who must meet the objective. What are these? How can they be determined? Some of the ways to make that determination are:

- *Use past performance, with trend exploration*—In some instances, use last year's performance and adjust for experienced improvement. This method must be used with caution, since previous performance levels may be quite poor in relation to the rest of the industry; using such previous performance as a future goal may set the company at a competitive disadvantage.
- *Adjust past performance for the impact of expected forces*—Recognition is given to the result of expected changes, both internal and external, such as: product obsolescence, government regulations, new product developments, competitive actions, industry sales forecasts, and so on.
- *Analyze competitors*—With 10K reports from competitors, analyses can be made of competitive performance. Return on assets, gross margin percentage, sales volume trends, funds spent on R&D, selling expenses, individual competitor data, or group data can be used as a basis for calculating desired performance on some measurable item.
- *Employ environmental, situational, and strategic analyses*—In the analytical study of operations, certain comparative relationships will become evident. The impact of expanding the more productive or effective ones can be judged or calculated on such matters as sales volume (for example, the impact of advertising, or the use of a certain channel of distribution, changing prices). The best methods used in one area might be applied to other areas. In turn, these actions could affect the objective.

In any event, there are several bases and supporting statistical analyses of various types that can aid in the selection of suitable long-term planning objectives.

DEVELOPING LONG-RANGE STRATEGIES

After the basic mission and long-range planning objectives have been determined, the next step is to search out those strategies best able to achieve the objectives. As used herein, "strategy" means the way, or means, by which the company deploys its human and financial resources and its physical assets to achieve the business purpose.

A great deal has been written about identifying and evaluating strategies. However, the process is largely an art, and developing a successful strategy often involves a great deal of luck. In strategic planning the emphasis usually is on products, markets, and marketing. In developing successful strategies, it is desirable that the company's creative talents be enlisted to suggest the most ingenious and comprehensive strategies possible. This development task may be assigned to gifted individuals or groups in marketing, planning, or other departments who have a reasonable knowledge of the operations. Sources that may provide clues for potential alternative strategies include:

- A review of company reports and records.
- Observation and discussion of the company's operations, including its known or alleged strengths and weaknesses.
- A review of competitive or comparable businesses.
- Discussion of the situation and alternatives with people who are familiar with the industry and the company or who have encountered similar problems, such as consultants, educators, members of boards of directors, and think tanks.

When the list of alternative strategies has been developed, they should be screened by knowledgeable people (perhaps the CEO and other members of top management) to eliminate the impractical strategies. Then the remaining strategies should be evaluated on both a qualitative and quantitative basis. Qualitative factors include the impact on other product lines or organizational units or on the corporate image. Quantitative measures may include contribution margin, cost effectiveness, return on assets, market share, and operating profit.

This art of determining the strategy requires a good insight into the company's strengths and weaknesses, good judgment and intuition, and a willingness to examine some new ideas.

Specifically, strategy development demands:

- Comprehending the current status of the business and where continuance of the same policies and strategies will take it. This involves identifying such factors as:
  — Major products.
  — Major markets.
  — Important strengths and weaknesses of the company as compared to the competition.
  — Present major strategies.
  — Knowing the economic contribution (e.g., cash flow and operating profit) of the various segments by product, market, and profit center.
- Understanding the company objectives and how they may differ from results of continuing the present activity.
- Recognizing some of the strategies that may or could be involved in the strategic planning, and selecting the practical ones for study.
  — *Product strategies*—Product design, new product development, adding new products by purchase or acquisition, product obsolescence, life cycle of products.

- *Market strategies*—Adding or dropping markets; changing distribution channels, methods of sales, prices, terms of sale, delivery methods, advertising media, promotional methods.
- *Manufacturing strategies*—Plant locations, subcontracting, foreign sources, manufacturing techniques, material content, quality control.
- *R&D strategies*—University affiliations, joint ventures, licensing, purchase of rights.
- *Financial strategies*—Inventory financing, credit terms, debt structure, ESOPs, stock issues, control systems, the planning system, inflation hedging, foreign exchange practices, leasing instead of purchasing fixed assets.
- *Human resource strategies*—Organization structure, style of management, decentralization, downsizing, recruitment policies, training programs, wage and salary levels, executive replacement.
- Evaluating the proposed individual strategies and judging how they will assist in meeting the business objective.

From the listing of the basic types of strategies, some alternative strategies may be deduced. However, the following list provides a few specific illustrations of strategies undertaken. What strategies must be employed or changed obviously depends on the problems to be overcome. The strategies appear in typical groupings of product strategies, market strategies, and operating efficiency.

Products:

1. Change the style of packaging to appeal to middle-aged customers
2. Change packaging to smaller quantities to attract elderly singles.
3. Add a related product that would use the same distribution channel and methods as the other products.
4. Drop line Y, which provides no contribution margin.
5. Modify the product so it will serve a function not now recognized.
6. Consider private brands in the Southeast.

Markets and marketing:

1. Enter the growing European market through a joint venture.
2. Change prices to meet the competition of the "R" chain.
3. Increase local advertising to cover TV in markets W, X, and Y.
4. Change from sales representatives to agents in the Northwest territory.
5. Reduce the promotional effort on product "T" in the marketplace because of its declining stage in the life cycle.

Operating efficiency:

1. Switch to the "just-in-time" inventory control method in Los Angeles and San Francisco.
2. Establish a warehouse in Denver.
3. Enforce terms of sale in order to increase receivables turnover.
4. Dispose of the Kansas City subsidiary because of losses and the lack of growth prospects.
5. Sell the Chicago office building. In the present inflated market, reduce space requirements, and move to a less expensive location.

4

LONG-RANGE FINANCIAL PLAN

The preceding chapter provided an overview of strategic planning. In this chapter, the strategic plan becomes more specific through numerical examples as the following topics, which are segments of the long-range plan, are examined:

- Trend of revenues and profits
- Capital investments
- Cash flows and financing requirements
- Key statistics
- Risk analysis
- Breakdown by business unit/product line/geography
- Financial position

LAYOUT AND PURPOSE

The elements of the business plan that were described in the preceding chapter did not address the means by which the plan could be achieved. Targets were set, but there was no discussion of how the company would get from its present situation to the new targets. The long-range plan shows anticipated growth rates from the present to the targets, as well as the capital expenditures and capital requirements needed. The plan is backed up by a set of key statistics that indicate changes in such areas as coverage of loan covenants and liquidity.

The long-range plan also includes an in-depth risk analysis. The risk of significant revenue and profit changes are listed, along with probabilities of the changes occurring. It is possible from this analysis to infer the risk of the corpo-

Table 4–1: Differences Between the Annual and Long-Range Plans

Task	Long-range Plan	Annual Plan
Lists costs by individual account	No	Yes
Includes subsidiary budgets (purchasing, labor, etc.)	No	Yes
Used for monthly comparison to actual results	No	Yes
Has cash budget	Yes	Yes
Has P&L and balance sheet budgets	Yes	Yes

ration's not meeting its goals, and to gain a general idea of the risk of financial loss that the company is willing to undertake to achieve its goals.

Finally, the plan should include subsidiary plans that categorize projected sales and profits by strategic business units, product lines, and geographical regions, helping to determine where the greatest risks and opportunities lie in the plan.

The long-range plan differs significantly from the annual plan (as described in the following chapter). The differences are noted in Table 4–1.

After examining the table, you may conclude that the long-range plan is not as large or detailed as the annual plan; that is a correct assessment. The long-range plan deals with long-term needs and key statistics, and does not concern itself with low-level detailed costs. The plan is meant to be easily modified for "what if" analysis, and a relatively small model with linked graphics is best for that purpose.

The *purpose* of the long-range plan is to give management a "rough-cut" analysis of whether or not its business plan is achievable, and of the risks and funding involved. Also, the long-range plan can be discussed with investors in order to bolster the stock price. Finally, the plan is used to assist lenders in determining the risk involved in lending to the company.

The controller is responsible for the long-range plan, in the absence of a CFO. The plan quantifies the goals and strategies enumerated in the business plan, and numerical analysis logically falls into the realm of the controller. However, input into the long-range plan must come from all departments. For example, all departments must submit capital requests. The sales department must contribute minimum/maximum expected revenue figures by product. The engineering department must contribute estimated margin information by product.

TRENDS OF REVENUES AND PROFITS

The business plan will itemize a target sales level to be reached by a specified date, or an average growth rate. The long-range plan must specify the anticipated growth by individual year. This growth does not have to be a steady trend-line from year to year. Instead, the plan should tie revenue levels to new products coming onto the market, new business units being created, or new geographical areas being reached.

Similarly, the trend of profits should be tied to the anticipated costs of creating new products, capital expenditures, marketing campaigns, or other growth-related costs.

The format of this section of the plan should be graphical, with numerical backup if needed. Examples of such graphs are shown in Figures 4–1 and 4–2. Each example shows both actual revenues and profits for the last few years of operations as well as projections through the period of the business plan.

CAPITAL INVESTMENTS

The long-range plan should include a listing of capital investments required to attain the revenue and profit objectives. The investment amount should also include working capital requirements (cash invested in receivables and inventories, less the amount of accounts payable). There is a growing trend in industry toward eliminating working capital by shrinking inventories and receivables. If the company plans to pursue such a strategy, that goal should be built into the business plan, since it will have a significant impact on capital requirements.

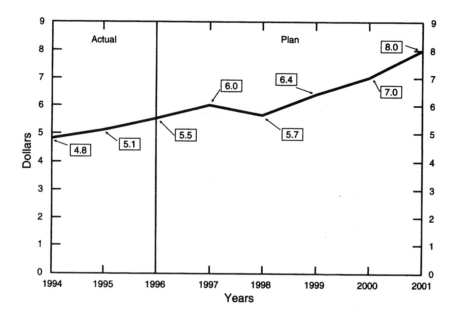

Figure 4–1: The Hi-Tech Corporation 1997–2001 Strategic Plan Consolidated Net Sales (dollars in billions)

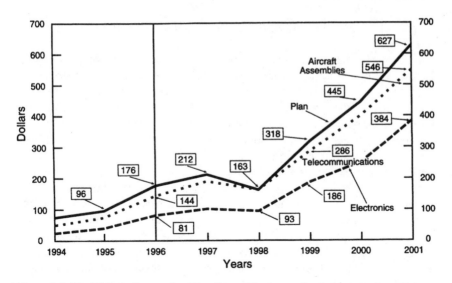

Figure 4–2: The Hi-Tech Corporation Consolidated Net Income By Strategic Business Unit 1997–2001 Strategic Plan (dollars in millions)

Capital requirements should be listed by product, business unit, or geographical area, so that management can easily determine the costs associated with launching a new product or business unit or selling into a new geographical area. A typical capital plan is shown in Table 4–2.

Capital requirements are especially useful when determining returns on investment and strategy risks, as discussed later in the Risk Analysis section of this chapter.

Table 4–2: Capital Requirements

	The New Technology Company 19XX-20YB Strategic Plan
Aircraft Product A	
Assembly Line	34.1*
Assembly Building	17.2
Working Capital	43.0
Total	94.3
Communications Product B	
Assembly Line	11.0
Assembly Building	14.1
Working Capital	29.3
Total	54.4

dollars in millions

CASH FLOWS AND FINANCING REQUIREMENTS

The long-range plan should include cash requirements for each year of the plan. This is one of the most crucial parts of the long-range plan, for management must know about the risk of future indebtedness as well as the need to issue stock or bonds. If stock is issued, then management must be aware of the projected impact on earnings per share (since an increased number of shares outstanding will water down the earnings per share in the absence of additional earnings). In addition, management must be aware of the company's projected debt/equity mix, since this will affect the cost of capital.

If future indebtedness is more than management is comfortable with, then the capital requirements part of the long-range plan can be reviewed to determine where the requirements are coming from. For example, if $150 million of additional debt or equity is required over the course of the long-range plan and capital requirements are as shown in Table 4–2, then management may want to review the benefits of Aircraft Product A in great detail, since that product is responsible for the majority of capital requirements.

Product profitability assumptions are a key component of projected cash flows; the strategic plan should contain assumptions regarding expected competition that may reduce margins, and internal quality or other initiatives that may increase margins. Figure 4–3 shows earnings per share under several scenarios.

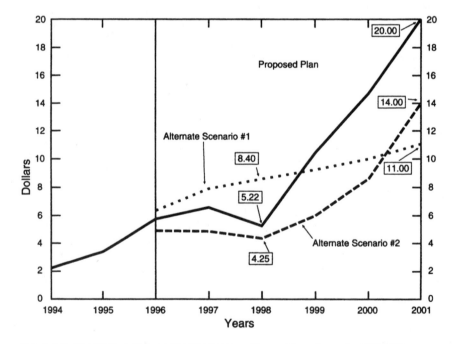

Figure 4–3: The Hi-Tech Corporation Earnings per Share – Three Scenarios 1997–2001 Strategic Plan

Table 4-3: The Hi-Tech Corporation Statement of Consolidated Cash Flows 1997–2001 Strategic Plan (Dollars in Millions)

	Present Year (Indicated Final)	Plan Year				
		1997	1998	1999	2000	2001
Cash Flows from Operating Activities						
Net Earnings	$ 176	212	163	318	445	$ 627
Depreciation and Amortization	174	214	244	240	250	200
Deferred Taxes, etc.	4	4	—	—	—	—
Working Capital Provided by Operations	354	430	407	558	695	827
Increase (Decrease) in Operating Related Working Capital Items	255	149	(221)	(7)	(55)	(45)
Net Cash Flows from Operating Activities	99	281	628	551	640	872
Cash Flows from (Used by) Investing Activities						
Equity Interest—Corp. X	—	—	—	—	—	(800)
Capital Expenditures	(118)	(420)	(100)	(50)	(50)	(50)
Proceeds from Asset Sales and Retirements	1	—	20	—	—	—
Net Cash Flows Used in Investing Activities	(117)	(420)	(80)	(50)	(50)	(850)
Cash Flows from (Used by) Financing Activities						
Dividends to Shareholders	(52)	(53)	(53)	(58)	(58)	(63)
Change (reduction) in Short-Term Bank Debt	116	(135)	(200)	(150)	—	—
Additions to Long-Term Debt	—	500	—	—	—	—
Reduction in Long-Term Debt	(21)	(42)	(50)	(250)	(240)	(350)
Net Cash Flows from (Used by) Financing Activities	43	270	(303)	(458)	(298)	(413)
Increase (Decrease) in Cash and Cash Equivalents	25	131	245	43	292	(391)
Cash and Equivalents at Beginning of Year	172	197	328	573	616	908
Cash and Equivalents at End of Year	$ 197	328	573	616	908	$ 517

This kind of chart is very useful to management, since decisions regarding addition or elimination of products will directly affect earnings per share. Table 4–3 shows a simple calculation of cash flows for a long-range plan.

KEY STATISTICS

The long-range plan should include overall statistics that indicate changes in the company's market value, changes that may break loan covenants, and changes that may increase the company's risk to unacceptable levels. Some of the most common ratios are listed below (for ratio formulas, refer to Chapter 19, Performance Measurement and Trends).

- *Percentage return on average assets*—This ratio is a good measure of how well the company is utilizing its assets to achieve the greatest possible return. Management should alter the long-range plan to maximize this ratio, since the best possible return on average assets requires the most frugal use of expensive capital. See Figure 4–4.
- *Percentage return on average shareholder's equity*—This ratio estimates the return on investment to the shareholder. It is useful for calculating the impact of the business plan on the shareholders' future returns. See Figure 4–5.
- *Ratio of long-term debt to net worth*—This ratio is used in loan covenants. Management must be careful to construct a long-range plan that does not break the covenants contained in its loan agreements. See Figure 4–6.

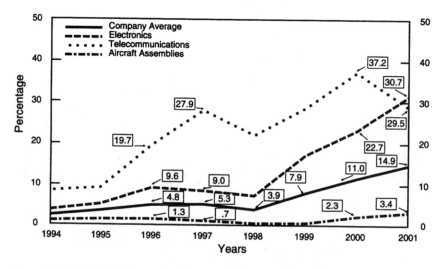

Figure 4–4: The Hi-Tech Corporation Percentage Return on Average Assets 1997–2001 Strategic Plan

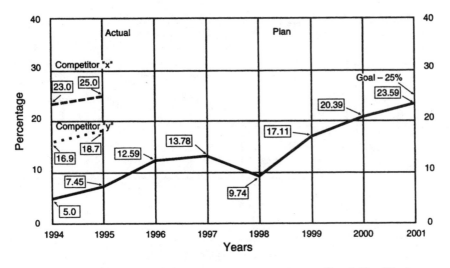

Figure 4–5: The Hi-Tech Corporation Percentage Return on Average Shareholders' Equity 1997–2001 Strategic Plan

- *Current ratio*—This ratio is used in loan covenants. Management must be careful to construct a long-range plan that does not break the covenants contained in its loan agreements. See Figure 4–7.

- *Number of times fixed charges are earned*—This ratio is a measure of risk. An excessive amount of debt payments may put the company in a difficult liquidity situation if revenues or margins are lower than anticipated.

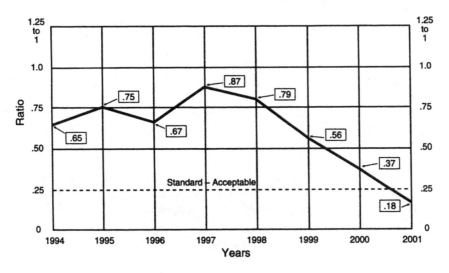

Figure 4–6: The Hi-Tech Corporation 1997–2001 Strategic Plan Ratio of Long-Term Debt to Net Worth

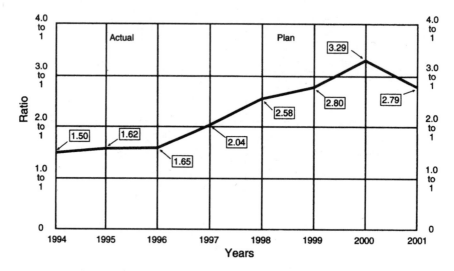

Figure 4–7: The Hi-Tech Corporation 1997–2001 Strategic Plan Current Ratio

Ratios can also be used to support specific objectives within the business plan. For example, if management wants to reduce capital requirements by reducing working capital, then appropriate ratios to monitor would be the Average Collection Period and Inventory Turnover (see Chapter 18, Performance Measurements and Trends, for details). If working capital is currently $50 million and management wants to reduce it by 50%, then the plan may generate a required inventory turnover rate of 20 turns per year. Management must then either find a way to achieve the inventory turns goal, or find other means of reducing working capital, such as aggressively collecting receivables or extending payables.

RISK ANALYSIS

The long-range plan should include an in-depth assessment of the risks that will occur as a result of the business plan. The commentary should include some or all of the following topics:

- *Competitive response*—Competitors will have a response to any new product introduction or expansion into a new geographical area. The response may be price cuts, lawsuits, or lobbying for government regulation.
- *Capital cost overruns*—Construction projects have been known to exceed their budgets. A worst-case scenario could help management anticipate funding requirements.
- *Nationalization of facilities*—Some countries have a history of nationalizing certain industries with little or no compensation to the previous owners of

expropriated facilities. If management becomes aware of such a problem, then it may wish to relocate its new facilities.

- *Ecological costs*—Some companies, notably in the asbestos and tobacco industries, have been targets of lawsuits due to products that were later found to be unsafe. In addition, any product or process that has significant chemical waste byproducts should be brought to the attention of management, since resulting lawsuits or government fines could destroy any profits from sale of the product.
- *Sales fluctuations*—Sales projections are sometimes inaccurate. Management should be aware of the worst and best case scenarios. The worst case may result in significant losses to the company, and the best case (as recently experienced by several personal computer manufacturers) may require construction of additional production facilities.
- *Raw material scarcity*—Some raw materials are in short supply (computer chips) or are tightly controlled by the producer (oil by OPEC in the 1970s). If so, sales projections may fall short due to the inability of the company to produce enough of the product to meet demand.
- *Deterioration of margins*—Competing products may come onto the market that will cause margins to deteriorate due to price cuts. The company should make some attempt to identify this risk from both national and international competitors and derive a likely range of margin percentage reductions to factor into the long-range plan.
- *Technological advances*—Advances in technology may make a product obsolete (e.g., as slide rules were made obsolete by calculators). Though these advances may be hard to predict, some news of experimental technology can be found in trade literature that will allow the company to forecast a decline in its market. For example, the movie video rental market is projected to decline after the turn of the century as on-demand movie rentals become available through cable television companies.

The risk assessment section of the long-range plan is among the most crucial parts of the plan. Some of this information can be researched during the construction of the business plan (see the preceding chapter), but the long-range plan attempts to quantify the cost associated with each of the factors noted above. Armed with this information, management can then alter the business plan as necessary both to reduce the company's risk to an acceptable level and to maximize its profits.

BREAKDOWN BY BUSINESS UNIT/PRODUCT LINE/GEOGRAPHY

The long-range plan should include capital expenditure, revenue, margin, and profit breakdowns so that management can determine where it can expect its greatest returns as well as its greatest risk of loss. Following are typical detailed breakdowns:

- *Business Unit*—The business plan frequently categorizes sales and profits by business unit. A breakdown of this kind may highlight projected problems in specific business units that management can correct.
- *Product Line*—The business plan may include the rollout of a new product. If so, a summary of the costs associated with the new product (e.g., marketing, advertising, R&D, and capital costs) should be listed. An attached commentary should include an assessment of minimum/maximum/expected sales levels, probability of capital cost overruns, and possible competitive responses to introduction of the new product.
- *Geography*—The business plan may include expansion into geographical areas. If so, the cost of advertising and marketing campaigns should be itemized. If the areas are in other countries, the company may have to build production facilities in those locations; if so, the capital cost should also be included. Finally, the working capital cost of the expansion should be included. The breakdown should utilize all of these "hard" numbers in a summary that includes risk assessments of such factors as nationalization of facilities, minimum/maximum/expected sales levels, and possible capital cost overruns.

FINANCIAL POSITION

The long-range plan should include a profit and loss statement as well as a balance sheet for each year of the long-range plan. This information is not just for internal use. Lenders want this information to determine corporate risk when approving loans; investors want this information to determine their investment positions with the company.

The long-range plan should simply extend the typical P&L and balance sheet through the number of years covered by the plan. Examples of those statements are shown in Tables 4–4 through 4–6.

Some companies include a statement of financial highlights with their standard financial statements. The highlights usually include estimates of projected backlogs, sales, earnings, a few key expenses, and the return on assets or equity. An example of a financial highlights statement is shown in Table 4–7. Finally, the projected earnings per share and the projected net earnings are the items of most concern to investors. As such, they are commonly graphed to draw the attention of investors to them. Examples of graphed earnings per share and projected net earnings are shown in Figures 4–8 and 4–9.

Table 4-4: The Hi-Tech Corporation Statement of Consolidated Financial Position at Year End 1997–2001 Strategic Plan (Dollars in Millions)

	Actual		At Plan Year End				
	12/31/95	12/31/96 (Indicated Final)	1997	1998	1999	2000	2001
Assets							
Current Assets							
Cash and Equivalents	$ 172	197	328	573	616	908	$ 517
Receivables	576	614	640	510	550	650	600
Inventories	1,037	1,320	1,400	1,200	1,300	1,200	1,200
Prepaid Items	46	44	40	40	40	40	40
Total	1,831	2,175	2,408	2,323	2,506	2,798	2,357
Long-Term Assets							
Minority Interests (Corp. X)	—	—	—	—	—	—	800
Property, Plant and Equipment	2,407	2,522	2,942	3,022	3,072	3,122	3,172
Less: Accumulated Depreciation and Amortization	792	966	1,180	1,404	1,644	1,894	2,094
Net	1,615	1,556	1,762	1,618	1,428	1,228	1,078
Other Assets	75	80	80	80	80	80	80
Total	1,690	1,636	1,842	1,698	1,508	1,308	1,958
Total Assets	$ 3,521	3,811	4,250	4,021	4,014	4,106	$ 4,315

Table 4-5: The Hi-Tech Corporation Statement of Consolidated Financial Position at Year End 1997–2001 Strategic Plan (Dollars in Millions)

	Actual		At Plan Year End				
	12/31/95	12/31/96 (Indicated Final)	1997	1998	1999	2000	2001
Liabilities and Equity							
Current Liabilities							
Notes Payable to Banks	$ 319	435	300	100	—	—	$ —
Current Portion of Long-Term Debt	21	21	—	50	50	50	50
Accounts Payable	563	590	610	540	590	500	500
Accrued Items	187	212	200	160	170	190	170
Income Tax Payable	17	34	43	37	65	90	100
Other Current Liabilities	26	27	28	15	20	20	25
Total	$ 1,133	1,319	1,181	902	895	850	$ 845
Long-Term Obligations							
Senior Debt—Existing	$ 863	842	800	750	500	300	$ —
Senior Debt—New	—	—	500	500	500	450	400
Other Long-Term Obligations	142	140	110	110	110	120	120
Total	$ 1,005	982	1,410	1,360	1,110	870	$ 520
Deferred Income Taxes	$ 47	50	40	30	20	10	$ 10
Shareholders' Equity							
Paid-in Capital	$ 310	310	310	310	310	310	310
Retained Earnings	1,026	1,150	1,309	1,419	1,679	2,066	2,630
Total Equity	$ 1,336	1,460	1,619	1,729	1,989	2,376	$ 2,940
Total Liabilities and Equity	$ 3,521	3,811	4,250	4,021	4,014	4,106	$ 4,315

Table 4-6: The Hi-Tech Corporation Statement of Consolidated Earnings 1997–2001 Strategic Plan (Dollars in Millions)

Item	Actual		Plan Year				
	Past Year	This Year (Indicated Final)	1997	1998	1999	2000	2001
Net Sales	$ 5,052	5,500	6,000	5,700	6,400	7,000	$ 8,000
Operating Costs							
Manufacturing	$ 4,461	4,815	5,204	4,995	5,420	5,791	$ 6,544
Marketing	40	41	39	40	42	46	52
Research and Development	50	55	120	114	128	140	160
General and Administrative	41	39	37	38	42	43	44
Total	$ 4,592	4,950	5,400	5,187	5,632	6,020	$ 6,800
Operating Margin	$ 460	550	600	513	768	980	$ 1,200
Other Expenses							
Interest Expense	$ 181	223	200	190	180	100	$ 50
Other (Net)	111	15	15	(10)	10	10	10
Total	$ 292	238	215	180	190	110	$ 60
Earnings Before Income Taxes	$ 168	312	385	333	578	870	$ 1,140
Income Taxes	72	136	173	170	260	425	513
Net Earnings	$ 96	176	212	163	318	445	$ 627

Table 4-7: The Hi-Tech Corporation Financial Highlights 1997–2001 Strategic Plan (Dollars in Millions Except per Share)

Item	Actual		Plan Year				
	Past Year	This Year (Indicated Final)	1997	1998	1999	2000	2001
New Orders	$ 3,800	3,600	2,500	8,470	6,400	7,500	$ 8,200
Sales Backlog (year end)	5,650	3,750	250	3,020	3,020	3,520	3,720
Net Sales (consolidated)	5,052	5,500	6,000	5,700	6,400	7,000	8,000
Net Earnings							
Amount	96	176	212	163	318	445	627
Percent of Sales	1.9%	3.2%	3.5%	2.9%	5.0%	6.4%	7.8%
Per Share	3.09	5.66	6.79	5.22	10.16	14.22	20.00
Capital Expenditures	115	115	420	100	50	50	50
Research and Development Expense	50	55	60	57	64	69	70
Book Value per Share (year end)	$ 43.03	46.93	51.87	55.38	63.57	75.91	$ 93.78
Return on Average Equity—%	7.45%	12.59%	13.78%	9.74%	17.11%	20.39%	23.59%
No. Common Shares Outstanding (thousands)—year end	31,050	31,110	31,210	31,220	31,290	31,300	31,350

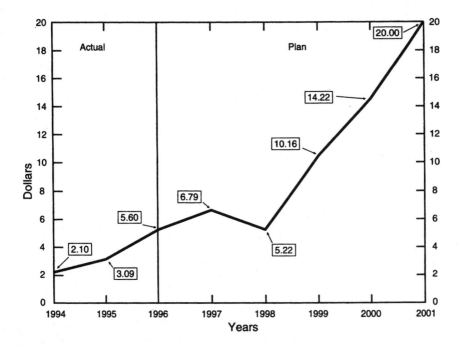

Figure 4–8: The Hi-Tech Corporation Earnings per Share 1997–2001 Strategic Plan

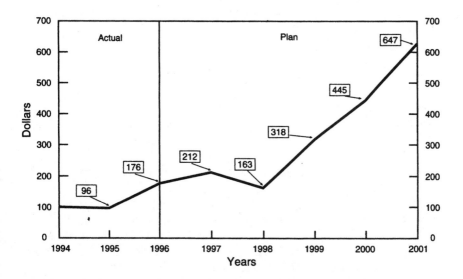

Figure 4–9: The Hi-Tech Corporation Consolidated Net Earnings 1997–2001 Strategic Plan
(dollars in millions)

5

ANNUAL PLAN

The purpose of this chapter is to explain the budgeting procedure, and how the many subsidiary plans interlock to form the complete budget. Since the capital budgeting process is a complex part of the overall budget, it is discussed in Chapter 14, Property, Plant, and Equipment. After an overview of the planning process, we give special emphasis to the sales planning process, since the accuracy of that budget determines the accuracy of the rest of a company's final budget. Finally, we describe a basic tool in evaluating a budget's reasonableness—the break-even analysis; the description includes the impact of changes in sales mix, sales price, and product cost on a company's break-even level.

NEED FOR PLANS

The fundamental purpose of business budgeting is to find the most profitable course through which the efforts of the business may be directed in meeting its primary service objective. Guided by the budget, management tries to hold the business on its charted course as nearly as possible.

Although it is easy to speak in theory of the desirability of budgeting, the advantages in an actual case are not always so apparent. Conditions change rapidly in business; the actions of customers and competitors cannot be entirely controlled, and after they become known a business must govern itself accordingly, regardless of any previously developed program. Plans, when made intelligently, require exhaustive study and research, and this constitutes an expensive procedure. What, then, are the specific advantages to be gained?

The benefits of budgeting lie in three fields of business activity; first, directly in *planning;* second, in the *coordinating* phase; and third, in the *control* area.

These activities are each very wide in scope and contain several supplemental or detailed advantages.

Many of these specific advantages are very closely related to all three primary reasons for budgeting. Considering each reason in more detail will give advantages of business planning and budgeting.

Planning

1. *To base action on thorough investigation.* Perhaps the cardinal advantage of systematic budgeting is that it trains executives to study their problems early and instills in the organization the habit of careful study before a decision is made. This habit is not easy to achieve. Intensive study is to many a distasteful exercise. Most of us prefer to postpone difficult decisions until necessity compels us to act. Businesses, like individuals, tend to become opportunists; they wait until a decision is forced, and then turn quickly, often without time for careful study of the problems, in the direction offering the easiest escape from troubles.

   If executives, from general manager to foreman, know that their plans must be formally expressed and that they will be charged with the responsibility for the execution of those plans, they can be encouraged to make an earlier and more intensive study of the problems at hand.

   This habit of making plans will benefit every activity: financial requirements, inventory levels, production facilities, production, purchasing, advertising, selling, sales promotion, product development, organization expansion, and labor relations.

2. *To enlist the assistance of the entire organization in determining the most profitable course.* When budgeting is undertaken with ample time and on a regular schedule, there is the opportunity to enlist the assistance of foreman, salespeople, branch managers, department heads, and all operating officials. In some lines of business the suggestions and counsel from such sources are essential to the development of the best operating plans, and in most lines of business such assistance is highly desirable. The final plans should express the combined judgment of the entire organization, thereby eliminating bias that frequently affects the judgment of individual departments.

3. *To serve as a declaration of policies.* Nothing so restrains the enthusiasm of an organization as uncertainty. The budget procedure provides a vehicle through which basic policies are periodically reexamined and set forth as guiding principles for the organization. Basic policies, not temporary expediency, should be the guiding factors of a business, and the organization should be schooled in such policies.

4. *To define objectives.* The company's personnel will follow the executive staff when they realize that it has a sensible plan of action and define objectives in mind. Such objectives should be clearly expressed and, to a certain

degree, should stand as goals of attainment for the entire organization. Objectives, however, must not be the product of hope but rather the logical consequence of carefully laid plans.

5. *To stabilize employment.* No employer of labor can disregard the welfare of the corporate staff. We have passed the time when workers can be set aside at will when not needed. To be sure, the firm's responsibility to the workers must be balanced with the responsibility to investors, and the welfare of both must be considered, but the business program must consider stability of employment. Intelligent budgeting rather than governmental regulation offers the greatest hope for providing stability of employment.

6. *To make more effective use of equipment.* During the course of planning, the excess cost of idle capacity will be revealed. Moreover, in considering those plans that offer the greatest profit, the maximum use of available facilities will inevitably be a factor. The result normally would be the elimination of some of the excess capacity costs related to the uneconomical use of physical facilities.

Coordination

1. *To coordinate human effort within the business structure*—In some respects this is the most important purpose of budgeting. In many companies there is a definite lack of coordination of effort. Only when the effort of all divisions is properly coordinated can the full power of united action be secured. If unforeseen situations arise that alter the operations of one division, the machinery must be available for quick readjustment of the program in other divisions affected thereby.

   The success of business budgeting should be measured not so much by how close the ultimate results are to the original plans as by the extent to which all executives are familiar with the immediate program and their respective parts therein. There must be no uncertainty if the organization is to function with full power.

2. *To relate the activities of the business to the expected general trend of business conditions*—Profits are frequently the result of changes in fundamental conditions of competitive efficiency. Business moves through periods of high and low activity and there are frequent signals of the movements of a particular business. These signals must be watched and the plans of the business must reflect courage or caution, depending on the expected trend.

3. *To direct capital and effort into the most profitable channels by means of a balanced and unified program*—Before spending money, serious study should be given to the amount that can be profitably spent, where it is to come from, just how it should be spent, and what results may be reasonably expected. A certain amount of funds must be directed toward equipment and inventories and a certain amount to the promotion of sales, but these amounts

must be kept in proper balance. No more ambitious project should be attempted than that for which there is available capital, no more products should be made than those which can be sold profitably, and no sales program should be developed beyond that needed for the planned production. When such a balance of factors is directed toward a definite objective, even though it can seldom be fully achieved in practice, its attainment will be more likely the result of careful advance planning. Without such planning, inventories are likely to be out of proportion to sales and production requirements, excessive amounts of credit may be extended to customers, and irregularities are likely to arise in the use of production facilities.

4. *To reveal weaknesses in organization*—As plans are made and the responsibility for their execution delegated, weaknesses in organization will be revealed. Executives will not accept responsibility unless lines of authority are so delineated that they will be unhampered in the execution of their tasks. Where joint responsibilities are necessary, provision must be made in advance for an orderly procedure of joint action. No management activity so quickly reveals weakness in organization as the procedure of systematic budgeting.

Control

1. *To control specific expenditures*—Some expenditures are subject to very definite control. It may be decided, for example, that $200,000 should be invested in plant expansion, that $100,000 should be appropriated for various sales promotion projects related to a new product, that 1,000 units of the new product should be sold during the period under consideration, and that these units should be manufactured at a cost of $200 each. Assuming that the plans have been predicated on careful study and the considered judgment of the entire organization, the foundation has been laid for a certain degree of control. The investment in the plant can be rigidly held to the prescribed limits in spite of the enthusiasm of production officials to go beyond that limit. Likewise, the expenditure for sales promotion can be definitely held to the predetermined plan. To be sure, the orders for 1,000 units may not be realized. In such cases the budget provides a certain degree of control. Expenditures are limited and directed into channels that offer the most promise. If external conditions beyond the control of management change, the program must be promptly revised. If such conditions do not change and the failure of execution lies within the organization, the budget serves as a very definite tool of control. The failure of sales and production performance to meet expectation provides the signal for corrective action.

2. *To prevent waste*—An inquiry into every contemplated expenditure and the reason for it will constitute an effective way to prevent waste.

Table 5–1: The Sales Budget

Product	No. of Units	Unit Selling Price	Total Sales
R	20,000	$33.00	$660,000
S	30,000	54.50	1,635,000
T	50,000	21.25	1,062,500
U	5,000	78.50	392,500
Total	105,000		$3,750,000

SYSTEM OF PLANS

At the highest level, the annual budget is the method by which the company implements its long-range plan. The goals set forth in the long-range plan are used as the basis for the annual budget, given such restrictions as funding limitations, legal issues, and general economic conditions. In the budgeting process, revenues, costs, levels of operations, facilities, financial resources, and personnel are all considered and interrelated. The appropriateness of levels and types of costs and expenses are analyzed and interrelated, and modeling is used to predict the financial impact of alternative operating decisions. Thus budgeting is a repeating process that aids the manager in revising plans until an acceptable one is reached.

The budget contains the following subsidiary budgets:

1. *Sales budget*—The sales forecast is the starting point in budget preparation. Table 5–1 shows an abbreviated sales budget.
2. *Production budget*—Once the tentative estimate of sales has been agreed on, the next step is a determination of the quantities of finished goods that must be produced to meet both the sales and inventory requirements. This calculation of units to be produced is illustrated in Table 5–2:
3. *Purchases budget*—After the levels of production have been set, the next job to be undertaken is the sometimes laborious task of determining the quantities of raw material needed to meet the production and inventory

Table 5–2: The Production Budget

Description	Product R	Product S	Product T	Product U
Quantity required for sale	20,000	30,000	50,000	5,000
Desired ending inventory	5,000	5,000	10,000	500
Total requirements	25,000	35,000	60,000	5,500
Less:				
Beginning inventory	3,000	2,000	8,000	1,000
Required production	22,000	33,000	52,000	4,500

Table 5–3: Unit Purchasing Requirements Based on Production Budget

| Raw Material | Finished Product | | | | Total Unit Requirements |
	R	S	T	U	
AA	11,000	33,000	–	9,000	53,000
BB	22,000	–	52,000	9,000	83,000
CC	11,000	66,000	104,000	4,500	185,500

requirements. This function is, first, a matter of extending the units of production times the units of each raw material needed, as shown in Table 5–3.

Then, after usage has been calculated, the value of needed purchases, in light of existing inventories, can be set. The dollar value is determined on the basis of expected unit cost prices that may be furnished by the purchasing department. The purchases budget is constructed basically in the format shown in Table 5–4.

Very often it is necessary to group purchases by class of material rather than to enumerate each individual type of material. In particular, this practice is used where unit prices are small.

4. *Labor budget*—Another budget dependent on the production budget is that of direct labor. The accuracy of this budget is highly dependent upon the accuracy of the labor routings (detailed analyses of the labor needed to build a product) for each product. Also, if a product's bill of materials is not accurate, then more labor is required to assemble the product, thereby affecting the labor budget. Finally, the labor content of the labor routing is strongly influenced by the assumed length of the production run, which in turn is dependent upon the equipment setup time. Since the controller is probably not qualified to evaluate the accuracy of a labor routing, it would be wise to bring together a team of experienced engineers to regularly review the setup times and assumed length of production runs for accuracy. The budget is computed as shown in Table 5–5.

Table 5–4: The Purchases Budget

| Raw Material | Requirements | | | | | | |
	Production	Ending Inventory	Total	Less: Beginning Inventory	Quantity to be Purchased	Unit Price	Purchases Budget
AA	53,000	2,000	55,000	3,000	52,000	$4.00	$208,000
BB	83,000	5,000	88,000	10,000	78,000	2.00	156,000
CC	185,500	20,000	205,500	20,000	185,000	1.00	185,500
Total							$549,500

Table 5–5: The Labor Budget

Product	Quantity	Standard Labor Hours per Unit	Total Standard Labor Hours	Direct Labor Budget (at $6 per Standard Labor Hour)
R	22,000	1.0	22,000	$132,000
S	33,000	2.5	82,500	495,000
T	52,000	.5	26,000	156,000
U	4,500	2.5	11,250	67,500
Total			141,750	$850,500

5. *Manufacturing expense budget*—Total manufacturing expenses for the expected production level must be ascertained on the basis of the activity of each type of expense and/or each department or cost center. The final estimate, arbitrarily assumed to be 50% of direct labor for this overly simplified illustration, is summarized in Table 5–6. A more accurate budget would have elements that varied with production volume; for example, variable expenses such as supplies would have a different budget depending upon the amount of product produced. Some companies also use a step-type budget, in which new, predetermined budgets are used for different levels of production activity.

6. *Inventory budget*—All information necessary to calculate the investment in inventories is now available. The value of the finished inventory is computed as demonstrated in Table 5–7. A similar procedure is followed with respect to raw materials, supplies, and work in process. The total value of inventories is then summarized as in Table 5–8.

The following steps should be taken in budgeting the major individual items of materials and supplies:

• Determine the physical units of material required for each item of goods to be produced during the budget period.

Table 5–6: The Manufacturing Expense Budget

Description	Amount
Indirect labor	$125,000
Payroll taxes and insurance (40%)	50,000
Provision for vacation wages	43,250
Utilities	52,000
Supplies	25,000
Repairs and maintenance	67,000
Depreciation	47,000
Property taxes	10,000
Property insurance	6,000
Total	$425,250

Table 5–7: The Computation of Finished Goods Inventory

Product	Quantity	Unit Cost	Total Sales
R	5,000	$14.00	$70,000
S	5,000	28.50	142,500
T	10,000	8.50	85,000
U	500	35.50	17,750
Total			$315,250

- Accumulate these into total physical units of each material item required for the entire production program.
- Determine for each item of material the quantity that should be on hand periodically to enable the production program to run smoothly with a reasonable margin of safety. The calculation of the minimum quantity on hand should include the size of the most economic order quantity.
- Deduct material inventories that are expected to be on hand at the beginning of the budget period to ascertain the total quantities to be purchased.
- Develop a purchase program which will ensure that the quantities will be on hand at the time they are needed. The purchase program must give effect to such factors as economically sized orders, economy of transportation, and margin of safety against delays.
- Test the resulting budget inventories by standard turnover rates.
- Translate the inventory and purchase requirements into dollars by applying the expected prices of materials to budgeted quantities.

The inventory of goods actually in the process of production between stocking points can be best estimated by applying standard turnover rates to budgeted production. Control over the work-in-process inventories can be exercised by a continuous check of turnover rates. Where the production capacity of individual processes, departments, or plants are revealed to be excessive, they should then be subjected to individual investigation.

The budget of finished goods inventory must be based on the sales budget. If, for example, it is expected that 500 units of item A will be sold during the budget period, it must be ascertained what number of units must be kept in stock to support such a sales program. When reviewing inventories for con-

Table 5–8: The Inventory Budget

Statement of Estimated Ending Inventories as of December 31, 19XX

Raw materials	$38,000
Supplies and parts	4,000
Work in process	97,500
Finished goods	315,250
Total	$454,750

trol purposes, it is not wise to control based on the total inventory amount, since the inventory levels of individual stock items are bound to be either too high or too low—each major inventory must be reviewed separately for reasonableness.

7. *Selling, general, and administrative budget*—Through detailed budgeting and summary by individual departments, the other expenses of the business are estimated. They are summarized in Table 5–9, which shows an administrative-type budget. This budget assumes relatively fixed costs, and is useful when the expense level should not be influenced by day-to-day sales levels, but rather by long-term output (depending on the industry, some sales may take a year to close), and is composed primarily of personnel costs. General and administrative expenses can be judged based on a comparison to the previous year's expenses, its relationship to sales as a percentage, and a comparison with the industry average.

8. *Research & development budget*—The R&D budget differs from the other budgets because the amount of funds allocated to it can be a very subjective issue. Funding can be based on the following criteria:

   • The amount of funds available.

   • The budgets of current R&D projects.

   • The R&D activities of competitors, and the company's need to match competitive R&D expenditures.

   • The need for R&D in the strategic plan.

   Once the total R&D amount has been allocated, the funds must be allocated to individual projects, and the controller should help create budgets for the individual projects.

9. *Capital assets budget*—Based on a detailed review of facility requirements and the availability of cash, a budget for capital expenditures is shown in Table 5–10.

Table 5–9: The Selling, General, and Administrative Budget

Items	Selling Expense	General and Administrative Expense	Financial Expense
Salaries—executives	$74,000	$90,000	$—
Salaries—salespeople	198,000	—	—
Commissions—agents	17,500	—	—
Fringe benefits	108,800	36,000	—
Advertising space	50,000	—	—
Bad debts	—	10,000	—
Traveling expenses	220,000	9,500	—
Rent	12,000	3,000	—
Supplies	21,000	7,000	—
Interest expense	—	—	1,900
Discount on sales	—	—	18,000
Total	$701,300	$155,500	$19,900

Table 5–10: The Capital Assets Budget

Capital Expenditures Budget for the Year Ending December 31, 19XX

Buildings	$120,000
Machinery and equipment	132,500
Total	$252,500

10. *Cost of goods sold budget*—The requisite information is now available to prepare a tentative statement of income and expense. First, of course, the statement of estimated cost of goods sold is computed, as shown in Table 5–11.

11. *Cash budget*—This is a projection of the anticipated cash receipts and disbursements and the resulting cash balance. A cash budget is used for the following reasons:

   • To point out peaks or seasonal fluctuations in business activity that necessitate larger investments in inventories and receivables.

   • To indicate the time and extent of funds needed to meet maturing obligations, tax payments, and dividend or interest payments.

   • To assist in planning for growth, including the required funds for capital investments and working capital.

   • To indicate well in advance of needs the extent and duration of funds required from outside sources and thus permit the securing of more advantageous loan terms.

   • To determine the extent and duration of funds available for investment.

Table 5–11: The Cost of Goods Sold Budget

Statement of Estimated Cost of Goods Sold

Raw materials	
Inventory, January 1, 19X5	$52,000
Add: purchases (Figure 5–4)	549,500
Total available	601,500
Less: inventory, December 31, 19X5	38,000
Transfer to work in process	563,500
Direct labor (Figure 5–5)	850,500
Manufacturing expense (Figure 5–6)	425,250
Total charges to cost of production	1,839,250
Add: work in process, January 1, 19XX	97,500
Total	1,936,750
Less: work in process, December 31, 19XX	97,500
Transfer to finished goods	1,839,250
Add: finished goods inventory, January 1, 19XX	202,500
Total	2,041,740
Less: finished goods inventory, December 31, 19XX (Figure 5–8)	315,250
Estimated cost of goods sold	$1,726,500

- To plan the reduction of bonded indebtedness or other loans.
- To permit the company to take advantage of cash discounts, thereby increasing its earnings.

The cash budget is created by projecting each cost element involving cash. It is very useful for controlling cash flow by comparing actual and forecasted performance. A cash budget is shown in Table 5–12.

The *sources of cash receipts* are collections on account, cash sales, royalties, rent, dividends, sale of assets, sale of investments, and new financing. These items can be predicted with reasonable accuracy. Usually, the most important recurring sources are collections on account and cash sales. Experience and a knowledge of trends will indicate what share of total sales probably will be for cash. For example, assume that an analysis of collection experience for June sales reveals the collection data shown in Table 5–13.

If next year's sales in June could be expected to fall into the same pattern, then application of the percentages to estimated June credit sales would deter-

Table 5–12: The Cash Budget

Item	Year Total
Cash and cash equivalents at beginning of period	$1,330,000
Cash receipts	
From operations:	
Collections on account	47,946,000
Cash sales	1,730,000
Interest receivable	205,000
Insurance proceeds	360,000
Miscellaneous	240,000
Total from operations	50,481,000
From other activities:	
Common stock issue	2,000,000
Short-term borrowings	4,725,000
Long-term debt issue	1,000,000
Total from other activities	7,725,000
Total cash receipts	58,206,000
Total cash available	59,536,000
Cash disbursements	
For operations:	
Accounts payable and accrued items	24,089,000
Payrolls	13,700,000
Interest	2,170,000
Federal and state income taxes	7,185,000
Total from operations	47,144,000
For other activities:	
Repayment on long-term debt	3,496,000
Dividends	2,600,000
Capital expenditures	3,500,000
Total for other activities	9,596,000
Total cash disbursements	$56,740,000
Cash and cash equivalents at end of period	$2,796,000

mine the probable monthly distribution of collections. The same analysis applied to each month of the year would result in a reasonably reliable basis for collection forecasting. These experience factors must be modified, not only by trends developed over time but also by the estimate of general business conditions as reflected in collections, as well as contemplated changes in terms of sale or other credit policies.

If a complete operating budget is available, the control should have little trouble in assembling the data into an estimate of *cash disbursements.* The usual cash disbursements in a company consist of payroll, materials, taxes, dividends, traveling expenses, other operating expenses, interest, purchases of equipment, and retirement of stock.

The cash budget plays a vital role in the budgeting process, because it is a check on the entire budgeting program. If the operating budget goals are achieved, the results will be reflected in the cash position. Failure to achieve budgeted performance may require the treasurer to seek additional sources of cash.

The subsidiary budgets converge, or roll up, into a set of planned financial statements, described below.

1. *The statement of planned income and expense*—A sample statement of income and expense is shown in Table 5–14. In practice, this statement might be detailed by product lines, territories, or channels of distribution.

2. *The statement of planned sources and uses of cash*—A sample statement of sources and uses of cash is shown in Table 5–15. This statement is extremely useful in determining the viability of a company. If the controller sees that more cash is required than is being generated by operations for several future periods, then the budget may need further enhancement to boost cash flow.

3. *The statement of planned financial position*—The final effect of all the planning is reflected in the statement of planned financial position at the close of the budget period. Usually, such a statement is prepared in comparative form with the actual or expected position at the beginning of the budget period as well as at the close. The statement and the related statement of retained earnings are illustrated in Tables 5–16 and 5–17.

Table 5–13: Distribution of Bad Debt Losses

Description	% of Total Credit Sales
Collected in June	2.1
July	85.3
August	8.9
September	2.8
October	.3
Cash discounts	.5
Bad debt losses	.1
Total	100.0

Table 5–14: The Statement of Planned Income and Expense

Statement of Planned Income and Expense	
Net Sales (Table 5–1)	$3,750,000
Cost of goods sold (Table 5–11)	1,726,500
Gross profit	2,023,500
Operating expenses:	
Advertising and selling (Table 5–9)	701,300
General and administrative (Table 5–9)	155,500
Total operating expenses	856,800
Operating profit	1,166,700
Other income—discount on purchases	5,000
	1,171,700
Other expenses	
Interest expense (Table 5–9)	1,900
Discount on sales (Table 5–9)	18,000
	19,900
Profit before income taxes	1,151,800
Income taxes (40%)	460,720
Net income	$691,080

ANNUAL PLANNING CYCLE

In a company with several operating divisions, an overview of the process of developing a plan is described below.

First, specific guidelines concerning the plan are issued by the company management to the operating divisions and the corporate executives involved. The guidelines are intended to assure that:

Table 5–15: The Statement of Planned Sources and Uses of Cash

Cash balance, December 31, 19XX		$460,000
Estimated cash receipts:		
Collections on accounts receivable	$3,672,500	
Proceeds from sale of common stock	500,000	
Proceeds from notes payable	50,000	
Total estimated receipts		4,222,500
Total cash available		$4,682,500
Estimated cash disbursements:		
Accounts payable—materials and supplies	$580,600	
Accounts payable—other	428,000	
Notes payable	300,000	
Salaries and wages	1,330,000	
Accrued income taxes	785,050	
Items—other	202,050	
Interest expense	1,900	
Dividends	210,000	
Capital assets	252,500	
Total estimated disbursements		4,090,100
Estimated cash balance, December 31, 19XX		$592,400

Table 5–16: The Statement of Planned Financial Position

Assets				
	Actual December 31, 19XX		*Estimated* December 31, 19XX	
Current assets				
Cash		$460,000		$592,400
Accounts receivable	$250,000		$322,500	
Less: Reserve for doubtful accounts	15,000	235,000	20,000	302,500
Inventories:				
Raw material	$52,000		$38,000	
Supplies	4,000		4,000	
Work in process	97,500		97,500	
Finished goods	202,500	356,000	315,250	454,750
Prepaid items		3,000		3,000
Total current assets		$1,054,000		$1,352,650
Fixed assets				
Land	$25,000		$25,000	
Buildings	375,000		495,000	
Machinery & equipment	625,000		757,500	
Total	$1,025,000		$1,277,500	
Less: Reserve for depreciation	210,000	815,000	257,000	1,020,500
Total assets		$1,869,000		$2,373,150

Liabilities and Shareholder's Equity		
Current liabilities		
Accounts payable	$60,000	$80,400
Notes payable	300,000	50,000
Accrued salaries and wages	30,000	55,000
Accrued income taxes	370,400	46,070
Accrued items—other	28,000	80,000
Total current liabilities	$788,400	$311,470
Ownership equity		
Common stock	$250,000	$350,000
Capital contributed for common stock in excess of par value	500,000	900,000
Retained earnings	330,600	811,680
Total ownership equity	$1,080,600	$2,061,680
Total liabilities and shareholders' equity	$1,869,000	$2,373,150

Table 5–17: The Statement of Planned Retained Earnings

Balance, December 31, 19XX	$330,600
Add: Estimated net income for the year 19XX	691,080
Total	$1,021,680
Less: Dividends to be paid in 19XX	210,000
Estimated balance, December 31, 19XX	$811,680

- Actions taken during the year will be consistent with corporate policy and strategy as decided in the strategic plan.
- The financial assumptions will be consistent and realistic (e.g., tax rates, inflation rates, capital expenditure levels).

When received, the division plans are consolidated to form the total company picture. The division plans are prepared by function (i.e., sales, facilities, human resources, and so on). Then the consolidated plan, and that of each division, is evaluated in the corporate office. Some reiteration may be necessary to arrive at an acceptable plan. In fact, after each of the detailed budgets is prepared by the accounting staff, the figures are compared with past experience and tested by checking significant relationships. Discussions are held with the functional supervisors or department heads to clarify any seemingly out-of-line condition.

When the overall picture is judged satisfactory at top management and board of director levels, the division is notified of the approved plan. However, when the plan is presented to the board of directors for approval, it should include summaries of key statistics, major assumptions, and risk assessments.

Once the budget is approved, the business enters a new phase. The budget must be attained, so the budget becomes a control tool. For this purpose, actual operating results of the period are compared with the budget. Variances are analyzed, and corrective action is taken wherever necessary. Quite often, economic and competitive pressures force the company's results away from its plan; if so, the budget must be revised.

ROLE OF THE CONTROLLER

The controller plays a major role in assisting management in the plan development phases. He or she must:

- Provide the basic financial guidelines by which the plan should be constructed, including:
  — Allowable capital commitments.
  — Tax rates, including those on income, sales, and property.
  — Bases for estimating accounts payable, inventory levels, receivables, and so on.
  — Interest expense rates.
  — Guidance on accounting practices to be used.
- Provide the format for all major financial statements, including supporting detail statements, so that appropriate analysis may be made. This is necessary to permit the analysis of data and consolidation of the financials.
- Analyze segments of the plan for reliability and reasonableness of information.
- Analyze areas that appear questionable, in a financial sense, so that suggestions can be made for improving profitability.

- Consolidate the financials to form the company's overall financial position.
- Evaluate the overall plan against targets or financial measures, and recommend changes where appropriate.
- Summarize all important aspects of the plan for presentation to top management for approval.

Sales Planning: The Base of All Business Plans

The sales plan is the foundation of the entire system of plans; the production plan, marketing plan, R&D plan, administrative expense plan, facilities plan, working capital plan, and financing plan. The sales plan is so fundamental that the company must develop the best possible sales plan in order to create adequate subsidiary plans.

The sales manager will often view the market as threefold, and will estimate sales in accordance with this view:

1. Sales of existing products and/or services to existing customers.
2. Sales of existing products and/or service to new customers.
3. Sales of new products to existing as well as new customers.

All of these sales may be necessary to avoid a natural decline in sales over a period of time, and to reach the long-term corporate sales objective.

Steps in Developing the Near-Term Sales Plan

The planning steps listed below are typical when industry estimates of future sales levels are available, or when some useful external data may be reliable, and when the involved executives are accustomed to being provided with relevant sales and gross profit analyses.

- The sales manager requires the following starting information for developing the sales plan:
  — Worksheets in the proper format for providing the sales estimate, by month and by product or salesperson, for the planning year.
  — Sales performance for the last year by salesperson in monetary and physical units.
  — Industry data on expected next-year total sales.
  — Any other analyses based on external information, developed by the market research department or economist or the controller, giving a clue to expected business conditions for the coming plan year.
  — Any other data the sales manager needs to help in developing sales estimates.

— Analyses giving the estimated sales impact of planned sales promotions, and reasons for the cause or precise location of below-plan performance in the sales area.

- The sales executive provides a detailed (e.g., by product, salesperson, or territory) estimate of sales for the planning year. Ideally, the sales manager will do this with the advice of the sales staff. When doing so, the sales manager will advise the sales staff on such issues as the percent sales increase expected, the estimated impact of promotional campaigns, and the actions of competitors.

- At the top executive level, the estimates are consolidated and company totals determined. The summarized sales plan is shown in Table 5–18.

- The proposed sales level is discussed by the executive management in terms of its reasonableness.

- When the sales budget is tentatively approved (an iterative process), the data are provided to other functional executives to develop their segments of the annual plan. Several iterations can take place, based on such issues as adjustments for capacity, competitive actions, and the possible lack of raw materials, until an operating plan is agreed upon.

- The operating budget and capital budget, together with the related financial statements, are consolidated and tested for financial acceptability. Further iteration may be necessary if financial concerns arise.

- When the board of directors approves the plan, each segment becomes a commitment for the plan period by the responsible executive.

METHODS FOR DETERMINING THE SALES FORECAST

The methods used to arrive at the sales forecast in the sales plan will influence the quality of the information. Weight must be given to both internal and external factors. External factors, such as general economic conditions, industry trends, total market potential, and competitive reactions, are beyond the company's con-

Table 5–18: The Sales Plan by Territory

Sales Territory	This Year	Total	Quarter 1	2	3	4
West	$212,400	$230,000	$46,000	$63,720	$79,040	$41,240
Rockies	75,000	78,750	15,750	23,620	31,500	7,880
Southwest	134,600	150,750	37,690	45,200	45,200	22,660
Central Plains	53,400	56,100	14,000	16,900	16,900	8,300
Middle West	171,300	186,700	33,600	65,300	50,000	37,800
Southeast	91,400	95,100	19,000	28,500	21,000	26,600
Total	$738,100	$797,400	$166,040	$243,240	$243,640	$144,480

trol, but may greatly affect the sales potential. Internal factors—conditions within the company—include production capacity, product quality, sales experience and history, special advertising programs, and pricing policy.

In this section, some of the more common methods of estimating sales are discussed. What system is used may depend on several related factors:

- *Time*—The time span available and the frequency of the data.
- *Resources needed or available*—Human resources, computers, financial sophistication, and cost.
- *Data input*—What data is needed, and the consistency, availability, and variability of that data.
- *Output*—Reliability, extent of detail, capability of detecting trend changes, and capability of revealing direction changes that have taken place.

The most commonly used forecasting techniques are described in the following sections.

Statistical methods. Basically, a statistical technique is applied to a series of relevant numbers to arrive at a forecast of sales for the industry or company. Then this forecast is modified by the expected impact of sales efforts, promotional campaigns, and so on, to arrive at a sales plan for the company. Among these techniques are:

- *Time series analysis*—Using the least-squares method, an existing series of values is converted into a trend and extrapolated for a future time period. The analysis account for cyclical movements and seasonal patterns to arrive at the forecast.
- *Correlation*—A series is located with which the company sales, or sales of a particular product line, seem to correlate or move sympathetically. The annual product sales are plotted against the index and, based on the leading factor, calculated for the planning period.

Judgmental methods (nonstatistical). The judgmental method involved gathering estimates from several groups. Sometimes, for example, *estimates of salespersons* are used. The sales staff is supplied with actual unit and dollar sales for the past few years, and creates estimates based on that information and their personal knowledge of their territories and customers. This method has the advantage of using knowledgeable people as well as letting the sales staff have a say in creating the forecast. On the other hand, sales personnel tend to provide optimistic forecasts, the sales staff may not give weight to broad economic indicators, and estimates may be deliberately reduced if compensation is based on the quotas that will be derived from the sales forecast.

Additionally, *customer surveys* may be made. The sales staff can ask their customers for purchase estimates for the upcoming year. This is used when other methods of forecasting are not reliable. It is useful when the number of customers is small, so that a few make up a large proportion of the company's business. However, the method is time consuming, and users may be uncooperative.

Finally, *executive opinion composites* can be developed. The executive staff is familiar with the industry and company sales picture. The method involved is to secure the estimates from a group of executives, and then jointly combine the opinions. However, if the executives really do not know the market, then the opinion is one big guess, based on few facts.

Other methods. For some types of products the total market is well known. In addition to the industry total unit volume and/or dollar volume, the rate of growth has been calculated, and often the estimated sales for the next year or two have been determined—perhaps by the industry association. In any event, the planner knows what *share of the market* the company has secured in the past. This market share is then adjusted for the estimated impact of special sales promotions, or estimated competitive activity is applied to the projected total market to arrive at the company portion of the estimated industry sales for the coming year.

The *end-use analysis* technique depends on having a sound estimate of the total end-use market for which products the company's articles serve as component parts or elements. To use the automotive industry as an example, if the expected unit sales of automobiles are known or have been estimated, then the supplier company can estimate its probable sales during the planning period for its product. This market, plus the estimated replacement business, can be combined to arrive at sales expectations. This method bears a close relationship to the customer survey procedure.

The *product line analysis* makes use of the fact that often major products are sold through different channels of distribution or methods of sales than other products, and the sales and sales effort may be managed by product line. Under these circumstances, a company's internal sales analyses by product, subanalyzed by territory, may be the starting point of determining the sales estimate, supplemented by some of the other techniques to arrive at the sales plan.

The *market simulation* technique involves the use of a computer and the construction of a mathematical model of the market. Modifying input for the different factors that influence the market permits the calculation of various sales estimates.

Of practical value in creating market forecasts are these three groups of indicators:

1. *Leading indicators*—Series that usually reach peaks or troughs before general economic activity. Some leading indicators are:
   - *The length of the average work week*—Employers find it more economical to increase the number of hours worked each week before hiring additional employees. These longer work weeks may lead to an upturn of one or more months, or they may coincide with the change.
   - *The number of unemployment claims*—The number of persons who sign up for jobless benefits reflects the change in present or anticipated busi-

ness activity. The fewer who sign up, the better. This index usually turns up before a turning point in economic activity.

- *The gain in new orders for consumer goods*—When new orders are received, materials and supplies are purchased, workers are hired, and output increases. Recoveries have occurred as much as four months after gains in new orders.
- *The increase in stock prices*—A rise in the Standard & Poor's Corporation index of 500 companies usually indicates higher actual and expected profits. Advances in the stock market have preceded improvements in business activity by three to eight months.
- *The number of new housing starts*—From the time a building permit is issued until commencement of construction, several months pass. Gains in building permits issued have led business upturns by zero to ten months.
- *The number of new orders for plant and equipment*—When such orders are received, construction and manufacturing activity increases. These signals have preceded economic upturns by as much as six months, but also have trailed such change by up to nine months.
- *The net change in inventories*—As companies expect an increase in sales, they tend to build their stocks of inventory on hand. This index has led business recoveries by zero to eight months.

2. *Coincident indicators*—Series that tend to move with aggregate economic activity. Some coincident indicators are the number of employees on the nonagricultural payroll, personal income, and manufacturing and trade sales.

3. *Lagging indicators*—Series that reach turning points after the aggregate economic activity has already turned. Some lagging indicators are the ratio of consumer credit to personal income, the prime rate charged by banks, and the average duration of unemployment.

Many sales forecasting professionals do a good job of predicting domestic sales, but have difficulty with international projections. Some of the reasons for less than sensational sales results in the global marketplace include:

- *Inadequate market research*—Marketing executives sometimes think that the experience in one market is automatically transferable to others.
- *Tendency to overstandardization*—Instead of encouraging some local innovation, some salespersons think the same product or packaging applies to all markets.
- *Inflexibility in the entire marketing program*—The same programs are forced on every business unit. Yet experience has shown that some facets are unacceptable in local markets. While some central guidance is desirable, forced adoption, without listening to local arguments, destroys local enthusiasm.
- *Lack of adequate follow-up*—While there may be impressive kickoff programs, momentum is lost because local progress is not monitored.

If a company is alert to the advantages of globalization and is desirous of taking advantage of economies of scale in marketing, manufacturing, R&D, distribution and purchasing, then it needs to avoid the deficiencies mentioned above.

USEFUL SOURCES FOR FORECASTING INFORMATION

There is no definitive set of general economic indicators that will tell the forecasting staff what sales will be in the upcoming period. However, some indicators are used as components of corporate forecasting models. The controller should be aware of external sources of sales forecasting data in case some of this information is to be used in the company's forecasting model.

A partial listing of information sources is as follows:

1. *Government Sources.*
   - Department of Commerce
     — Bureau of Economic Analysis
     — Department of Labor (Bureau of Labor Statistics)
     — Department of Agriculture
     — Bureau of Mines
     — U.S. Government Printing Office
2. *Commercial Banks (economic forecasting departments).*
3. *Other Sources.*
   - Trade associations
   - State governments
   - Federal Reserve Board
   - Universities (economics departments and schools of business)
   - Financial services providing economic data for pay
   - Business magazines, such as *Forbes, Fortune, Business Week,* and *Management Accounting*
   - Libraries

BREAK-EVEN CHART

The profit structure of a company is often presented in the familiar break-even chart form. Management uses this chart to understand the interrelationship of cost, profit, and volume. Figure 5–1 is based on the assumptions: that prices will remain unchanged; that fixed costs will remain the same up to the maximum capacity of the plant; that variable costs will vary in direct ratio to volume; and that income taxes will be 50% of all income before taxes. Figure 5–1 clearly presents the following information for management:

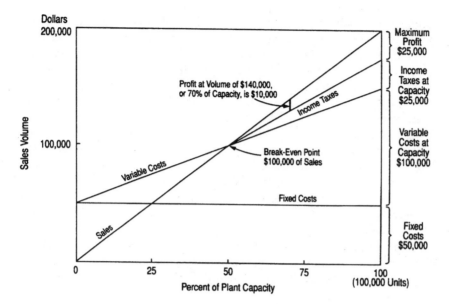

Figure 5–1: Break-Even Chart Illustrating the Interrelationship of Costs, Volume, and Profit.

- Fixed costs of the business are $450,000 monthly.
- Under present tax laws, and with present facilities, the maximum net profit is $25,000 per month or $300,000 per year.
- At present prices, a monthly sales volume of $100,000, or 50,000 units, is required to break even. This makes no provision for dividends to the stockholders.
- To realize a new profit of $10,000 per month will require a sales volume of $140,000 per month.
- Plant capacity expressed in sales dollars under existing prices and processes is $200,000 per month.

Net profit is measured by the vertical line between sales income and income taxes. Income taxes have been figured only from the break-even point.

It is not necessary to draw a chart to find the break-even point of a business. This can be done with the following calculation:

$$\text{Break-even point} = \frac{\text{aggregate fixed expense}}{\text{ratio of variable income to sales}}$$

Any controller who has had the task of determining an overall break-even point for the company and then has determined the break-even point by product lines has perhaps been confused by the fact that the sum of the individual break-even points usually did not equal the overall break-even point. The reason for this is that the overall break-even point has been based on a specific volume mix of product sales. The individual break-even points of the various product lines must be weighted for their proportion of total sales in order to add up to the company's break-even point.

The controller can use a break-even analysis to find answers to the following questions.

Selecting the most profitable products. Use the analysis to determine the marginal profit of the company's various products, so that the most profit is garnered. However, the controller must also factor in the cost of receivables and inventories that may be needed for some products and not for others.

The minimum selling price. The minimum selling price is the variable cost. Such costs set the floor, and anything above this is making a contribution toward fixed expenses.

Unit costs at different volume levels. Suppose, for example, that management desires to know what the unit cost would be at various sales volume levels, with prices remaining fixed. It may be assumed that, in the illustration at hand, the selling price is $2 per unit. What would be the unit cost were the sales to be increased to $240,000? It is assumed that the present sales consist of 50,000 units and that the present unit cost is $2.40, consisting of $0.80 of fixed costs and $1.60 of variable costs. The proposed volume is 120,000 units ($240,000/$2). The new unit cost would be:

$$= \frac{\text{fixed costs}}{\text{Proposed unit volume}} + \text{present variable unit cost}$$

$$= \frac{\$40,000}{120,000} + \$1.60$$

$$= \$1.933$$

At a sales volume of $240,000, the unit cost is $1.933.

Advisability of plant expansion. If a company wishes to add facilities in anticipation of higher sales, the break-even analysis is most useful in pointing out the risks associated with a plant expansion. The break-even analysis will show the additional amount of base-level sales required to cover the cost of the new facilities, as well as the maximum profit that can be obtained by using all of the productive capacity of the new facility. As a result of this analysis, management may become more interested in outsourcing production or expanding in smaller stages.

Most profitable use of scarce materials. Assume, for example, that only a part of the required inventory is available for a chemical common to five products. How should the chemical "X" be distributed, considering only the greatest net profit to the company? It is assumed that rates of production are about the same and that all products are manufactured with the same facilities. The solution is evident from the example in Table 5–19.

Table 5–19: Marginal Profit per Pound of Product

	Unit				
Product	Selling Price	Variable Cost	Marginal Income Contribution	Pounds of "X" per Lb. of Product	Marginal Profit per Lb. of "X"
1	$2.00	$1.00	$1.00	.5	$2.00
2	2.50	1.50	1.00	.3	3.33
3	4.00	2.50	1.50	.5	3.00
4	3.00	1.00	2.00	1.5	1.33
5	5.00	2.50	2.50	2.0	1.25

Product 2 yields the greatest profit per pound of "X" and these requirements should be met first, all other factors being equal.

CHANGES IN THE SALES MIXTURE

Most companies have a variety of product lines, each making a different contribution toward fixed expenses. Changes in the break-even point as well as the operating profit can result from shifts in the mixture of products sold, even though the sales prices are unchanged and the total dollar sales volume meets expectations. Such results can occur also from changes in distribution channels or sales to different classes of customers if the rearrangement affects the contribution of the product over and above variable costs. Actually, when a break-even chart is used, an underlying assumption is that the proportion of each product sold, or sales through each channel of distribution, is unchanged. Very often this does not happen; the proportionate drop is not the same for all products. The higher-priced lines, for example, may decline much more rapidly than others. Such changes must be recognized in evaluating the data.

The effect of a change in sales mixture is illustrated in the calculations shown in Table 5–20. Assume the following proportion of sales among three products, the indicated variable costs, fixed costs, and profit.

Table 5–20: Impact of a Change in Sales Mix on Profits

	Sales			Marginal Income over Variable Costs	
Product	%	Amount	Variable Costs	Amount	% of Net Sales
A	40.00	$4,000.00	$2,600.00	$1,400.00	35.00
B	50.00	5,000.00	4,000.00	1,000.00	20.00
C	10.00	1,000.00	875.00	125.00	12.50
Total	100.00	$10,000.00	$7,475.00	2,525.00	25.25
Fixed Costs				1,200.00	
Operating Profit				$1,325.00	

The break-even point can be calculated as follows

$$\frac{\$1,200}{.2525} = \$4,752$$

If, however, sales increase on the higher-margin items, the break-even point would decrease. Such a change is illustrated in Table 5–21.

The break-even point can be calculated as follows:

$$\frac{\$1,200}{.28625} = \$4,192$$

This break-even point has dropped by $560 as a result of the changes in sales mixture.

CHANGES IN THE SALES PRICE

It should be clear that a change in selling price affects the break-even point and the relationship between income and variable costs. The controller should also be aware that a change in selling price may have an even greater effect on marginal income than a corresponding percentage increase in variable costs. For example, in Table 5–22, a 10% drop in selling prices is equivalent to an 11.1% increase in variable costs as regards the break-even point and marginal income.

Sales were reduced by 10% of $50,000 to a level of $45,000. As variable costs were not changed, these costs as a percent of sales are 44.44%, an increase of 11.1%. Computing the revised variable cost as a percent of net sales based on the original $50,000 of sales produces a variable cost of $22,222. This is 11.1% higher than the original variable cost.

Table 5–21: Impact of Change in Sales Mix on Break-Even Point

Product	Sales %	Sales Amount	Variable Costs	Marginal Income over Variable Costs Amount	% of Net Sales
A	60.00	$6,000.00	$3,900.00	$2,100.00	35.00
B	35.00	3,500.00	2,800.00	700.00	20.00
C	5.00	500.00	437.50	62.50	12.50
Total	100.00	$10,000.00	$7,137.50	2,862.00	28.625
Fixed Costs				1,200.00	
Operating Profit				$1,662.50	

Table 5–22: Impact of Price Change on Break-Even Volume

	Present Selling Prices		With a 10% Reduction in Sales Price		Equivalent Increase in Variable Costs	
Sales	$50,000	100.00	$45,000	100.00	$50,000	100.00
Variable costs	20,000	40.00	20,000	44.44	22,222	44.44
Marginal income	30,000	60.00	25,000	55.56	27,778	55.56
Fixed costs	15,000	30.00	15,000	33.33	15,000	30.00
Operating profit	15,000	30.00	10,000	22.23	12,778	25.56
Break-even volume	$25,000		$27,000		$27,000	

CHANGES IN THE COST

An increase or decrease in the amount of fixed cost changes the operating profit by a like amount, while the break-even point is changed by a like percentage. To illustrate, assume a case where fixed costs are reduced by $10,000, or 33.3%. The operating profit and break-even points are shown in Table 5–23.

In the example, with a reduction of $10,000 in fixed costs, the operating profit naturally increased by a like amount. Moreover, fixed costs were reduced by 33.3%, and so the break-even point declined by 33.3%, from a $75,000 sales volume to $50,000.

This calculation assumes that no change would take place in variable costs, but in practice a change in fixed costs may be accompanied by a change in the variable. For example, installation of a labor-saving device may increase depreciation and maintenance charges and decrease direct labor costs and related payroll charges. If an increase in fixed costs is being discussed, the probability of an increased sales volume should be reviewed. Furthermore, alternatives should be examined, such as subcontracting or renting of space and equipment in lieu of purchasing. The acquisition of permanent assets will decrease the firm's ability to adjust its costs to lower levels should a reduced sales volume ever necessitate such action. Opportunities for the reduction of fixed expenses should not be

Table 5–23: Impact of Cost Changes on Break-Even Sales

	Present		Fixed Costs Reduced by $10,000	
	Amount	% of Net Sales	Amount	% of Net Sales
Net sales	$200,000	100	$200,000	100
Variable costs	120,000	60	120,000	60
Marginal income	80,000	40	80,000	40
Fixed costs	30,000	15	20,000	10
Operating profit	50,000	25	60,000	30
Break-even sales	$75,000		$50,000	

overlooked in any attempt to reduce costs. A lowering of fixed costs increases the margin at any sales level and, by reducing the break-even point, the company is able to withstand a greater drop in income before losses appear.

Changes in unit variable costs or expenses also affect the break-even point. Most cost reduction programs center around this category, because here a great many possibilities are open for cost reduction. For example, changes in the type of material used, or the purchase price of material, or the amount of scrap or waste can affect variable costs. Changes in manufacturing processes, hourly labor rates, plant layout, or employee training methods, or the introduction of incentive payments can all affect the labor costs. General economic conditions may influence the ability of a firm to reduce variable costs. Very often the reduced sales volume permits more effective maintenance of equipment in the shutdown periods. Then, too, in such periods the labor turnover rate and material prices are usually reduced. Of course, such conditions may force sales price reductions, which negatively affect the company's profits.

6

SALES

Sales management is a dynamic area, constantly facing new problems. The controller has a great impact on the resolution of these problems. An extensive review of sales and distribution costs can help sales executives make prudent decisions consistent with the company's goals.

The controller may be asked to provide input about any of the following topics:

- *Product*—What product is to be sold and in what quantity? Is it to be the highest quality in its field or lower? Is the product to be a specialty or a staple?
- *Pricing*—At what price is the article to be sold? Shall the company follow a policy of meeting any and all price competition? What are the terms of sale?
- *Distribution*—To whom shall the product be sold—shall the firm sell directly to the ultimate consumer or through others, such as wholesalers? What channels of distribution should be used?
- *Method of sale*—How shall the goods be sold? Is it to be by personal solicitation, advertising, or direct mail? What sales promotion shall be used?
- *Organization*—How shall salespeople be selected, and how shall they be trained? What is to be the basic organizational setup? Are there to be branch offices? Will sales supervisors handle all lines of product, or will each specialize? Into what departments shall the sales organizations be divided? How many salespeople should be employed?
- *Planning and control*—How are sales territories to be set up? Shall sales standards be used as measuring sticks of performance? How will salespeople be compensated—salary, commission, or bonus? What controls will be employed?

This chapter discusses the controller's role in relation to the sales department, as well as typical kinds of analyses to apply to sales, the applicability of standards to the sales staff, issues regarding product pricing, and reports that are useful for describing the performance of sales revenue, margins, and costs.

ROLE OF THE CONTROLLER

The controller's skills are useful in sales accounting and analysis to assist marketing executives in the following areas:

- *Problems of product*—The initial selection of the product or consideration of changes in the line, sizes, and colors should generally be based on the collective judgment of the sales manager (for marketing considerations), the manufacturing executive (production problems), and the controller (cost considerations). The controller should be able to indicate the probable margin on the product, as well as the effect of volume on the margin or the effect of changes in quality, composition, and manufacturing processes on the cost to make or sell. In the continuing review of sales trends, the controller may be able to identify unfavorable trends that could require a redirection of the sales effort or a change in the product.

- *Problems of price*—In many companies, pricing procedures are not reviewed on a periodic basis. The pricing procedure may not be responsive to increased costs. Although cost is not the only determining factor, it must be considered in maximizing the return on investment. The controller must be able to provide all the available cost information. Total costs, marginal or differential costs, out-of-pocket costs, or cost differences must be considered in developing the price structure. This is true for competitive bids or for establishing price lists for the usual type of sale.

  In an analysis of sales volume and related prices, it may be revealed that unfavorable variances often result from salespersons having too much authority in setting prices. Obviously, as production costs change, the information should be communicated to the sales executives for consideration of appropriate price changes. Also, assistance should be provided in setting volume price-breaks for different sizes of orders.

- *Problems of distribution*—The controller contributes the cost analysis necessary, as well as a review of statistics for unfavorable trends. The controller should also research differences in the selling cost through different channels of distribution, as well as in different customer accounts and sizes of orders. Controller input is needed on such issues as:
  - The minimum order size to accept.
  - Restriction of the sales effort on large volume accounts that purchase only low-margin products.
  - Desirability of servicing particular types of accounts through jobbers, telephone solicitation, mail order, and so on.

— Discontinuance of aggressive sales efforts on accounts where annual sales volume is too low.

— The best location for branch warehouses.

• *Problems relating to the method of sale*—The controller can assist the sales manager by providing information on historical costs and preparing alternative cost scenarios for various selling methods. For example, such analyses can include the impact of distributing samples, using various advertising programs, and costs of market tests.

• *Problems of organization*—Because the sales management function is dynamic, organizational changes are necessary to satisfy the new requirements. In making these changes, information related to potential sales by product or territory may assist in reassigning or hiring new salespeople.

• *Problems of planning and control*—The controller can be active in any of the following areas:

— *Sales budgets and quotas.* Detailed records about the distribution of sales by territory, product, and customer, coupled with the sales manager's knowledge of product changes and trends, provide basic information necessary in an intelligent setting of sales budgets, quotas, and standards. The controller also may provide services in connection with forecasting and market studies.

— *Distribution expense budget and standards.* A history of past expenses as recorded in the accounting department provides much-needed data in setting budgets and standards for the measurement and control of the selling effort.

— *Periodic income and expense statements.* These can be by territory, commodity, method of sale, customer, salesperson, or operating division. Increasing levels of detail can spotlight specific levels of weakness.

— *Special analyses to reveal performance problems.* Typical special reports cover sales incentive plans (to see which plan will motivate the staff to sell the most profitable products), branch office and warehouse expenses, customer development expense, and salesperson's compensation in comparison with sales garnered and the industry pay structure. The controller also has the responsibility to see that adequate procedures are followed and that the sales planning and control is sound from a financial viewpoint.

SALES ANALYSIS

The evidence is unmistakably clear in any business that average sales revenue and expense information is not sufficient. Such general information is of little value in making key marketing decisions and directing sales efforts. The data must be specific and directly related to the problem under examination.

Types of Sales Analyses Needed

There are many types of sales analysis. Some analyses chart past sales performance, while others involve determining trends in comparison with past periods,
the relationship to budget, to gross profit, selling expense, or net profit. Analyses
may be expressed in physical units or dollar volume. Typical analyses are by
product, territory, channel of distribution, method of sale, customer, size of order,
terms of sale, organization, and salesperson. These analyses may be developed,
not merely with regard to sales, but from gross profit to profit after direct selling
expense, or ultimately to the net profit of the segment being measured. Other
analyses related to unrealized sales may be useful, such as unfilled orders, cancellations, and lost sales.

The controller may find that the sales manager can use certain of these analyses monthly or periodically—for example, sales by territory, by product lines, or
by salesperson. Other analyses may be made only for a special investigation,
when it is expected that the tabulation will reveal out-of-line conditions. In any
event, it is the controller's responsibility to design and install procedures and
records in such a fashion (for example, by reorganizing the chart of accounts)
that the maximum information is made available with a minimum of effort. It is
axiomatic that in many situations the faster a company gets its information, the
better its competitive position.

Deductions From Sales

In any analysis of sales, the importance of sales deductions should not be overlooked. Although reviews may relate to net sales, the clue to substandard profits
may lie in the deductions—high freight cost, special allowances, or discounts.
These factors may reveal why unit prices appear too low. In particular, it may be
helpful to prepare an analysis of deductions by responsibility: the manufacturing
division, for defective products; the traffic department, for erroneous freight
allowances; and the sales division, for allowances to retain customer goodwill.

Typical Conditions Found by Sales Analyses

Many businesses find that a large proportion of the sales volume is done in a small
share of the product line. Likewise, a small proportion of the customers will provide the bulk of the business. Such conditions reflect the fact that only a small part
of the selling effort is responsible for most of the business. This information may
prove useful in permitting the concentration of sales effort and the consequent
reduction in selling expenses or redeployment of the sales staff to different customers or territories. When product analysis reveals unsatisfactory conditions, a
simplification of the product line may be indicated. Although the line may not be
limited to only volume items, many sales managers are beginning to realize that
not all varieties need be carried. Smart executives will let their competitors have
the odd sizes or odd colors and concentrate on the more profitable articles.

The controller can use the drill down technique to pinpoint specific areas that cause problems. For example, the controller notes that sales are $20,000 lower than expected in the period. By drilling down to the next level of detail, the problem is more clearly defined as being caused by the Northeast region. By drilling down to the next level of detail, the controller finds that salesperson X in the Northeast region has fallen far short of the sales goal. Even further detail may show which specific items in the product line are not being sold by salesperson X. This kind of analysis allows the sales manager to correct the low sales problem with specific actions.

Other Uses of Sales Analysis

The controller can perform many simple sales analyses to guide the sales effort. Here are a few:

- *Sales planning and setting of quotas*—Past experience is a factor.
- *Inventory control*—To properly plan inventories, a business should be familiar with past sales and probable future trends in terms of seasonal fluctuations and type of product.
- *Setting sales standards*—Past experience is a factor.
- *Enhancing the distribution of sales effort*—The company may be concentrating its effort in too restrictive an area. Consideration of potential sales, competitive conditions, and cost factors may dictate a wider coverage. Alternatively, analysis might reveal that the territory is not being fully covered.
- *Enhancing the sales effort on products*—A study of sales and the potentials may reveal the restriction of sales effort to certain products, resulting in the neglect of other and more profitable ones. Also, a comparison of sales by product with previous periods will reveal trends.
- *Enhancing the sales effort in terms of customers*—Analysis of consumer buying trends should reveal information about the types of merchandise purchased by each customer. Also, comparison with the sales of a similar period for the previous year will reveal whether the company is making headway in securing the maximum amount of profitable business from the customer. Analysis by customer account, coupled with other information and discussions with the sales manager, will show certain accounts that cannot possibly provide a profitable volume, even if developed. This may permit greater utilization of the sales effort elsewhere.

Sales and Gross Profit Analysis

Sales efforts should be directed and focused on profitable volume. To accomplish this, sales executives must be provided with all the facts related to profit. Therefore, analyses of sales must include a detailed analysis of gross profit. For example, a salesperson's report should indicate the comparative gross profit by periods as well as sales. Although high gross profit does not necessarily signify a high net profit (since the selling costs may be excessive), it is an indicator.

Variations in gross profit may result from changes in the selling price, product sales mixture, returns, or volume, largely controlled by the sales executive, or from changes in manufacturing efficiency controlled by the production executive. These facts should be recognized when reviewing changes in gross profit. The causes of variances should be divided into those that are the responsibility of the sales executive and of the production executive. The best measure of sales performance will be standard gross profit. When the standard eliminates the manufacturing efficiency factor, then the sales department is responsible for the result, as well as the volume variance.

SALES STANDARDS

A standard is a scientifically developed measure of performance. The most widely used sales standard is the quota, which is the amount of dollar or physical volume of sales assigned to a sales unit. The quota may involve other considerations, such as gross profit, new customers, collections, or traveling expenses, thereby representing a composite standard of performance. Sales standards are frequently not appreciated by sales managers, who are of the opinion that standards substitute impersonal statistics for sales leadership. However, sales standards reveal weaknesses in performance, are a basis for rewarding merit, and set a stimulating goal for each salesperson to achieve. The primary requirements in developing tools for the sales executive are threefold:

1. *Sales standards are the result of careful investigation and analysis of past performance, taking into consideration expected future conditions.* Sales standards represent the opinion of those best qualified to judge what constitutes satisfactory performance. Judgment about detailed operations must rest largely with the sales executives. Opinions about expected general business conditions should represent the combined judgment of the executive staff, including the chief executive, the sales manager, and the controller.

2. *Sales standards must be fair and reasonable measures of performance.* Nothing will be so destructive to morale as a sales quota, or any other standard, set much too high. Experience shows that such standards will be ignored. The standards must be attainable by the caliber of salesperson the company expects to be representative of its sales staff.

3. *Sales standards will need revision from time to time.* Because sales conditions change frequently, the measuring stick must change to keep pace.

The sales representative should be thoroughly informed about the method of arriving at the quota and convinced that the amount of assigned sales is justified according to the existing conditions. Then, and only then, will the salesperson exert all efforts to meet the quota.

Actual experience with sales quotas, as with all standards, will reveal that sales representatives react to them somewhat differently, particularly at first. Some are stimulated to their highest efficiency, whereas others are discouraged. Some sales executives place considerable emphasis on this human element in setting their quotas.

The objection sometimes raised—that efforts are lessened after quotas are reached—is seldom valid if performance is properly rewarded. The chief difficulty arises when quotas are exceeded as a result of some fortuitous circumstance in which the sales representative has had no part or for which the representative's share of the credit is uncertain. The solution here rests with extreme fairness in handling individual cases and with the development of confidence in the knowledge and integrity of sales executives.

Illustrations of Sales Standards

Sales standards may be expressed in terms of effort, results, or the relation of effort to result. For example, a salesperson may be required to make three calls a day or 15 calls a week. If the calls are made, the standard is met. Again, as a result of these calls, 10 orders must be received for every 15 calls made. Another standard is to simply secure a certain dollar volume from a given territory, regardless of the number of calls made or the percentage of orders per call.

Although the applicability of sales standards to various industries and types of trading concerns may differ, standards the controller may consider discussing with the sales manager are as follows:

- *Standards of effort*
  - — Number of calls made per period
  - — Number of calls made on prospective customers
  - — Number of dealers and agencies to be established
  - — Number of units of sales promotional effort to be used
- *Standards of results*
  - — Percentage of prospects to whom sales are to be made
  - — Number of customers to whom new articles are to be introduced or sold
  - — Number of new customers to be secured
  - — Amount of dollar volume to be secured
  - — Number of Physical units to be sold
  - — Amount of gross profit to be secured
  - — Amount of profit to be secured
  - — Amount to be sold to individual customers
  - — Dollar or physical volume of individual products to be sold
  - — Percentage of gross profit to be returned
  - — Average size of order to be secured
  - — Relation of sales deductions to gross sales

- *Standards expressing relationship of effort and result*
  - — Number of orders to be received per call made
  - — Number of new customers to be secured per call made on prospects
  - — Number of inquiries or orders to be received per unit or per dollar of sales promotional effort expanded
  - — Relation of individual direct selling expense items to volume or gross profit
  - — Relation of sales administration or supervision costs to volume or gross profit

Revision of Sales Standards

Some standards of sales performance can be set with a high degree of exactness. The number of calls a salesperson should make, the percentage of prospects to whom sales should be made, and the physical units that should be sold to each customer are illustrative of performances that frequently lend themselves to accurate measurements. However, there are many factors in sales performance that are so governed by conditions beyond the control of the salespeople that the standards must be revised promptly to meet important changes in such conditions. Where a salesperson is given some latitude in price setting, the gross profit may vary with competitive conditions beyond his or her control. Strikes, droughts, and floods may suddenly affect the sales possibilities in a particular territory. If the sales standards are to be effective measures of sales performance, they must be promptly revised as conditions change. Careless measurement of performance soon leads to discouragement, resentment, and disinterest in the task.

Method of Expressing Sales Standards

Quotas should be broken down into their detailed elements. This helps to show the sales representative where, how, and to whom the goods should be sold. To illustrate, a company may give each of its sales representatives the following quota details:

The proportion of the quota assigned to each product line.

The part of the quota that represents an expected increase in business from new customers.

The part of the quota that represents an expected increase in business among old customers.

The part of the quota to be secured in cities of various sizes.

The part of the quota assigned to particular kinds of outlets or classes of customers.

The part of the quota to be secured from special sources.

The distribution of the quota among the months of the year.

Although such a plan entails considerable work, it tends to balance the sales effort and to assist the sales representative in directing his or her work most effectively.

It should be realized that such plans require the necessary detailed analysis of past performance by the controller's staff. Furthermore, such detail is indicative of a well-developed program. Many firms, particularly the small and medium sized, will express quotas in general terms only—so many dollars of sales or so many overall units. Where quotas are relatively new, the controller should proceed cautiously and develop the details gradually so that the sales executives can be guided step by step. Only when the data are available and the sales staff realizes the advantages of detailed planning can the quota type of standard serve most usefully.

It frequently happens that the quota cannot be fairly expressed directly in money or physical volume. For example, a sale of $100 of class A goods may deserve more credit than a like amount of class B goods, or a sale to a new customer may deserve more credit than a similar sale to an old customer. In such cases, the quota may be expressed in points that give effect to a weighting for different types of sales performance. Thus a sale of $100 class A goods may be counted as 10 points, whereas $100 of class B goods would be counted as only 5 points. The "point" system may likewise be extended to include other types of service, such as calls on new prospects, demonstrations, or collections.

The final requirement for effective standards is an adequate method of compensation as a reward for good performance.

SALES REPORTS

It is the function of the controller to furnish the sales executives with the sales facts. However, it is one thing to furnish the information, and another to see that it is understood and acted on. To assure the necessary understanding, the controller must adapt the report to the reader. Information for the needs of the chief executive will be different from that for the sales manager, and reports for subordinate sales executives will differ even more. The extent of the information required and the form of presentation will depend on the capabilities of the individual, the individual's responsibilities, the type of organization, and the philosophy of sales management.

Some sales managers can effectively use vast amounts of statistical data, whereas others prefer summarizations. Accordingly, the controller should offer to develop reports to meet individual requirements. The use of charts, graphs, and summaries will greatly enhance the communication of the sales data to sales management. In many instances, a narrative report citing the significant issues or problems is the most effective tool. Depending on the seriousness of the problem, or where major actions are being recommended, a meeting may be in order. It is up to the controller to make sure that the information provided is understood and can be properly used.

The matters that may be included in a sales report may cover any of the following items.

- Actual sales performance, with month or year-to-date figures.
- Budgeted sales for both the period and year-to-date.
- Comparison of actual sales by firm with industry figures, including percentages of the total.
- Analysis of variances between budgeted and actual sales and reasons for differences.
- Sale–cost relationships, such as cost per order received.
- Sales standards—comparison of actual and quota sales by salesperson.
- Unit sales price data.
- Gross profit data.

These data may be expressed in physical units or in dollars. Aside from actual or standard sales performance, some may relate to orders, cancellations, returns, or lost sales.

Top sales executives should receive information in summary fashion. For example, a comparison of actual and planned sales by product line or territory is appropriate information for the sales manager. Trend reports that show increasing or declining sales by major category are useful. Also, an orders-on-hand report gives the sales manager information about the likely short-term direction of sales. Such a chart is shown in Table 6–1.

For control purposes, the performance of each segment of the sales organization should be made known to the supervisor responsible. It follows, therefore, that reporting must be available for each division, district, area, branch, and salesperson. As reports relate to increasingly lower levels of management, such information can become massive in extent. To avoid lengthy reports, the controller can use "exception" reports. This method eliminates data where performance was satisfactory and details only that which did not reach acceptable levels. Such a report could list only those salespeople who were 5% or more under budget, or only those customers on which a loss was realized. These reports can

Table 6–1: Report on Sales Order Activity

		Orders on Hand				
Description	Order on Hand, 6/30/XX	Orders Received	Orders Canceled	Orders Delivered	Units	Sales Value in $
Vehicles						
Type A	50	25	5	10	60	120.0
Type B	100	—	5	20	75	262.5
Type C	150	50	—	5	195	838.5
Type D	60	10	—	5	65	97.5

use either direct costs only, or also include allocated overhead costs. An exception report for salespeople is shown in Table 6–2.

PRODUCT PRICING

In the field of product pricing, the controller can exert some preventive accounting control by bringing facts to bear on the problem before unwise decisions are made. This control activity is closely related to profit planning: the influence of prices on company profits is obvious, and the best controls on costs and expenses will not succeed in producing a profit if selling prices are set incorrectly. The controller can perform the following product pricing functions.

- Help establish a pricing policy that will be consistent with the corporate objectives.
- Provide unit cost analysis as one factor in price-setting.
- Project the effect on earnings of proposed price changes and alternatives.
- Gather pertinent information on competitive price activity.
- Analyze the historical data on prices and volumes to substantiate probable trends as they may influence proposed price changes.
- Determine for management the influence on profits of changes in price, product mix, sales volume, and so on.

Cost Basis for Pricing

Over the long term, no company can sell all or most of its products at less than cost; therefore, adequate cost information is indispensable. In the short term, the

Table 6–2: Exception Report—Salesperson Performance

Description	Actual Sales	Under Budget Amount	%
Performance satisfactory	$827,432	$112,610	15.8
Under budget performance			
Abernathy	32,016	1,760	5.2
Bristol	17,433	1,390	7.4
Caldwell	19,811	1,320	6.2
Fischer	24,033	1,470	5.8
Gordon	8,995	480	5.1
Inch	27,666	1,820	6.2
Long	4,277	600	12.3
Mather	39,474	3,800	8.8
Owens	43,189	4,400	9.6
Subtotal	216,894	17,040	7.9
District total	$1,044,326	$95,570	9.2

role played by the cost factors depends on the circumstances. For example, if the product is built to order, then costs will be more important. Furthermore, if competition is weak or if the company is a price leader, then cost information will play a larger role than if the opposite situations exist.

The question then arises, "What kinds of costs are required?" For different purposes, different types of costs may be desirable. One type of cost may be suitable for a short-range decision and quite another type for long-term purposes. Moreover, for pricing, the usual historical cost approach may not meet the requirement. In short, the controller should be aware of the several costing methods and the limitations of each and select that concept most suited to the purpose at hand.

Before reviewing several alternative costing techniques, some general observations are useful. First, prices relate to the future. Therefore, costs to be used in determining prices must be prospective. Recognition should be given to cost levels expected to prevail in the period under review. Probable raw material and labor costs should be considered. Prospective changes in process ought to be reflected in cost estimates.

Obviously, inflation must be considered, and the best available information should be obtained to recognize what future rates of inflation can be expected. In this forecasting, the controller should utilize, to the extent practicable, the modern scientific tools of statistical sampling, simulation methods, decision analysis techniques, and price level analysis. Consideration should also be given to the replacement cost of the productive capacity or capital assets. Prices must provide for the future replacement of these productive assets at the projected costs.

The controller should assist in determining the sales price that will produce the greatest net profit over a long period of time. Too high a profit over the short term may invite competition or governmental regulation. The basic procedure is for the controller to secure from the sales manager the probable number of units that can be sold at various price levels. Then the unit cost and total cost at the corresponding production levels are calculated. That volume at which the greatest total profit is secured can then be determined.

Finally, all costs related to a product should be considered, not merely the cost to manufacture. It defeats the purpose if manufacturing costs are carefully calculated but selling or other expenses are applied as an overall percent without regard to the direct expense and effort specifically applicable to the product.

Although many costing methods are in use, there are four approaches that warrant discussion:

1. Total cost method Under this concept the cost of the product is determined, and to this figure is added the desired profit margin. Such a calculation is shown in Table 6–3. The total cost method has the advantage of being easy to calculate and being able to recover all costs. However, it does not distinguish between direct costs and total costs (critical for short-term pricing decisions), and ignores the possibility of using even higher prices to achieve a greater return.

2. Direct cost method This approach recognizes only the incremental costs of a product. These are the costs directly associated with the product that would not

Table 6–3: The Total Cost Method

	Product A Unit Cost and Selling Price
Cost and expenses	
Raw material	$10.00
Direct labor	4.00
Manufacturing overhead	6.00
Total manufacturing cost	20.00
Research and development expense (10% of manufacturing cost)	2.00
Selling and advertising expense (20% of manufacturing cost)	4.00
General and administrative expense (10% of manufacturing overhead)	.60
Total cost	26.60
Desired profit margin (25% of total cost)	6.65
Proposed selling price	$33.25

be incurred if the product were not manufactured or sold. Any selling price received above this floor represents a contribution to fixed expenses. Applying this principle to Product A described under the total cost method produces the information shown in Table 6–4.

If the product must be sold for the incremental costs or less, then the company would not earn less profit, and might possibly earn a higher profit, by not manufacturing and selling the product. Full consideration must be given, however, to lost business if the withdrawal of the product would cause the loss of other business.

This costing method is of most use when additional sales may be made at reduced prices (for example, to private brand business), when idle plant capacity can be utilized only at reduced prices, and when these added sales do not create problems in the regular market place.

The use of marginal costs is for short-term decisions only. The great danger is the tendency to secure a larger and larger volume of sales on an incremental basis, with an ultimate deteriorating effect in the market and a large share of business that does not return its proper share of all costs. Furthermore, under

Table 6–4: The Direct Cost Method

	Product A Unit Cost and Selling Price
Cost and expenses	
Raw material	$10.00
Direct labor	4.00
Variable manufacturing expense	1.50
Variable selling expense	1.50
Variable administrative expense	.30
Total variable or incremental cost	17.30
Fixed expense applicable to the product	2.50
Total direct costs	$19.80

such conditions there is no profit from the products that are priced only to cover their costs.

3. *Return on assets method* This method maximizes the return on assets employed. It gives attention to the capital invested in manufacturing or sales facilities or working capital. The following formula may be used to calculate the sales price required to produce a return on assets employed:

$$\text{unit price} = \frac{\dfrac{\text{cost} + (\text{desired \% return} \times \text{fixed assets})}{\text{annual sales volume in units}}}{1 - (\text{desired \% return})(\text{variable assets as \% of sales volume})}$$

In the formula, cost represents the total cost of manufacturing, selling, administrative, and research expenses. The percent return represents that rate desired on assets employed. The fixed assets represent plant and equipment. The variable assets represent the current assets that are a function of volume and prices. Applying some assumptions, a unit price of Product A may be calculated in this manner:

$$= \frac{\dfrac{\$2,660,000 + (.20 \times \$300,000)}{100,000}}{1 - (.20 \times .30)}$$

$$= \frac{\$2,720,000/100,000 \text{ units}}{1 - .06}$$

$$= \frac{27.20}{.94} = \$28.936$$

The proof is computed as follows:

Income and costs	
Sales (1,000,000 units at $28.936)	$2,893,600
Costs	2,660,000
Income before taxes	$233,600
Assets employed	
Variable (30% of $2,893,600)	$868,080
Fixed	300,000
Total assets employed	$1,168,080
20% return on assets employed of $1,168,080	$233,600

In a multiproduct company, there is a problem with allocating capital employed to the various product lines. This problem can be solved by allocating assets to the product lines. Some methods of prorating assets to product lines are shown in Table 6–5.

Table 6–5: Methods Used to Allocate Corporate Assets to Product Line

Item	Possible Bases
Cash	In ratio to total product cost
Accounts receivable	In ratio to sales, adjusted for significant differences in terms of sale
Raw material	In ratio to actual or expected usage
Work in process	In ratio to actual or expected usage
Finished goods	In ratio to cost of manufacture
Fixed assets	In ratio to conversion costs (labor and variable manufacturing overhead) or labor hours

4. Target cost method This method is considerably different from the other costing methods. Target costing means that the new product design team determines the price at which the product must sell, and then designs a product with a cost to fit that price level. The controller's role is to be involved in the initial cost determination before the product is produced, to ensure that planned costs allow for an adequate profit margin. The controller will also be involved in later cost studies to see if actual costs match the planned costs.

The prior discussion on product pricing has to do principally with establishing prices for unrelated customers under competitive conditions. A special aspect of product pricing relates to international transfer prices—the value assigned to goods or services produced in one country for the use or benefit of a related company in another country.

Transfer prices, which should be reflected in the sales plans and planned net income of both the producing and receiving companies, probably should be established through the joint efforts of the sales executive and a member of the controller's department. The reason for this is that complicated IRS regulations relate to actual or expected costs, capital employed, functions performed by each party, and the risks involved. Proper cost accounting is essential.

The setting of product prices is complex and includes the evaluation of many variables. It is the task of the controller to provide all pertinent facts for management's judgment. The various costing methods must be considered and the most appropriate applied to each company's unique set of circumstances. In addition to the applicable costs, other factors in setting product prices should be summarized for management's review:

- Return on invested capital or assets employed.
- Assets employed and turnover.
- Percent of plant capacity utilized.
- Percent of product line for each product.
- Percent of market.
- Competition pricing and percent of market.

7

DISTRIBUTION EXPENSES

The costs of getting the manufactured products to the customer have become relatively more significant in recent years, as the cost of manufacturing products has generally declined. In fact, for some companies, the total costs of distribution of the products are in excess of the production or procurement costs.

Although in most companies more effort has been directed toward analysis and control of production costs, the costs of distribution have either not been available in usable form or not communicated to marketing management for decision making. Executives responsible for distribution of the products must be made aware of the cost components to effectively plan and carry out a proper distribution system effort. The controller must develop the control mechanisms, secure the facts and interpret them, and communicate the information to the marketing executives. To be effective, the marketing executive must understand the accounting control information and use it to develop better marketing plans. The increasing costs of distribution can be effectively controlled and even reduced if the controller works with the sales and marketing management to develop the necessary control techniques.

Any controller who tackles distribution cost control will find that the problems usually are much more complex than those relating to production costs. First, the psychological factors require more consideration. In selling, the attitudes of the buyer and the salesperson are variable, and competitive reaction cannot be overlooked. This is in sharp contrast to production, where the worker is generally the only human element. Moreover, in marketing activities the methods are more flexible and more numerous than in production, and several agencies or channels of distribution may be used. Such conditions make the activities more difficult to standardize than production activities. Also, the constant changes in method of sale or channel of distribution are factors that make it harder to secure basic information. Even when the information is secured, great care must be taken in its interpretation. Where indirect or allocated costs are significant, the analyses may require a more relative marginal or incremental cost approach.

The bulk of this chapter covers the detailed analysis and control of distribution costs.

DEFINITION

Distribution costs are the costs relative to all activities from the time goods are produced (or purchased, for a nonmanufacturing company) until the products reach the customer—the cost of storing, marketing, selling, and shipping the product. This section discusses those expenses that are normally under the control of the marketing or sales executive. They include the following general classifications:

Direct selling expenses—All the direct expense of order-getting costs, including direct expenses of salespersons; sales management and supervision; branch sales offices; and sales service, the expenses related to soliciting orders.

Advertising and sales promotion expense—All media advertising expenditures, sales promotions, marketing development, and publicity.

Transportation expense—All transportation charges on outbound goods to customers and returned sales and costs of managing and maintaining the operation of outbound transportation facilities.

Warehousing and storage expense—Includes all costs of warehousing, storing, inventory handling, order-filling, and packaging and preparation for shipment.

Market research expense—The expenses of various project studies, including the expenses of administering the department activity, undertaken to test or obtain information on the various products, markets, channels of distribution, or other distribution segments.

General distribution expense—All other expenses related to distribution functions under sales management that are not included in the foregoing items. They may include general sales management expenses, recruitment and training, and staff functions such as accounting, if applicable.

ROLE OF THE SALES MANAGER

The sales manager is responsible for the requisite sales volume of the right products, and the planning and control of distribution costs. These may seem like two diametrically opposed objectives. However, the situation is a problem of balance; if more money is spent for the distribution effort, what does the business receive in return? Usually, the sales manager is under pressure to increase sales while reducing selling expenses. Thus, he or she must know whether distribution costs are really too high, and if they are too high, just where: What salesman? What territory? What expense? The sales effort must be carefully guided, and this can only be done with the correct accounting information coming from the controller. The sales manager must have an intelligent analysis of distribution costs as a basis from which to work.

ANALYZING DISTRIBUTION COSTS

There are several ways to analyze distribution costs:

- *By the nature of the expense or object of expenditure*—This information is recorded in the general ledger, and can easily be converted into trends in raw expenses, or expenses as a percentage of revenue. However, the controller must dig deeper in order to tell the sales manager why certain expenses are too high, who is responsible for the excess costs, and what can be done to improve the situation.
- *By contribution margin*—This is calculated by deducting from sales income those direct costs incurred in obtaining that segment of the sales income being analyzed. The expenses not deducted from revenues in computing the contribution margins are those not changed by the decision under review. It is used for short-term tactical decisions, but is not good for long-term decisions, because it does not factor in the recovery of total costs, which includes overhead. This approach has the following advantages:
  — Measurement of the immediate gain to the company's overall profit by the transaction under review.
  — Facilitation of management's decision because those costs to be changed are already separated from costs not affected.
  — Avoidance of errors and controversy that arise by reason of cost allocations.
  — Simplicity of application, since direct costs are identifiable more readily than total costs, including the necessary allocations.
  — Data can be secured more quickly and with less effort.
- *By functions or functional operations performed*—This kind of analysis requires the following steps:
  — Establish the functional operations to be measured, such as sales calls, shipments from the warehouse, and circular mailings.
  — Segregate the costs of the functions for measurement. This can either be through specific accounts in the general ledger, or through allocations.
  — Establish units of measurement of functional service. For example, the pounds of shipments might be the measure of the shipping expense, or the

number of the salespeople's calls might serve as one measurement of direct field selling expense.

— Calculate a unit cost of operation by dividing the total controllable functional cost by the number of units.

— Take corrective action if significant cost variances occur.

• *By matching revenues to functions*—This matches expenses with related revenues, so the controller can demonstrate the results of a specific distribution effort. This kind of analysis requires cost distributions for direct and indirect costs. Direct costs are fairly obvious, but indirect costs are exceedingly difficult to spread among the various cost objects. The controller would be wise to spend a considerable amount of time subdividing the indirect costs into smaller pieces and using different allocation bases to apportion the costs in a logical manner among the cost objects. The degree of sophistication of the allocation may depend on whether or not the analysis is short-range or long-range. All costs must be included for long-range analysis, so all allocated costs must be identified. If, on the other hand, decisions are of limited scope and for a short period, such as the sale to a private brand customer for the next year, then perhaps only direct expenses ought to be considered.

The effective direction of the sales effort usually requires all of these types of analysis if the sales manager is to be furnished with the necessary information.

ANALYZING BY APPLICATION

There has been sufficient experience with distribution cost analysis to prove its value. Although the degree of refinement may vary in different companies, the general approach is as follows:

• Determine which type of analysis is required for a particular situation, such as an analysis by method of delivery.

• Classify distribution costs according to those that are direct and indirect.

• Select and apply the allocation bases to the indirect expenses. This includes a segregation and proper treatment of variable, as opposed to fixed, costs.

• Prepare the analysis and commentary for the appropriate executive. This involves the following steps in arriving at significant cost and profit relationships:

— Determine the gross profit by segment.

— Accumulate the direct expense by segment, and deduct this from gross profit to arrive at the profit after direct expense.

— Prorate the indirect expense to arrive at the final net profit.

— Prepare the necessary subanalyses to pinpoint the conditions needing correction.

The following sections discuss the steps required to perform detailed analyses by territory, product, customer, and size of order.

Analysis by Territory

A territory is any geographical area used by a company for sales planning, direction, or analysis. Where goods are sold has a great effect on net profit, because there are striking differences between territories in terms of sales potential, gross margins, and net profit. If goods are sold free on board (f.o.b.) a central point and at the same price, then the gross profit is unchanged. However, if the product is sold on a delivered price basis, then the gross margin is different because of transportation charges. Also, the total distribution costs (including marketing and selling) are different in different territories. The cost to sell in densely populated New York is different from the cost to sell in western Texas. Because of these dissimilar conditions, executives must have an analysis of distribution costs by territory. Such information permits the sales manager to rearrange the sales effort where necessary and to direct the sales effort into the most profitable areas.

Since analysis by territory applies when a large geographical area is covered, a manufacturer covering a national market would greatly benefit from such an analysis, whereas a retail store probably would not. Exactly what type of territorial analysis needs to be made depends on the problem and type of organization. If a territorial sales executive is responsible for costs and results, then a complete analysis by this responsibility area is desirable. Or, if the problem is one of the cost to sell in a small town versus a city, such a segregation must be made.

Once the points of weakness are discovered through analysis, correction action must be taken. Here are some possibilities:

Reorganize territories to allow efforts to be more in line with potentials.

Rearrange territory boundaries to reduce selling expenses and secure better customer coverage.

Shift salespeople to different areas.

Increase emphasis on neglected lines or customers in the territory.

Change the method of sale or channel of distribution (e.g., switch from a salesperson to an agent).

Change the warehouse locations in the territory.

Eliminate unprofitable territories.

Change the advertising policy or expenditure in the territory.

Analysis by Product

In today's economy, the design, style, or type of product a firm sells may change constantly. Hence every company is sooner or later faced with the problem of what products it should sell. Will the firm sell the best or the cheapest line? Will it promote the use of a new plastic? Should it introduce a silent airplane motor? The answer to questions like these is twofold. First, through market analysis, a determination must be made about what the customers want and what price they will pay. Then through cost analysis it must be determined whether the company can make and sell the article at a profit. Therefore, an analysis by products is desirable.

Many firms, in order to increase sales volume, often add new products to the line. Sometimes these new products fit into the line and permit certain economies. Often, however, the different products require new services in varying degree. For this reason, too, an analysis by product is necessary to determine the cost to sell, as well as the net profit.

Generally speaking, the sales effort should be directed toward those products with the greatest net profit possibilities, and cost analysis is necessary to know just which products these are. This is not to say that a company should drop a low-margin item; it may be contributing more than out-of-pocket costs, or it may be necessary for customer convenience. Furthermore, there may be little possibility of selling a high-margin item to a customer. For example, there may be no chance of selling any quantity of a high-profit glue instead of a low-margin paint product to a paint manufacturer. There are more factors in selling than merely cost considerations, but such conditions must be watched and held within reasonable limits. Distribution cost analyses by commodity, then, are of use in the direction of the sales effort.

Many controllers may find, in making product cost analyses, that the net profit on an entire line of products is not great enough, or even that losses are being sustained. When such conditions are revealed, usually steps are taken to increase that margin because the firm may not be in a position to drop an entire line. This is but another way of saying that analysis is a means of controlling costs, because the manufacturing or distribution costs may be too high.

Finally, product cost analyses help to set selling prices when the company is in a position to use cost as a major price-setting guide. Such analyses are desirable in conjunction with determining maximum price differentials to particular customers.

It is self-evident to most controllers that a product analysis of distribution costs should be made when the characteristics of the commodity or their methods of distribution are such that a uniform basis of allocation is not indicative of the effort or cost to sell. In this case, pounds or units of sale or sales dollars may be a fair measure of selling expense. However, there are numerous circumstances when such an apportionment is inaccurate or misleading:

- *If there are differences in the time or amount of sales effort required*—Product A that sells for $0.60 each may require about three times the effort of product V which sells at $0.30 each. Neither sales dollars nor units would be a fair basis. Perhaps one product would require a higher degree of technical assistance and more frequent callbacks, when compared with another. Again, specialty salespeople may merchandise one product, and general-line salespeople may handle another. All such circumstances result in different costs to sell, and should be so reflected in the analyses.

- *If there are differences in the method of sale*—Obviously, if one product is sold exclusively by mail order and another by salespeople, the selling cost cannot be prorated on a sales dollar or unit basis.
- *If there are differences in the size of the order*—When one product is sold in 10-pound lots and another is sold in tank cars, many of the distribution costs can be different.
- *If there are differences in channels of distribution*—One product may be sold directly to retailers, whereas another is distributed through wholesalers. Here, also, there is a difference in distribution costs.

The analysis by product ordinarily will reveal areas of weakness where some correction action can be taken, such as the following:

Shifting the emphasis of the sales effort to more profitable lines or bringing effort in line with sales potential.

Adjusting sales prices.

Eliminating certain unprofitable lines, package sizes, colors, and so on.

Adding new product lines related to the family, with consequent sharing of the fixed distribution expense.

Changing the method of sale or channel of distribution.

Changing the type, amount, and emphasis of advertising.

Revising packaging, design, quality, and so on.

Analysis by Customer

It costs more to sell to some types of customers than to others and more to one customer within a type than to another. Some customers require more services, such as warehousing, delivery, or financing. Some customers insist on different pricing, particularly when different size orders or annual purchases are factors. Again, the types of products sold to some classes of customers differ from others. All these are reasons why analyses by customers are necessary to measure the difference in net profit. Aside from use in the direction of sales effort, these analyses serve in setting prices and controlling distribution costs.

In most firms the analyses by customers will not be continuous. The sales manager may be interested in whether money is being made on a particular account, or changes may be contemplated only on certain groups of accounts. On these occasions special analyses can be made.

Although analyses may be made by individual customers, particularly when there are a few high-volume accounts, by and large the analyses will relate to certain groups or categories. The two basic factors in selecting the classification to be used are the amount of distribution services required (this is the primary reason for differences in distribution costs) and the practicability of segregating the distribution costs. Classifications that have proved useful are these:

- Amount of annual purchases.
- Size of orders.
- Location.
- Frequency of salespeople's calls.
- Type of agent (retailer, wholesaler, or jobber).
- Credit rating of customers.

In making an analysis by classification of customer, one approach is to gather all customers in the applicable group and determine total costs for that group. This may be time-consuming. Another method involves a sampling procedure, wherein representative customers in each category are selected and the cost of servicing them is determined. A modification of this approach is to make a thoroughly detailed analysis in some areas and a sample run in other areas.

It will be appreciated that relatively few distribution cost items can be charged directly to customers and that allocations must be made. Statistical data from various reports will be necessary, such as the number of calls made to customers, the time spent with customers, or the number of orders.

Occasions will arise when a decision must be made about whether business with a specific customer should be continued or whether the method of sale to the customer ought to be changed. For example, changing the selling method from field calls to a phone basis may result in retaining valuable business while securing a contribution margin in line with normal operating requirements.

An analysis by customer provides information of great value to the sales manager. It gives a clear view of the number of accounts in various volume brackets and the average value of orders. In using this information for corrective action, consideration must be given to the production volume needed to cover fixed production costs. The information will furnish facts for executive discussion regarding the following issues:

- Discontinuance of certain customer groups.
- Price adjustments.
- Need for higher margins for certain groups.
- Changes in the method of sale.

Analysis by Size of Order

Another analysis is by size of order. One of the causes of high distribution costs and unprofitable sales is the small order—not because it is small but because the revenue is not high enough to cover all the related transaction costs and still make a profit. There are many instances when small orders cannot be discontinued; however, corrective action can be taken to bring the problem under control. The controller's first step is to get the facts through an analysis of distribution costs by size of order.

The problem is naturally more important in some companies than in others, especially when the order-handling costs are relatively large or fixed.

The procedure for analyzing distribution costs by size or order is similar to that for other analyses. It involves segregating order handling costs into fixed costs and variable costs. In this case, certain costs will be recognized as fixed for all sizes of orders, others will vary with the money volume, and still others will vary with physical volume. The five steps to be followed are:

1. Determine the size of the order groups to be studied (e.g., below $25, $26 to $50, and so on).
2. Classify the costs according to those that vary with the size of the order (e.g., packing), those that are uniform for orders of all sizes (e.g., accounts receivable bookkeeping), and those that must be considered as general overhead (e.g., advertising and supervision costs).
3. Identify the factors that govern the amount of the variable expense applicable to orders of different sizes (e.g., dollar value, weight, or handling size).
4. Apply the factors of variability to the variable expenses and add the uniform costs, thereby arriving at a direct cost of orders by sizes.
5. Apply the overhead costs by some suitable factor, such as hundredweight or dollar value, to arrive at the total order cost.

Other Analysis Issues

The following analyses may also prove useful:

- *By channel of distribution*—Useful where a choice in channel of distribution may be made in order to direct sales into the most profitable channel. The analysis needs to be made from time to time as cost trends change.
- *By method of sale*—The same comments as in the case of analysis by channels of distribution are applicable.
- *By salesperson*—For the purpose of measuring the salesperson's performance in terms of profit and to better direct salespeople in their activities.
- *By organization or operating division*—Useful when there are separate selling divisions. Such an analysis is used to measure performance of the divisional executive. Examples are analyses by departments in a department store, by stores in a retail chain store company, or by branches in a manufacturing organization.

In making recommendations based on the distribution cost analysis, before the decision is reached, every possible effect on every activity of the business must be considered. When deciding whether or not a certain territory must be dropped, the net effect on profit, the change in factory volume with the same fixed expense, and the resulting differences in unit cost must be considered.

SETTING THE DISTRIBUTION BUDGET

The advertising and sales promotion expense often is planned and controlled on a project basis. As such, some boards of directors prefer to approve these projects in a manner similar to capital budget requests. The reasons for this kind of approval are varied. For many companies—retail stores or consumer goods producers like Proctor & Gamble or Coca-Cola Inc., for example—advertising and promotion is a major expenditure. Moreover, it is difficult to measure the effectiveness of advertising or sales promotion programs, and the results of the program may be less immediate and less direct than other types of marketing effort, such as direct selling. Finally, advertising sales promotion is usually organized as a separate department or as an outside agency, unlike other selling efforts.

The purpose of advertising varies in different circumstances. While the general purpose is to support the broad marketing objectives, more specific goals include the following:

- Educate consumers in the use of the product or service.
- Reduce the cost of other selling efforts.
- Increase sales.
- Establish or maintain trademarks or brand names.
- Develop new markets.
- Meet or outdo competition.
- Maintain prices.
- Introduce new products or services.
- Create favorable public opinion.
- Avoid unfavorable legislation.

Two methods, explained below, are used to establish an advertising sales promotion budget.

1. *The lump-sum appropriation method.* This method entails authorizing the expenditure for advertising and sales promotions related to some factor. Its advantage is simplicity. Though it lacks a scientific basis, there may be a perceived long-term relationship between advertising expenditures and the sales level. Under this plan the total amount to be spent could be based on:
   - A percentage of planned or budgeted sales.
   - A percentage of the prior year sales or perhaps an average of several past years.

- A fixed amount per unit of product expected to be sold.
- An arbitrary percentage increase over the prior year's expenditure.
- A percentage of gross profit on the product for the prior year or the planning year.
- A percentage of net income of the prior year or planning year.

2. *The estimated amount required to attain certain objectives.* Under this method, strategies and tactics are determined so that the relevant costs for each tactic can be estimated to derive a total cost for the year. In some cases the marginal or gross profit from the additional units estimated to be sold can be compared with the advertising expense to determine if the project seems to make financial sense. This can be done on an incremental advertising expense and quantity basis to ascertain at which point, if any, the incremental unit advertising cost exceeds the incremental marginal profit after all direct costs. Such an analysis is shown in Table 7–1.

We must know that the business is being operated efficiently, and this requires measuring sticks: *standards.* A complete analysis of past operations must be the starting point. By this analysis we may determine that 1,000 calls have been made by salespeople in a given territory, at a cost of $5 per call, and with certain sales results. But the questions are left unanswered about how many calls should have been made by the sales staff and what the cost per call should have been. These elements also must be ascertained if effective control of the sales effort is to be exercised. We may know that 1,000 orders have been handled at a clerical cost of $0.50 per order, but we also need to know what the cost would have been if the clerical work had been efficiently directed. In brief, we need standards by which to judge the distribution performance and signal its weaknesses.

It would be foolish to contend that all distribution activities can be highly standardized. In fact, it is never possible to completely standardize production activities. However, it is possible to establish standards for a large number of dis-

Table 7–1: Incremental Advertising Expense and Profit Margin

Incremental Block	Incremental Advertising Expense	Additional Units Estimated to Be Sold	Estimated Marginal Unit Income	Incremental Unit Advertising Cost	Unit Increment (Decrement) to Profit	Total Margin
1	$0	20,000	$1.00	$—	$1.00	$20,000
2	25,000	30,000	1.20	.83	.37	11,100
3	25,000	70,000	1.30	.36	.94	65,800
4	25,000	50,000	.90	.50	.40	20,000
5	25,000	50,000	.80	.50	.30	15,000
6	25,000	30,000	.70	.83	−.13	−3,900
7	25,000	30,000	.60	.83	−.23	−6,900
8	25,000	20,000	.50	1.25	−.75	−15,000
9	25,000	10,000	.40	2.50	−2.10	−21,000

tribution activities. After all, if no one is competent to judge what distribution effort is necessary to secure certain results and what it will cost to do it, then management is indeed in a helpless position.

If many cost and performance factors are not under constant control, the executive's profit goal is almost certain to be unmet. But such control implies standards. Warehouse labor hours never appear too high in the absolute; they become too high only when measured against what they should be under the circumstances—that is, only when a standard is applied.

Distribution cost standards may be either of a general nature or in units that measure individual performance. Cost standards that are of a general nature are as follows:

- Selling cost as a percentage of net sales.
- Cost per dollar of gross profit.
- Cost per unit sold.
- Cost per sales transaction.
- Cost per order received.
- Cost per customer account.

These standards are useful indicators of trends for the entire distribution effort and also can be applied to individual products, territories, branches, or departments.

However, these general standards do not necessarily indicate points of weakness in terms of individual responsibility. If costs are to be controlled, the performance of the individual must be measured. Consequently, the controller must set standards for controllable costs of individual cost items or functions. For example, standards in the warehouse could be the cost per item handled or cost per shipment. Standards for the direct sales force could be the cost per mile traveled or cost per day.

How to Set Distribution Standards

The *first* step in setting distribution cost standards is to classify the costs according to functions and activities expressive of individual responsibility. The cost of such major functions as direct selling, advertising, transportation, warehousing, credit and collection, and financing can be separated in most businesses and subjected to individual study and control. The costs of the major functions should be further classified by individual activities that make up the functional service. For example, the credit and collection costs may be separated into credit approvals, posting charges, posting credits, and writing collection letters.

The *second* step is to select units or bases of measurement through which the standards can be expressed. The measure may apply to the effort used, to cost, to results achieved, or to the relationship of these factors. For example, salespeople are each expected to make a certain number of sales calls per day. This constitutes a measure of effort used; the unit of measure is the call. The cost of writing orders in the order department can be measured in terms of the number of orders or order lines written. This is a measure of costs, and the unit of measurement is the order or order line. Salespeople are expected to produce a certain number of orders or to secure a certain number of new accounts. This is a measure of results, and the units of measurement are orders and new accounts. Finally, salespeople may be required to hold their direct costs to within 8% of their sales volume. Here the measurement is in terms of the relationship of particular costs to the results in the sales volumes, and the basis of measurement is the ratio of one to the other.

Although such specific units of measurement are not available for all distribution activities, some basis must be selected before the standards can be applied. Where specific units are not available, more inclusive or composite bases must be used. For example, the entire credit and collection cost may be measured by the number of accounts carried, or the entire advertising cost may be measured by its ratio to dollar sales volume.

The *third* step is to analyze past experience relative to the cost of the functions and the specific activities involved with a view to selecting the best experience and the best procedure. This may involve intensive study of individual methods of operation similar to that employed in the development of production standards.

The *fourth* step is to consider the effect on costs of expected changes in external conditions and of the planned sales program. If increased sales resistance is expected, an estimate must be made about its effect on such costs as advertising and direct selling. If the program calls for a lengthening of the installment credit period, the effect on the financing cost must be estimated.

The *final* step is to summarize the judgment of those executives whose experience and training qualify them to judge the measures of satisfactory performance.

Standards as finally set will result in much overlapping. Thus a standard cost might be applied to the warehousing function as a whole. Within this general function many individual cost standards may be applied that relate to specific activities such as clerical costs of order handling and physical assembling.

Keep in mind that different standards must be set for different territories, products, channels of distribution, classes of customers, departments, and so on, wherein different conditions prevail.

Additional Information Needed to Use Standards

To use standards effectively, a company must regularly record and store information about items quite dissimilar from the usual accounting information. The following data are illustrative of the items to be recorded:

- Analyses of sales in physical units.
- Number of sales transactions classified in terms of size, hour of day, and so on.
- Number of quotations made.
- Number of orders classified in terms of size, period in which received, and so on.

- Number of order lines written.
- Average number of salespeople.
- Number of salesperson-days.
- Number of calls on old and new customers.
- Number of days salespeople travel.
- Number of miles salespeople travel.
- Average number of customers classified with regard to location, annual volume, and so on.
- Number of labor hours of salespeople, advertising and display people, warehouse workers, truck drivers, delivery personnel, maintenance workers, and clerical workers.
- Number of returns and allowances classified in terms of cause.
- Number of units of advertising space or time used in the various advertising media.
- Number of advertising pieces mailed; letters, circulars, folders, calendars, and so on.
- Number of pieces of advertising material distributed: window cards, store displays, inserts, and so on.
- Number of samples distributed.
- Number of demonstrations performed.
- Number of inquiries received.
- Number of new customers secured.
- Number of shipments.
- Analyses of shipments in physical units.
- Dollar value of shipments.
- Number of ton-miles units of shipping.
- Number of deliveries.
- Number of parcels delivered.
- Number of miles of truck operation.
- Number of shipping claims handled.
- Physical volume of goods handled in warehouses.
- Average size of physical inventory carried.
- Rates of turnover in dollars and physical units.
- Average number of accounts carried.
- Number of invoices.
- Number of invoice lines.
- Number of remittances received.
- Number of credit letters sent.
- Average number of days accounts are outstanding.

- Average amount of receivables carried.
- Number of mail pieces handled.
- Number of postings.
- Number of letters written.

Many of the foregoing items must be further classified by territories, commodities, and departments to supply the full information needed.

Such information will be useful for many purposes in the direction of distribution activity, but it is essential to a program of standards. Many firms have in the past neglected to accumulate and use such information. It is not uncommon to find a company that has the most exacting records of a production machine, such as its purchase date, cost, working hours, idle hours, and maintenance cost. However, those same firms may have been employing a salesperson whose total cost has greatly exceeded the cost and maintenance of the machine, but about whom little detailed information has been kept. The salesperson's activity report can provide some of these data.

In many firms the distribution data is entirely too meager. More information must be collected if the distribution program is to be wisely directed.

8

DIRECT MATERIALS AND LABOR

The cost of a product is split among direct materials and labor, overhead, distribution, and general and administrative costs. All of these costs can contribute a significant amount to the total cost of a product, but direct materials and labor traditionally have been the largest cost elements for most products. Thus, the controller should be mindful of any control systems that will allow tight monitoring of these costs.

Controlling direct materials and labor costs is the subject of this chapter. In addition, there are many references in the text to the impact of just-in-time (JIT) systems on cost controls, which call into question the need for some traditional (and extensive!) control systems, such as those used for direct labor tracking. This chapter also includes a discussion of the deleterious effects on production results of several traditional variance reports, and why these results occur.

OBJECTIVES

A manufacturing cost accounting system is an integral part of the total management information system. In analyzing costing systems, the controller must recognize the purpose of the manufacturing cost accounting system and relate it to production or operating management problems. The objectives must be clearly defined if the system is to be effectively utilized. There are fundamental purposes of a cost system that may vary in importance from one organization to another; however, they may be summarized as follows:

- *For control of costs.* Control of costs is a primary use of manufacturing cost accounting and cost analysis. The major elements of costs—labor, material, and manufacturing expenses—must be segregated by product, by type of cost and by responsibility. For example, the actual number of parts used in the assembly of an airplane section, such as a wing, may be compared to the bill for materials and correction action taken when appropriate.

- *For planning and performance measurement.* Closely related to cost control is the use of cost data for effective planning and performance measurement. Some of the same information used for cost control purposes may be used for the planning of manufacturing operations. For example, the standards used for cost control of manufacturing expenses can be used to plan these expenses for future periods with due consideration to past experience relative to established standards. Cost analysis can be utilized, as part of the planning process, to determine the probable effect of different courses of action. Again, a comparison of manufacturing costs versus purchasing a particular part or component can be made to help with make-or-buy decisions. The use of cost analysis would extend to many facets of the total planning process.

- *For price setting.* A critical reason for supplying cost data is to establish selling prices. The manufactured cost of a product is not necessarily the sole determinant in setting prices, since the desired gross margin and the price acceptable to the market are also significant factors. As more companies realize that direct labor and materials are relatively fixed costs, management will concentrate on designing the product to fit a specific price, cost, and gross margin; the controller should be included in this process to advise management in regard to indirect and direct costs.

- *For inventory valuation.* One of the key objectives of a costing system is the determination of a product unit cost and the valuation of inventories. This is also a prerequisite to an accurate determination of the cost of goods sold in the statement of income and expense. The manufacturing cost system should recognize this fact and include sufficient cost details to accomplish this purpose.

ROLE OF THE CONTROLLER

A fundamental responsibility of the controller in the product cost area is to ensure that the manufacturing cost systems have been established to serve the needs and requirements of the production executives. The controller is the fact-finder regarding costs and is responsible for seeing that factory management is furnished with sufficient cost information on a timely basis and in a proper format to effect control and planning. It is imperative that the cost data be accurate and that production management be provided with a clear interpretation of the facts. Merely presenting the facts is not enough; the cost information must be communicated in an understandable manner, since many production executives are not fully aware of the ramifications. The controller should develop educational techniques to aid the factory management in the utilization of cost data for effective decision making. It is necessary that a sound cost philosophy be adopted at all levels of responsibility. The controller's staff should have a thorough understanding of the factory operations and how the products are manufactured and should be able to relate the cost figures to various products. This takes extra effort and cooperation between the controller's staff and the operating personnel.

To carry out this responsibility and serve production management properly, the controller must be assured that the right cost system has been designed and adequate implementing procedures have been developed to accumulate and record the cost information. The cost system must be flexible so that changes can be made as the needs of factory management vary. This includes provision for additional cost information in special circumstances or during alternative cost analyses. As variances are analyzed and out-of-line conditions are reported, production managers can change methods or vary their cost information requirements. Emphasis should be placed on areas requiring improvement; less time should be devoted to on-standard operations.

Unfortunately, under a just-in-time (JIT) system, manufacturing managers need feedback regarding costs far more frequently than on a monthly basis. JIT products are manufactured with little or no wait time, and consequently can be produced in periods much shorter than was the case under the line manufacturing concept. Therefore, if a cost problem occurred, such as too many direct labor hours required to finish a part, then the formal accounting system would not tell the line managers until well after the problem had happened.

Fortunately, JIT principles stress the need to shrink inventories and emphasize overall cleanliness, thereby making manufacturing problems highly visible *without* any product costing reports. A subset of JIT is cellular (group) manufacturing, in which equipment is generally arranged in a horseshoe shape, and one employee uses those machines to make one part, taking the piece from machine to machine. Consequently, there is little or no work-in-process (WIP) to track, and any scrapped parts are immediately visible to management, because they cannot be hidden in piles of WIP. Based on this kind of manufacturing concept, line managers can do without reports, with the exception of daily production reports concerning actual quantities versus budgeted quantities that meet quality standards.

Just-in-time manufacturing places the controller in the unique position of looking for something to report on. Since direct labor and materials costs are now largely fixed, the controller's emphasis should switch to planning the costs of new products and tracking planned costs versus actual costs. Since the JIT manufacturing environment tends to have small cost variances, the controller should question the amount of effort to be invested in tracking direct labor and materials variances versus the benefit of collecting the data.

Another area in which the controller can profitably invest time-tracking information is the number of items that increase a product's cycle time, or the non-value-added cost of producing a product. Management can then work to reduce the frequency of these items, thereby reducing the costs associated with them. Here is a limited list of such items:

Number of material moves

Number of part numbers used by the company

Number of set-ups required to build a product

Number of products sold by the company, including the number of options offered

Number of product distribution locations used

Number of engineering change notices

Number of parts reworked

Also, if a process is value-added, then the controller can initiate an operational audit to find any bottlenecks in the process, thereby improving the capacity of the process. For example, engineering a custom product is clearly value-added; internal auditors could recommend new hardware or software for designing the product to allow the engineering department to design twice as many products with the same number of staff.

Under JIT, there are several traditional performance measures that the controller should be careful *not* to report:

- If there is a report on machine efficiency, then line managers will be encouraged to create an excessive amount of WIP in order to keep their machines running at maximum utilization.

- If there is a report on purchase price variances, the materials staff will be encouraged to purchase large quantities of raw materials in order to get volume discounts, thereby bloating inventory.

- If there is a report on head count, the manufacturing manager will be encouraged to hire untrained contract workers, who may produce more scrap than full-time, better-trained employees.

- If the firm includes a scrap factor into a product's standard cost, then line managers will take no corrective action unless scrap exceeds the budgeted level, thereby incorporating scrap into the production process.

- If there is a report on labor variances, then the accountants will expend considerable labor in an area that has relatively fixed costs and not put time into areas that require more analysis.

- If there is a report on standard cost overhead absorption, then management will be encouraged to overproduce to absorb more overhead than was actually expended, thereby increasing profits, increasing inventory, and reducing available cash.

TYPES OF COSTING ANALYSIS

The question will often arise about what type of cost data is to be presented. Just how should production costs by analyzed? This will depend, of course, on the purpose for which the costs are to be used, as well as the cost experience of those who use the information.

Unit costs or total costs may be accumulated in an infinite variety of ways. The primary segregation may be any one of the following: product or class of product, operation, department, machine or machine center, process, customer order, responsible worker, or cost element.

Each of the primary segregations may be subdivided a number of ways. For example, the out-of-pocket costs may be separated from the "continuing costs"—those that would be incurred whether or not a particular order or run was made. Again, production costs might be segregated between those which are direct or indirect; that is, those attributable directly to the operation and those prorated. Thus the material used to fashion a cup might be direct, whereas the power used to operate the press would be indirect. Sometimes the analysis of costs will differentiate between those that vary with production volume and those which are constant within the range of production usually experienced. For example, the direct labor consumed may relate directly to volume, whereas depreciation remains unchanged. The controller must use judgment and experience in deciding what type of analysis is necessary to present the essential facts.

The mix of product cost components has shifted away from direct labor and material dominance to overhead dominance, as depreciation, materials management, and engineering time have taken up a greater proportion of a typical product's cost. Because of this change in mix, the controller will find that product cost analyses will depend heavily on how to assign overhead costs to a product. Activity-based costing (ABC) is of considerable use in this area. For more information about ABC, please refer to Chapter 9.

TYPES OF COST SYSTEMS

Experience in determining costs in various industries has given rise to several types of cost systems that suit the various kinds of manufacturing activities. A traditional costing system known as a "job order" system is normally used for manufacturing products to a specific customer order or unique product. For example, the assembly or fabrication operations of a particular job or contract are collected in a separate job order number. Another widely used costing system is known as a "process cost" system. This system assigns costs to a cost center rather than to a particular job. All the production costs of a department are collected, and the departmental cost per unit is determined by dividing the total departmental costs by the number of units processed through the department. Process cost systems are more commonly used in food processing, oil refining, flour milling, paint manufacturing, and so on.

No two cost accounting systems are identical. There are many factors that determine the kind of system to use, such as product mix, plant location, product diversity, number of specific customer orders, and complexity of the manufacturing process. It may be advisable to combine certain characteristics of both types of systems in certain situations. For example, in a steel mill the primary system may be a process cost system; however, minor activities such as maintenance may be on a job cost basis. The controller should thoroughly analyze all operations to determine the system that best satisfies all needs.

There are two issues currently affecting the job order and process costing systems that the controller should be aware of:

1. JIT manufacturing systems allow the controller to reduce or eliminate the record-keeping needed for job cost reporting. Since JIT tends to eliminate variances on the shop floor by eliminating the WIP that used to mask problems, there are few cost variances for the cost accountant to accumulate in a job cost report. Therefore, the time needed to accumulate information for job costing may no longer be worth the increase in accuracy derived from it, and the controller should consider using the initial planned job cost as the actual job cost.

2. One of the primary differences between process and job shop costing systems is the presence (job shop) or absence (process flow) of WIP. Since installing a JIT manufacturing system inherently implies reducing or eliminating WIP, a JIT job shop costing system may not vary that much from a process costing system.

MEASURING DIRECT MATERIAL COSTS

Direct material refers to material that can be definitely or specifically charged to a particular product, process, or job, and that becomes a component part of the finished product. The definition must be applied in a practical way, for if the material cannot be conveniently charged as direct or if it is an insignificant item of cost, then it would probably be classified as *indirect material* and allocated with other manufacturing expenses to the product on some logical basis. Direct material also should include the cost of packing supplies necessary to deliver the goods to the customer, as well as any normal losses due to scrap, evaporation, spoilage, or shrinkage. Excessive amounts of scrap should be expensed or charged to the overhead account.

In its broadest sense, material planning and control is simply the providing of the required quantity and quality of material at the required time and place in the manufacturing process. By implication, the material secured must not be excessive in amount, and it must be fully accounted for and used as intended. The extent of material planning and control is broad and should cover many areas, such as plans and specifications; purchasing; receiving and handling; inventories; usage; and scrap, waste, and salvage. In each of these phases, the controller has certain responsibilities and can make contributions toward an efficient operation.

Because material is such a large cost item in most manufacturing concerns, effective utilization is an important factor in the financial success or failure of the business. Proper planning and control of materials with the related adequate accounting has advantages in that it:

reduces inefficient use or waste of materials,

reduces production delays by reason of lack of materials,

reduces the risk from theft or fraud,

reduces the investment in inventories,

reduce the required investment in storage facilities,

provides more accurate interim financial statements,

assist buyers through a better coordinated buying program,

provides a basis for proper product pricing, and

provides more accurate inventory values.

CONTROLLING DIRECT MATERIAL COSTS

Before describing direct material cost controls, we must define those costs. Direct material costs include the invoice price for the direct material, the inbound freight cost, sales taxes and duties, and the cost of delivery pallets or other freight containers. Any discounts should be taken from the material cost, while licensing or royalty payments should be added to the cost.

With respect to materials, as with other costs, control in its simplest form involves the comparison of actual performance with a measuring stick—standard performance—and the prompt rectification of adverse trends. However, it is not simply a matter of saying "350 yards of material were used, and the standard quantity is only 325" or "The standard price is $10.25 but the actual cost to the company was $13.60 each." Many other refinements are involved: the standards must be reviewed and better methods found, or checks and controls must be exercised before the cost is incurred. The central theme, however, is still the use of a standard as a point of measurement.

Although the application of controls will vary in different firms, some of the considerations that must be handled by the controller are described below.

Purchasing and Receiving

- Establishment and maintenance of internal checks to assure that materials paid for are received and used for the purposes intended. Since some purchases are now received on a just-in-time basis, the controller may find that materials are now paid for based on the amount of production manufactured by the company in a given period, instead of a large quantity of paperwork associated with a large number of small-quantity receipts.
- Audit of purchasing procedures to ascertain that bids are received where applicable. A JIT manufacturing system uses a small number of long-term suppliers, however, so the controller may find that bids are restricted to providers of such services as janitorial duties and copier repairs.

- Comparative studies of prices paid for commodities with industry prices or indexes.
- Measurement of price trends on raw materials. Many JIT supplier contracts call for price decreases by suppliers at set intervals; the controller should be aware of the terms of these contracts and audit the timing and amount of the changes.
- Determination of price variances on current purchases through comparison of actual and standard costs. This may involve purchases at the time of ordering or at the time of receipt. The same approach may be used in a review of current purchase orders to advise management in advance about the effect on standard costs. In a JIT environment, most part costs would be contractually set with a small number of suppliers, so the controller would examine prices charged for any variations from the agreed-upon rates.

Material Usage

- Comparison of actual and standard quantities used in production. A variance may indicate an incorrect quantity on the product's bill of materials, misplaced parts, pilferage, or incorrect part quantities recorded in inventory.
- Preparation of standard cost formulas, to emphasize major cost items and as a part of a cost reduction program.
- Preparation of reports on spoilage, scrap, and waste compared with standard. In a JIT environment, no scrap is allowed for and is certainly not included in the budget as a standard.
- Calculation of costs-to-make versus costs-to-buy.

This list suggests only some of the methods available to the controller in dealing with material cost control.

CONTROLLING DIRECT MATERIAL QUANTITIES

Standards of material usage may be established by at least three procedures:

1. By engineering studies to determine the best kind and quality of material, taking into account the product design requirements and production methods.
2. By an analysis of past experience for the same or similar operations.
3. By making test runs under controlled conditions.

Although a combination of these methods may be used, best practice usually dictates that engineering studies should be made. To the theoretical loss must be added a provision for those other unavoidable losses that are impractical to eliminate. In this decision, past experience will play a part. Past performance alone, of course, is not desirable in that certain known wastes may be perpetuated. This engineering study, combined with a few test runs, should give fairly reliable standards.

Quantity standards are based on certain production methods and product specifications. It would be expected, therefore, that quantity standards should be modified as these other factors change, if such changes affect material usage. For the measuring stick to be an effective control tool, it must relate to the function being measured. However, the adjustment need not be carried through as a change in inventory value, unless it is significant.

In the best material quantity control scheme, the firm knows in advance how much material should be used on the job, frequently secures information about how actual performance compares with standard during the progress of the work, and takes corrective action where necessary. The supervisor responsible for the use of materials, as well as his or her superior, should be aware of these facts. At the lowest supervisory level, details of each operation and process should be in the hands of those who can control usage. At higher levels, of course, only overall results need be known.

The method to be used in comparing the actual and the standard usage will differ in each company, depending on several conditions. Some of the more important factors that will influence the controller in applying control procedures to material usage are:

- The production method in use.
- The type and value of the materials.
- The degree to which cost reports are utilized by management for cost control purposes.

One of the most important considerations is the nature of the production process. In a job order or lot system, such as an assembly operation in an aircraft plant, where a definite quantity is to be produced, the procedure is quite simple. A production order is issued, and a bill of material or "standard requisition" states the exact quantity of material needed to complete the order. If parts are spoiled or lost, it then becomes necessary to secure replacements by means of a nonstandard or excess usage requisition. Usually, the foreman must approve this request, and, consequently, the excess usage can be identified immediately.

If production is on a continuous process basis, then periodically a comparison can be made of material used in relation to the finished product. Corrective action may not be as quick here, but measures can be taken to avoid future losses.

Just as the production process is a vital factor in determining the cost accounting plan, so also it is a consideration in the method of detecting material losses. If losses are to be localized, then inspections must be made at selected points in the manufacturing process. At these various stations, the rejected material can be counted or weighed and costed if necessary. When there are several distinct steps in the manufacturing process, the controller may have to persuade the production group of the need and desirability to establish count stations for control purposes. Once these stations are established, the chief contribution of the accountant is to summarize and report the losses over standard.

Another factor in the method of reporting material usage is the type and value of the item itself. A cardinal principal in cost control is to place primary emphasis on high-volume items. Hence valuable airplane motors, for example, would be identified by serial number and otherwise accurately accounted for. Items with less unit value, or not readily segregated, might be controlled through less accurate periodic reporting.

Management is often not directly interested in dollar cost for control purposes, but only in units. There are no differences in the principles involved, only in the applications. Under these conditions, the controller should see that management is informed of losses in terms of physical units. In this case, the cost report would be merely a summary of the losses. Experience will often show, however, that as the controller gives an accounting in dollars, the other members of management will become more cost conscious.

The essence of any control program, regardless of the method of reporting, is to follow up on standard performance and take corrective action.

A variation on using quantity standards and materials variation reporting is JIT variance reporting. One of the cornerstones of the JIT concept is that you only order what you need, and that means that you won't waste what you use, and *that* means that there should be no materials variances. Of course, even at world-class JIT practitioners such as Motorola and Toyota, there is scrap; however, there is much less than would be found at a non-JIT company. Consequently, the controller must examine the cost of collecting the variance information against its value in correcting a small number of scrap causes. The conclusion may be that JIT does not require much materials variance reporting, if any.

In comparing actual and standard material costs, the use of price standards permits the segregation of variances as a result of excess usage from those incurred by reason of price changes. By and large, however, the material price standards used for inventory valuation cannot be considered as a satisfactory guide in measuring the performance of the purchasing department. Prices of materials are affected by so many factors outside the business that the standards represent merely a measure of what prices are being paid compared with what was expected to be paid.

A review of price variances may, however, reveal some informative data. Exceedingly high prices may reveal special purchases for quick delivery because someone had not properly scheduled purchases. Or higher prices may reveal shipment via express when freight shipments would have been satisfactory. Again, the lowest-cost supplier may not be utilized because of the advantages of excellent quality control methods in place at a competing shop. The total cost of production and the impact on the marketplace need to be considered—not merely the purchase price of the specific item. A general guide for controllers is that the exact cause for any price variance must be ascertained before valid conclusions can be drawn.

One negative result of recording a purchase price variance is that the purchasing department may forego close supplier relationships in order to get the lowest part cost through the bidding process. Part bidding is the nemesis of close supplier parings (a cornerstone of JIT), since suppliers know they will be kicked off the supplier list, no matter how good their delivery or quality, unless they bid the lowest cost.

In practice, the responsibility for setting price standards varies. Sometimes the cost department assumes this responsibility on the basis of a review of past prices. In other cases the purchasing staff gives an estimate of expected prices that is subject to a thorough and analytical check by the accounting staff. Probably, the most satisfactory set-up is through the combined effort of these two departments.

Where products are quite costly, and relatively few in number, it may be found useful to provide management periodically with both the changes in standard prices and an indication about the effect of price changes on the standard cost of the product. Such statements may stimulate thinking about material substitutions in processes or specifications.

MEASURING DIRECT LABOR COSTS

Labor accounting and control are important. As automation and the use of robots become more prevalent, what was once called direct labor may no longer be important. But labor is still a significant cost. Likewise, those costs that are closely related to labor costs have grown by leaps and bounds: costs for longer vacations, more adequate health and welfare plans, pension plans, and increased social security taxes. These fringe benefit costs now approximate 40% to 50% of many payrolls. For all these reasons, the cost of labor is an important cost factor.

The objectives of labor accounting are twofold:

1. A prompt and accurate determination of the amount of wages due the employee.
2. The analysis and determination of labor costs in such manner as may be needed by management (e.g., by product, operation, department, or category of labor) for planning and control purposes.

The advent of JIT manufacturing systems has called into question the need for reporting the direct labor utilization variance. This variance revolves around the amount of a product that is produced with a given amount of labor; thus, a positive labor utilization variance can be achieved by producing more product than may be needed. An underlying principle of JIT is that you only produce as much as you need, so JIT and labor utilization variance reporting are inherently at odds with each other. If JIT has been installed, then the controller should consider eliminating this type of variance reporting.

CONTROLLING DIRECT LABOR COSTS

As with direct materials cost controls, we must first define direct labor costs before considering controls. Direct labor is that labor which can be specifically identified with providing a service, completing a project, or building a product. Such costs include assembly, inspection, processing, and packaging. When accounting for a large project, direct labor will typically include many types of labor that fall into the overhead classification in other forms of production; this is because nearly all positions, such as janitorial and maintenance, can be directly associated with the project. Nonproductive time that cannot be associated with a specific service, product, or project will become part of overhead. For example, break time for an employee who is working on one product can logically be assigned to that product; however, clean-up time for a factory that produced multiple products should be assigned to overhead.

The cost of labor has a number of components, and these are assigned to either direct labor cost or overhead cost. The governing criteria in assigning a cost to either direct labor or overhead is that a labor cost component should be assigned to direct labor if the cost is incurred because the company uses direct labor to produce a service, product, or project. In other words, most employee benefits will not be incurred unless direct labor is performed, and therefore those costs must fall into direct labor. Typical employee benefit costs that fall into this category are:

- Productivity bonuses (both individual and group)
- FICA
- Cost of living allowances
- Health insurance
- Group life insurance
- Holiday pay
- Vacation pay
- Pension costs
- Worker's compensation insurance costs
- Unemployment insurance compensation (state and federal)

The assignment of these costs to direct labor or overhead will vary depending on the situations of individual firms, so the controller should consult with the company's external auditors for an opinion on this matter.

In controlling direct labor costs, as with most manufacturing costs, the ultimate responsibility must rest with the line supervision. Yet this group must be given assistance in measuring performance, and certain other policing or restraining functions must be exercised. Herein lie the primary duties of the controller's organization. Among the means at the disposal of the chief accounting executive in labor control are the following:

- Institute procedures to limit the number of employees placed on the payroll to that called for by the production plan.
- Provide preplanning information for use in determining standard labor crews by calculating required standard man-hours for the production program.
- Report hourly, daily, or weekly standard and actual labor performance. This reporting would not be necessary in a JIT environment.
- Institute procedures for accurate distribution of actual labor costs, including significant labor classifications to provide informative labor cost analyses. This reporting would not be necessary in a JIT environment.
- Provide data on past experience with respect to the establishment of standards. This reporting would not be necessary in a JIT environment.
- Keep adequate records on labor standards and be on the alert for necessary revisions.
- Furnish other supplementary labor reports, such as these:
  — Hours and cost of overtime premium, for control of overtime.
  — Cost of call-in pay for time not worked to measure efficiency of those responsible for call-in by union seniority.
  — Comparative contract costs (old vs. new union contracts).
  — Average hours worked per week, average take-home pay, and similar data for labor negotiations.
  — Detailed analysis of labor costs over or under standard. This reporting would not be necessary in a JIT environment.
  — Statistical data on labor turnover, length of service, and training costs.
  — Union time—cost of time spent on union business.

A JIT manufacturing environment creates significant changes in direct labor costs that the controller should be aware of. When a manufacturing facility changes from an assembly line to manufacturing cells, the labor efficiency level drops, because machine set-ups become more frequent. A major JIT technique is to reduce set-up time to minimal levels, but even the small set-up times required for cellular manufacturing require more labor time than the zero set-up times used in long assembly-line production runs. Consequently, if management is contemplating switching to cellular manufacturing, the controller should expect an increase in the labor hours budget. Also, if the labor cost does not increase, the controller should see if the engineering staff has changed the labor routings (standard hours required to produce a product itemized by skills required and department) to increase the number of expected set-up times.

The following discussion on labor standards does not apply to a JIT manufacturing environment, especially one that uses cellular (i.e., "group") manufacturing layouts. Labor utilization standards can be improved by increasing the amount of production for a set level of labor, and this is considered to be good in an assembly line environment. Under JIT, however, producing large quantities of parts is not considered acceptable; under JIT, good performance is producing the exact quantity of parts that are needed, and doing so with quality that is within present tolerance levels. Once the correct quantity of parts is produced, the direct labor staff stops production; this creates unfavorable labor utilization variances. Therefore, measuring a JIT production facility with a labor utilization variance would work against the intent of JIT, since the production manager would be encouraged to produce more parts than needed, and would not be mindful of the part quality.

The improvement of labor performance and the parallel reduction and control of costs require labor standards—operating time standards and the related cost standards. Setting labor performance standards is a highly analytical job that requires a technical background of the production processes as well as a knowledge of time study methods. This may be the responsibility of a standards department, industrial engineering department, or cost control department. Occasionally, it is under the jurisdiction of the controller. Establishment of the standard operation time requires a determination of the time needed to complete each operation when working under standard conditions. Hence this study embodies working conditions, including the material control plan, the production planning and scheduling procedure, and layout of equipment and facilities. After all these factors are considered, a standard can be set by the engineers.

In using time standards for measuring labor performance, the accounting staff must work closely with the industrial engineers or those responsible for setting the standards. The related cost standards must be consistent; the accumulation of cost information must consider how the standards were set and how the variances are analyzed.

Generally, performance standards are not revised until a change of method or process occurs. Since standards serve as the basis of control, the accounting staff should be on the alert for changes put into effect in the factory but not reported for standard revision. If the revised process requires more time, the production staff will usually make quite certain that their measuring stick is modified. However, if the new process requires less time, it is understandable that the change might not be reported promptly. Each supervisor naturally desires to make the best possible showing. The prompt reporting of time reductions might be stimulated through a periodic review of changes in standard labor hours or costs. In other words, the current labor performance of actual hours compared with a standard should be but one measure of performance; another measure is standard time reductions, also compared with a goal for the year.

It should be the responsibility of the controller to see that the standards are changed as the process changes to report true performance. If a wage incentive system is related to these standards, the need for adjusting process changes is emphasized. An analysis of variances, whether favorable or unfavorable, will often serve to indicate revisions not yet reported.

Although standard revisions will often be made for control purposes, it may not be practical or desirable to change product cost standards. The differences may be treated as cost variances until they are of sufficient magnitude to warrant a cost revision.

Effective labor control through the use of standards requires frequent reporting of actual and standard performance. Furthermore, the variance report must be by responsibility. For this reason the report on performance is prepared for each foreman as well as for the plant superintendent. The report may or may not be expressed in terms of dollars. It may compare person-hours or units of production instead of monetary units, but it always does compare actual and standard performance.

In a JIT environment, the manufacturing departments are tightly interlocked with minimal WIP between each department to hide problems caused by reduced manpower. In other words, if an area is understaffed, then downstream work stations will quickly run short of work. Consequently, the most critical direct labor measure in a JIT environment is a report of absent personnel, delivered promptly to the production managers at the start of the work day, so they can reshuffle the staff to cover all departments and contact the missing personnel.

Generally speaking, labor rates paid by a company are determined by external factors. The rate standard used is usually that normally paid for the job or classification as set by collective bargaining. If standards are set under this policy, no significant variances should develop because of base rates paid. There are, however, some rate variances that may be created and are controllable by management. Some of these reasons, which should be set out for corrective action, include:

- Overtime in excess of that provided in the standard.
- Use of higher-rated classifications on the job.
- Failure to place staff members on incentive pay, such as additional payments when objectives are achieved.
- Use of a crew mixture that is different from the standard (more higher classifications and fewer of the lower, or vice versa).

The application of the standard labor rate to the job poses no great problem. Usually, this is performed by the accounting department after securing the rates from the personnel department. Where overtime is contemplated in the standard, it is necessary, of course, to consult with production to determine the probable extent of overtime for the capacity at which the standard is set.

Labor requirements can be preplanned in some firms. The degree to which this preplanning takes place depends on the industry and particular conditions within the individual firm. Are business conditions sufficiently stable so that some reasonably accurate planning can be done? Can the sales department indicate with reasonable accuracy what the requirements will be over the short run? A useful preplanning application might be a machine shop where thousands of parts are made. If production requirements are known, the standard hours worked necessary can be calculated and converted to manpower. The standard hours worked may be stored in a computer by skills required and by department (i.e., a labor routing). After evaluating the particular production job, an experienced efficiency factor may be determined. Thus if 12,320 standard hours worked are needed for the planned production but an efficiency rate of only 80% is expected, then 15,400 actual hours worked must be scheduled. This requires a crew of 385 employees (at 40 hours per week for one week). This can be further refined by skills, or an analysis can be made of the economics of authorizing overtime. Steps should be taken to assure that only the required number is authorized on the payroll for this production. As the requirements change, the standard person-hours should be reevaluated.

In a Material Requirements Planning (MRP) environment, labor routings must be at least 95% accurate, and the firm must strictly adhere to a master production schedule. If the controller works in such an environment, then labor requirements can easily be predicted by multiplying the related labor routings by the unit types and quantities shown on the master schedule.

Wage Incentive Plans

In an effort to increase efficiency, a number of companies have introduced wage incentive plans, with good results. The controller is involved through the payroll department, which must calculate the monetary effect of such a plan. His responsibilities for the system are best left to authorities on the subject. One facet of an incentive plan, however, is germane to the costing process and should be discussed. When an incentive wage plan is introduced into an operation already on a standard cost basis, a problem arises about the relationship between the standard performance level at which incentive earnings commence and the standard performance level used for costing purposes. Moreover, what effect should the wage incentive plan have on the standard labor cost and standard manufacturing expense of the product? To cite a specific situation, a company may be willing to pay an incentive to labor for performance that is lower than that assumed in the cost standard (but much higher than actual experience). If such a bonus is excluded from the cost standard, the labor cost at the cost standard level will be understated. Further, there may be no offsetting savings in manufacturing expenses since the costs are incurred to secure performance at a lower level than the cost standard. These statements assume, of course, that the existing cost standard represents efficient performance even under incentive conditions. On the other hand, if the effect of the incentive plan is to increase sustained production levels well above those contemplated in the cost standards, it may be that the product will be overcosted by using present cost standards and that these standards are no longer applicable. How should the cost standards be set in relation to the incentive plan?

In reviewing the plan, several generalizations may be made. First, there is no necessary relationship between standards for incentive purposes and standards for costing purposes. The former are intended to stimulate effort, whereas the latter are used to determine what the labor cost of the product should be. One is a problem in personnel management, whereas the other is strictly an accounting problem. With such dissimilar objectives, the levels of performance could logically be quite different.

Then, too, the matter of labor costing for statement purposes should be differentiated from labor control. As we have seen, labor control may involve nonfinancial terms—pieces per hour, pounds per hours worked, and so on. Labor control can be accomplished through the use of quantitative standards. Even if costs are used, the measuring stick for control need not be the same as for product costing. Control is centered on variations from performance standards and not on product cost variations.

A thorough consideration of the problem results in the conclusion that labor standards for costing purposes should be based on normal expectations from the operation of a wage incentive system under standard operation conditions. The expected earnings under the bonus plan should be reflected in the standard unit cost of the product. It does not necessarily follow that the product standard cost will be higher than that used before introduction of the incentive plan. It may mean, however, that the direct labor cost will be higher by reason of bonus payments. Yet, because of increased production and material savings, the total unit standard manufacturing cost should be lower.

TARGET COSTING

The main point of this chapter has been to control production costs *after* a product design reaches the factory floor. However, by this time the components being used in the product have already been fixed and the design is one that must be produced using specific manufacturing methods. By the time it reaches production, there really is not a great deal that the controller (or anyone else) can do to reduce product costs beyond a few percentage points that can be garnered from the extra efficiencies already noted in this chapter. A better approach that attacks costs before the design is finished is called target costing.

In essence, target costing requires many departments to become involved in the design stage, where they work together to create products that meet specific target costs that will create tolerable margins at predetermined product price points. If a product design cannot attain its target cost, then it is shelved. The methodology starts with a review of the market to see what prices are being charged by competing products, or what prices customers think they would pay if a new product design were to be sold. Then the accounting staff backs out a company-standard profit margin from the sale price, which leaves us with a target cost. This may actually be a range of costs, since the sales and marketing staff may conclude that the product price will drop over time as competition increases, which will require a matching drop in costs if margins are to be maintained.

The target cost then goes to the design group that includes not just the usual engineers but also a cost accountant and representatives from the production, marketing, and purchasing staffs. This group then breaks down the target cost further and assigns a target cost to sub-components of the product, each of which is then worked on by a subgroup of the design team. All members of the groups pitch in to determine new ways to meet their cost targets, such as new production methods or the use of a small number of parts that can be purchased in sufficiently high volume to result in lower per-unit part prices from suppliers. The design team will go through a number of milestone reviews to see if it is coming close to its target cost. The team must prove in each succeeding review that it is coming closer to the target, or else the project will be cancelled. For example, if the team can come within 12% of its target cost during the first milestone review, then the project is allowed to continue to the next milestone where the team must be within 9% of its goal, and so on. This rigorous approach keeps the project on track and avoids any sudden surprises.

The role of the cost accountant is to continually re-compile the cost of the product as it passes through its various design milestones (which may be a great deal of work if the product has a large number of component parts), and to feed this information back to the design team, which uses it to spot high-cost parts that will be subject to further design work. In addition, the cost accountant must continue to review product costs after the completed design is released to production, so that management can see if the designed cost is the same as the manufactured cost. This subsequent analysis should not just be a simple variance that gives management no clue regarding why costs have changed; instead, it should specifically note what internal processes or external part prices are causing the variances. Finally, there may be plans to continually reduce product costs over time, in which case the cost accountant will be responsible for tracking the progress of cost reductions and notifying management of specific problems in achieving these goals.

9

OVERHEAD

The indirect manufacturing expenses, or overhead costs, of a manufacturing operation have increased significantly as business has become more complex and as the utilization of more sophisticated machinery and equipment has become more prevalent. As the investment in computer controlled machinery has increased, improving productivity and reducing direct labor hours, the control of depreciation expense, power costs, machine repairs and maintenance, and similar items has received a greater emphasis by management.

Manufacturing overhead has several distinguishing characteristics compared with the direct manufacturing costs of material and labor. It includes a wide variety of expenses, such as depreciation, property taxes, insurance, fringe benefit costs, indirect labor, supplies, power and other utilities, clerical costs, maintenance and repairs, and other costs that cannot be directly associated with a process or job. These types of costs behave differently from direct costs, as the volume of production varies. Some will fluctuate proportionately as production increases or decreases, and some will remain constant or fixed and will not be sensitive to the change in the number of units produced. It may be observed that some costs are semivariable and for a particular volume level are fixed; however, they may vary with volume, but not absolutely proportionately with volume, and probably can be segregated into their fixed and variable components.

In the midst of this plethora of fixed, variable, and semivariable costs, the controller must control costs as well as account for costs by process or job. This chapter provides an overview of how the controller can manage these tasks.

THE NEED FOR OVERHEAD CONTROLS

The diverse types of expenses in overhead and divided responsibility concerning their management may contribute to the incurrence of excessive costs. Furthermore, the fact that many cost elements seem to be quite small in terms of consumption or cost per unit often encourages neglect of proper control. For example, it is natural to increase clerical help as required when volume increases to higher levels, but there is a reluctance and usually a delay in eliminating such help when no longer needed. The reduced requirement must be forecasted and anticipated and appropriate actions taken in a timely manner. There are numerous expenses of small unit-cost items that may be significant, but in the aggregate can make the company less competitive: excessive hours worked for maintenance, use of special forms or supplies when standard items would be sufficient, personal use of supplies, or indiscriminate use of communications and reproduction facilities. All types of overhead expenses must be evaluated and controls established to achieve cost reduction wherever possible.

Although these factors may complicate the control of manufacturing overhead, the basic approach to this control is fundamentally the same as that applying to direct costs: the setting of budgets or standards, the measurement of actual performance against those standards, and the taking of corrective action when those responsible for meeting budgets or standards repeatedly fail to reach the goal.

Standards may change at different volume levels; in other words, they must have sufficient flexibility to adjust to the level of operations under which the supervisor is working. To this extent the setting and application of overhead standards may differ from the procedure used in the control of direct material and direct labor. Also, the controller can use activity-based costing (ABC) to assign costs to products (or other cost elements, such as production departments or customers). Activity-based costing is a process that summarizes costs, allocates those costs to activities, and then charges the fully costed activities to those products or processes that use the activities. This approach is better than the traditional method of assigning a uniform overhead rate to all production, since using ABC results in more accurate product costing.

RESPONSIBILITIES OF THE CONTROLLER

In formulating and reporting on overhead information, the controller should heed these suggestions to make the information more useful to the manufacturing executive:

- The budget (or other standard) should be based on technical data that are sound from a manufacturing viewpoint, and should be agreed to in advance by the manufacturing manager. As manufacturing processes change, the standards must change. Adoption of just-in-time (JIT) techniques may require, for example, a different alignment of cost centers. Further, with the increased use of robots or other types of mechanization, direct labor will play a less important role, while manufacturing expense (through higher depreciation charged, perhaps more indirect labor, higher repairs and maintenance, and power) will become relatively more significant.

- The manufacturing department supervisors, who will do the actual planning and control of expenses, must be given the opportunity to fully understand the system, including the manner in which the budget expense structure is developed, and to generally concur in the fairness of the system.
- The account classifications must be practical, the cost departments should follow the manufacturing organization structure, and the allocation methods must permit the proper valuation of inventories, as well as proper control of expense.
- The manufacturing costs must be allocated as accurately as possible, so that the manufacturing executive can determine the expense of various products and processes. This topic is covered in more detail later in this chapter, in the "Activity-Based Costing: An Introduction" section.
- Where a budgeting process is operational, procedures must be in place that facilitate the preparation of the planning budget in an effective and timely manner (by provision of adequate forms, instructions, schedules, etc.).
- Where flexible budgets are in use, either identify or assist in the identification of the fixed and variable portions of costs.
- Determine that the costing methods provide reliable and acceptable accumulation and allocation by cost object and that variances are properly analyzed.
- Work with industrial engineers who will provide the technical data required for the development of standards, such as manpower needs, power requirements, expected downtime, and maintenance requirements.
- Work with the manufacturing executive to develop information collection procedures for assigning costs to activities and tracking product usage of those activities if an activity-based costing system is in place.

ACCOUNT CLASSIFICATIONS

One requirement for either adequate cost control or accurate cost determination is the proper classification of accounts. Control must be exercised at the source, and since costs are controlled by individuals, the primary classification of accounts must be by individual responsibility. This generally requires a breakdown of expenses by factory departments that may be either productive departments or service departments, such as maintenance, power, or the tool crib. Sometimes, however, it becomes necessary to divide the expense classification more finely to secure a proper control or costing of products—to determine actual expenses and expense standards by cost center. This decision about the degree of refinement will depend largely on whether improved product costs result or whether better expense control can be achieved.

A cost center, which is ordinarily the most minute division of costs, is determined on one of the following two bases:

1. One or more similar or identical machines.
2. The performance of a single operation or group of similar or related operations in the manufacturing process.

The separation of operations or functions is essential because a foreman may have more than one type of machine or operation in his or her department—all of which affect costs. One product may require the use of expensive machinery, and another may need only some simple hand operations. The segregation by cost center will reveal this cost difference. Different overhead rates are needed to reflect differences in services or machines required.

If the controller chooses to install an activity-based costing (ABC) system, then a very different kind of cost breakdown will be required. The ABC method collects costs by activities, rather than by department. For example, under ABC, information might be collected about the costs associated with engineering change orders, rather than the cost of the entire engineering department. If management decides that it wants both ABC and departmental cost information, then the controller must record the information twice—once by department and again by activity.

The accounts that are capitalized into the overhead account are well-defined by GAAP, and are presented in Table 9–1.

Most of the debate surrounding the content of the overhead cost pool is about the segments of inventory to which the overhead should be applied. Overhead is not normally applied to raw materials, but arguments have been presented in favor of the following two issues:

1. *Inbound transportation costs.* Where the cost of getting the goods to the factory site is identifiable with particular material or lots, the cost may properly be added to the raw material. If such allocation is impractical, it may be considered part of the manufacturing overhead.
2. *Purchasing department expense.* The cost of this department generally would continue at the same level from period to period regardless of receipts, so allocating the cost to raw materials would not be a proper matching of expenses with effort expended. The cost may be more properly treated as manufacturing overhead.

The overall discussion of overhead issues will become less important as more companies adopt just-in-time inventory systems. As inventories shrink, there will be only small quantities of work-in-process or finished goods on hand, so most overhead costs will flow directly to the income statement.

Table 9–1: Allocation of Costs to Expenses or Capital Accounts

Description	Capitalize	Expense
Advertising expenses		XXX
Costs of strikes		XXX
Depreciation and cost depletion	XXX	
Factory administration expenses	XXX	
General & administrative expenses related to overall operations		XXX
Income taxes		XXX
Indirect labor and production supervisory wages	XXX	
Indirect materials and supplies	XXX	
Interest		XXX
Maintenance	XXX	
Marketing expenses		XXX
Officers' salaries related to production services	XXX	
Other distribution expenses		XXX
Pension contribution related to past service costs		XXX
Production employee's benefits	XXX	
Quality control and inspection	XXX	
Rent	XXX	
Repair expenses	XXX	
Research and experimental expenses		XXX
Rework labor, scrap, and spoilage	XXX	XXX
Salaries of officers related to overall operations		XXX
Selling expenses		XXX
Taxes other than income taxes related to production assets	XXX	
Tools and equipment not capitalized	XXX	
Utilities	XXX	

Source: Adapted from *Analysis: Tax Reform Act of 1986,* Coopers & Lybrand LLP, New York, 1986, p. 176.

FIXED AND VARIABLE COSTS

Another step in controlling manufacturing overhead is the segregation of costs into two groups: fixed or variable. Variable costs increase or decrease in direct proportion to the volume of work. Control is exercised by keeping the expense within the limits determined for the particular level of activity. Fixed costs do not vary with activity but remain much the same over a relatively short period of time. Control over this kind of expense rests with the executives who determine policy with respect to plant investment, inventory level, and size of organization. It will be observed that failure to distinguish between these two types of expenses can result in failure to control overhead. This is because one cannot tell whether increased costs result from higher unit fixed costs as a result of lower volume or from failure to keep variable costs within proper bounds.

The segregation of fixed and variable expenses permits the adoption of the *flexible budget,* which is a budget that allows expenses to vary with the activity level of the department involved. The opposite kind of budget is the *fixed budget,* which is planned for a fixed activity level. Activity rarely stays at one level in practice, so fixed budgets can be of little use if the volume level changes.

Another classification of manufacturing expenses is the semivariable expense. This expense varies with the volume of production, but not in direct proportion to that volume. To control these expenses two techniques are available. One method is to determine for each semivariable expense in each department just what the costs should be at various operating levels. For example, if the expected range is between 60% and 90% of capacity, costs should be budgeted at every 5% level (i.e., 65%, 70%, 75%). The budget applicable to the actual volume level would be selected and interpolated between the 5% ranges if necessary. Then actual costs would be compared to the budget and corrective action taken.

Another method of applying budgetary control to semivariable expenses is to resolve them into their fixed and variable portions and treat each accordingly. The fixed portion could be considered the necessary expense at the lower level of the expected volume, and the difference between this and the higher level could be treated as variable.

A good starting point in determining the fixed and variable components of costs is past experience. This review should encompass not only total costs but also various measures of activity. It is necessary to determine how much costs vary, as well as the best tool or factor for measuring activity. For example, past activity may be related to standard direct labor hours, actual direct labor hours, or units of production. Review of past experience must be supplemented by good judgment in applying the data to future periods. Changes in wage rates, material costs, or supervisory staff, for example, must be considered in modifying the data for standard purposes.

The following list contains examples of fixed costs:

- *Fixed by general management decisions:*
  — Depreciation on buildings and machinery
  — Real and personal property taxes
  — Insurance (property and liability)
  — Salaries of production executives
  — Patent amortization
- *Fixed by production executive decisions:*
  — Salaries of factory supervisory staff
  — Factory administrative expense
  — Safety expenses

Examples of variable costs include:

- Royalties on units produced
- Small tool expense
- Supplies

- Testing expense
- Salvage expense

The following list contains examples of semivariable costs (i.e., those costs that contain both fixed and variable elements):

- Repairs and maintenance
- Factory office salaries and expense
- Payroll taxes and insurance
- Utilities

Using the High–Low Method

The illustrative separation of the fixed and variable elements of a manufacturing expense by a simple method is shown next. Assumptions for the example are as follows:

1. At a level of 50% of normal capacity, the maintenance department expense is $80,000 per month, whereas experience shows that at a level of 80% of capacity, the cost is $128,000.
2. The variable factor, or measuring stick, is standard hours of production worked.
3. At an 80% capacity, the standard hours worked are 160,000.

The variable costs are $48,000, and the variable budget allowance is $0.80 per standard hour worked, calculated as follows:

	Capacity	
% Normal Activity	Standard Hours Worked	Cost
80%	160,000	$128,000
50%	100,000	80,000
Variable	60,000	$48,000
Unit variable cost ($48,000/60,000)		$0.80

On such a budget structure, the maintenance department allowance for a month of 120,000 standard hours of production worked will be the following:

Fixed portion	$80,000
Variable ($0.80 × 120,000 − 100,000)	16,000
Total	$96,000

Note that the variable allowance is granted only for standard hours worked in excess of what was considered the lowest probable level of activity. However, the entire cost might be treated as variable within the same budget (120,000 × $0.80 = $96,000).

Graphic Determination of Fixed and Variable Costs

The use of only a few points to determine the variable expense is of limited value, since only a few levels are considered. If more accuracy is desired, another convenient approach is to use a scatter chart. For example, assume that the data in Table 9–2 on personnel department costs are available.

These numbers are then plotted on a chart as in Figure 9–1. The vertical axis represents the dollar costs, and the horizontal axis represents the factor of variability—standard hours worked in the illustration. After the points are plotted, a line of best fit may be drawn by inspection, in such a manner that half of the points are above it and half of the points are below it. Any highly variant items should be disregarded. For a higher degree of refinement the method of least-squares may be used. The least-squares method is a mathematical technique that derives a line of best fit with more precision than can be achieved by visually plotting the line.

The point at which the line of best fit intersects the vertical axis indicates the fixed cost that might be expected if the plant were in an operating condition but producing nothing. The total cost of any level of activity is determined by reading the chart. For example, at a level of 25,000 standard hours worked, the budget expense would be $13,400. This is made up of $5,500 fixed and $7,900 variable elements. The variable rate is $0.316 per standard hour worked.

The slope of the line on the chart indicates the degree of variability. Thus a horizontal line represents a fixed cost, whereas a line that goes through the point of origin indicates a completely variable cost. Sometimes, in constructing a

Table 9–2: Comparison of Costs to Standard Hours Worked Activity Measure

Month	Factory Standard Hours Worked	Total Departmental Costs
January	20,000	12,200
February	16,000	10,600
March	13,000	9,400
April	14,000	9,800
May	17,000	10,400
June	19,000	12,000
July	21,000	12,400
August	23,000	12,600
September	25,000	13,600
October	22,000	12,200
November	18,000	11,800
December	19,000	11,600

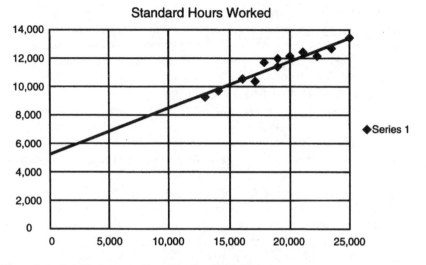

Figure 9–1: Graphic determination of fixed and variable costs

chart, the points show no tendency to arrange themselves along a line. If this situation does exist, then either the control of costs has been absent or a poor choice has been made about the factor of variability. Another factor should be tested to ascertain the cause.

A significant consideration in the control of manufacturing overhead expense through the analysis of variances is the level of activity selected in setting the standard costs. While it has no direct bearing on the planning and control of the manufacturing expenses of each individual department, it does have an impact on the statement of income and expenses, as well as on the statement of financial position. As for the income statement, it is desirable to identify the amount of manufacturing expense absorbed by or allocated to the manufactured product, with the excess expense identified as variance from the standard cost. This variance or excess cost ordinarily should be classified as to cause. As for the statement of financial position, the normal activity level has a direct impact on inventory valuation and, consequently, on the cost-of-goods-sold element of the income statement, in that it helps to determine the standard product cost. It should be obvious that the fixed element of unit product costs is greatly influenced by the total quantity of production assumed. Of equal importance is the necessity for a clear understanding by management of the significance of the level selected, because in large part it determines the volume variance.

Generally speaking, there are three levels on which fixed standard manufacturing overhead may be set:

1. *The expected sales volume for the year, or other period, when the standards are to be applied.* All costs are adjusted from year to year. Consequently, certain cost comparisons are difficult to make. Furthermore, the resulting

statements fail to give management what may be considered the most useful information about volume costs. Standard costs would be higher in low-volume years, when lower prices might be needed to get more business, and lower in high-volume years, when the increased demand presumably would tend toward higher prices. Another weakness is that the estimate of sales used as a basis would not be accurate in many cases.

2. *Practical plant capacity, representing the volume at which a plant could produce if there were no lack of orders.* Practical plant capacity as a basis tends to give the lowest cost. This can be misleading because sales volume will not average this level. Generally, there will always be large unfavorable variances, the unabsorbed expense.

3. *The normal or average sales volume, herein defined as normal capacity.* This is the utilization of the plant that is necessary to meet the average sales demand over the period of a business cycle or at least long enough to level out cyclical and seasonal influences. This basis permits stabilization of costs and the recognition of long-term trends in sales. Each basis has advantages and disadvantages, but normal capacity seems to be the most desirable under ordinary circumstances.

Where one unit is manufactured, normal capacity can be stated in the quantity of this unit. In those cases where many products are available, it is usually necessary to select a common unit for the denominator. Productive hours are a practical measure. If the normal productive hours for all departments or cost centers are known, the sum of these will represent the total for the plan. The total fixed costs divided by the productive hours at normal capacity results in the standard fixed cost per productive hour.

Volume variances can also cause costing problems in an activity-based costing (ABC) environment. Activity costs are derived by dividing estimated volumes of activity drivers into activity cost pools to derive costs for individual activities. If the estimated volume of an activity driver deviates excessively from the actual amount, then the activity cost applied to a product may significantly alter the product's ABC cost. For example, there are estimated to be 1,000 material moves associated with a product in a month, and the total cost of those moves in a month is $10,000, which is $10 per move. If the actual number of moves associated with the product is 2,000, then the cost per move that is applied to product costs is off by $5 per move. However, if the ABC system collects actual activity driver volume information for every accounting period, then the volume variance will not occur.

COST ALLOCATION

The following section discusses traditional cost allocation systems, the need for activity-based costing (ABC), problems with the ABC model, and ways to report

ABC information to management. We also briefly outline an ABC installation, ABC software models, analyzing non-value added processes, and converting indirect costs to direct costs. The ABC topic is much larger than this abbreviated discussion, so we recommend that a reader who wishes to implement such a system consult one of the many books available on the subject.

Traditional Cost Allocation

A traditional cost allocation system seeks to assign all indirect production costs to cost objects. Where possible, the indirect costs are assigned based on the use of those costs by the cost objects. If no usage relationship can be established, then the indirect costs will be assigned based on some broad allocation measure.

A cost is considered *indirect* if it cannot be directly assigned to a cost object with minimal effort. For example, one firm may consider an engineer's salary to be indirect if he works on numerous projects at once. However, another firm might expand additional effort to track that engineer's time, so that the salary cost can be directly assigned to cost objects. In the first case, the salary is considered an indirect cost. In the second case, the salary is considered a direct cost. Examples of costs that are generally considered to be indirect are repairs and maintenance, utilities, and depreciation.

A *cost object* is the item being measured. For example, the controller may wish to find the cost of a product, a department, or a geographical sales region. Each can be a cost object, because the controller must accumulate a different, discrete set of cost information about each item.

The method for allocating costs is the *overhead rate*. This is a constant rate per unit of the application base. For example, the total amount to be allocated is $100,000, and the allocation base is units of production. If 10,000 units are expected to be produced, then $10 will be allocated for each unit produced. These overhead rates are usually determined at the beginning of the year in order to avoid seasonal fluctuations in the rate and to avoid the extra work needed to recalculate the rate for each accounting period. The overhead rate estimate is based on the projected amount of indirect cost divided by the expected volume of the allocation base. Since the rate is based on two estimates, it is obvious that incorrect overhead rates are fairly common. If the controller deems the overhead rate to be materially incorrect, then a mid-year correction is appropriate. For lesser cases of under- or over-absorbed overhead, the variance should be factored into the current period's financial statements.

The base selected should be the one that best allocates costs. However, the "best" method is a matter of opinion in many cases, so that indirect labor is frequently misapplied. For those organizations with a large amount of indirect costs, an incorrect allocation base can have serious repercussions on product costing. For example, a cost that is reported too low may cause management to take steps to increase sales of that item, when it should be emphasizing the sales of other, more profitable products.

A typical allocation process is as follows:

1. *Accumulate costs for all production cost centers and service cost centers.* An example of a product cost center is a sheet metal bending department. An example of a service cost center is a maintenance department.

2. *Assign the cost of all service cost centers to the production cost centers.* For example, the maintenance department fills out timesheets which indicate that 30% of its labor and parts costs were used in maintaining the sheet metal bending department. If the maintenance department's total assigned cost is $100,000, then $30,000 of the $100,000 will be charged to the sheet metal bending department.

3. *The total cost of the production cost centers are assigned to the cost objects produced in those centers.* For example, if half of the sheet metal bending department's time is spent producing bird feeders, then half of that department's total cost is assigned to the total production of bird feeders.

Sometimes service centers perform work for other service centers. When this happens, costs may be assigned from one service center to another. The reader should consult a cost accounting textbook for examples of the step-down allocation method. Service centers invariably have "leftover" costs that cannot be directly assigned elsewhere. An example of this is the salary of the supervisor, who is not directly involved in providing a service to a cost object. In such cases, there are many bases the controller can use to allocate the costs-to-cost objects. For example, common allocation bases are the number of people, labor hours, labor dollars, machine hours, square footage, volume of transactions (e.g., number of material moves, parts ordered, engineering change orders), or total revenues/costs (e.g., based on total revenue or expenses dollars).

Activity-Based Costing: An Introduction

Traditional cost accounting systems apply overhead to products based on the amount of direct labor they use. When direct labor was a significant proportion of the value being added to a product, this did not skew product costs significantly. However, as direct labor was gradually replaced by automation, the direct labor component dropped while overhead costs increased. As a result, many businesses find that their overhead rates are at 300% or more of their direct labor costs. Consequently, a slight change in a product's direct labor charge yields a significant product cost variation as the applied overhead amount swings dramatically up or down.

To combat this overhead application problem, several companies began to apply overhead based on other, more relevant, factors than direct labor. This resulted in multiple overhead rates being used at one time, and required additional data collection for the different overhead application bases. Eventually, activity-based costing (ABC) was invented. ABC is not a direct offshoot of the multiple overhead rate system. Instead, it assumes that costs are assigned based on resources consumed, so that resource costs are identified and then assigned to products based on their use of those resources. The ABC information is then accumulated into reports by product, customer, geographic region, or other reporting entities.

An ABC system requires a large amount of data collection. Cost data must be accumulated in ways that are usually not the same as the traditional by-department chart of accounts system. The controller must therefore recombine costs into "cost pools." In addition, the ABC system must derive a cost for various activities, and then the use of those activities by the reporting entity (products, customers, geographic regions, etc.) must be measured. This data collection is either handled on a project basis, so that ABC costs are only derived once, or built into a new costing system that either supersedes or exists beside the traditional costing system. Also, the ABC system must be carefully designed so that the data collection is not too burdensome. The ABC team should keep the number of cost pools and activity measures to a minimum. Once an ABC system is operational, the ABC team can analyze the model's accuracy and selectively add or delete items requiring data collection.

The information derived from an ABC model can be used to provide product cost information, inventory valuations, and control non-value added costs. One of its greatest benefits is to assist management in determining the true costs of products that are otherwise buried in overhead and misapplied elsewhere. As a result, management has better gross margin information, and can more intelligently add or delete products or options with that information. If the ABC information is not presented to management, then its benefits will not be significant.

The information provided by the traditional costing system may conflict with the information provided by the ABC system. If, for example, management bonuses are calculated based on the results of the traditional system, then the ABC results may be ignored. Also, if a company has several divisions and ABC is not implemented in all of them, then the corporate controller will have incomplete comparative costing information. As a result, management action based on cost comparisons would not be possible.

Developing an ABC Model

For the purposes of this discussion, we will assume that costs are only being accumulated to report on product costs. To develop an ABC model, the following eight steps must be completed:

1. *Identify activities.* This step has the following components:
   - *Define the boundaries of the project*—An ABC analysis can involve all aspects of the company, but completing such a project may take too long to retain management's interest. Instead, the ABC project leader should consider a small, important target area for the initial ABC analysis, and

then expand the process at a later date. For example, the initial project could include the engineering and materials departments, but exclude marketing.

- *Document process flows*—List all activities within each target area. This information is usually recorded on a flowchart. Activities may cross over department boundaries. For example, the materials ordering process begins with the bill of materials in the engineering department before it moves to the materials department where the actual ordering occurs. The flowcharts should be reviewed with key personnel from the areas being studied, so that flaws in the model can be corrected.

2. *Identify all direct costs.* Traditional costing methods already track direct costs in some detail, so this is an easy step if there are existing costing systems in place. If not, then identify the direct labor and materials costs that are associated with individual products. Accurate labor routings and bills of material are needed for proper direct cost identification. If there is an existing Material Requirements Planning (MRP) system in place, then routings and bills of material should already be available.

3. *Assign indirect costs to cost pools.* Use the flowcharts developed during the first step to identify logical clusters of costs. This can be a very time-consuming step, for the costs in the general ledger are organized to support a traditional costing system, not an activity-based system that requires a different chart of accounts. As a result, many general ledger accounts will have to be subdivided into smaller pieces that are then summarized into cost pools. A sample list of cost pools that a manufacturing company might use includes:

- Accounts payable
- Depreciation
- Maintenance labor
- Material movement
- Plant management
- Production control
- Purchasing
- Quality control
- Receiving
- Rework
- Scrap
- Utilities

4. *Identify output measures.* Use the flowcharts developed during the first step to identify activities that consume costs. These activities measure the frequency and volume of demand placed on an activity by the product or service being produced. For example, every time a product is moved, costs are incurred for the labor of the forklift driver and depreciation expense for the forklift. Other examples of output measures are:

- Number of parts
- Number of suppliers
- Number of units reworked
- Number of material moves
- Number of purchase orders
- Number of customer orders
- Number of engineering change requests

5. *Collect output measures.* Most companies use ABC on a project basis, so that output measures are only collected once. Those companies assume that output measures do not vary significantly in the short term, and thus rely on ABC information for which the foundation data was only collected once. The alternative, and more accurate, approach is to collect the output measure information for each reporting period. Doing so requires information collection systems for items that were not previously tracked. Some output measures are difficult to track, so management must commit in advance to the extra time and cost of doing so.

6. *Calculate activity costs.* Divide the output measures into the cost pools to derive activity costs. For example, an output measure may be that 210 invoices were paid by accounts payable in a period. The cost of the accounts payable labor for that period was $1,672, so the cost per accounts payable activity (paying the invoice) was $7.96.

7. *Calculate product costs.* There are several layers of costs to add to a product under the ABC model:

   - *Add direct costs*—These are the direct labor and material costs that are directly attributable to a product, and are usually derived from labor routings and bills of material.

   - *Add activity costs*—Add the costs of all costed activities to the product cost. For example, if 32 invoices were paid in order to produce a product, then the cost of the payables activity for that product (using the $7.96 amount from the previous example) would be $7.96 multiplied 32 times, or $254.72.

   - *Add other cost pools*—Other costs can be added from cost pools for areas such as marketing and general and administrative expenses. For example, if costs by geographic region are desired, then advertising costs can be subdivided by region and added to the total cost of products sold in each region.

8. *Use the information.* Review product costs based on the traditional costing system versus the new costing system. An ABC review will highlight costs that would otherwise have been lost in the total overhead cost. Typical management actions to reduce the overhead cost are listed below:

   - *Reduce the number of product options*—The cost of designing, scheduling, and building product options is located in overhead and can be reduced by cutting the number of product options.

- *Reduce the number of parts used*—The cost of designing, "sourcing" (the process of identifying and obtaining parts from a source or supplier), and purchasing parts is located in overhead and can be reduced by cutting the number of product options.
- *Reduce the number of material moves*—The cost of moving parts is located in the materials department part of the overhead cost and can be reduced by cutting the number of material moves (which also cuts the cycle time!).
- *Reduce the number of engineering change requests*—The cost of redesigning parts, sourcing new suppliers, and expediting purchases is located in the overhead cost and can be reduced by cutting the number of engineering change requests.
- *Reduce the number of suppliers*—The cost of sourcing and qualifying new suppliers is located in the materials department portion of the overhead cost and can be reduced by cutting the number of suppliers.

Note that the list of possible management actions is identical to the activities used in the ABC model. The ABC model is designed in this manner to focus attention on activities in the production cycle. If management reduces the number of activities, then not only is the "traditional" overhead cost reduced, but also the production cycle time is slashed.

Special issues may arise when developing an ABC model, or the controller may decide to extend an existing ABC model to cover additional activities. Examples of these special situations are the use of ABC in the budgeting process, converting indirect costs to direct costs, and implementing a bill of activities. The following list may help the controller to deal with special ABC problems, as well as to enhance existing ABC applications.

- *Convert indirect costs to direct costs*—If indirect costs can be converted to direct costs, then product costs will be more accurate. One area for such improvement is converting to a cellular manufacturing arrangement from an assembly line arrangement. Product costing for an assembly line can be inaccurate because many product types may pass through specific workstations or departments. As a result, costs are accumulated by workstation or department and then assigned to products based on labor hours or machine hours. In a cellular manufacturing environment, a small number of products are built by a small number of workers using a cluster of workstations that are reserved for producing that set of products. Consequently, costs are more easily assigned to products, and the costs of those grouped workstations can be considered direct instead of indirect.
- *Purchase an ABC software package*—Many companies build ABC systems that are separate from their traditional accounting systems. Another approach to building ABC systems is to use the alphanumeric fields sometimes provided with general ledger packages to store output measures for each reporting period.

- *Review non-value-added processes*—The controller can add a function to the process review phase of ABC, and review the process flowcharts for value-added versus non-value-added activities. A value-added activity converts resources into products or services. A non-value-added activity can be eliminated with no reduction in a product or service's functionality or quality. This added step allows the controller to target non-value-added processes for elimination. The non-value-added processes can be ranked in importance by the time or cost required for each one. Armed with that information, management can then prioritize them for elimination or reduction. Examples of non-value-added activities are:
  — Inspection
  — Rework
  — Moving
  — Storage
  — Queue time

  A value-added analysis also notes the company's value-added activities. The controller can highlight this information and encourage an engineering team to reduce or eliminate any bottlenecks in those operations. This action increases the company's production capacity.

- *Implement a bill of activities*—To create an on-line ABC system, the company should create a bill of activities (BOA) that is similar to the bill of materials (BOM) already used for its products. The BOA lists the types and quantities of activities used during the production of a product. Management can focus on the BOA to discern the primary sources of activity-based costs, and act to reduce those costs. Also, the BOA is needed to roll up activity costs for each period's cost reports, just as the BOM is used to roll up direct costs for each product.

- *Using ABC for budgeting*—Activity-based costing is rarely used for budgeting, but if the controller wishes to use it, then BOA's and BOM's should be used as the foundation data for standard costs. Multiplying the planned production quantities by the activity costs found in the bills of activity and direct costs found in the bills of lading will yield the bulk of all anticipated manufacturing costs for the budget period. The appropriate management use of budgeted activity costs is to target reductions in the use of activities by various products, as well as to reduce the cost of those activities. For example, the cost of paying a supplier invoice for a part used by the company's product can be reduced by either (1) automating the activity to reduce its cost, or (2) reducing the product's use of the activity, such as by reducing the number of suppliers, reducing the number of parts used in the product, or grouping invoices and only paying the supplier on a monthly basis.

CONTROLLING OVERHEAD

The basic approach in controlling overhead is to set standards of performance and operate within the limits of these standards. Two avenues may be followed to accomplish this objective: one involves the preplanning or preventive approach; the other, the after-the-fact approach of reporting unfavorable trends and performance.

Preplanning can be accomplished on many items of manufacturing overhead expense in somewhat the same fashion as discussed in connection with direct labor. For example, the crews for indirect labor can be planned just as well as the crews for direct labor. The preplanning approach will be found useful where a substantial dollar cost is involved for purchase of supplies or repair materials. It may be found desirable to maintain a record of purchase commitments, by responsibility, for these accounts. Each purchase requisition, for example, might require the approval of the budget department. When the budget limit is reached, then no further purchases would be permitted except with the approval of much higher authority. Again, where stores or stock requisitions are the source of charges, the department manager may be kept informed periodically of the cumulative monthly cost, and steps may be taken to stop further issues, except in emergencies, as the budget limit is approached. The controller will be able to find ways and means of assisting the department operating executives to keep within budget limits by providing this kind of information.

The other policing function of control is the reporting of unfavorable trends and performance. This involves an analysis of expense variances. Here the problem is somewhat different compared with direct labor or material because of the different levels of activity. Thus, the variance due to business volume must be isolated from that controllable by the departmental supervisors.

The *volume variance,* regardless of cause, must be segregated from the controllable variances. The volume variance is defined as the difference between budgeted expense for current activity and the standard cost for the same level. It arises because production is above or below normal activity and affects primarily the fixed costs of the business. The variance can be caused by seasonal or calendar factors, such as the varying numbers of days in each month.

The controllable variances may be defined as the difference between the budget at the current activity level and actual expenses. They must be set out for each cost center and analyzed in such detail that the supervisor knows exactly what caused the condition. At least two general categories can be recognized. The first is the rate of *spending variance;* this variance arises because more or less than standard was spent for each machine hour, operating hour, or standard labor hour. This variance must be isolated for each cost element of production expense. An analysis of the variance on indirect labor, for example, may indicate what share of the excess cost is due to (1) overtime, (2) an excess number of workers, or (3) use of higher-rated workers than standard. The analysis may be detailed to show the excess by craft and by shift. As another example, suppliers may be analyzed to show the cause of variance as (1) too large a quantity of certain items, (2) a different material or quality being used, or (3) higher prices than anticipated.

Another general type of controllable variance is the *efficiency variance.* This variance represents the difference between actual hours used in production and the standard hours allowed for the same volume. Such a loss involves all elements of overhead. The controller should analyze the causes, usually with the assistance of production personnel. The lost production might be due to mechanical failure, poor or insufficient material, or inefficient labor. Such an analysis points out weaknesses and paves the way for corrective action by the line executives.

The accounting staff must be prepared to analyze overhead variances quickly and accurately to keep the manufacturing supervision and management informed. The variance analysis should focus on overhead losses or gains for which unit supervision is responsible and include such features as:

- The expenditure or rate variance for each cost element as an over- or under-the-budget condition for the reporting period and year to date. The budgeted amount for controllable expenses may be calculated by multiplying the operating hours by the standard rate per cost element and compared to the actual.
- The departmental variance related to the level of production.
- The amount of fixed costs, even though the particular supervisor may not be responsible for the incurrence.
- Interpretative comments about areas for corrective action, trends, and reasons for any negative variances.

It is not sufficient just to render a budget report to the manufacturing supervisors; this group must be informed about the reasons for the variances. A continuous follow-up must also be undertaken to see that any unfavorable conditions are corrected. This may take the form of reviewing and analyzing weekly or even daily reports. Abnormal conditions such as excess training, overtime, absenteeism, and excessive usage of supplies must be isolated and brought to the attention of the responsible individuals who can take remedial action. There also may be other data available, such as repair records, material and supplies usage reports, and personnel statistics records (e.g., turnover and attendance), that are useful in determining variances.

One of the purposes of budgetary control is to maintain expenses within the limits of income. To this end, common factors of variability are standard labor hours or standard machine hours—bases affected by the quantity of approved production. If manufacturing difficulties are encountered, the budget allowance of all departments on such a basis would be reduced. The controller might hear arguments by the maintenance foreman, for example, that he should not be penalized in his budget because production was inefficient or that plans once set cannot be changed constantly because production does not come up to expectations. Such a situation may be resolved in one of at least two ways: (1) the forecast standard hours could be used as the basis for the variable allowance, or (2) the maintenance foreman could be informed regularly if production, and therefore the standard budget allowance, will be lower than anticipated. The first suggestion departs somewhat from the income-producing sources but does permit a budget allowance within the limits of income and does not require constant changes of labor force over a very short period. The second suggestion allows for more coordination between departments.

An important consideration is not *how* flexibility is introduced into the standard or budget but rather that it *is* introduced. Whether charts or tables are used to determine the allowable budget on a more or less automatic basis or whether the budget is adjusted monthly or quarterly on the basis of special review in relation to business volume is not essential. Either method can be employed successfully. The goal is to secure an adequate measuring stick that also keeps expenses at the proper level in relation to activity or income.

Many manufacturing executives in particular industries know from observation that certain expense relationships are the key to a profitable operation. Their experience has led to the use of a number of standards or standard relationships for manufactured expenses. These ratios are usually collected and distributed by industry trade associations or magazines devoted to the affairs of specific industries. Some comparisons often used can be seen in Table 9–3.

PRODUCTION REPORTS

The supervisory staff of the production organization extends over several levels of authority and responsibility from the assistant foreman, foreman, general foreman, division head, plant superintendent, and so on, up to the vice president of manufacturing. Likewise, the matters of the supervisory staff controls involve materials, labor, and overhead, and each of these subjects has special aspects to be reported on. It is obvious, then, that production reports must cover a wide field of subject matter for the readers. Effective production control is possible only when the production executives are aware of the necessary facts related to the plant operations, and the further the executive is from the actual production, the more he or she must rely on reports. As a result, a system of reports has been

Table 9–3: Operational Standards Used to Track Expenses

Item	As Related to
Total manufacturing expenses	Total direct labor costs
	Total direct costs
Indirect labor expense	Total standard direct labor
	Per direct labor hour
	Per actual direct labor hour
	Per machine hour
	Total manufacturing expense
Repair and maintenance expense	Per machine hour
Power	Per operating hour
Supplies	Per hour worked
Shipping and receiving	Per ton handled
Downtime expense	Per operating hour

developed in most industrial organizations for presenting the pertinent facts on the production activities.

Recent developments in computer systems permit an improved monitoring of operations, allowing much information to be available on a real-time basis. With the advent of personal computers, interesting combination reports consisting of commentary, charts, and graphs are now possible.

The number of variance reports that are used by manufacturing management will decline as cellular manufacturing becomes the standard form of production. Since cellular manufacturing uses minimal work-in-process (WIP), month-end variance reports from the accounting department will arrive far too late for the information to be useful. For example, if a machine produces a part out of specification, then a production worker operating in a cellular layout will immediately detect the problem, because the part will not be hidden in a pile of WIP. Consequently, management can detect and correct the problem immediately without the need for a report.

Reports will differ by industry and company so that no standardized reports can be used for business in general. However, they may be divided into two general categories according to their purpose: (1) control reports and (2) summary reports. As the name implies, control reports are issued primarily to highlight substandard performance so that corrective action may be taken promptly. These reports deal with performance at the occurrence level and are therefore usually detailed in nature and frequent in issuance. On the other hand, summary reports show the results of performance over a longer period of time, such as a month, and are an overall recapitulation of performance. They serve to keep corporate executives aware of factory performance and are, in effect, a summary of the control reports.

Indicative of the subjects the reports may cover are the following:

- *Material*—Inventories, spoilage and waste, unit standard costs, material consumed, and actual vs. standard usage.
- *Labor*—Total payroll, unit output per hour worked, total production in units, average hourly labor rates, overtime hours and costs, bonus costs, and turnover.
- *Overhead*—Actual vs. budgeted costs, idle facilities, maintenance costs, supplies used, the cost of union business, and subcontracted repairs.

In a production environment that has adopted just-in-time (JIT) manufacturing systems, reports will no longer include standards, because JIT assumes that most cost improvements can be managed in the design phase, not in the production phase, and that collecting variance information costs more in effort than is gained in tangible results. Thus, a set of JIT reports would include the following items not related to standards:

- Inventory turnover
- Unit output per hour worked

- Total production in units
- Staff turnover
- Actual purchased costs versus planned costs
- Inventory accuracy
- Bill of material accuracy
- Bill of activities accuracy

Production executives will make good use of data bearing on their operations provided certain fundamental rules are followed:

1. Reports should be expressed in the language of the executive who is to use them and in the form preferred by him or her (e.g., charts, graphs, or commentary).
2. Reports should be submitted promptly enough to serve the purpose intended. Control reports are of little value if issued too late to take corrective action.
3. The form and content of the report should be in keeping with the responsibility of the executive receiving it. Mid-level executives are interested in details, whereas higher executives are interested in departmental summaries, trends, and relationships.

10

GENERAL AND ADMINISTRATIVE EXPENSES

The category of expenses known as general and administrative (G&A) expense relates primarily to the costs of the various top management functions at the headquarters level having to do with overall policy determination, and direction of the business. This chapter discusses the accounts included in the G&A category, allocation of cost, and G&A cost control.

FUNCTIONS INVOLVED

The typical medium- to large-sized company would include the cost of these departments in the G&A expense category:

- Office of the chairman of the board
- Office of the president
- Financial organization:
  - Office of the chief financial officer
  - Officer of the controller
    - Accounting department
    - Tax department
    - Financial planning and control department
    - Financial information systems

— Office of the treasurer
  • Cash administration
  • Risk management
  • Retirement plan investments
— Office of the chief internal auditor
  • Financial auditing
  • Systems auditing
  • Special reviews
• Legal department:
  — Office of the vice president—legal
    • Office of the corporate secretary
    • Litigation
    • SEC relations
    • Patents and trademarks
  • Corporate offices for the direction and control of these major functions:
  — Marketing
  — Manufacturing
  — Research and development
  — Human resources
  — Management information systems
  — Public relations
  — Strategic planning

To the extent that the purpose of the preceding departments or organizational units have to do with the overall policy determination, planning, direction, and control, they probably would be classified as G&A in the annual report to shareholders. Comparable expenses at the division or subsidiary level might or might not be so classified (although the methods of planning and control would be similar to those for the corporate activity).

ACCOUNTING FOR AND ALLOCATING ADMINISTRATIVE EXPENSES

The controller is responsible for developing and maintaining an accounting system that serves, among others, the following purposes:

• Permits the reporting of expenses for external purposes in accordance with generally accepted accounting principles.
• Allows the accumulation of costs by natural category in such a way as to facilitate planning and control.
• Accumulates costs on a "responsibility" basis so that a specific individual may be assigned responsibility for the planning and control of the costs.

- Where appropriate, permits the allocation of expenses on some acceptable basis, such as benefits received, to cost objects—which might include divisions or cost centers or products that use the service.
- Gives due weight to internal control concerns.

Methods of allocation, and when costs should be allocated, are of special concern in the planning and control of assets. A basic tenet for responsibility accounting is that expenses should not be allocated to a department unless the supervisor can exercise control over such costs. If such control is present, then the following allocation methods are possible:

- Allocate costs based on the amount of the resource consumed by the cost center receiving the service. For example, if a division uses a financial analyst's time to evaluate a prospective acquisition, then that analyst's time should be charged to the applicable division.
- Allocate costs using a common activity base, but only if the direct charge method noted above is not feasible. Costs can be charged based on many activity bases, such as sales, assets employed, payroll, number of new hires, square feet used, and the number of purchase orders issued. It is desirable to have a number of cost pools that are allocated using a number of different activity bases, *as long as costing accuracy is materially improved* by expending the extra effort on record-keeping.
- Allocate variances between standard and actual costs to the same cost centers using the same allocation bases that were used for the initial allocation. The variances can be allocated in proportion to the costs allocated previously using standard rates.
- Allocations should not be performed based on ability to bear the cost (e.g., the most profitable division is charged with most of the expenses), since it can have a counterproductive effect on management behavior.

If supervisors have no control over the costs that are allocated to them, then the allocated costs should be separated from the revenues and costs for which the supervisor is responsible, especially if profit goals and bonuses are involved. Otherwise, managers will have no incentive to achieve their targeted goals when imposed allocated costs cuts into their targets.

"UNIQUE" EXPENSES

This section examines those expenses that are in some ways unique to headquarters or central unit activities, and that are not found charged to most departments.

Charitable contributions. In most companies, charitable contributions are approved by the board of directors as a separate budget item. Therefore, this approved list, sometimes plus an approval allowance for contingencies, is the basis for planning and control. It presents no special problem. There will be instances where a specific contribution is for the benefit of a division or subsidiary, and may be charged to it.

Incentive pay. Many companies have established incentive pay systems for the officers and top management, accruing the estimated expense in the G&A category (office of the chairman). Since the formula is known, the anticipated expenses can be planned and accrued on the basis of the expected relevant factors.

Audit fees. The cost of the annual audit by the independent accountants can be estimated, included in the planned expenses, and accrued. In many instances, the share attributable to the separate subordinate units of the entity can be charged to them and included in their budgets.

Legal fees. If certain litigation is under way or imminent, the cost can be estimated and accrued. Based on past history, if other litigation is likely, a contingency provision might be made. Again, if the legal costs relate to a particular organizational unit (and not the corporate entity as a whole), then the provision for the accrual and budget may be made in that unit.

Interest expense and income taxes. Interest expense, being directly related to borrowed funds, is kept within limits through the control of business indebtedness. Control of interest-bearing obligations affects control of interest expense. When the financial budget of the company has been established, the amount of interest expense can be calculated on the basis of predicted borrowings, payments, and similar facts.

There are very few control problems in connection with income taxes. The first requirement is to establish a proper tax plan to minimize tax payments, to estimate monthly the amount due, and to make the proper accruals in accordance with generally accepted accounting practice. Another function of the controller is to review carefully methods and transactions, securing tax counsel where necessary, to comply with all technicalities and thus secure the greatest tax advantage. Other than this, the controller's responsibilities relate to keeping the required records and substantiating data to support tax claims, advising on capital gain and loss transactions, and arranging the capital structure, as well as the investments, to secure the maximum benefits under the tax laws. Quite aside from the tax problems of the individual company, the chief accounting officer can actively promote equitable tax laws directly or through associations.

Corporate expenses. There are numerous corporate expenses that must be assigned to particular executives for control purposes—for example, state and federal capital stock taxes, franchise taxes, fees of fiscal agents, stock transfer taxes, and fidelity bonds and insurance. There is no particular problem of control.

Excess facility costs. Occassionally, some companies find themselves in pos-session of distribution or production facilities that are too large for its production or storage needs. Usually, the facilities were built or acquired without a sound analysis of the potential demand for the company's products or because of other errors in executive judgment. Whatever the reason, it is unwise to burden the cur-rent manufacturing or distribution operations with the charge. The costs are often carried as a separate administrative expense until the property can be disposed of. The continuing expenses usually consist of depreciation, taxes, insurance, and a certain amount of maintenance. It is a relatively simple matter to estimate the cost and establish a budget to cover it. Management generally should be alert either to dispose of the property on favorable terms or to rent it.

Bad debt losses. Another item of expense peculiar to the financial group is bad debt loss. Obviously this loss is not the sole criterion of the efficiency of the credit department. Any bad debt losses could be eliminated either by making only cash sales or by restricting credit sales only to the financially strongest firms. Such a policy would drive business to competitors who are willing to take reasonable credit risks. Any discussion of bad debt losses must therefore assume that a company is competitive from the standpoint of extending credit. Under such circumstances there are some measuring sticks to be applied to loss experi-ence over a period of time. These include:

- Percentage of bad debt losses to total sales–This is to be used where the cash sales are relatively insignificant. Such a basis avoids the necessity of segre-gating cash and credit sales if solely for this purpose.
- Percentage of bad debt losses to total net credit sales.

If warranted, these bases can be refined through a segregation by different classes of customers, methods or terms of sales, or by different territories. Con-trol of the expense, of course, rests on effectively policing accounts receivable to discover evidence of slow payments.

Other income and expense. Most business firms have various items of income and expense that are of a nonoperating nature. The income may include interest income, royalties, rental income, dividends received, and income from sales of scrap. The expenses include loss on the sale of fixed assets and sales discounts. Based on past experience and knowledge about projected changes, reasonable estimates of these elements of income and expense can be made. Otherwise, con-trol of a limited nature is exercised through the judgment of the official to whom the accounts are assigned.

COST VARIABILITY

In most companies, G&A expense is not budgeted as a percentage of sales, since it is relatively fixed and does not vary with sales. However, many G&A functions can be viewed as step costs. For example, accounts receivable volume will decline as sales drop; if there is a significant reduction in sales volume, then the budget for a receivables position would be eliminated. However, there are many fixed costs. For example, director expenses are fixed, since the same number of board meetings will occur, no matter how much sales volume may vary. Table 10–1 splits G&A expenses into discretionary, variable, step, and fixed costs.

Table 10–1 shows that there are almost no variable costs to budget. However, there are many discretionary costs. Withholding expenditures on discretionary items can have a marked impact on profits, so a separate analysis of discretionary G&A costs should be made available to management, especially if profitability is expected to be a problem.

Areas where costs may verge on becoming variable costs instead of step costs are the salaries of the payroll, cost accounting, standards, cashier's, and internal audit departments.

CONTROLLING COSTS

Accounting costs can also be controlled through standards of performance and cost. These standards can be applied to many office functions just as they have been applied to manufacturing and sales functions. They are not applicable to all accounting activities, and do not give the same degree of accuracy as in the fac-

Table 10–1: Break-Down of Costs into Levels of Variability

Cost Description	Discretionary	Variable	Step	Fixed
Salaries			XXX	
Fringe benefits			XXX	
Travel & entertainment	XXX			
Telecommunications			XXX	
Repairs & maintenance	XXX			
Rent				XXX
Dues & subscriptions	XXX			
Utilities				XXX
Purchased services			XXX	
Depreciation				XXX
Insurance				XXX
Incentive pay	XXX			
Director fees & expenses				XXX
Outside legal fees	XXX			
Audit fees			XXX	
Charitable contributions	XXX			
Consultant fees	XXX			
Gain/loss on sales of assets	XXX			
Cash discounts		XXX		
Provision for doubtful accts.		XXX		
Interest expense				XXX

tory. But in many offices, the possible cost savings for certain clerical activities are sufficient to justify the effort of establishing the standards. The application of setting standards to the measurement of clerical work is a six-step process.

1. *Preliminary observation and analysis*—This step is fundamental in securing the necessary overall understanding of the problem and in selecting those areas of activity that may lend themselves to standardization. Also, it assists in eliminating any obvious weakness in routine.
2. *Selection of functions on which standards are to be set*—Standards should be set only on those activities sufficient in volume to justify standards.
3. *Determination of the unit of work*—A unit must be selected in which the standard may be expressed. This will depend on the degree of specialization and the volume of work.
4. *Determination of the best method and setting of the standard*—Time and motion studies can be applied to office work, with sufficient allowance being given for fatigue and personal needs.
5. *Testing of the standard*—After the standard has been set, it should be tested to see that it is practical.
6. *Final application*—This involves using the standard and preparing simple reports that the supervisor and the individual worker can see. It also requires a full explanation to the employee.

Illustrative accounting and clerical functions that lend themselves to standardization and the units of work which may be used to measure performance are shown in Table 10–2.

In addition to performance standards, unit cost activities can be applied to measure an individual function or overall activity. Thus, applying cost standards to credit and collection functions may involve various functions and units of measurement depending on the extent of mechanization, as shown in Table 10–3.

Table 10–2: Accounting and Clerical Functions Subject to Measurement

Function	Unit of Standard Measurement
Order handling	Number of orders handled
Mail handling	Number of pieces handled
Billing	Number of invoice lines
Check writing	Number of checks written
Posting	Number of postings
Filing	Number of pieces filed
Typing	Number of lines typed
Customer statements	Number of statements
Order writing	Number of order lines

Table 10–3: Accounting Activities and Related Cost Standards

Functional Activity	Unit Cost Standard
Credit investigation and approval	Cost per sales order
	Cost per account sold
	Cost per credit sales transaction
Credit correspondence records and files	Cost per sales order
	Cost per letter
	Cost per account sold
Preparing invoices	Cost per invoice line
	Cost per item
	Cost per invoice
	Cost per order line
	Cost per order
Entire accounts receivable records, including	Cost per account
posting of charges and credits and preparation	Cost per sales order
of customers' statements	Cost per sales transaction
Posting charges	Cost per invoice
	Cost per shipment
Preparing customers' statements	Cost per statement
	Cost per account sold
Posting credits	Cost per remittance
	Cost per account sold
Calculating commissions on cash collected	Cost per remittance
Making street collections	Cost per customer
	Cost per dollar collected
Window collections	Cost per collection

The potential savings that may be realized through the reduction of G&A expenses are usually not as great as those in the factory or sales operations. This is natural because the major expenses of a business are concentrated in the two functions of production and distribution. However, depending on the size of the gross margin percentage, it is far more effective to reduce costs to increase profits than to increase revenues to increase profits. Table 10–4 shows the revenues required to cover the cost of a person with a $40,000 salary.

Table 10–4 shows that it is very much in the interest of a low-margin company to work hard to reduce G&A expenses to a bare minimum in order to enhance its net profits.

The previous section described various standards that can be used to measure performance in G&A areas. Standards tell the controller about the current level of efficiency, but do nothing to suggest improvements. The controller must explore many methods for cost control, methods quite independent of budgets or standards. Specific points by which administrative or office expenses may be reduced through observation and analysis are these:

- *Clean up the area*—The first step in finding waste is being able to see it. Therefore, clean up all G&A areas by moving old files to storage and instituting a clean desk policy.

Table 10–4: Revenues Needed to Support Specific Costs

Salary Level	Gross Margin	Revenue Required
$40,000	90%	$ 44,444
$40,000	80%	$ 50,000
$40,000	70%	$ 57,143
$40,000	60%	$ 66,667
$40,000	50%	$ 80,000
$40,000	40%	$100,000
$40,000	30%	$133,333
$40,000	20%	$200,000
$40,000	10%	$400,000

- *Eliminate duplicate documents*—Review stored documents and eliminate duplicate items. For example, if an invoice is being stored alphabetically, numerically, and by customer code, then eliminate all but one. This step cuts filing costs.
- *Eliminate reports*—Reports are frequently created to meet a one-time need, but are then continually produced because no one ever notified the sender. Consequently, report users should be contacted periodically to see if they still need reports. Also, the information contained in ongoing reports can sometimes be combined into one report.
- *Consolidate forms*—Most companies have too many forms. Some forms can be combined, thereby reducing the number of approvals and paperwork required to complete transactions.
- *Eliminate multiple approvals*—The time and effort required to get multiple approvals for anything usually exceeds the benefit obtained by the additional approvals.
- *Eliminate duplicate tasks*—Tasks are frequently cross-checked by supervisors; this is a duplication of tasks, and should be eliminated. The reason for the cross-checking is usually because supervisors are looking for and correcting errors. The way to eliminate the need for cross-checking is to make the process mistake-proof. For example, staff can receive better training, and tasks can be either fully or partially automated.
- *Apply automation*—As technological advances reach the marketplace, utilize them to reduce the need for staffing. For example, the advent of voice mail systems reduces the need for a receptionist. Computerized word processing systems allow managers to write their own memos and reports, and reduces the need for secretaries. Computerized time clocks reduce the need for manual tracking of pay hours by payroll clerks.
- *Reduce cycle time*—Cycle time is the total time required to complete a process. Analysis of most processes reveals that the bulk of the cycle time is the wait time between tasks versus time spent adding value to the process. Flowchart key processes and itemize the time required to perform each

process. Then work to remove the "dead time" from each process. As cycle times shrink, the need for staffing is reduced. For example, one company has elected to pay suppliers as soon as bills are received. It compared the cost of money from paying bills early to the cost of reprocessing paperwork for a month until the bills were due for payment. The company concluded that it was cheaper to pay immediately.

- *Rearrange work space*—After the closing process has been cleaned up and the paperflow made more efficient, the controller should review the work space. If the work space can be rearranged to reduce paper movement to a minimum and cut the level of nearby traffic (thereby reducing interruptions), then moving the staff is justified.

- *Review reproduction costs and locations*—Most firms have a small number of large copiers. A review of the situation usually reveals that most advanced copier functions are not needed. Instead, consider having a minimal number of high-end copiers in central locations for "power" users, and then buy a large number of inexpensive tabletop copiers to spread throughout the building. The benefits will be reduced capital costs and vastly reduced walking time by the staff to reach the nearest copier. Also, all copiers should be purchased from the same manufacturer in order to reduce the number of supplier contacts and the complexity of copier contract administration.

- *Install LAN fax card*—If your company has a local area network (LAN), then consider purchasing a LAN fax card, so that employees can send and receive documents without ever leaving their computer workstations. However, non-computer documents are also sent from time to time, so either a document scanner or a low-end fax machine should be retained for such items.

- *Train the staff*—One of the best ways to reduce errors is to train the staff. At a minimum, training must involve detailed instruction in current company procedures. Too often, management issues a procedure modification in a memo, and assumes that the staff will follow the change. Such procedural changes usually fail because follow-up training did not occur. If the controller wants to avoid costly errors, than training must take place. Also, one can upgrade low-level personnel into more demanding tasks by using additional training.

- *Staff for low or average work loads*—Reduce staff levels to the point where they are always busy at normal or low transaction volumes. If the work load increases, then use either overtime or temporary help. However, staff efficiency tends to decrease if overtime exceeds 10% for extended periods.

- *Outsource functions*—Outsourcing G&A functions is becoming more popular. Some functions where this has proved effective are:
  — Payroll
  — Check-cashing (on site, but by bank or ATM)
  — Messenger service
  — Travel arrangements

In the above situations, the company should first verify that the change will actually result in real savings to the company. Traditional make–versus–buy studies must be performed as part of the original decision process and then rechecked periodically to determine that the original savings were achieved as planned.

- *Shut down office to match factory*—If the production facility is closed, such as during the holiday season, it may then be possible to shut down the G&A area as well.
- *Call in the internal auditors*—Have the internal audit staff review G&A functions and suggest process improvements to reduce costs. An additional audit task is to periodically review telephone records for private phone calls, and to recommend procedures to control this problem.
- *Reduce per-minute phone costs*—The elimination of the long-distance phone monopoly has sparked a great deal of competition. Some companies buy large blocks of phone time from the primary phone companies and resell it at considerably reduced prices. Contact a local phone time reseller for a comparison of rates. Also, "800" line service can now be moved among the phone companies without having to change the "800" number, so the controller can also do comparison shopping in this area.
- *Institute direct purchasing of office supplies*—The cost to requisition an item, source a supplier, create a purchase order, and receive the item has been estimated at about $150. For office supplies, this is not a cost-effective process. Instead, employees can order their own supplies with a preprinted ordering form (containing pre-approved items) that is faxed to a predetermined supplier.
- *Benchmark G&A*—After all of the above recommendations have been implemented and management is running out of cost reduction ideas, try comparing the company's G&A costs against those of other companies. Sometimes a consultant must be brought in to manage the benchmarking effort as a neutral third party. Be sure to contact firms that are outside of the company's industry, since the best performers may be located elsewhere.

Although some of these points may seem minor in reducing costs, savings can be quite sizable in the aggregate.

As reductions are implemented, the argument may arise that the talent needed to perform the essential functions must be retained at a minimum level. It cannot be terminated for a temporary downturn or transferred to low-skill positions. However, as departments shrink to apparently minimum levels, one can combine departments and cross-train staff to achieve an additional level of staff reduction.

Finally, the controller should review G&A costs on the balance sheet. The two primary items are office equipment and working capital. Careful attention to these areas will result in lower capital needs, lower depreciation and insurance costs, and a higher return on investment.

Office equipment. As noted previously, the mix of copier equipment can be changed to favor low-end equipment, and fax machines can be replaced by a LAN fax card. Also, obsolete phone, copier, and fax equipment should be immediately removed from the fixed asset register in order to keep the company's insurable and taxable asset valuation as low as possible. Finally, office space should heavily favor cubicles over offices, because cubicle furnishings are cheaper and more staff can be contained in a smaller work space, thereby reducing occupancy costs.

Working capital. The working capital a company needs is the value of its inventory and accounts receivable, less the amount of its accounts payable. There is a growing trend in businesses to strive for zero working capital or even negative working capital. The main item under partial control of G&A is accounts receivable. The controller can work to reduce the days of receivables by closely reviewing the billing process to ensure that products are billed immediately following shipment. Also, the controller should send the collections staff to training classes offered by numerous credit collections firms such as Dun & Bradstreet. Finally, close management of the collections function will ensure that overdue accounts are tightly monitored.

11

CASH AND INVESTMENTS

Most business executives have long been aware of the need for cash. Supplier bills must be paid in cash. Payrolls must be met with cash. Recently, the ability of the company to generate adequate cash has assumed more importance. Witness the attention to leveraged buyouts or other proposed mergers or acquisitions.

Sound cash management is a basic financial function. While it is usually the responsibility of the senior financial officer, the controller has an important role to play. This chapter reviews phases of cash management that the controller either handles or has a direct interest in.

OBJECTIVES OF CASH MANAGEMENT

Cash is a particularly vulnerable asset because, without proper controls, it is easily concealed and readily negotiable. Cash management has these following objectives:

- Provide adequate cash for both short- and long-term operations.
- Utilize company funds effectively at all times.
- Establish accountability for cash receipts and provide adequate safeguards until the funds are placed in the company depository.
- Establish controls to assure that disbursements are made only for approved and legitimate purposes.

- Maintain adequate bank balances to support proper commercial bank relations.
- Maintain adequate cash records.

ROLE OF THE CONTROLLER

With respect to cash management, a cooperative relationship should exist between the controller and treasurer. Duties and responsibilities will vary, depending on the type and size of the company. The treasury staff has custody of cash funds and administers the bank accounts. The treasurer is responsible for maintaining good relations with banks and other investors, providing the timely interest and principal payments on debt, and investing the excess cash. In addition, the treasurer usually has responsibility for cash receipts and disbursement procedures.

The controller may have four responsibilities related to cash in companies large enough for separate treasury and controllership functions:

1. Develop the cash forecasts.
2. Review the internal controls system with respect to both receipts and disbursements to assure its adequacy and effectiveness.
3. Reconcile all bank accounts.
4. Prepare periodic cash reports.

The following list outlines the investment functions often performed by the controller:

- Ascertain that the proper accounting principles are applied in valuing and recording investments.
- Assure that the proper detail records are maintained to provide proper accountability for investments.
- Determine that the proper reports are issued to measure performance and otherwise provide the accounting information needed to properly oversee the management of investments.
- Perform such reviews as are required to ascertain that an adequate internal control system exists for the protection of investments.
- Periodically ensure the existence of investments by taking a physical inventory of evidence of their ownership.

CASH COLLECTIONS

One of the primary objectives of financial management is the conservation and effective utilization of cash. From the cash collection viewpoint, there are two phases of control: the acceleration of collections (see next section), and proper internal control of collections (covered in a later section of this chapter).

Acceleration of Cash Receipts

Two methods are commonly used to speed up the collection of receivables. They are known as the lock-box system and area concentration banking.

The lock-box system involves establishing depository accounts in the various geographical areas of significant cash collections so that remittances from customers will take less time in transit—preferably not more than one day. Customers mail remittances to the company at a locked post office box in the region served by the bank. The bank collects the remittances and deposits the proceeds to the account of the company. Funds in excess of those required to cover costs are periodically transferred to company headquarters. Supporting documents accompanying remittances are mailed by the bank to the company. Collections are thus accelerated through reduction in transit time, with resultant lower credit exposure. Arrangements must be made, however, for proper control of credit information.

Under the system of area concentration banking, local company units collect remittances and deposit them in the local bank. From the local bank, usually by wire transfers, expeditious movement of funds is made to a few area or regional concentration banks. Funds in excess of compensating balances are automatically transferred by wire to the company's banking headquarters. This techniques reduces in-transit time.

While checks are the predominant means of collecting accounts receivable, an increasing amount of business is handled through electronic funds transfer (EFT). Moreover, there are various combinations of methods and instruments that speed collections. The controller may wish to review some of the selected references dealing with aspects of these different collection methods:

- Lockbox.
- Depository transfer check (DTC).
- Automated clearing house (ACH transfer).
- Wire transfer.
- Preauthorized draft (PAD).

CASH DISBURSEMENTS

The controller should maintain careful control over the timing of disbursements to ensure that bills are paid only as they are due and not before. In such a manner, cash can be conserved for temporary investment.

Another consideration in payment scheduling is the conscious use of the cash float. By recognizing in-transit items and the fact that ordinarily bank balances are greater than book balances because of checks not cleared, book balances of cash may be planned at lower levels. The incoming float may be balanced against the outgoing payments.

The relationship between the time a check is released to the payee and the time it clears the bank (i.e., the disbursement float) contains three elements:

1. The time needed for the check to travel by mail or other delivery from the issuer to the payee.
2. The time required by the payee to process the check.
3. The period required by the banking system to clear the check (i.e., the time from the deposit by the payee to the time the item is charged to the issuer's account).

In controlling this float, it is often helpful to trace the time interval of large checks to estimate the proper allowance for the time period required for checks to clear. Many banks now offer modern access to their databases of cleared check information, so the controller knows the exact amount of cleared checks.

The controller can also maintain a zero balance account. With this system, the clearing account is kept at a zero balance. When checks are presented for payment, arrangements are such that the bank is authorized to transfer funds from the corporate general account to cover the items. Payment may be made by draft. Comparable arrangements can be made for the treasurer to make wire transfers to the zero bank account on notification of the items being presented for payment. Zero bank balance arrangements can facilitate control of payments through one or a limited number of accounts. The system may facilitate a quick check of the corporate cash position.

Automatic balance accounts use the same account for receipts and disbursements. When the account is above a specified maximum level, the excess funds are transferred to the central bank account; conversely, when the balance drops below a minimum level, the bank may call for replenishment.

INVESTMENT OF SHORT-TERM FUNDS

In most companies, surplus or excess funds not needed for either operating purposes or compensating bank balances are available for investment. Prudent use of these funds can add to income. Although the financial officer will direct the investment of those funds, the controller should be concerned with adequate investment reporting and control.

Criteria for Selecting Investments

Given the opportunity for earning additional income from temporary excess funds, there are five criteria to be considered when selecting an investment vehicle.

1. *Safety of principal*–A primary objective should be to avoid instruments that might risk loss of the investment.
2. *Price stability*–If the company is suddenly called on to liquidate the security to acquire funds, price stability would be important in avoiding a significant loss.
3. *Marketability*–The money manager must consider whether the security can be sold, if required, rather easily and quite quickly.
4. *Maturity*–Funds may be invested until the demand for cash arises—perhaps as reflected in the cash forecast. Hence maturities should relate to prospective cash needs. Temporary investments usually involve maturities of a day or two to as much as a year.
5. *Yield*–The financial officer of course is interested in optimizing the earnings or securing at least a comparative return on the investment and is thus interested in the yield. This is not necessarily the most important criterion, because low-risk, high-liquidity investments will not provide the highest yield.

The importance attached to each of these factors will depend on the management philosophy, condition of the market, and inclinations of the investing person. Is the investor conservatively inclined or not? Of course, restrictions placed on the operation will influence the weighting of each. An example of short-term investment guidelines is shown in Table 11–1.

Investment Restrictions

Sometimes the board of directors or the senior financial officer will place restrictions on how short-term funds may be invested. Subjects covered should include maximum security, credit rating of the issuer, and maximum investment in selected types of securities by issuer, type of instrument, country, and currency.

Instruments for investment vary widely, and market conditions may dictate the most desirable at any particular time. Typical money market instruments include:

- U.S. Treasury bills.
- U.S. Treasury notes and bonds.
- Negotiable certificates of deposit.
- Banker's acceptances.
- Selected foreign government issues.
- Federal agency issues.
- Repurchase agreements.
- Prime commercial paper.
- Finance company paper.
- Short-term tax exempts.

Table 11–1: Guidelines for Short-Term Investments

Objective: To invest excess cash in only top-quality short-term investments, for optimum total return, commensurate with corporate liquidity requirements.

Liquidity: Liquidity shall be provided by minimum and maximum limits as follows:

1. At least $80 million shall be invested in overnight investments and in negotiable marketable obligations of major U.S. issuers.
2. No more than 50% of the total portfolio shall be invested in time deposits or other investments with a lack of liquidity such as commercial paper for which only the dealer and issuer make a market.

Diversification: Diversification shall be provided through a limit on each nongovernment issuer (as listed next). These are general limits, and in each case quality review may result in elimination of a lower limit for the issuer. Overnight or repurchase investments must meet quality criteria but are not subject to limits on the amount invested.

1. U.S. Government and agencies—no limit.
2. Domestic bank certificates of deposit, time deposits and banker's acceptances—$30 million limit for banks with capital accounts in excess of $800 million (top 10 banks); $20 million for banks with capital accounts of $350 to $800 million (second 11 banks); $5 million for all other banks with capital accounts in excess of $250 million (11 banks).
3. U.S. dollar (or fully hedged foreign currency) obligations of foreign banks, each with capital accounts exceeding $500 million—limited to $15 million each for Canadian banks and $10 million each for other foreign banks, subject to an aggregate limit of $75 million for non-Canadian foreign banks.
4. Domestic commercial paper with P–1/A–1 rating only—$20 million limit for issuers with long-term senior debt rating of Aa or better; $10 million for issuers with a debt rating of A; and $10 million for commercial bank-holding companies with capital accounts in excess of $500 million, within the overall limit of the flagship bank described in 2 above.
5. Foreign commercial paper unconditionally guaranteed by a prime U.S. issuer and fully hedged, subject to the guarantor's issuer limit described in 4 above.
6. Obligations of savings and loan associations, each with capital accounts exceeding $250 million—limited to $10 million each.

Operating procedure: Payments shall be made only against delivery of a security to a custodian bank. Securities shall be delivered from custody only against payment. Due bills by a bank will be accepted for delivery only under exceptional conditions. No due bills issued by a dealer will be accepted.

Maturity limits: The average maturity of the entire fund shall be limited to an average of two years. The maximum maturity for each category is as follows:

U.S. government	5 years
Municipal obligations	2 years
Bank CDs, and banker's acceptances	1 year
Bank time deposits	90 days
Commercial paper	270 days

MARKETABLE SECURITIES

A company generally invests in marketable securities for two reasons. One is to profitably employ available cash that would otherwise be idle in order to provide a return to the company while it is awaiting opportunities to reinvest in the business (e.g., receivables, inventory, fixed assets, etc.). These temporary investments are usually in bank certificates of deposit, treasury notes, stocks, and so on, and, since they are easily convertible to cash, are called cash equivalents. As such they are considered current assets of the company. A second reason is that an enterprise may choose to invest excess cash in opportunities that offer a higher rate of return than an investment in the company's normal product lines. Sometimes these alternatives involve the purchase of high-interest, long-term bonds, both government and corporate. Sometimes they involve the acquisition of equity securities representing an interest in other businesses. These investments are also in marketable securities but since the intent is to maintain the investment for the long term, these assets are not current assets of the company and should not be reported as such.

For a security to be classified as marketable, there must be evidence that it can readily be bought or sold. For purposes of accounting, all investments are classified in two ways based on *purpose* and *nature*.

As for the purpose of the investment, is it a short-term investment or a more permanent one? This distinction is based on the intent of management. If the intention is to convert the investment into cash during the operating cycle (defined as up to one year), then it is considered a temporary investment. Most temporary investments also have a ready market and so are called marketable securities. A temporary marketable security is a current asset and therefore part of working capital. It is important that the permanent investments not be included in current assets, thereby overstating working capital. Such misclassifications can result in serious errors in cash planning and financing strategies. All current marketable securities are to be valued for balance sheet purposes at the lower of cost (the price paid for the security plus other expenses incidental to the acquisition, such as brokerage fees or taxes), or market value as of the balance sheet date (the amount that the security could probably be sold for).

Permanent investments must be further divided by nature into:

- *Marketable equity securities.*
  - Investments in unconsolidated affiliates, which are accounted for by the equity method.
  - Other equity investments, which are accounted for by the cost method.
- *Other investments*—These are accounted for by the cost method.

Equity and Cost Methods of Accounting

The *equity method* should be used to account for investments when the investor has the ability to exercise significant influence over the investee even though the investor holds less than 50% of the voting stock. This significant influence exists when the investor owns 20% to 50% of the stock of the investee. When an equity investment represents less than 20% of the stock of the investee, then the *cost method* should be used to account for it. The cost method requires that the investor record the investment at the lower of cost or current market value. Of course, if an equity investment provides the investor with control of the investee (over 50% ownership of voting stock), then the financial statements must be prepared on a consolidated basis.

The controller can use the following nine-step procedure to account for marketable securities:

1. The securities should be classified into two portfolios, current securities and noncurrent securities. The current portfolio should include all securities to be traded within a year; the noncurrent portfolio shou]ld include all other securities.

2. The cost of the items in each portfolio should be recorded and the total portfolio calculated. The cost will include the amount paid to the seller for the security plus all expenses of the purchase, such as brokerage commissions and sales taxes.

3. The current market value of each portfolio should be determined as of the balance sheet date.

4. The carrying amount of each portfolio is the lower of its aggregate cost or market value.

5. Unrealized losses on the current portfolio, that is, the difference between aggregate cost and a lower aggregate market value, are deducted on the income statement for the period. The credit side of the entry is to a valuation account that will be reported as a reduction of the cost of the current portfolio for balance sheet presentation purposes.

6. Unrealized losses on the noncurrent portfolio, which are calculated in the same manner as for the current portfolio, are reported separately as a reduction of stockholder's equity. The credit is also to a valuation account identified as an allowance against the noncurrent portfolio. If a security in the noncurrent portfolio has a decline that is judged to be not temporary, then the security should be written down to market value and the loss included in the income statement for the period.

7. Subsequent unrealized gains or losses on the portfolio are reported the same way, that is, the current portfolio through the income statement, the noncurrent through the equity section of the balance sheet. However, neither portfolio can ever be valued in excess of the original aggregate cost of the portfolio.

8. If a security is transferred from one portfolio to another, the carrying value is the lower of cost or market on the date of the transfer, and it becomes the new cost basis of the security.

9. A sale of a security from either portfolio at an amount different from its carrying cost results in a realized gain or loss that is reported in the income statement for the period.

The following disclosures are required with respect to marketable securities. The information may be presented either in the body of financial statements or in the footnotes thereto.

As of the date of the balance sheet:

- The aggregate cost of the marketable securities.
- The aggregate market value of the marketable securities.

This information is shown for the current portfolio, the noncurrent portfolio, and the total of both portfolios, that is, the total unrealized gains (gross) and the total unrealized losses for each portfolio and the total of both.

For each income statement presented:

- The net realized gain or loss for the period.
- The basis on which cost was determined in computing the realized gain or loss.
- The change in the valuation allowance that affects the determination of income and the equity section of the balance sheet.

Financial statements should not be adjusted for gains and losses occurring after the balance sheet date but before the financial statements are issued. However, significant activity during this period should be disclosed.

With the complexity of the problem and the many aspects involved, these limited comments have been made so readers will be aware of the guidelines. For application in their own companies, controllers are referred to the relevant AICPA and FASB publications.

Equity and Cost Methods of Accounting

The *equity method* should be used to account for investments when the investor has the ability to exercise significant influence over the investee even though the investor holds less than 50% of the voting stock. This significant influence exists when the investor owns 20% to 50% of the stock of the investee. When an equity investment represents less than 20% of the stock of the investee, then the *cost method* should be used to account for it. The cost method requires that the investor record the investment at the lower of cost or current market value. Of course, if an equity investment provides the investor with control of the investee (over 50% ownership of voting stock), then the financial statements must be prepared on a consolidated basis.

ACCOUNTING FOR RECORDS OF INVESTMENT

A systematic manner of recording information relative to the purchase or sale of investments is required. In addition to the data required for "lower of cost or market" valuations, detailed records are necessary to provide the information needed to manage the portfolio, as well as to establish and support gains or losses for tax purposes.

The file of invoices or statements from the broker may be sufficient in some cases. Indeed, these documents are the source of much information. Generally, however, the controller should establish a control account for investments in securities and support it with a securities ledger. This ledger should contain the following information:

- Stock ledger information:
  - Description of the issue—Name, type, par value, certificate numbers.
  - Dividend dates.
  - Record of purchase—Date, number of shares, price, commission, tax, total cost, broker.
  - Date and amount of dividends received.
  - Record of sale or disposition—Date, broker, number of shares, sale or call price, commission, and net proceeds.
  - Dividends in arrears.
  - Loss or gain.
- Bonded ledger information:
  - Description of issue—Name, interest rate, maturity date, interest dates, serial numbers, tax position.
  - Record of purchase—Date, broker, price, accrued interest, commission, tax, total cost, maturity value.
  - Date and amount of interest received.
  - Amortization of premium or discount.
  - Record of disposition—Date, broker, redemption or sale price, accrued interest, commission, net proceeds.
  - Loss or gain.

Reports on Cash and Investments

In some companies a simple daily cash report is prepared for the CEO and treasurer. It summarizes the cash receipts and cash disbursements, as well as balances of major banks. An example is shown in Table 11–2. From the control viewpoint, it is desirable to know how collections and disbursements compare with estimates. Such information is shown in Table 11–3. In addition to comparing actual and forecasted cash activity, it is also useful to periodically compare book balances with those required to meet the service charges or compensating balance requirements of the company's banks. Such a report compares the "object" balance with actual book and actual bank balances. This type of report provides effective cash utilization by recording the absence of excessive balances and by keeping bank balances adequate to fairly compensate the financial institution. Such a report is shown in Table 11–4.

Table 11–2: Daily Cash Report.

Daily Cash Report
as of the close of business, June 16, 19XX

Balance, June 15, 19XX	$135,300
Receipts	10,200
Total	145,500
Disbursements	15,300
Balance, June 16, 19XX	$130,200

Bank Balances, etc.

National City Bank	$65,900
Commerce National Bank	22,100
Ohio Trust Company	30,500
Total	118,500
Petty Cash and Payroll Funds	11,700
Total	$130,200

The activity in investments for most industrial firms normally will be quite limited and few reports need be prepared. Periodic reports to management should include the name of each security, its cost, current market value, effective yield, and any dividends received. For the overall portfolio, the controller should report

Table 11–3: Comparison of Actual and Estimated Cash Activity.

Weekly Cash Report
for the week ended November 16, 19XX

	Month to Date	
Description	Actual	Estimated
Beginning cash balance	$32,511	$32,510
Cash Receipts		
Government	18,310	18,000
Wholesale	67,730	65,500
Retail	21,100	23,400
Total	107,410	106,900
Cash Disbursements		
Accounts payable—expenses	12,860	12,300
Payrolls	37,010	36,900
Material purchases	19,340	14,300
Federal Taxes	8,640	8,920
Capital expenditures	39,990	40,190
Other	2,030	2,000
Total	119,870	114,610
Ending cash balance	$19,781	$24,800
Estimated month-end balance		$30,000

Table 11–4: Actual and Objective Bank Balances.

Quarterly Report on Bank Balances

Bank	Actual per Books	Objective	(Over) Under Objective	Balances per Bank Statement
Chase Manhattan	$17,440	$17,800	$360	$19,120
Morgan Guaranty	16,850	16,500	(350)	17,180
Bank of America	14,310	15,700	1,390	15,810
National Bank of Commerce	2,890	3,000	110	3,020
Other Local	490	=====	(490)	520
Total Cash in banks–U.S.	51,980	53,000	1,020	55,650
Subsidiaries–foreign	8,190	7,000	(1,190)	8,600
Cash funds	760	750	(10)	=====
Total cash	$60,930	$60,750	$(180)	$64,250

on the overall cost, market value, and rate of return. A typical report on investment position is shown in Table 11–5.

CASH AND INVESTMENT CONTROLS

Cash enters a firm through the following sources: mail receipts, over-the-counter
cash sales, sales or collections made by salespeople or solicitors, and over-the-
counter collections on account. Naturally, all businesses have other cash transactions of a less routine nature, such as from the sale of fixed assets, that may be
handled by the officers or require special procedures. Most of the cash problems
will center on the transactions listed in Table 11–3 because the more unusual or
less voluminous cash receipts are readily susceptible to a simple check.

Regardless of the source of cash, the very basis for the prevention of errors or
fraud is the principle of internal check. Such a system involves the separation of the
actual handling of cash from the records relating to cash. It requires that the work of
one employee be supplemented by the work of another. Certain results must always
agree. For example, the daily cash deposit must be the same as the charge to the

Table 11–5: Report on Investment Position.

Security	Number of Shares	Market Value	Purchase Price	Rate of Return	Total Dividends for YTD
ABC Corporation	500	$37,000	$31,000	5.2%	$800
Atlas Construction	100	2,400	2,400	6.3	75
National Co.	1,000	30,000	31,000	6.5	1,000
USA Corporation	1,000	65,500	64,000	7.8	2,000
JPC Corporation	100	1,900	1,875	7.5	70
Security Co.	500	42,000	38,000	5.3	1,000
Total or average		$178,800	$168,275	6.5%	$4,945

cash control account. This automatic checking of the work of one employee by another clearly discourages fraud and locates errors. Under such conditions, any peculations are generally restricted to cases of carelessness or collusion.

The system of internal control must be designed for each organization. However, there are some general suggestions that will be helpful to the controller in reviewing the situation in his or her own company:

- All receipts of cash through the mails should be recorded in advance of transfer to the cashier. Periodically, these records should be traced to the deposit slip.
- All receipts should be deposited intact daily. This procedure might also require a duplicate deposit slip to be sent by the bank or person making the deposit (other than the cashier) to an independent department, for use in subsequent audits.
- Responsibility for the handling of cash should be clearly defined.
- Separate the functions of receiving cash and disbursing cash.
- Separate the handling of cash from cash record maintenance. Cashiers should not have access to these records.
- Tellers, agents, and field representatives should be required to give receipts, while retaining a duplicate.
- Bank reconciliations should not be made by those handling cash or keeping the records. Similarly, the mailing of statements to customers, including the checkoff against the ledger accounts, should be done by a third party. The summarizing of cash records also may be handled by a third party.
- All employees handling cash or cash records should be required to take a periodic vacation, and someone else should handle the job during such absence. Also, at unannounced times, employees should be shifted to other jobs to detect or prevent collusion.
- All employees handling cash or cash records should be adequately bonded.
- Mechanical and other protective devices should be used where applicable to give added means of check—cash registers, the tape being read by a third party; duplicate sales slips; daily cash blotters.
- Where practical, cash sales should be verified by means of inventory records and periodic physical inventories.

Common Methods of Misappropriating Cash

The following common methods of misappropriating cash can be a guide to the controller in designing control systems.

- *Mail receipts:*
  - Lapping—diverting cash and reporting it some time after it has been collected; usually, funds received from one account are credited against another account from which cash has been diverted earlier.

— Borrowing funds temporarily, without falsifying any records, or simply not recording all cash received.
— Overstating discounts and allowances.
— Charging off a customer's account as bad debt and pocketing the cash.
— Withholding miscellaneous income, such as insurance refunds.

- *Over-the-counter sales:*
  — Failing to report all sales and pocketing the cash.
  — Underadding the sales slip and pocketing the difference.
  — Falsely representing the refunds or expenditures.
  — Registering a smaller amount than the true amount of the sale.
  — Pocketing cash overages.
- *Collections by salespeople:*
  — Conversion of checks made to cash.
  — Failure to report sales.
  — Overstating amounts of trade-ins.
- *Disbursements:*
  — Preparing false vouchers or presenting vouchers for payment twice.
  — Raising the amount on checks after they have been signed.
  — Cashing unclaimed payroll or dividend checks.
  — Altering petty cash vouchers.
  — Forging checks and destroying them when received from the bank—substituting other canceled checks or charge slips.

Where adequate internal control is used, most of these practices cannot be carried on without collusion.

In addition to the segregation of duties that has been described, certain other practices may be adopted to further deter any would-be embezzler. One of these tools is surprise audits by the internal auditor, as well as by public accountants. Another is the prompt follow-up of past-due accounts. Proper instructions to customers about where checks should be mailed, and a specific request that they be made payable to the company, and not to any individual, also will help. Bonding of all employees, with a detailed check of references, is a measure of protection. Special checking of unusual receipts of a miscellaneous nature will tend to discourage irregularities.

Controlling Disbursements

Once the cash has been deposited in the bank, it would seem that the major problem of safeguarding the cash has been solved. Indeed, it is quite true that control of cash disbursements is a relatively simple matter, if a few rules are followed.

After the supplier's invoice has been approved for payment, the next step usually is the preparation of the check for executive signature. If all disbursements are subject to this top review, how can any problem exist? Yet it is at this point that the greatest danger is met. Any controller who has had to sign numerous checks knows that it is an irksome task—the review to ascertain that receiving reports are attached, the checking of payee against the invoice, and the comparison of amounts. Because it is such a monotonous chore, it is often done in a perfunctory manner. Yet this operation is essential to the control of disbursements. There are too many instances where false documents and vouchers used a second time have been the means of securing executive signatures. Prevention of this practice demands careful review before signing checks, as well as other safeguards. Those who sign the checks must adopt a questioning attitude on every transaction that appears doubtful or is not fully understood. Indeed, the review of documents attached to checks will often bring to light foolish expenditures and weaknesses in other procedures.

The opportunities for improper or incorrect use of funds are so great that a controller cannot unduly emphasize the need for proper safeguards in the cash disbursement function. The following suggestions may be of use in determining safeguards:

- Except for petty cash transactions, all disbursements should be made by check.
- All checks should be prenumbered, and all numbers accounted for as either used or void. One can avoid preprinted check stock completely by using unnumbered check stock that is numbered during printing by the computer system. The computer printer can even print the authorized signature onto the check (though this raises concerns about access to the computer system instead of the check stock).
- All general disbursement checks for amounts in excess of $1,000 should require two signatures. Update signature cards regularly, so that people who leave the firm or move on to other positions in the company are not authorized to sign checks.
- Responsibility for cash receipts should be divorced from responsibility for cash disbursements. Split the cash functions among several staff members. For example, whoever opens the mail should not be the person who applies payments against receivables records. Also, the person who approves payables for payment should not be the person who creates checks. The person who performs the bank reconciliation should not be involved with other cash activities.
- All persons signing checks or approving disbursements should be adequately bonded.
- Bank reconciliations should be made by those who do not sign checks or approve payments.
- The keeping of cash records should be entirely separate from the handling of cash disbursements.

- Properly approved invoices and other required supporting documents should be a prerequisite to making every disbursement.
- Checks for reimbursement of imprest funds and payrolls should be made payable to the individual and not to the company or bearer.
- After payment has been made, all supporting documents should be perforated or otherwise mutilated or marked "paid" to prevent reuse.
- Mechanical devices such as check writers should be used to the extent practical.
- Annual vacations or shifts in jobs should be enforced for those handling disbursements.
- Approval of vouchers for payment usually should be done by those not responsible for disbursing.
- Special authorizations for interbank transfers should be required, and a clearing account for bank transfers should be maintained.
- All petty cash vouchers should be written in ink or typewritten.
- It may be desirable to periodically and independently verify the bona fide existence of the regularly used suppliers of recurring services, such as janitorial services, lawyers, and consultants.
- Have the company create a file of all checks created, and send it (preferably daily) to its bank. The bank then matches presented checks against the check file to see if any checks are unauthorized. The bank can also reserve the process by making available a list of each day's cleared checks, which the company can then reconcile to its list of printed checks.
- Secure the check stock and review it regularly. Anyone can create a check to themselves with stolen check stock.
- Purchase check stock that has been treated with special chemicals that deface the check if it is chemically tampered with or is photocopied.

Bank Reconciliations

An important phase of internal control is the reconciling of the balance on the bank statement with the balance recorded on the company's books. If properly done, the task is much more than a listing of outstanding checks, deposits in transit, and unrecorded bank charges. For example, the deposits and disbursements as shown on the bank statement should be reconciled with those on the books. Also, compare endorsements with the payee and check the payee against the record. Bank reconciliations should be handled by someone independent of any cash receipts or disbursements activities. The job can be handled by the controller or may be performed by the bank itself. Particular attention should be paid to outstanding checks of the preceding printing and to deposits at the end of the month to detect kiting—issued without a corresponding decrease in the company's cash balance.

Petty Cash Funds

Most businesses must make some small disbursements. To meet these needs, petty cash funds are established that operate on an imprest fund basis, so that balances are fixed. At any time the cash, plus the unreimbursed vouchers, should equal the amount of the fund. Numerous funds of this type may be necessary in the branch offices or at each plant. A procedure should be provided including limits on individual disbursements through this channel, proper approvals, and so on. If it is practicable, the person handling cash receipts or disbursements should not handle petty cash. Other safeguards would include surprise cash counts, immediate cancellation of all petty cash slips after payment, and careful scrutiny of reimbursements. Although the fund may be small, very considerable sums can be expended. The controller should not neglect checking this activity.

Payrolls

In most companies, payroll disbursements represent a very sizable proportion of all cash payments. Proper safeguards for this disbursement are particularly desirable. The use of a special payroll account is a very common procedure. A check in the exact amount of the total net payroll is deposited in the payroll account against which the individual checks are drawn. This has advantages from an internal control standpoint, and it may facilitate the reconciling of bank accounts.

The preparation of the payroll, of course, should be separate from the actual handling of cash. Special payroll audits are advisable to review procedures, verify rates, check clerical accuracy, and witness the payoff.

Investments

Many corporations contract with a major bank to serve as custodian of the securities, to make payment on incoming delivery, and to receive funds on outgoing delivery. The form of contract should provide maximum safeguards to the company.

Because opportunities for fraud exist, given telephonic transactions and the wire transfer of funds, care must be exercised in the form and nature of confirmation secured and the internal controls used in authorizing payment.

12

RECEIVABLES

Accounts receivable are an important item in the balance sheets of most business concerns, and must be carefully controlled to avoid excessive working capital requirements. Proper procedures and adequate safeguards on these accounts are essential not only to the continued success of the enterprise but also to satisfactory customer relationships. Control of accounts receivable begins before the agreement to ship the merchandise, continues through the preparation and issuance of the billing, and ends with the collection of all sums due. The procedure is closely related to cash receipts control and inventory control, acting as the link between the two. This chapter introduces ways to measure, manage, and control the receivables function.

MEASURING RECEIVABLES

The receivables balance should be tested regularly to determine the reasonableness of the balance. A degradation in performance will attract management attention, possibly involving many of the changes outlined later in this chapter.

One test of accounts receivable is the number of days' sales outstanding (DSO). The formula is:

$$\text{average number of days' sales outstanding} = \frac{\text{average receivables}}{\text{annual sales on credit}} \times 365$$

For example:

$$\frac{\text{average receivables}}{\text{annual credit sales}} = \frac{\$204,510,000/12}{\$122,220,000 - \$98,400} \times 365 = 36.5 \text{ days}$$

An increase in the DSO beyond 36.5 days indicates a worsening receivables situation, whereas a smaller DSO indicates that receivables are being collected more rapidly.

Another receivables measurement is the receivables turnover ratio. The formula is:

$$\frac{\text{net sales}}{\text{customer receivables}} = \frac{\$122,220,000}{17,070,000} = 7.16 \text{ times}$$

The calculation shows that receivables have been collected, or "turned over," 7.16 times during the year. An increase in the turnover number indicates more rapid receivables collection.

A well-managed collection operation should maintain a days' sales outstanding figure that is about one-third beyond the terms of sale. For example, if invoices are due in thirty days, then an acceptable days' sales outstanding figure would be forty days. If the ratio indicates poor collection performance, then the following items should be checked.

Review prospects in advance. Work with the sales department to create a list of prospects and review the financial condition of those firms before contacting them regarding a sale. Not only does this avoid future collection problems, but also makes more efficient use of salespeople's time. Without this up-front effort, sales made to marginal customers may lengthen the days' sales outstanding.

Bill promptly. Bill as soon as you ship! Slow billing will cause excessive days' sales outstanding. To avoid this common problem, review the billing paper flow at least once a year. If you do not find that invoices are being issued to customers within one day of shipment, then change the work flow to achieve this goal.

Track overdue accounts closely. Create a log of contracts with payments overdue and update it religiously. If a customer tells you that a check will be mailed by the fifteenth of the month and you do not receive it, then call the customer a few days later to follow up—don't wait too long! If a customer realizes that you will badger the account until payment is received, then you will have a much better chance of receiving the cash. Quick-paying customers reduce the days' sales outstanding. Also, a frequently updated aging report is critical, since customer balances can be spotted the moment they become overdue.

Review and terms of sale. Periodically review the actual sale terms granted to customers. You may find that special deals are being offered, possibly because prospective customers were not reviewed in advance (see first item). When sales are made to marginal accounts, extended terms are sometimes used to secure the sale. Long payment terms increase the days' sales outstanding.

Remove other receivables from the receivable account. The days' sales outstanding account is typically based on the accounts receivable account (as opposed to the aging report total). If the account includes officer notes or taxes receivable, then the days' sales outstanding figure will be skewed, showing excessive days' sales outstanding.

FUNCTIONS OF THE CREDIT DEPARTMENT

The credit manager should assist in stimulating business through a wise extension of credit, and also keep bad debt losses at a reasonably low level. The credit manager is also responsible for collecting receivables. In detail, the department's tasks are as follows:

- *Establish credit policies*—This involves such questions as the class of risk to accept, rigidity of credit term enforcement, and adjustment policies to be followed.
- *Investigate credit*—This requires a continuous procedure for securing and analyzing information concerning the responsibility of present and prospective customers. Information about customers can be collected from:
  — Commercial credit reporting agencies, such as Dun & Bradstreet
  — Trade references supplied by the customer
  — Banks that hold a customer's loans, investments, and checking accounts
  — Collection agencies
  — The SEC's reports on any companies that issue stock or bonds to the public
  — The annual financial report files of the stock exchanges for those companies they list for trade
- *Approve credit*—This requires a procedure by which the credit department definitely approves new customers and the continuance of old ones.
- *Establish credit limits*—Usually, approval is limited to a certain amount, and a plan must be designed to check the extension of credit at this point, or at least to notify the proper authority when the limit is reached. In addition, there will be situations when credit terms should not be granted, but the sale can still be made. In these cases, one can either sell for cash or have backup guarantees by either an individual, a second corporation, or a standby letter of credit.

- *Enforce discount terms*—Discounts offered for prompt payment are frequently taken by customers after the time allowed. A policy must be established and a procedure designed for the enforcement of the discount terms.

- *Collect receivables*—Definite collection steps must be arranged for slow and delinquent accounts. This involves schedules of collection letters, follow-up procedures, and suspension of accounts from approved lists. In addition, the collections staff should be updated regularly on special collection techniques (such as attention-getting telegrams) and sent to trade association meetings to swap information with collection personnel from other companies.

- *Adjust credit*—This involves settlement of accounts, participation in creditors' committees, and representation in receivership and bankruptcy proceedings. Also, responsibility for writing off bad accounts must begin with the credit departments, although final approval may be required from the treasurer or controller, in the interest of sound internal accounting control.

- *Maintain credit records*—Files, reports, and ratings must be maintained as part of the credit analysis and collection effort.

- *Manage the collection process*—The following items contribute to a tightly managed collections process:
  - *Rapid billings*—Quick billings lead to shorter days' receivables outstanding, whereas extremely delayed billings may be difficult to collect.
  - *Rapid cash application*—The job of the collections clerk is greatly improved when cash receipt information is quickly updated and forwarded to the collections staff. This avoids unnecessary calls on supposedly delinquent accounts that have actually already been paid.
  - *Tickler file*—This file informs the collections clerk of the need to call customers on specific dates.
  - *Confirmation letters*—When a collection agreement is complicated, it is best to immediately summarize the agreement terms in a letter and send it to the customer, so there will be no confusion regarding payment.

- *Measure the collection process*—One must gain an understanding of the collection department's performance not only through quantitative measures such as days' sales outstanding and the percentage of overdue invoices. In addition, a review of bad debt write-offs will indicate other problems, such as the reasons why credit was granted to customers who later defaulted. If these problems are tracked and corrected, then the volume of collection items will decline, thereby enhancing the quantitative performance measures.

An in-depth knowledge of the business may reveal reasons for large receivables balances that have nothing to do with high-risk customer accounts. For example, the days' sales outstanding can be skewed by one very large invoice, or by a large cluster of billings that occur at one time, such as at month-end. Also, a factoring arrangement may cause an abnormally low DSO.

The credit analyst typically makes credit decisions with the assistance of customer financial statements.

When doing so, items to look for are:

- *Ratios*—These ratios show where cash is being tied up in a customer's organization, thereby not allowing cash availability for debt payments:
  - *Days' sales outstanding*—If the customer's DSO is greater than its days of selling terms plus a third, then too much cash is tied up in receivables.
  - *Quick ratio*—If the customer's quick ratio falls below 2 to 1, then the ability to pay may be hindered.
  - *Inventory turnover*—If the customer's inventory turns are worse than the industry norm, then too much cash is being tied up in inventory. The presence of obsolete inventory is sometimes indicated by low inventory turns accompanied by a good current ratio (since the excessive inventory appears in the numerator of the current ratio calculation). Alternatively, if a company has good inventory turns but a poor current ratio, the company may have too little working capital to support the level of business being transacted (called *over-trading*); if so, look for high debt levels or call the customer's bank for information. This type of company is a dangerous trading partner, for its heavy debt load may cause it to crash quickly if its level of business drops.
  - *Debt ratio*—If the customer's total liabilities are greater than 100% of equity, then the equity cushion available for payments to creditors is too small.
- *Seasonality*—A company's books are typically closed during the slowest time of the year, when inventories are at their lowest, receivables have been collected, and debt has been paid down. If a company chooses to have its year-end in a different month than other companies in its industry, then its key ratios may vary dramatically from industry norms, even though it may operate in a similar manner.
- *Trends*—If possible, obtain the last three annual financial statements from your key customers, and look for the following danger signs that indicate where cash is being used, and is therefore not available for payments:
  - *Decrease in inventory turnover*
  - *Increase in the collection period*
  - *Increase in the ratio of total liabilities to equity*
  - *Increase in the rate of working capital turnover*—this is when sales increase, but the amount of working capital remains the same. Debt is usually substituted for the needed working capital, which increases fixed costs and therefore the risk to the creditor.

SHORTENING THE RECEIVABLES CYCLE

The cash manager is interested in getting cash payments into the company bank accounts as quickly as possible. The credit manager and the accounting department require transaction data that permit application of the payment to the proper account and invoice. Hence, cash acceleration procedures must address both of these concerns. The following methods are used to accelerate collections.

Lockbox. A lockbox is a post office box opened in the name of the seller but accessed and serviced by a remittance processor. Banks and others who process the remittances usually do so in a manner and at the time of day that allows funds to be more readily available to the depositor. Lockboxes offer these advantages over processing deposits at the premises of the seller:

- Faster availability of the funds
- Greater security over the remittance
- Reduced processing costs
- Greater reliability in deposit processing
- Greater reliability in capturing necessary remittance data. Image processing involves capturing the image of the check and temporarily storing it in digital form. This enables the bank to immediately dispatch the check for clearing, while the image is used to complete work required by the bank.

Wire transfer. This is a series of telegraphic messages between two banks, usually through a Federal Reserve bank wherein the sending bank instructs the Federal Reserve bank to charge the account of the receiving bank, and advises the receiving bank of the transfer.

ACH transfer. This system, operating under the auspices of the National Automatic Clearing House Association, is a method for the commercial banks to exchange electronic payments without the high cost of Federal Reserve wires. In most instances the payroll initiates a payment for credit to the bank account of the payee.

Depository transfer check (DTC). Under this system, a bank prepares a DTC check on behalf of its customer against the customer's depository account in another bank. It is a means of more quickly getting funds from depository accounts into concentration accounts.

Preauthorized Draft (PAD). This is a draft drawn by the payee against the bank account of the payor. The method often is used by insurance companies or other lenders where the payment is fixed and repetitive. The payor must authorize its bank to honor the draft, which may be in either electronic or paper form.

Accelerating the cash collections is one means of reducing the receivables. In fact, if sales personnel are involved in collections, an incentive based on customer payment habits might be considered. However, the amount of funds tied up in receivables may result in part from antiquated or slow procedures in the order and billing process and not in the collection cycle. A detailed review of the procedures from receipt of the customer order, through shipment, to cash collection might be helpful in spotting areas for improvement. For example, in a typical manufacturing company, each step in the procedures from receipt of the customer order until final collection should be studied for means of expediting. Thus, the following events ought to be analyzed for means of speeding up the process:

- Order receipt steps, such as processing the customer order from receipt in the mailroom or order department to the sales department.
- Order processing steps in the sales department, such as separation of stock orders from custom orders.
- Credit approval steps, such as the segregation of orders to be expedited, and the separation of orders for known creditworthy customers.
- Order shipping procedures, such as reviews by the shipper of a credit hold list prior to shipping product.
- Order paperwork flow from the shipping department to the billing department.
- Invoice preparation and mailing procedures.

In this connection, given the advent of the microcomputer and the development of related software that integrates the financial system, the advantage of a simple computerized system should be considered. The advantages are many. For example, *billings and month-end statements may be sent out more promptly.* The more quickly invoices are sent out, the more quickly they are paid. Invoices should always be mailed within one day of the shipment date. Moreover, *up-to-date records make management information more accurate.* Customers may be incorrectly dunned for overdue payments, when funds may have already been received, but not recorded. A computer system will not avoid this problem if records are not updated by the clerical staff, but it will make the process easier. Also, *billings can be sent by electronic data interchange (EDI).* EDI allows the company to send invoices electronically to a central computer clearinghouse, where the invoice is electronically stored. Customers access the clearinghouse by modem, and receive the invoice electronically.

RESERVE FOR DOUBTFUL ACCOUNTS

The accounts receivable investment includes providing a reserve for estimated doubtful accounts. This may be accomplished in one of two ways when actual sales are made. First, set aside a percentage of monthly sales (or credit sales) based on past experience. Second, review the accounts receivable aging and reserve for any probable uncollectible accounts. When dealing with the long-term business plan, the estimated percent of sales is the method most commonly employed.

RECEIVABLES FRAUD AND CONTROL

The controller's first experience with fraud may be the review of "what went wrong" following the loss of assets. To avoid this problem, we provide a list of typical receivables frauds that the controller can prepare for through proper control systems, which are also mentioned. With proper controls, it should be much more difficult to perpetrate many of the frauds listed below.

Receivables Fraud

The following examples should not be considered the only possible types of receivables fraud; dishonest people will continue to derive new methods of removing money from a company; so the controller must remain watchful.

- Ship materials to a false address and do not issue an invoice. Collusion is usually required, with one person in accounting and one person in the shipping department.
- Issue an invoice to a customer at a high price and record an invoice for the company's records at a lower price; when payment is received, the employee pockets the difference between the price paid and the price recorded. To do this, an employee must have control over the billing and cash receipts functions.
- Increase receivable balances with bogus transactions in order to procure loans secured against receivables. This can be accomplished by one billings person.
- Write off artificial discounts and adjustments; when full payment comes in, pocket the difference between the discounts and the full payment. To do this, an employee must have control over the billing and cash receipts functions.
- Write off receivables as bad debts; when full payment comes in, pocket the written-off amount. To do this, an employee must have control over the billing and cash receipts functions.

Receivables Controls

The vast number of shipments to customers from most business concerns gives rise to the danger that not all goods are properly charged to customers' accounts receivable. Further, even though an invoice is prepared, the customer may be billed for an incorrect amount because of differences in the quantity shipped, price, or extensions. The controller must institute proper procedures to ensure that such risks are minimized. The following procedures may be useful in controlling these receivables problems:

- *Compare source information*—Invoices to customers are compared to prenumbered shipping memos by an independent party. This comparison includes both the quantity and description of goods shipped, and all shipping memo numbers must be accounted for.

- *Audit prices and extensions*—Prices appearing on invoices are independently checked against established price lists, and all extensions and footings are checked.
- *Compare detail to summary records*—Periodically, the detail of the accounts receivable is checked against the general ledger total and reconciled, preferably by an internal auditor or other independent party.
- *Confirm balances*—Surprise mailings of monthly statements and confirmation requests should be made by third parties.
- *Segregate duties*—All handling of cash should be segregated from the maintenance of receivable records.
- *Review special adjustments*—All special adjustments for discounts, returns, or allowances should have special approval.
- *Review bad debts*—A special record should be kept of all bad debts written off, and a follow-up should be made on those items to minimize the danger of collections being received and not recorded.
- *Mail invoices separately*—Invoices may be mailed tocustomers by a separate unit.

13

INVENTORY

Inventory can be one of the largest dollar items listed on the balance sheet. It can be the cause of large and unexpected adjustments in the year-end financial statements, due to unexpected amounts of obsolete and missing stock. In fact, supporters of just-in-time (JIT) manufacturing systems consider inventory to be a liability, since it is expensive in terms of insurance, storage space, moving costs, obsolescence, shrinkage, tracking costs, and working capital. Under the JIT system, minimal inventory reduces all of the above costs. Since minimal inventory and highly accurate inventory records are critical under *any* manufacturing system, this chapter focuses on installing inventory tracking systems, which can then be used to pinpoint inventory problems and lead to smaller inventories. In addition, this chapter discusses the valuation of inventories, the physical inventory procedure, and inventory fraud.

INVENTORY MANAGEMENT SYSTEMS

Inventory management systems are a topic of considerable debate, as JIT systems gradually supplant material requirements planning (MRP) and various reorder point systems. In this section the following will be examined:

The turnover statistic, which is the most universally used benchmark for analyzing the performance of an inventory management system.

Overviews of each management system, as well as the advantages and disadvantages of each one.

The cost of carrying inventories, as well as where responsibility for inventory systems should lie.

Turnover

Turnover is the most universal measure of the manufacturing system's efficiency in using inventory. It is derived by dividing the usage factor by the average inventory. For example, the turnover of various inventories would be determined as follows:

- *Finished goods*—Cost of goods sold/average inventory of finished goods
- *Work-in-process*—Cost of goods completed/average inventory of work-in-process
- *Raw materials*—Materials placed in process/average inventory of raw materials
- *Supplies*—Cost of supplies used/average supply inventory

The result is the number of "turns," usually measured in turns per year. Turnover statistics must be analyzed with caution, for several factors can cause the same result. A slow turnover can indicate overinvestment in inventories, obsolete stock, or declining sales. A very high turnover can indicate improved utilization through conversion to a JIT or MRP system, or it may be caused by keeping an excessively small amount of stock on hand, resulting in lost sales or increased costs due to fractional buying.

The purpose of business is turning a profit, not turning inventory. Evaluating a company's performance based on a turnover is not wise without more detailed information. If turnover is used to evaluate the performance of a new manufacturing system, such as MRP or JIT, then it is useful. If it is used to compare performance between accounting periods, then it is useful as an indicator of underlying problems or improvements that must be researched further to determine the exact causes of any changes in the statistic.

Reorder Points

When there are known requirements, the MRP and JIT systems will indicate when materials need to be ordered, and inventories can be planned accordingly. When there is greater uncertainty, as in job-lot work, estimates of the volume level must be made, and a provision for error, through the use of safety stock, may be used. The reorder point is then calculated by multiplying the anticipated lead time in weeks by the estimated demand in units per week, plus a safety stock quantity. Reorder point systems tend to result in excess inventories and obsolete materials, because parts will automatically be ordered even though the need for them may be declining. Typical turnover rates to be expected are three to six turns, though this statistic will vary widely by industry.

At the time the stock level reaches the reorder point, a requisition is issued for additional inventory. Some of the more widely used means of signaling the time to reorder include:

- *Minimum–maximum system*—This method is used in connection with the inventory record. The minimum quantity level is the reorder point; the maximum level is the minimum quantity plus the economical order size.
- *Reserve stock method*—Under this system, the stock is divided into two parts: one for immediate use, and one as a reserve. When use of the reserve is commenced, additional stock is reordered. This system may involve two bins (one with the reserve stock) or one bin with the reserve stock identified (e.g., in a separate bay).
- *Visual check system*—When the manager checks the stock level, with direct knowledge of the business activity, he or she can judge when to reorder.
- *Reservation method*—This method recognizes the available stock as well as the physical stock. Available stock is defined as stock on order, plus physical stock, less the unfilled requirement. The reorder point is based on the available stock rather than the physical stock.

Material Requirements Planning

Inventory is handled differently under the material requirements planning (MRP) system. An MRP system schedules production through a master schedule. The system then multiplies the master schedule quantities by the bills of material for each item on the schedule to determine the gross part requirements for production needs. The gross requirements are then reduced by unallocated parts currently in stock to derive the list of parts to be ordered. The to-be-ordered list is grouped into convenient lot sizes, and the parts are ordered. Typical turnover rates to be expected are six to fifteen turns, though this statistic will vary widely by industry.

The MRP system improves inventory turns and brings order into unsystematic manufacturing systems by requiring high data accuracy levels. However, it can require considerable computer processing time. Also, an MRP system is designed to work with long set up times, long production runs, and long cycle times, and accepts scrapped parts; a JIT system, on the other hand, works toward short setups, short production runs, short cycle times, and zero scrapped parts. Finally, an MRP system results in excess inventory, since orders are placed for standard lot sizes, rather than for the exact amounts required.

Just-In-Time Systems

A just-in-time (JIT) system involves many changes to a typical manufacturing system, which result in vastly reduced inventories. Turnover rates can be as high as eighty, though twenty turns is more typical; this statistic will vary widely by industry. Some of the changes are described below.

Purchasing. A traditional system processes bids from many suppliers, takes the lowest bid, and orders in bulk, leaving leftover parts in the warehouse for future use. A JIT system uses a small number of long-term suppliers, and orders only as much as is immediately needed, so that no extra parts are stored in the warehouse, and suppliers deliver parts directly to the assembly area. There is no room for defective parts in a JIT system, so supplier quality systems are tested by company terms to ensure that parts will be delivered within specifications.

Delivery. A traditional system builds to stock and released finished goods as orders are received. A JIT system closely links its production schedule to suppliers' delivery schedules, thereby reducing its finished goods stocking requirements.

Manufacturing. A traditional system produces long runs of one product before shutting down, resting the equipment, and producing another long run. A JIT system works to reduce setup times, so that (ultimately) it is economical to produce one item in a production run. Also, machines are rearranged into clusters called manufacturing cells, so that small jobs move rapidly through a common routing over several types of machines; this process reduces work-in-process inventories. It also improves quality, since one worker is responsible for the part through several production steps, and can spot quality problems quickly, before many parts are produced. *Kanbans* are authorization cards that allow a worker to produce a set amount of parts for an upstream workstation, thereby controlling the amount of WIP in the system.

Warehousing. A traditional system receives supplier parts, stocks the parts, and issues them to the assembly floor based on a pick list. A JIT system avoids the warehouse entirely, and sends the parts directly to the assembly floor.

Quality. A traditional system accepts a set percentage of defective products, and overproduces to allow for the variance. A JIT system uses statistical process control to identify upward or downward trends in variances, thereby predicting when a process will exceed its within-specification boundaries. In addition, supplier quality systems are closely tracked to ensure that received products are free of defects.

Inspection. A traditional system inspects products after they have been produced, and eliminates or reworks any defective products. A JIT system builds quality into the process, so that no inspection staff is needed.

Cycle time. A traditional system has a long cycle time, because parts sit in the warehouse before being kitted (removed from storage and clustered together for use in a production run), where they sit again, and between manufacturing work-stations, where they sit in piles of work-in-process (WIP). A JIT system sends received parts directly from the receiving dock to the assembly area, where WIP is reduced by using manufacturing cells and kanbans.

Accounts payable. A traditional system will not pay a supplier until an invoice is received and matched to receiving documentation from the receiving department. Under a JIT system, suppliers are paid based on how many units the manufacturer produces in each period; the number of parts that must have been received is calculated by multiplying the number of parts in the finished product by the quantity of the product that was produced. The traditional system would not work in a JIT environment, since an immense amount of paperwork would be needed to process the increased number of small-volume receipts.

Working capital. A traditional system requires working capital for inventories. Some JIT systems are now approaching negative working capital levels, because their inventory requirements are so low. This challenge allows the company to more profitably invest its cash flow in other activities.

Cost accounting. A traditional system records variances on the shop floor, which are then summarized and reported back to the manufacturing managers by a cost accountant. A JIT system emphasizes cycle time and recording cost information during production slows down cycle time. Also, JIT systems function with so little WIP that quality problems become obvious and can be corrected well before the cost accountant can summarize variance information and send it back to the manufacturing staff for corrective action. Thus, a JIT system uses minimal variance reporting.

Product/Costs. A traditional system measures variances caused by the manufacturing facility that affect the cost of a product. The JIT system has removed most variances from the manufacturing system, so the cost accountant's focus becomes setting a target cost during the design stage and assigning targeted subsidiary part costs to suppliers. The cost accountant then reports on variances caused by suppliers not meeting their cost targets.

A JIT system's biggest problem is replacing the existing system; it is so radically different that the existing system may come to a complete stop before the new system is properly implemented, thereby losing valuable production time. This problem is avoided by implementing the JIT system from the delivery end of the process, and working backwards toward the receiving function. Also, some JIT concepts, such as manufacturing cells, can be implemented and fitted into an existing system without unduly affecting production performance. As for its advantages, JIT systems require minimal computing power and working capital, and can create products with far less cycle time than any other system.

The Cost of Carrying Inventories

The cost of carrying inventories is significant. First, working capital is required to pay for inventory; the interest cost of working capital is easily calculated when money is borrowed to obtain inventory or working capital. Interest may also be imputed by using a rate commensurate with the return on investment in other alternatives. Also, when funds are used to purchase inventory, the money is no longer available for other, possibly more worthwhile, projects. There are other inventory costs that must also be recognized, such as insurance, taxes, warehousing, storage and handling, pilferage, spoilage, and obsolescence. The total of these costs can easily range from 25 to 40% of the inventory value on annual basis.

Inventory also causes a product's cycle time to increase. The total cycle time is the time required to build a product; reducing the cycle time increases the firm's speed to market, so that customer orders can be handled more rapidly. When parts must be received, moved into storage, kitted, and then moved to the assembly area for production, critical time is added to the production process. Just-in-time (JIT) systems move the inventory straight from the receiving dock to the production floor, thereby reducing the cycle time drastically.

Responsibility for Inventory

The responsibility for inventory may generally be assigned as follows, with variations based on the company's organizational structure and products. *Manufacturing-related inventories,* such as raw materials, manufacturing supplies, and work-in-process, should be the responsibility of the chief manufacturing executive, so that the position has complete command over the materials needed to manufacture the finished product. *Sales-related inventories,* such as finished goods, can be the responsibility of either the chief manufacturing executive or the sales executive. The reason for assigning these inventories to the sales executive is that a better job of estimating sales requirements will result. Moreover, greater attention will be paid by the sales executive to disposing of obsolete or slow-moving items.

Regardless of who is assigned the responsibility, the assignment must be clear, so that inventories are kept at manageable levels. There must also be full coordination between the purchasing, engineering, and production functions, so that parts are purchased only as needed, and based on accurate bills of material. The controller is rarely responsible for the inventory, but should be responsible for related internal control issues and inventory valuation methods.

INVENTORY TRACKING

If perpetual inventory records are maintained with high accuracy, then no physical inventory need be conducted. An increasing number of companies are turning to this method for the following reasons:

- *Avoid wasted time*—Staff time is not being efficiently utilized during the physical inventory process, because they could be involved in other activities. Also, the production facility is shut down, allowing no revenue-generating products to be manufactured.
- *Improve product delivery performance and reduce freight costs*—High inventory record accuracy allows companies to promise shipments to customers with greater confidence, because products can be built without delays due to missing parts. Also, rush charges for missing parts are avoided.
- *Achieve higher accuracy with ongoing counts*—Inventory counts should be done by the experts—the warehouse staff—and should be done at their leisure, which will ensure higher count accuracy. If a complete plant-wide physical inventory is performed, then accuracy drops due to counts by less experienced non-warehouse staff and the short timeline required to complete the count.
- *Avoid year-end surprises*—Many companies have been unpleasantly surprised by unexpected changes in inventory levels at year end. These surprises can be avoided by constantly monitoring inventory levels with a perpetual inventory system.
- *Use data to reduce inventory and cut costs*—The transaction history that is a byproduct of a perpetual inventory system allows the materials manager to make informed decisions regarding deletions of parts from stock. This is of value to the controller, since cash requirements for additional inventory are reduced and can be enhanced as inventory is sold back to suppliers. As inventory is reduced, the staff needed to track it and the insurance needed to cover it can both be reduced, thereby improving the company's cash flow a second time.

A physical inventory can be eliminated if accurate perpetual inventory records are available. Many steps are required to implement such a system, requiring considerable effort. The controller should evaluate the company's resources prior to embarking on this process, and adjust those resources accordingly in order to complete the project. In addition, the controller must realize that, once high accuracy levels are achieved, continued monitoring is needed to maintain those levels.

The steps needed to implement an accurate perpetual inventory system are:

- *Select and install inventory tracking software*—The primary requirements for inventory tracking software are that it:
  — *Track transactions*—One of the primary uses of a perpetual inventory system is the ability to list the frequency of product usage, which allows the materials manager to increase or reduce selected inventory quantities.
  — *Update records immediately*—The perpetual inventory data must always be up-to-date, because production planners must know what is in stock

and because cycle counters must have access to accurate data. Batch updating of records is not acceptable.

— *Report inventory records by location*—Cycle counters need inventory records sorted by location in order to most efficiently count the inventory.

• *Test inventory tracking software*—Create a set of typical records in the new software, and perform a series of transactions to ensure that the software functions properly. In addition, create a large number of records and perform the transaction again, to see if the response time of the system drops significantly. If the software appears to function properly, continue to the next step. Otherwise, fix the problems with the software supplier's assistance, or acquire a different software package.

• *Train the warehouse staff*—The warehouse staff should receive software training immediately before using the system, so that they do not forget how to operate the software. Enter a set of test records into the software, and have the staff simulate all common inventory transactions, such as receipts, picks, and cycle count adjustments.

• *Revise rack layout*—It is much easier to move racks prior to installing a perpetual inventory system, because no inventory locations must be changed on the computer system. Create aisles that are wide enough for forklift operation, and cluster small parts racks together for easier parts picking.

• *Create rack locations*—A typical rack location is, for example, A-01–B-01. The meaning of this location code is as follows:

— A = Aisle A

— 01 = Rack 1

— B = Level B (numbered from the bottom to the top)

— 01 = Partition 1 (optional—subsection of a rack)

As one progresses down an aisle, the rack numbers should progress in ascending sequence, with the odd rack numbers on the left and the even numbers on the right. This layout allows an inventory picker to move down the center of the aisle, efficiently pulling items based on sequential location codes.

• *Lock the warehouse*—One of the main causes of record inaccuracy is removal of items from the warehouse by outside staff. To stop such removal, all entrances to the warehouse must be locked. Only warehouse personnel should be allowed access to the warehouse. All other personnel entering the warehouse should be accompanied by a member of the warehouse staff to prevent the removal of inventory.

• *Consolidate parts*—To reduce the labor of counting the same item in multiple locations, group common parts in one location.

• *Assign part numbers*—Have several experienced personnel verify all part numbers. A mislabeled part is as useless as a missing part, since the computer database will not show that it exists. Mislabeled parts also affect the inventory cost; for example, a mislabeled engine is more expensive than the item represented by its incorrect part number, which identifies it as, say, a spark plug.

- *Verify units of measure*—Have several experienced personnel verify all units of measure. Unless the software allows multiple units of measure, the entire organization must adhere to one unit of measure for each item. For example, the warehouse may desire tape to be counted in rolls, but the engineering department had rather create bills of material with tape measured in inches instead of fractions of rolls.

- *Pack the parts*—Pack parts into containers, seal the containers, and label them with the part number, unit of measure, and total quantity stored inside. Leave a few parts free for ready use. Only open containers when additional stock is needed. This method allows cycle counters to rapidly verify inventory balances.

- *Count items*—Count items when there is no significant activity in the warehouse, such as during a weekend. Elaborate cross-checking of the counts, as would be done during a year-end physical inventory, is not necessary. It is more important to have the perpetual inventory operational before warehouse activity increases again; any errors in the data will quickly be detected during cycle counts and flushed out of the database. The counts must include the part number, location, and quantity.

- *Enter data into computer*—Have an experienced data entry person input the location, part number, and quantity into the computer. Once the data is input, another person should cross-check the entered data against the original data for errors.

- *Quick-check the data*—Scan the data for errors. If all part numbers have the same number of digits, then look for items that are too long or short. Review location codes to see if inventory is stored in nonexistent racks. Look for units of measure that match the part being described. For example, is it logical to have a pint of steel in stock? Also, if item costs are available, print a list of extended costs. Excessive costs typically point to incorrect units of measure. For example, a cost of $1 per box of nails will become $500 in the inventory report if nails are listed as individual units.

- *Initiate cycle counts*—Print out a portion of the inventory list, sorted by location. Using the report, have selected staff count blocks of the inventory on a continuous basis. They should look for accurate part numbers, units of measure, locations, and quantities. The counts can concentrate on high-value or high-use items, but the entire stock should be reviewed regularly. The most important part of this step is to examine why mistakes occur. If a cycle counter finds an error, the cause of the error must be investigated and then corrected, so that the mistake will not occur again.

- *Initiate inventory audits*—The inventory should be audited frequently, perhaps as much as once a week. This allows the controller to track changes in the inventory accuracy level and initiate changes if the accuracy drops below acceptable levels. In addition, frequent audits are an indirect means of telling the staff that inventory accuracy is important, and must be maintained. The minimum acceptable accuracy level is 95%, with an error being a mistaken part number, unit of measure, quantity, or location. This accuracy level is needed to ensure accurate inventory costing, as well as to assist the materials department in planning future inventory purchases. In addition, establish a tolerance level when calculating the inventory accuracy. For example, if the computer record of a box of screws yields a quantity of 100 and the actual count reveals a quantity of 105, then the record is accurate if the tolerance is 5% but inaccurate if the tolerance is 1%. The maximum tolerance should be 5%, and this figure could be reduced for high-value or high-use items.

- *Post results*—Inventory accuracy is a team project, and the warehouse staff feels more involved if the audit results are posted against the results of previous audits.

- *Reward staff*—Accurate inventories save a company thousands of dollars in many ways. Therefore, it is cost-effective to encourage the staff to maintain and improve the accuracy with periodic bonuses based on reaching higher levels of accuracy with tighter tolerances.

The previous section dealt with the basic steps needed to implement an accurate perpetual inventory system. However, there are several special cases that require additional steps. Some of the more common cases are:

- *Customer-owned inventory*—Customer-owned inventory cannot be valued, since the company does not own it. There are different solutions for different companies. For example, one can avoid assigning a cost to the part, assign different part numbers to a part based on who owns it, or segregate the materials in an uncounted area. In these cases, be careful when assigning several part numbers to the same part, for engineering drawings and bills of material usually list only one part number for a part.

- *Consignment inventory*—One technique used by materials departments to improve the production process is to turn over some items to suppliers, who then have title to their own inventory in the production area. Because it is owned by suppliers, it should not be costed. To avoid incorrect costing, this consignment inventory should be stored in clearly marked areas, and should not appear in the inventory database.

- *Materials at supplier locations*—Company-owned materials are sometimes kept at supplier or customer locations. These items can constitute a large unseen part of the inventory, and can easily escape an otherwise rigorous inventory tracking system. It is the responsibility of the materials department to track this inventory. Track these items by using a special location code for the off-site location, and verify the item quantities with the customer or supplier as part of the cycle count and periodic audit process.

- *Floor stock*—Floor stock is defined as the fasteners kept on the shop floor to assemble product. These are typically kept in uncounted bins, and replenished from the warehouse as the bins empty. The easiest treatment of this material on the computer system is to avoid it. Floor stock is generally not expensive, and therefore has no significant impact on the accuracy of the financial statements if they are expensed instead of being capitalized into inventory. Also, the cost to count floor stock may not be worth the additional level of record accuracy in the perpetual inventory.

Another approach to floor stock is to return as much of it as possible to the warehouse. A close review of floor stock turnover typically reveals that some of it turns slowly. If so, those items can be returned to stock and later requisitioned back to the shop floor as needed. This technique reduces the amount of uncounted floor stock.

- *Work in process*—Work in process must be tracked in the perpetual inventory system, because it can be large enough to have a significant impact on the financial statements. The easiest approach to this problem is to utilize cell manufacturing to reduce the work in progress in the manufacturing process— if it isn't there, you don't have to count it. However, because cell manufacturing is beyond the job scope of most controllers, the next approach may be more appropriate: encourage data collection at each job station on the assembly floor.

Data collection is difficult outside of the warehouse, where the staff is usually less well trained in data entry methods. Several methods are possible, based on the controller's level of confidence in the staff's ability to enter data. One method is to have each manufacturing station log in those items entering its area, and log out those items leaving its area. This is a time-consuming process that can move faster with bar coding.

A different method could work if bills of material are accurate. Then the progress of jobs through the shop can be tracked by simply logging in the stage of completion of the job. If the inventory tracking software is sophisticated enough, the WIP cost is calculated by comparing the job's reported stage of completion to the bill of materials.

PHYSICAL INVENTORY PROCEDURE

The physical inventory is a manual count of all inventory on hand, and is used to obtain an inventory valuation for the period-end financials. Physical inventories are still used by many companies; even those who have converted to perpetual systems may find that sections of the inventory located outside of the warehouse, such as work-in-process, require a periodic physical count. Companies using such advanced systems as manufacturing cells may still require a physical count of work-in-process, unless all production is allowed to flow through the manufacturing process and into finished goods prior to conducting the count.

Preplanning the inventory is critical. The following points will ease the counting process:

- *Use trained personnel*—The inventory counters should all be experienced warehouse personnel, because they are familiar with the parts, as well as their related part numbers and units of measure. The front-office staff has no place in the counting process, because they do not know the parts, part numbers, or units of measure.

- *Use "deal time"*—It is difficult to count while production operations are occurring. Consequently, using weekend or evening time will hasten the counting process.

- *Clean up in advance*—A messy counting area means that the counting team must find the stock before counting it; save time by organizing the inventory in advance, clearly labeling part numbers and units of measure, and cleaning the counting areas.

- *Train the staff*—The physical inventory teams must be trained in counting procedures, as well as proper cutoff procedures and completion of forms. The training may require detailed written instructions.
  - *Cutoffs*—Items received after the cutoff period must be marked "do not count" and segregated. Items shipped must leave the dock by the cutoff period, or they will be included in inventory. No parts will move in or out of the warehouse while the count is being performed.

- *Assign the staff*—Allocate inventory locations to specific counting items.

- *Organize*—The counting process involves the warehouse staff, the cost accountant(s), and the accounting staff. They must be tightly organized to achieve an accurate physical count. Because of the many departments involved, a person with significant experience and authority must lead the effort.

- *Create an inventory tag form*—The tag is used to record the inventory count for each item, and should include fields for the part number, description, location, unit of measure, counter's signature, and last job performed (if it is a work-in-process item). The tags must be *pre-numbered.*

The counting process should include the following steps:

- *Notify the auditors*—The auditors must be notified of the time and place of the physical inventory. An audit team will test counts, observe the procedure generally, and trace the counts to the inventory summary.
- *Assign counting teams to areas*—The following areas should be counted:
  - Central warehouse
  - Receiving inspection
  - Staging (kitting) areas
  - Finished goods area
  - Work-in-process areas
  - Shipping area

— Outside storage (e.g., in trailer storage or company-owned inventory located at other companies)
— Rework areas
— Packaging materials

Equally important, the following items should not be counted:

— Tools and equipment
— Material handling containers
— Written-off inventory
— Maintenance equipment
— Office supplies
— Departmental expense items (e.g., glue, solder, and tape)
— Consignment inventory

- *Count all areas*—Attach a prenumbered inventory tag to each area that has been counted, in order to prove that the count was completed. The tag should be a two-part form, so that one copy can be removed and used to summarize the inventory. The count is usually conducted by two-person teams, with one counting and the other recording the information.

- *Review counted areas*—Review the counted areas for missing or duplicate counts, and spot-check counts for correct quantities, part numbers, and units of measure. High dollar-value items should be 100% checked.

- *Control tags*—Collect all tags and look for missing or duplicate tag numbers; resolve any problems before summarizing the information in the next step.

- *Summarize tags*—Input the tag information into the computer, or record it manually on a summary sheet. The summary sheet should include all of the information contained on the tags. Whether an automated or manual report, the summary should include space to mark down the market value of each item, so that the cost of each item can be marked to the lower of cost or market for financial statement reporting purposes.

- *Look for discrepancies*—Problems can be unearthed with any of the following techniques:
  — Compare the physical inventory records with perpetual records (if such records are kept).
  — Review the extended costs for excessively large dollar values. Frequently, incorrect units of measure are the source of these errors.
  — Review the unit counts for excessively high counts. Once again, incorrect units of measure may be the culprit.
  — Compare expensive items in the inventory to the summary, to ensure that the correct quantities are recorded, and that their costs appear reasonable.

- *Review the cutoff*—Even with an excellent inventory count, the inventory can be severely misstated if inventory is included or excluded without a corresponding sale or liability entry in the accounting records. Review the receiving and shipping records for several days before and after the inventory count, and ensure that an accounting entry exists for each transaction.

INVENTORY VALUATION

The selection of the method to value has a significant impact on the reported earnings and financial condition of a company. Since the inventory is among the largest of the current assets, the method of valuing inventories is a very important factor in determining both the results from operations and the firm's financial condition.

The primary objective in choosing a cost basis for valuing inventories is to select that method which, under the circumstances, will most satisfactorily reflect the income of the period. In many instances, the units sold are not identifiable with the specific cost of the item, or such application is impractical. For this reason, a variety of cost applications have been developed that recognize differences in the relationship of costs to selling prices under various conditions. For example, the last in, first out (LIFO) method may be applicable where sales prices are promptly affected by changes in reproduction costs. Circumstances of the individual company or industry must govern, but uniform methods within the industry will permit useful comparisons.

The controller must develop management's awareness about the effect different methods of valuation have on profits. To do this, several inventory valuation methods should be applied and the results analyzed and interpreted for management's consideration. The board of directors or the chief executive may pick the method to be used, so they must be well-informed.

Inventory Valuation Methods

The more common inventory valuation methods are:

- *Identified or specific costs*—Under this method, purchases are not commingled but are kept separate. The issue or sale is priced at the exact cost of the specific item. Such a system is not widely adopted because it requires too much physical attention and accounting detail. It is sometimes used in costing perishable stock or nonstandard units that have been purchased for a specific job.
- *First-in, first-out (FIFO)*—This method is often known as the original cost method. It assumes that items first received are first issued. To illustrate the operation, assume an opening inventory of 50 units at $10 each, receipts on January 11 of 10 units at a cost of $15, and issues on January 3 and 12 of 40 units each. The issue on January 3 would be costed at $10 per unit, leaving a balance of 10 units at $10 each. The issue of January 12 would be priced as follows:

10 units at $10 each	$100
30 units at $15 each	450
Total	$550

The requisition must be priced on two bases since two different acquisitions were issued.

- *Simple arithmetic average cost*—The average is computed by dividing the total unit prices for the inventory on hand by the number of such prices, without regard to the quantities to which the prices relate. It is mathematically unsound.

- *Weighted average cost*—This procedure involves the determination after each receipt of the total quantity and value on hand. The total units are divided into the total value to secure an average unit cost. All issues are priced at this average cost until the next receipt, when the new average is computed.

The unit price must be carried out to sufficient decimal places to retain accuracy. Disadvantages of this method include the detailed calculations necessary and the length of time taken to reflect recent purchases in the average. It has the advantage of stabilizing costs when prices fluctuate.

- *Moving average cost*—This method uses an average price of a convenient period of time, such as three or six months. It is a variation of the weighted average method. The effect or price fluctuations is minimized.

- *Monthly average cost*—The total beginning inventory and the receipts for the month are divided into the aggregate cost to determine an average. This average is then applied to the issues for the period. The method has the advantage of eliminating some clerical work. The disadvantage is that the requisitions cannot be costed for the month until the new average cost is determined. Sometimes this disadvantage is avoided by using the previous monthly average.

- *Standard cost*—As the name implies, a predetermined or standard cost is used. The price variances on raw materials may be recognized when the material is received or when it is issued into process. Use of standard costs eliminates such clerical effort. No cost columns are needed on the ledger cards, and the repeated calculation of unit costs is avoided.

- *Last in, first-out cost (LIFO)*—The use of this method assumes that the last unit purchased is the first to be requisitioned. The mechanics used are very similar to the FIFO method, except that requisitions are priced at the cost of the most recent purchase. For example, assume that 100 units are purchased at $4 each and that, later, 50 units are purchased at $6 each. A requisition for 75 units would be priced as follows:

50 units at $6	$300
25 units at $4	100
75 Total	$400

The purpose of the LIFO method is to state, as closely as possible, the cost of goods sold at the current market cost. This method reduces unrealized inventory profits to a minimum.

There are two problems with LIFO. First, record-keeping is more extensive than that required for other valuation methods. If the oldest inventory is never used, then the company can have costing layers on that inventory that are many decades old. Second, if inventory levels drop to zero at period-end, the profit impact could be enormous, for the oldest cost layers may stretch back many years to times when product costs were significantly different. For example, Product A currently costs ten dollars. If the oldest Product A cost layer is only one dollar per unit and all of the inventory is used, then the cost of goods sold will be reduced to one tenth of its current level, creating significant taxable income.

If a company is using the LIFO valuation method and is installing a just-in-time manufacturing system, then the controller should know that the cost of goods sold percentage may vary drastically while the inventory is being reduced and old inventory layers with different costs are being eliminated.

- *Replacement cost*—By this method, the inventory is priced at the cost that would be incurred to replace it at current prices and in its current condition. The method is not the same as LIFO, for the latter uses the latest price on the books, which is not necessarily the replacement cost. The method has many practical difficulties, is not approved by the IRS, and is not considered a GAAP. If used for internal purposes, it must be adjusted for external reporting.
- *Retail inventory method*—This method is frequently used by department stores, where the inventories are marked item by item at selling price rather than cost. The average margin or markup is determined for the period, and this is applied against the ending inventory at retail to ascertain cost. It is a type of average costing.

In a stable price economy fewer questions of inventory valuation policy normally arise. It is in periods of rapid price change that the valuation base selected may have a significant influence on income determination. Obviously, the effect of price changes is not uniform in every industry or in every company. Certain characteristics of the inventory determine the effect of price changes on a company. Among these are the following:

- *Degree of selling price responsiveness to cost changes*—If prices bear little immediate relationship to costs, then the selling price to be realized on the disposition of the present inventory will not impair its value. There will be no cause for a write-down.
- *Relative share of investment in inventories*—The larger the inventory, the greater the risk and the more significant the write-down if values decline substantially. A firm whose major investment is in inventory is more vulnerable to market changes than one that requires a heavy investment in plant and equipment to conduct business.

- *Use of a price hedge*—Losses on the inventory are offset by gains on future sales in the commodities market.
- *Rate of inventory turnover*—If the turnover is rapid, then a shorter time will elapse between the sale of the goods and purchase of materials for additional sales. Thus, in periods of large market value changes, fluctuations in the inventory value will not be as marked.

Lower of Cost or Market, and Inventory Reserves

In some instances, a departure from the cost basis is justified. This occurs when the utility of the goods disposed of in the ordinary course of business is less than cost. Loss in value can occur by reason of damage, deterioration, obsolescence, changes in the price level, and other causes. Such loss should be recognized as a charge against the period in which it occurs. In these instances the goods should be valued at "market," which will be lower than cost. The market value of an item is the current cost of replacing it. One exception to this rule is when goods can still be sold at a fixed price, such as would be contained in a long-term contract with a customer.

Most companies establish an inventory loss reserve in expectation of finding obsolete or damaged inventory over a period of time. The reserve is usually established as a percentage of the inventory, and is based on historical or industry averages of actual losses. The reserve is deducted from the inventory on the balance sheet. As actual losses are uncovered, they are written off against the loss reserve. Since actual losses can be hidden on the balance sheet, each loss occurrence should be reported to management, in case any corrective action is necessary.

The controller must provide for a continuous review of procedures and transactions to assure that inventories are being properly valued. This will include procedures for notification when materials become unsaleable, and should include creating a materials review board (MRB) that would periodically review the inventory. A typical MRB has representatives from the accounting, quality control, engineering, sales, and materials departments. The combined expertise of this group can be relied on to identify unsaleable materials.

Consistency in Valuation

Irrespective of the method of pricing the inventory, an essential requirement of inventory valuation is consistency from period to period. Over the long run, the basis of valuing inventories will not affect the total profit or loss from operations. However, from quarter to quarter or year to year the effect on profits can be significant if the basis or method is changed. If circumstances require a change, the reason for the change and the effect on profit should be fully disclosed in the financial statements presented to management and the shareholders. Also, the following items can cause more subtle changes in the inventory valuation:

- Changes to a bill of material (BOM) or labor routing that affect the cost of an item.
- Changes in run sizes that affect labor routings from a previous period.
- Changes in labor dollars that affect overhead, since overhead is usually calculated as a percentage of labor.

INVENTORY FRAUD AND CONTROLS

As with other areas of a business, the controller should be aware of fraud schemes that are specific to the inventory area. The schemes, and the most basic inventory controls, are covered in this section.

Inventory Fraud

The year-end inventory count can be fraudulently increased in order to reduce the cost of goods sold and thereby create an artificially large profit. Also, company personnel may steal inventory and try to cover up the theft with artificially high inventory counts. Consequently, the counting team should look for the following fraudulent schemes that may have occurred during or before the inventory count:

- Empty or mislabeled boxes
- Incorrect units of measure
- Diluted liquid inventory
- Excessively advanced sites of WIP completion
- Customer-owned stock included in the inventory count

In addition, the controller should watch for the following fraudulent schemes that can occur when performing the inventory cutoff:

- Double-counting inventory that is in transit between two company-owned locations
- Counting inventory for which payables have not been recorded

An additional concern relates solely to JIT purchasing. Since JIT precludes competitive bidding, it may be possible for buyers to select suppliers who will kick back profits to the buyers in exchange for the business. This problem is real, but is mitigated somewhat by the amount of interaction between company employees and the supplier. The product design function under JIT purchasing requires that the company's design engineers work closely with suppliers, and therefore be able to recognize a sham supplier.

Inventory Controls

Inventory controls should include physical control over the stock plus accuracy of the inventory information and of the bills of material that describe the inventory.

The following controls can be used to *physically control* the inventory:

- Make the warehouse manager responsible for all inventory shortages.
- Erect fencing around all inventory storage locations, and lock all entrances.
- Permit only warehouse personnel into the warehouse, or require an escort for non-warehouse personnel.
- Record all transactions for items that enter or leave the warehouse, and require a signature from the receiving, kitting, or shipping person in the warehouse who handles each transaction.

The controller should also institute reviews of the *inventory information* by someone who does not report to the inventory manager. The ideal person would be the internal auditor; in the absence of such a person, the cost accountant or a person similarly knowledgeable about inventory should conduct the reviews. If a perpetual inventory is available, then the review should be conducted weekly. The reviewer should take a random sample from the inventory report (sorted by location and including extended costs), and review:

- that items physically in stock are listed on the report;
- that items listed on the report are physically in stock;
- that units of measure are correct;
- that high dollar value items are correct (sample 100% of these items).

The inventory report from the previous week should also be retained, so that the following items can be reviewed:

- that the total number of part numbers in stock does not vary significantly from the previous week, or that such variances can be identified and explained;
- that the total dollar value of inventory does not vary significantly from the previous week, or that such variances can be identified and explained.

To control the *bill-of-material information*, cross-check additional items that are requested from stock during a job's production, or returned to stock following a job's production. These transactions strongly indicate that a product's bill of materials is incorrect. Also, distribute forms to the production and kitting staffs, who can report on missing or duplicate parts. Finally, a review committee can systematically review all bills of material for inaccurate quantities, part numbers, and units of measure. Since the controller bases year-end inventory projections on product costs that in turn are based on bills of material, correcting the bills can eliminate the annoyance of larger year-end inventory variances.

Under a JIT manufacturing system, inventory is minimized, and, consequently, the risk of significant fraud is greatly reduced. However, to avoid collusion between buyers and suppliers (who no longer have to bid for work), the controller should periodically compare the company's supplier costs to a sample of costs from other suppliers. The controller should also review prices charged by suppliers versus prices contracted.

14

PROPERTY, PLANT, AND EQUIPMENT

Capital expenditure planning and control are critical to the long-term financial health of any company operating in the private enterprise system. Expenditures for fixed assets require significant financial resources, decisions are difficult to reverse, and the investment affects financial performance over a long period of time.

Investment in capital assets has other ramifications or possible consequences not found in the typical day-to-day expenditures of a business. Once funds have been used for the purchase of plant and equipment, it may be a long time before they are recovered. Unwise expenditures of this nature are difficult to retrieve without serious loss to the investor. Needless to say, imprudent long-term commitments can result in bankruptcy or other financial embarrassment.

Also, a substantial increase in capital investment is likely to cause a much higher break-even point for the business. Large outlays for plant, machinery, and equipment carry with them higher depreciation charges, heavier insurance costs, greater property taxes, and possibly an expanded maintenance expense. All these tend to raise the level of sales volume needed for the business to earn a profit.

In today's highly competitive environment, it is mandatory that companies make significant investments in fixed assets to improve productivity and take advantage of the technological gains being experienced in manufacturing equipment. The sophisticated manufacturing and processing techniques available make investment decisions more important; however, the sizable amounts invested allow for greater rewards in increased productivity and higher return on investment. This opportunity carries with it additional risks relative to the increasing costs of a plant and equipment.

These conditions make it imperative that wisdom and prudent judgment be exercised in making investments in capital assets. Management decisions must be made utilizing analytical approaches. There are numerous mathematical techniques to assist in eliminating uneconomic investments and systematically establishing priorities.

ROLE OF THE CONTROLLER

The controller's financial knowledge is needed to evaluate the capital asset requirements that are generated by the first-level management. In many cases, heavy losses have incurred because the acquisition decision was made with an optimistic outlook but without adequate financial analysis. The controller's staff must make an objective appraisal of the potential savings and return on investment.

After decisions have been made by the CEO and board of directors to make the investments, the controller must establish proper accountability, measure performance (procurement of the capital assets at the budgeted price), and institute recording and reporting procedures for control to ensure that the equipment has been received and installed, and is fulfilling its intended use.

The controller's tasks in relation to property, plant, and equipment are as follows:

- Establish a procedure for the planning and control of fixed assets.
- Establish hurdle rates on the types of fixed assets under consideration.
- Review all requests for capital expenditures to verify the probable rate of return.
- Ascertain that the plant and equipment expenditures required to meet the manufacturing and sales plans are included in the business plan, and that funds are available to pay for the expenditures.
- Establish controls to ensure that capital expenditures are kept within authorized limits.
- Review economic alternatives to asset purchases, such as leasing or renting, or buying the manufactured item from other suppliers.
- Establish a reporting system that informs managers about their equipment's maintenance costs, idle time, productivity, and actual costs versus budget.
- Maintain property records that identify all assets, describe their locations, track transfers and sales, and account for depreciation.
- Maintain a depreciation policy for each type of equipment for book and tax purposes.
- Ensure that proper insurance coverage is maintained for the fixed assets.
- Ensure that proper internal control procedures apply to the machinery and equipment.

CAPITAL BUDGETING

The principal part of this chapter will and should be devoted to the capital budgeting process. Most of the accounting and reporting duties are known to the average controller, but more involvement in the budget procedure should be encouraged. Given the relative inflexibility that exists once capital commitments are made, it is desirable that the CEO and other senior executives be provided a suitable framework for selecting the essential or economically justified projects from among the many proposals, even though their intuitive judgment may be a key factor. When the undertaking begins, the expenditures must be held within the authorized limits. Moreover, for the larger projects at least, management is entitled, once the asset begins to operate, to be periodically informed how the actual economics compare with the anticipated earnings or savings.

The nine steps in a well-conceived capital budgeting process are outlined below. These steps are not all performed by the controller, but rather by the appropriate line executive.

1. For the planning period of the short-term budget, determine a permissible range for capital commitments for the company as a whole, and for each major division. This tells management how much can be spent in the period.

2. Encourage the presentation of worthy capital investment projects. For major projects, the target rate of return should be provided, and any other useful guidelines should be furnished, such as corporate objectives and plans for expansion.

3. When the proposals are received, make a preliminary screening to eliminate those that do not support the strategic plan, or that are obviously not economically or politically supportable.

4. After this preliminary screening:
   - Classify all projects by urgency of need.
   - Calculate the economic benefits.

5. Review the project proposals for:
   - Validity of nontechnical data.
   - Rate of return and any related calculations.
   - Compatibility with the financial resources available and any capital budget criteria.

6. Present the data to the board of directors and secure approval in principle.

7. When the time approaches for starting a major project, the specific authorization should be reviewed and approved by the appropriate members of management. This process may require a review of the underlying data to be sure no fundamentals have changed.

8. Prepare periodic reports to indicate costs incurred to dates as well as the estimated cost to complete the project.

9. Conduct a post-completion audit to compare actual and estimated cash flow.

Establishing the Limit of the Capital Budget

The capital budgeting process begins with the setting of a maximum amount that may be spent on capital expenditures. The company's top management will set a capital budget amount, based on the following factors:

- Estimated internal cash generation.
- Availability and cost of external funds.
- Present capital structure of the company (i.e., too much debt?).
- Strategic plans.
- Stage of the business cycle.
- Short- and medium-term growth prospects of the company and the industry.
- Present and anticipated inflation rates.
- Expected rate of return on capital projects compared with the cost of capital or other hurdle rates.
- Age and condition of present plant and equipment.
- New technological developments and the need to remain competitive.
- Anticipated competitor actions.
- Relative investment in plant and equipment compared with industry or selected competitors. This can be measured by comparing the ratio of fixed assets to net worth; this ratio indicates how much of the net worth is used to finance plant and equipment versus working capital.

Supporting Information for Capital Expenditure Proposals

Every capital proposal must have sufficient supporting detail for top management to make an informed yes-or-no decision. The following information will be needed for these capital budgeting proposals:

For a *replacement* of existing equipment:

- The investment and installation cost of the new equipment.
- The salvage value of the old equipment.
- The economic life of the new equipment.
- The operating cost of the new item over its life.
- The reason for the expenditure.

For an *expansion* of facilities, the above information about new equipment is needed, plus the following information.

- The market potential for the new product.
- The probable sales quantity and value of the output.

- The marketing cost.
- The new equipment's salvage value.
- The project's rate of return (several alternative methods are discussed in this chapter).

Method of Evaluating Projects

Since most companies do not have sufficient funds to undertake all projects, some means must be found to evaluate the alternative courses of action. The evaluation of quantitative information must be blended with good judgment, and perhaps good fortune, to select the most appropriate capital proposals for completion. For those companies using analytical tools, the following three elements are essential:

1. An estimate of the expected capital outlay, as well as the amount and timing of the estimated future cash flow.
2. A technique for relating the expected future benefits to a measure of cost, such as the cost of capital.
3. A means of evaluating the risk, which includes the probability of attaining the estimated rate of return.

The more important valuation methods are the payback method and several rate of return analyses. These methods are reviewed in the following sections.

The Payback Method

The payback method calculates the time period needed to pay back a project's original investment from the project's cash flows. The payback method offers these advantages:

- It is useful when a business has minimal cash flow and must accept proposals that appear to promise a payback in a short time period.
- It is useful for appraising very risky investments where the threat of expropriation or capital wastage is high and difficult to predict.
- It is a simple computation and easy to understand.
- It is a rough indicator of profitability and, as such, allows the controller to reject obviously undesirable proposals.

However, the payback method also has the following disadvantages:

- It does not consider earnings after the initial outlay is recouped, even though the cash flow after payback is the real factor in determining profitability. Essentially, the method confuses recovery of capital with profitability.

- It places undue emphasis on liquidity, since the cash outflow must occur immediately after completion of the project in order to show a rapid payback. Thus, it has a tendency to reject highly profitable projects that do not have substantial cash flow in their early years.
- It does not recognize the gradual wastage of the asset. In other words, the time period over which the asset will be useful is of no importance, so assets that are discarded immediately after the payback has been achieved will be acceptable under this method.

The Operator's Method

The operator's method computes the return on investment, which is calculated by adding the annual earnings and depreciation, and dividing the sum by the original investment. The technique may be varied to include total required investment, including working capital. The operator's method has the following advantages:

- It is simple to understand and calculate.
- In contrast to the payback method, it gives some weight to the length of the project's life and overall profitability.
- It facilitates comparison with other companies or divisions or projects, especially when the life spans are roughly comparable.

The basic disadvantage is that it does not recognize the time value of cash flow. Competing projects have equal returns, but the distribution of earnings, plus depreciation, may vary significantly among them year by year. In addition, the total period over which equal returns are received may vary among projects.

The Accountant's Method

This technique compares earnings to the average outstanding investment rather than the initial investment or assets employed. It is based on the underlying premise that capital recovered as depreciation is therefore available for use in other projects and should not be considered a charge against the original project. The method may be varied to include the effect of income taxes and differing depreciation rates.

The accountant's method is shown in Table 14–1.

The accountant's method has two shortcomings. First, it is heavily influenced by the depreciation basis used. Double-declining balance depreciation will, of course, reduce the average investment outstanding and increase the rate of return. Second, it fails to reflect the time value of money. In the example, if the average investment were the same but income was accelerated in the early years and decelerated in later years, the rate of return would be identical. Its major advantage is that it is simpler to calculate than the discounted cash flow approach.

Table 14–1: The Accountant's Method

Year	Net Earnings Before Depreciation	Depreciation	Net Profit	Average Investment Outstanding
1	$300,000	$100,000	$200,000	$950,000
2	300,000	100,000	200,000	850,000
3	300,000	100,000	200,000	750,000
4	300,000	100,000	200,000	650,000
5	300,000	100,000	200,000	550,000
6	300,000	100,000	200,000	450,000
7	300,000	100,000	200,000	350,000
8	300,000	100,000	200,000	250,000
9	300,000	100,000	200,000	150,000
10	300,000	100,000	200,000	50,000
Total	$3,000,000	$1,000,000	$2,000,000	$5,000,000

$$\text{Rate of Return} = \frac{\text{Profit after Depreciation}}{\text{Average investment}} = \frac{\$2,000,000}{\$5,000,000} = 40\%$$

Discounted Cash Flow Methods

It is difficult to compare one project with another, particularly when the cash flow patterns vary. *When* cash is received becomes very important in that cash receipts may be invested and earn something. The discounted cash flow technique takes cash flow timing into account, and has therefore been adopted as an effective tool in ranking and judging the profitability of the investments. The technique is used in either of two methods, the internal rate of return (IRR) method and the net present value (NPV) method.

The IRR method involves the determination of that rate of return at which the sum of the stream of after-tax cash earnings, discounted yearly according to present worth, equals the cost of the project. In other words, the IRR is the maximum constant rate of return that a project could earn throughout its life and just break even.

We describe the method as follows. Assume that an investment of $1,000 is made and, over a five-year period, an annual cash flow of $250 is secured. What is the rate of return? By using present value tables, we arrive at 8%. The application of the 8% factor to the cash flow results in a present value of approximately $1,000, as seen in Table 14–2.

By trial and error, apply a range of discount factors until the proper one is found. Table 14–3 uses a 10% discount factor and a 40% discount factor, $1,000,000 investment, and $300,000 cash flow per year.

The four steps in applying the IRR method are as follows:

1. Determine the amount and year of the investment.
2. Determine, by years, the cash flow after income taxes coming from the investment.

Table 14–2: Derivation of the Present Value of a Predictable Cash Flow

Year	Annual Cash Flow (a)	Discount Factor (b)	Present Value (a) × (b)
1	$250	.926	$232
2	250	.857	214
3	250	.794	198
4	250	.735	184
5	250	.681	170
		Total present value	$998

Discounted Rate of Return:

$$10\% + (30\%(1{,}932 - 1{,}000)/(1{,}932) - 857)) = 36\%$$

3. Extend the cash flow by two discount factors to arrive at present worth.
4. Apply various discount factors until the calculation of one comes close to the original investment and interpolate to arrive at a more accurate figure.

The disadvantages of the discounted cash flow method are as follows:

- It is more complex than other methods.
- It requires more time for calculation.
- An inherent assumption is that reinvestment will be at the same rate as the calculated rate of return.

Table 14–3: Computation of the Internal Rate of Return

Years from Start of Operation	(Expenditure) or Income	10% Discount Rate		40% Discount Rate	
		Discount Factor	Discounted Amount (000s)	Discount Factor	Discounted Amount (000s)
0	$(1,000,000)		$(1,000)		
0 to 1	300,000	.953	285.9	.844	253.2
2	300,000	.866	259.8	.603	180.9
3	300,000	.788	236.4	.431	129.3
4	300,000	.716	214.8	.308	92.4
5	300,000	.651	195.3	.220	66.0
6	300,000	.592	177.6	.157	47.1
7	300,000	.538	161.4	.112	33.6
8	300,000	.489	146.7	.080	24.0
9	300,000	.444	133.2	.060	18.0
10	300,000	.404	121.2	.041	12.3
Total Cash Flow	$3,000,000				
		Discounted Cash Flow	$1,932.3		$856.8

The advantages of the method are as follows:

- Proper weighting is given to the time value of investments and cash flow.
- The use of cash flow minimizes the effect of arbitrary decisions about capital versus expenses, depreciation, and so on.
- It is comparable to the cost-of-capital concept.
- It allows the financial analyst to compare alternative projects.

The net present value (NPV) method of evaluating capital expenditures also considers the time value of money. The difference between NPV and IRR is that a preselected rate is used—the rate that the company considers the minimum rate of return for taking the risk of the capital investment. If the sum of the present values of the stream of cash exceeds the cost of the proposed investment, then the rate of return exceeds the target and meets the earnings requirements. If the NPV is negative, then the proposal fails to meet the required earnings rate, and the project should be rejected. An NPV calculation is shown in Table 14–4.

When a discounted cash flow method is used to evaluate investments in another country, the significant test is the cash flow to the parent, not to the foreign subsidiary. Among the impediments to cash flow to the parent, which must be considered in the decision, are such items as currency restrictions, fluctuations in the foreign exchange rate, political risk, inflation, and withholding taxes.

Hurdle Rates

A hurdle rate is the minimum rate of return that a capital project should earn if it is to be judged acceptable. It is not used for special projects, such as those required by law, no matter what the return on investment (if any) may be. Examples are pollution abatement or safety devices. Because of these special projects, a factor is commonly added to the hurdle rate, resulting in a slightly higher hurdle rate.

Table 14–4: Net Present Value Calculation

Year	Estimated Cash Flow	Discounting Factor at 22%	Present Worth
0	$800,000	1.000	$(800,000)
1	370,000	.820	303,400
2	350,000	.672	235,200
3	301,000	.551	165,851
4	215,000	.451	96,965
5	170,000	.370	62,900
6	110,000	.303	33,330
7	40,000	.249	9,960
8	10,000	.204	2,040
		Present value at 22% factor	$909,646

Some companies with multiple divisions use different hurdle rates for each line of business. This practice can be justified by the fact that among those businesses different business risks exist (e.g., threat of expropriation), rates of return expectations are markedly different, and differing business strategies may apply and require different hurdle rates.

The basis of the hurdle rate is the cost of capital. This is the rate that long-term debt holders and shareholders require in order to be persuaded to furnish the required capital. Thus, assume that:

1. A company capital structure target objective is $500,000 composed of 25% debt and 75% equity.

2. In the current market environment long-term bond holders require a 10% return (6% to the company after income taxes); a 17% return on equity is the going earnings rate.

The cost of capital would be calculated as shown in Table 14–5.

Based on the above analysis, if the company is to attract the capital required to stay in business, then, on average, all its capital investments should earn at least 14% after taxes. If this does not occur, then the shareholder return would be diluted.

Project Risk Analysis

It would be helpful for the decision maker to know not only the expected rate of return, but also the probability of receiving that rate, as well as the range of returns possible, together with the probability of each occurring. If there is a strong probability of cash flows dropping below the expected rate, then the board of directors should be presented with this information along with the rest of the capital budget request.

Sensitivity analysis is a mathematical technique wherein changes may be made in any of the input factors, and the consequent movement in the result observed. Those making estimates of return on investments know that the answers depend greatly on the assumptions. It is important to test how much an

Table 14–5: Cost of Capital Calculation

Structure	Capitalization	Required Rate of Return After Taxes	Required Amount of Return
Senior debt	$125,000,000	6.0%	$7,500,000
Common stock	375,000,000	17.0%	63,750,000
Total	$500,000,000		$71,250,000

$$\text{Cost of capital} = \frac{\$71,250,000}{500,000,000} = 14\%$$

error in an assumption can sway the result. Such knowledge can permit analysts to concentrate their attention on the more important variables. The technique can provide considerable insight into a capital budget proposal.

Investments are made in capital assets with the expectation that the return will be sufficiently high not only to recoup the cost but also to pass the hurdle rate for such an expenditure. But the nature of investment is changing, as are the attendant risks, in the new manufacturing environment. This new environment has the following characteristics:

- While automation is viewed as a primary source of additional income, this often is preceded by redesigning and simplifying the manufacturing process, before automation is considered. Many companies have achieved significant savings simply by rearranging the plant floor, establishing more streamlined procedures, and eliminating the non-value-added functions such as material storage and handling. After this rearrangement is accomplished, then automation might be considered.

- Investments are becoming more significant in themselves. While a stand alone grinder may cost $1 million, an automated factory can cost $50 million or $100 million. Moreover, much of the cost may be in engineering, software development, and implementation.

- The equipment involved often is increasingly complex, and the benefits can be more indirect and perhaps more intangible. If there are basic improvements in quality, in delivery schedules, and in customer satisfaction, then methods can be found to measure these benefits.

Because of the high investment cost, the period required to earn the desired return on investment is longer. This longer-term horizon, together with the intangibles to be considered and the greater uncertainty, require the controller to be more discerning in making the analysis. Usually the indirect savings and intangible benefits need to be recognized and included in the investment analysis.

Inflation

Those involved in analyzing capital investments may ponder how inflation should be handled. In the capital budgeting process, these questions should be considered:

- *Should adjustments be made for inflation in the cash flows?* Many companies do not adjust for inflation, because it is difficult to get a reliable rate estimate. Also, for the same reason, only one inflation rate is used for the term of the analysis, rather than differing rates for different years.

- *Should specific inflation rates be used on different cost factors (e.g., labor and materials)?* Specific price indices exist for some materials, or groups of materials, and for wages in particular industries.

- *Should the hurdle rate be adjusted for inflation?* If the cash flows in the analysis are adjusted for inflation, then the hurdle rate should also be adjusted.

Ranking Capital Projects

When the reviewed have been completed, one must rank the projects in some order of priority, because there are usually many more proposed capital expenditures than would normally be undertaken within the bounds of financial capability. A practical grouping that would be understood by management and operation executives alike is as follows:

- *Absolutely essential:*
  — Government-required installations, such as safety or pollution abatement devices.
  — Replacement of inoperable facilities without which the company could not remain in business.
- *Highly necessary:*
  — Equipment that contributes to increased product quality.
  — Equipment that reduces the cost of producing the product.
- *Economically justified projects:*
  — New facilities, robotics, and equipment needed to produce new or additional products.
- *All other:*
  — Projects that cannot be justified with an economic analysis, such as donations, parking lot lighting, and cafeteria facilities.

Projects based on economic return can be ranked by rate of return. The information is then presented to the board of directors for approval. When presented, the information should include the priority, rate of return, total cost, reasons for, benefits of, and risks attached to, each project. On a separate Gantt chart, the timing of all expenditures for all projects should be highlighted.

POSTPROJECT APPRAISALS

It happens in many companies that adequate analyses are made about the apparent economic desirability of a project, and acquisition costs are held within estimate, yet the project does not achieve the estimated rate of return. Some managements are unaware of such a condition because there is no follow-up on performance. For large projects, after a reasonable time period beyond completion, when all the "bugs" are worked out, a post-audit review should be made.

The review might be taken by the internal audit group, or perhaps a management team consisting of line managers involved with the project and some members of the controller's staff. The objective is to compare actual earnings or savings with the plan, ascertain why the deviation occurred, and what steps should be taken to improve capital investment planning and control. The scope might range from the strategic planning aspects through the detailed control procedures.

The following advantages may accrue from an intelligently planned post-audit.

- It may detect weaknesses in strategic planning that lead to poor decisions, which in turn impact the capital budgeting procedures.
- Environmental factors that influence the business but were not recognized might be detected.
- Experience can focus attention on basic weaknesses in overall plans, policies, or procedures as related to capital expenditures.
- Strengths or weaknesses in individual performance can be detected and corrected—such as a tendency to have overly optimistic estimates.
- It may enable corrections in other current projects prior to completion of commitments or expenditures.

The post-audit report commentary can focus on estimated cash flow through the date of the audit compared with actual cash flow, old versus new breakeven points, and planned versus actual operating expenses.

OTHER ASPECTS OF FIXED ASSETS

The largest issue surrounding property, plant, and equipment, covered earlier in this chapter, is the set of policies and procedures used to acquire it (i.e., capital budgeting). However, there are a host of other smaller issues that are touched upon in this section.

- *Working capital*—In many instances, a capital expenditure also requires an increase in working capital to pay for additional inventories and accounts receivable. These amounts should always be factored into the capital budgeting investment amount as well as the rate of return calculation.
- *Lease versus buy*—Use the NPV method to compare a lease acquisition against a buy acquisition. If the marginal (net of taxes) cost of funds to purchase the asset is known, the same discount rate can be applied to the stream of lease payments to arrive at the net present value. Usually the alternative with the lower NPV and the higher savings should be the one selected.
- *Funds for plant replacement and expansion*—Most companies do not establish funds for property expansion or replacement but use the general fund instead. However, such funds can be created, and some exponents believe

that public utilities and wasting asset industries, such as mining, should establish such funds.

- *Gain or loss on sale of assets*—The gain or loss on sale of a fixed asset should be charged off as incurred. It is essentially a correction of prior profits. The usual practice is to carry such gain or loss in the nonoperating section of the income statement.

- *Fully depreciated assets*—If fully depreciated assets are no longer in use, then their cost and related depreciation should be removed from the accounting ledger.

- *Obsolescence*—Equipment is likely to become obsolete before it is fully depreciated. This condition can occur because the product manufactured may be replaced by another, so that the need no longer exists for the facility. Or a new type of asset, one that produces at a much lower cost, may be developed to supersede present manufacturing equipment. In practice, the normal obsolescence will be combined with depreciation in both the provision and the reserve. A highly abnormal and significant obsolescence loss probably should be segregated in the income and expense statement.

- *Depreciation accounting*—Depreciation spreads the cost of an asset over its useful life. The determination of an asset's useful life is largely an engineering problem. However, the ramifications and implications of depreciation policy—such matters as treatment of obsolescence, accounting for retirements, determination of allocation methods, and selection of individual or group rates—are best understood by the controller.

- *Valuation of fixed assets*—Fixed assets are valued at cost, less the applicable allowance for depreciation, depletion, or amortization. Also, replacement cost information for production capacity is required to be included in the annual report form 10-K by the SEC.

- *Idle equipment*—The controller should inform management about losses from idle equipment and place responsibility in an attempt to eliminate the avoidable and unnecessary costs. This reporting may encourage the disposal of any permanently excess equipment, giving consideration to the medium-term plans. Losses resulting from unused plant facilities can include depreciation, property taxes, insurance, and utilities. There are three causes of idle time:

  1. *Those controllable by the production staff*—Some causes are poor planning; lack of materials, tools, or power; machine breakdowns; or improper supervision.

  2. *Those resulting from administrative decisions*—Management may decide to build additional capacity, which may lead to idle facilities in the short term, until demand builds to match the capacity.

  3. *Those arising from economic causes*—These causes are beyond the control of the company, such as seasonal demand or excess capacity in the industry.

Internal Control Requirements

There are a small number of control issues surrounding equipment; the controller should implement the following list:

- Identify all fixed assets, possibly by affixing a serial number to the item. Bar codes are sometimes used for easy scanning during fixed asset physical inventories.
- Transfer equipment between departments only with the written approval of the department head responsible for the physical security of the property.

This is necessary in order to track locations for insurance purposes and to properly charge depreciation to the correct departments.

- Prevent equipment from leaving the plant without a property pass signed by the proper authority.
- Perform a physical inventory on all fixed assets.
- Maintain detailed records on each piece of equipment, as described below.
- Review purchase requisitions to ensure that piecemeal acquisitions are not made simply to avoid obtaining approval of higher authority.
- Review retirements of fixed assets to see if the equipment can be used by other departments before scrapping or selling.
- Secure bids on sizable transactions.
- Provide for proper insurance coverage during construction of equipment as well as when it is completed.
- Review expenses to ensure that capital expenditures are not treated as expenses, thereby avoiding budget overruns.
- Track the following items for capital projects:
  — Amount authorized.
  — Actual commitments to date.
  — Actual costs incurred to date.
  — Estimated cost to complete.
  — Indicated total cost.
  — Indicated overrun or underrun compared to the project budget.

Plant and Equipment Records

Adequate plant and equipment records are a necessary adjunct to effective control. They provide a convenient source of information for planning and control purposes as well as for insurance and tax (e.g., personal and real property tax) purposes.

Detailed records must be designed to suit the individual needs of the company. Property records should include the following information:

- Name of the asset
- Type of equipment
- Control number
- Description
- Size
- Model
- Style
- Serial number
- Motor number
- Purchased new or used
- Date purchased
- Vendor name
- Invoice number
- Purchase order number
- Location (e.g., plant, building, floor, and department)
- Account number
- Transfer information
- Original cost information (e.g., purchase cost, freight, tax, installation, material, labor, and overhead)
- Additions to
- Date retired
- Sold to
- Scrapped
- Cost recovered
- Depreciation information (e.g., estimated life, annual depreciation, basis)

Plant and Equipment in Relation to Taxes

Many local communities and states levy real and personal property taxes or enforce payment of franchise taxes based on property values. Maintenance of adequate records can be a means of satisfying the taxing authorities on problems of valuation.

Plant and property values, through the resulting depreciation charges, are important from the federal income tax viewpoint. As mentioned previously, the depreciation allowance for tax purposes, if significantly different from depreciation for book purposes, can distort the profit before taxes and the tax charge. Where the estimate of useful life and the base for tax and book purposes are not significantly different, an effort should be made to bring the two in line. It may save the maintenance of a separate set of records. In any event, the burden of proof about the correctness of the depreciation claimed is placed on the tax-payer, who must keep the necessary records and other data to support the claim.

15

LIABILITIES

It has been said that the management, or planning and control, of a company's assets rests largely in the hands of the operating executives but that management of the liabilities and equity is primarily the responsibility of the financial executives. To an extent, this is true—the controller must closely plan and monitor liabilities to foresee changes in the company's liabilities.

This chapter discusses the practical considerations regarding liability planning, measurement, and control, as well as miscellaneous issues related to liabilities, such as bond ratings, debt capacity, debt capacity, and leverage.

DEFINITIONS

Liabilities are the economic obligations of a company that are recognized and measured in conformity with generally accepted accounting principles. However, there are many types of liabilities. The more common ones are:

- *Current liabilities.* Liabilities classified as current are those due to be paid within the operating cycle (usually one year). The importance of the proper segregation of current liabilities from other liabilities lies in the role played by various financial ratios, such as the current ratio, when funds are borrowed.
  - *Notes payable*—These represent the obligations of the company under legal instruments in which there exists an explicit promise to pay a specified amount at a specified time.

— *Accounts payable*—These are largely trade accounts payable and represent the obligations of the firm to its suppliers. Since these liabilities are recorded at the time the title to the goods passes or the services are received, the controller should be satisfied that clean cutoffs on the obligations exist.

— *Accrued expenses*—When an obligation exists by reason of the benefits having been received but that obligation is not yet due and payable, it normally will be recorded as an accrued expense. Included as such expenses would be accruals for wages, salaries, commissions, rents, royalties, pension costs, and income and other taxes.

• *Long-term liabilities*—Liabilities classified as long-term represent those obligations due in more than one year or those to be paid out of noncurrent assets.

— *Long-term leases*—Under present-day accounting, if at its inception a lease meets one or more of the following criteria, it will be classified as a capital lease by the lessee and placed on the balance sheet. Otherwise, it would be treated as an operating lease. The criteria for capitalization include:

The lease transfers ownership of the property to the lessee by the end of the lease term.

The lease contains a bargain purchase option.

The lease term is equal to 75% or more of the estimated economic life of the leased property.

The present value at the beginning of the lease term of the minimum lease payments equals or exceeds 90% of the fair market value of the property over the related investment tax credit retained or expected to be used by the lessor.

— *Bonds*—Bonds are essentially long-term corporate notes issued under a formal legal procedure and secured either by the pledge of specific properties, revenues, or the general credit of the issuer. Bonds differ from individual notes in that each represents a fractional interest of participation in a group contract, usually with a trustee acting as an intermediary. The terms of the control are set forth in the trust indenture.

— *Other long-term obligations*—Depending on circumstances, there may exist other obligations and like items that are classified either as long-term obligations or items carried in the long-term section of the balance sheet above the shareholders' equity. These may include such items as deferred income taxes, deferred compensation, accrued product warranties, negative goodwill, and minority interests.

OBJECTIVES

The purpose of liability management is to assure that the company has enough cash to meet funding requirements for any purpose significant to the long-term financial health of the company. Thus, it is not merely to avoid insolvency or bankruptcy. From the standpoint of the controller, the objectives of liability management are as follows:

- Recording and disclosing the company's financial obligations in accordance with generally accepted accounting principles.
- Reporting corporate liabilities in the proper form, as required by indentures and credit agreements.
- Maintaining a sound financial structure of debt in proportion to equity through effective planning and control.
- Securing necessary borrowed funds in a timely manner and at a cost that is competitive.
- Creating and maintaining controls that restrict commitments within well-defined limits so that they do not result in excessive liabilities.
- Enabling the company to be so well-regarded in the financial marketplace that its stock will command an acceptable price-earnings ratio, and that the stock will reflect a gradual increase in earnings per share and consequent long-term appreciation for the benefit of the owners.
- Permitting the company to maintain a prudent dividend policy.

Many of the above objectives of liability management are interrelated.

CONTROLS

Because of the differing nature of the various types of liabilities, it is practical in the accounting, planning, and control activities to treat each group separately. Here are some suggestions for what the controller can do to manage liabilities.

Current Liabilities

The controller can plan the liabilities by period. This is accomplished after the various asset levels (cash, receivables, inventories, plant, and equipment) are planned and when the operational plans (sales, manufacturing expenses, direct labor, direct material, selling expenses, and G&A) are completed. It is helpful to group the current liabilities according to the categories to be identified in the Statement of Estimated Financial Position, such as accounts payable, accrued salaries and wages, accrued expenses, accrued income taxes, and notes payable.

The controller can also test the plan for compliance with credit agreements or other internally developed standards such as the current ratio, inventory turns, net working capital, and the industry average or competitor performance.

As well, the controller can analyze each line item for ways to reduce the obligation. For example, he or she can use JIT inventory methods to reduce accounts payable or notes payable. Other ways to reduce inventory are to arrange with suppliers to receive goods on consignment or special payment terms. And the controller can monitor the period balances for any unfavorable developing trends, and take appropriate action. Finally, the controller can issue the appropriate control or informational reports, such as to the supervisor of accounts payable, the board of directors, or creditors. This might include updating the projected debt status to the year-end, summarizing contingent liabilities, or issuing information about a payables aging, unfunded pension plan liabilities, foreign currency exposure, or outstanding obligations on leases.

Long-Term Liabilities

The controller can plan the long-term debt, by appropriate category, for the annual plan. He or she can test the plan against credit agreement requirements, or standards for debt capacity, including that which might exist under the least favorable business conditions which are likely to prevail in the planning period. Moreover, he or she can monitor actual performance during the plan term for unfavorable developments, as well as report on the financial condition and outlook to the appropriate interests (e.g., bankers, bondholders, or the board of directors).

All Indebtedness Items

Here the controller can review the accounting to ascertain that GAAPs are followed. He or she can also check the internal controls to assure that the system is functioning properly. It would also be wise to keep reasonably informed about the status and probable trend of the debt market, and any new debt instruments, both short- and long-term. If appropriate, this includes foreign markets.

Also, routines must be instituted to see that all liabilities are properly certified or approved by designated authority. The proper comparison of receiving reports, purchase orders, and invoices by those handling the detail disbursement procedure eliminates many duties by the officers; but the liabilities not covered by these channels must have the necessary review. The controller, for example, must approve the payrolls before payment. The chief purchasing agent must approve invoices for services, because no receiving report is issued. Certain special transactions may require the approval of the president. Invoices for parts or services should be checked against the voucher file for duplicate payments. In summary, the controller should consider the system of recording payables somewhat independently of the disbursements procedure to give added assurance that the necessary controls exist.

Additionally, the controller should be sensitive to the impact of new debt issues on the holders of existing debt.

CREDIT AGREEMENT PROVISIONS

Indentures or credit agreements are usually tailored to fit the desires of both the lender and the borrower. However, a great many standard provisions apply to most loan agreements. The controller should be aware of the provisions that relate to indebtedness limits and certain uses of cash. The following list of provisions includes examples of typical limitations:

- *Current ratio requirement*—The company covenants that it will not permit current assets at any time to be less than, for example, 150% of the current liabilities.
- *Dividend limitation*—The company covenants that it will not pay or declare any dividends over a set amount. However, payments to preferred stock-holders are usually allowed.
- *Debt*—The company and its subsidiaries will not incur or guarantee additional debt. Also, a ratio such as tangible assets to debt is used to establish a maximum allowable debt amount. This ratio is highly variable by situation, but a ratio of 2 to 1 is acceptable in most instances. The ratio should also be calculated on a consolidated basis, since companies may shift debt among subsidiaries in order to make some subsidiaries theoretically debt-free, and therefore capable of acquiring more debt.
- *Subordinated debt*—the company covenants that it will not require additional debt that will act to lessen the claim of the current creditors on the company's existing assets.
- *Minimum working capital*—The company covenants that it will maintain a fixed amount of working capital to cover the firm's operating cash needs.
- *Negative covenants*—The company will not undertake to acquire additional debt without the permission of specific creditors or those creditors holding a minimum percentage of the company's debt.
- *Sale, lease, etc.*—The company will not sell or transfer any assets other than obsolete or worn-out property, provided the value of such transferred or sold items does not exceed a specific ratio, such as assets to equity. This clause is used to keep companies from liquidating those assets that are used as collateral on loans. Obviously, inventories are not included in this provision.

MEASUREMENTS

Current and planned liability levels should be tested for acceptability. The levels can be tested based on legal requirements, such as those in bank lending agreements or in bond indentures, as was discussed earlier in this chapter. Also, key ratios should be examined for reasonableness and compared to industry averages, or internal company benchmarks. Dun & Bradstreet, for example, periodically issues selected ratios on each industry, showing the median and upper and lower quartile for certain operating ratios and financial conditions. The controller can measure the company's ratios against these industry ratios, against the performance of selected competitors, or against standards used by commercial bankers or financial analysts. If these tests reveal unacceptable conditions, then corrective action should be taken.

Ratios used to measure the acceptability of current liabilities include the following:

- *Current ratio*—This is calculated by dividing the current assets by the current liabilities. It measures the protection the creditors have, even if the current assets prove to be less valuable than anticipated. A ratio of 2 to 1 is acceptable. With improved receivables and inventory control, even a ratio of 1.5 to 1 may be acceptable.
- *Quick ratio*—This measures the relationship of highly liquid assets (e.g., cash investments and accounts receivable) to current liabilities. This ratio, also known as the liquidity ratio or acid test, is an indicator of what very liquid assets are available to meet the demands of the short-term creditors.
- *Minimum net working capital*—This is an absolute amount; the difference between current assets and current liabilities. Some loan and credit agreements require a minimum amount of working capital at all times. The net amount indicates the extent to which the current assets could shrink and yet be sufficient to meet the current liabilities.
- *Current debt to net worth*—To the extent that assets are financed by the owners, there is more protection (i.e., more assets) for the creditors. A low current debt to net worth ratio is some measure of how the owners are supplying more relative funds.
- *Current debt to inventory*—A high ratio of current debt as related to inventory would suggest that goods are purchased, processed, and sold without payments being made to suppliers. Depending on the relative ratio, as compared to industry and trade practice, a high relationship would indicate inadequate financing.
- *Number of days' payables on hand (payables turnover)*—The number of days' payables on hand is determined by dividing the accounts payable balance by the amount of purchases, and multiplying by the days in the period. An unexpectedly low days' payables number indicates that early payment discounts are being taken.

DEBT CAPACITY

The goal of the financial executive should be to arrange the financing so that the owners of the business will receive the maximum economic benefit over the longer run, by increasing the share price and the level of dividends.

It can be demonstrated over a period of time, assuming normal profitability and the deductibility of interest expense for tax purposes, that prudent borrowing will increase the return to the shareholder. Given this potential for gain, there exists a powerful deterrent that discourages using long-term debt; that deterrent is the risk associated with servicing the debt. Debts and interest payments must be paid when due regardless of the company's financial condition, possibly resulting in unwelcome restraints or even the loss of the enterprise. These fixed payments also reduce a company's options to match the prices of competitors during price wars, resulting in reduced sales, lower margins, and possible losses.

With the deterrents to excessive debt loads being so severe, how is the controller to know what debt level is optimal? Some guidance in arriving at a decision may come from:

> *Institutional lenders*—Bankers negotiate long-term loans at rather frequent intervals in contrast to the financial officer of an industrial enterprise. Consequently, they will be more familiar with the terms of recent agreements. Presumably, they are also conservative and will tend to err in the conservative direction. They should be able to judge if proposed standards will be acceptable in the marketplace.
>
> *Action of competitors*—The financial statements and loan agreements of public companies are available. From such public information the controller can derive ranges of debt levels for comparison purposes.
>
> *Analysis of past practice*—Historical analysis of debt and income behavior in the company in times of adversity and under normal conditions may provide some guidance.

Conventionally, there are two types of standards by which to judge long-term debt capacity; they are a capitalization standard and an earnings coverage standard. In arriving at a debt policy for a company, each should be considered and interrelated. In working with internally generated data, the controller can make refinements ordinarily not possible with public data of other companies.

A widely used standard, often employed as a constraint in credit agreements, is the *long-term debt to equity ratio*. Thus long-term debt should not be more than, say, 25% of equity capital. It can also be expressed as a percent of total capitalization. In using such a standard, several determinations should be calculated, showing the impact, for example, of a 20% debt ratio versus a 25% debt ratio to judge the risk involved. Then, too, recognition must be given to the often wide variation between the principal of the debt and the annual debt service charge of interest and debt repayment. While the ratio of debt to equity may be the same for many years, the debt repayment burden may be substantially different if it is paid off in five years instead of thirty years.

The *earnings coverage standard* measures the total annual amount required for debt service to the net earnings available for serving the debt. By relating the annual cash outflow for debt service to the net earnings available for this purpose, it seeks to ensure that even in times of adversity there are sufficient funds to meet the obligation. Obviously, the greater the probability of change in cash flow, the higher the desired times–coverage ratio. The observed times coverages vary greatly by industry and by company. Typical well-financed companies may have a coverage of 15 times or more.

Debt coverage ratios should be calculated for a variety of economic circumstances, assuming both the worst possible cash flow and the most probable cash flow. The final analysis, debt policy, or appropriate capital structure can be determined only by an examination of the factors in the company and in the industry that influence the ability to repay debt; it is a matter of judgment and foresight regarding likely conditions.

BOND RATINGS

There is a significant difference in interest cost to a company, depending on the quality rating assigned to debt securities by the three rating agencies, and this is an important consideration in selecting aggregate debt limits. The three debt rating agencies—Standard and Poor's Corporation, Moody's Investor Service, and Fitch Investor's Service—assign ratings that characterize judgment about the quality or inherent risk in any given security. The rating will depend, among many other factors, on the debt coverage relationship.

The symbols Moody's uses for the highest four ratings are as follows:

Aaa   The best quality; smallest degree of investment risk.

Aa   Judged to be of high quality by all standards.

A   Higher medium grade obligations, with some elements that may be present to suggest a susceptibility to impairment at some time in the future.

Baa   Lower medium grade. Lacks outstanding investment characteristics and, in fact, has speculative characteristics as well.

The objective of many well-financed companies is to secure at least an Aa rating for its bonds. Presentations to secure bond ratings should be carefully prepared, because poor ratings are not easily overcome.

In determining a debt rating, the agencies need adequate financial data, such as the following:

- Consolidated balance sheets. Perhaps five years historical and five years projected should be presented.
- Consolidated statements of income and retained earnings for five historical years and five projected years. Included would be dividends paid and per share data, including:
  — Earnings
  — Dividends
  — Book value
- Consolidated statements of cash flows. Again five historical years and five prospective years should be presented.
- Product group statements for historical and projected data regarding sales, as well as the operating margin in dollars and as a percentage.

Table 15–1: Favorable Leverage

	100% Common Stock	Common Stock, plus Bond Capitalization
Capitalization		
Bonds (11%)		$20,000,000
Common stock	$100,000,000	$100,000,000
Total	$100,000,000	$120,000,000
Number of common shares	4,000,000	4,000,000
Income		
Income before taxes and interest	$37,000,000	$44,400,000
Bond interest	═══	2,200,000
Income before taxes	$37,000,000	$42,200,000
Income taxes (46%)	17,020,000	19,412,000
Net income for common	$19,980,000	22,788,000
Return on equity	19.98%	22.79%
Earnings per common share	$5.00	$5.70
Dividend (40% payout)	$2.00	$2.28

LEVERAGE

In considering capital structure, the controller must study the impact of leverage. Leverage involves financing an enterprise with senior obligations to increase the rate of return on the common equity. It is also known as "trading on the equity." An application of leverage is shown in Table 15–1. Assume that the management has been earning, before income taxes, 37% on capitalization; that it believes it can continue to achieve this same return; and that the company can borrow at an 11% rate. If it borrows 20% of equity and continues the rate of return on assets,

Table 15–2: Unfavorable Leverage

	100% Common Stock	Common Stock, plus Bond Capitalization
Capitalization		
Bonds (11%)		$20,000,000
Common stock	$100,000,000	$100,000,000
Total	$100,000,000	$120,000,000
Number of common share	4,000,000	4,000,000
Income		
Income before interest and taxes	$10,000,000	$10,000,000
Bond interest	═══	2,200,000
Income before taxes	$10,000,000	7,800,000
Income taxes (46%)	4,600,000	3,588,000
Net income for common	4,400,000	4,212,000
Return on equity	4.4%	4.21%
Earnings per common share	$1.10	$1.05
Dividend (40% payout)	$.44	$.42

the earnings per share, with favorable leverage, increases from $5.00 to $5.70 and the return on equity rises from 19.98% to 22.79%.

However, if under unfavorable leverage conditions management has been too optimistic and the earnings rate has been less than the bond interest rate, the results could be unsatisfactory—as illustrated in Table 15–2. Here, the rate of return on capitalization was less than the bond interest rate.

From an investor standpoint, in good times the leverage increases the earnings per share and the price of stock. However, in adverse times, the reverse condition exists, and the stock of a leveraged company becomes less attractive.

16

EQUITY

Shareholder's equity is the interest of the shareholders, or owners, in the assets of a company, and at any time is the cumulative net result of past transactions affecting this segment of the balance sheet. This equity is created initially by the owners' investment in the company, and may be increased from time to time by additional investments, as well as by net earnings. It can be reduced by distributions of the equity to the owners (usually as dividends). Further, it may also decrease if the enterprise in unprofitable. When all liabilities are satisfied the remainder belongs to the owners.

Basic accounting concepts govern the accounting for shareholders' equity as a whole, for each class of shareholder, and for the various segments of the equity interest, such as capital stock, contributed capital, or earned capital. This chapter does not deal with the accounting niceties regarding the ownership interest. It is assumed that the controller is well grounded in such proper treatment, or will become so. Our concerns relate to the shareholders' interest in total and not to any special accounting segments. Consequently, this chapter is restricted to such topics as the cost of capital, dividend policy, equity planning, and stock records.

ROLE OF THE CONTROLLER

The controller must properly account for the shareholders' equity, providing those analyses and recommending those actions that are consistent with enhancing shareholder value over the long term. Specifically, the following tasks must be performed:

- Accounting for shareholders' equity in accordance with GAAP. This includes the historical analysis of the source of the equity and the segregation of the cumulative equity by class of shareholder.
- Preparing the appropriate reports on the status and changes in shareholders' equity as required by agencies of the U.S. government, management, credit agreements, and other contracts.
- Making the necessary analyses to assist in planning the most appropriate source (e.g., debt or equity) of new funds, and the timing and amount required of each.
- Maintaining in proper and economical form the capital stock records of the individual shareholders, with the related meaningful analysis. In a larger firm, a separate department or outside service might perform these functions.
- Making the required analysis periodically on such matters as:
  - Dividend policy
  - Dividend reinvestment plans
  - Stock splits/dividends
  - Stock repurchases
  - Capital structure
  - Trend and outlook for earnings per share
  - Cost of capital for the company and industry
  - Tax legislation as it affects shareholders
  - Price action of the market price of the stock, and influences on it

EQUITY FORMULAS AND DEBT RATIOS

The rate of growth of equity is germane to establishing target rates of return on equity, selecting sources of capital, and monitoring dividend policy. The annual growth in shareholders' equity from internal sources may be defined as the rate of return earned on such equity multiplied by the percentage of the earnings retained. It is represented by the following formula:

$$G = R(1-P)$$

where

G = annual percentage rate of growth in shareholders' equity

R = annual net rate of return on shareholders' equity

P = the payout ratio or share of earnings annually paid out as dividends

As an example, if a company can earn 23% each year on its equity, and the payout ratio is 40%, the shareholders' equity will grow at 14% per year, calculated as follows:

$$G = .23(1-.40)$$
$$= .23(.60)$$
$$= .14, \text{ or } 14\%$$

Another facet of the shareholder's equity role is the relationship of the return on equity (ROE) to the rate of annual increase in earnings per share (EPS). Basically, the rate of return on shareholders' equity, when adjusted for the payout ratio, produces the rate of growth per year in EPS. It is expressed in the following formula:

growth per year in EPS = ROE × retention ratio

This relationship is illustrated in Table 16–1. Thus, assuming a constant return on equity of 20% and a constant dividend payout ratio of 25%, the EPS growth rate is calculated by means of the same formula as for the growth of shareholders' equity:

$$G = R(1-P)$$
$$= .20(1-.25)$$
$$= .20(.75)$$
$$= .15. \text{ or } 15\%$$

For illustrative purposes to management or the board of directors, these same factors can be translated into book value per share, earnings per share, and dividends per share, as shown in Table 16–2. In such terms, explanations about the shareholders' interest often are more easily understood.

Prudent financial planning will consider the impact of decisions on earnings per share. Management is concerned with the growth in EPS since one of its tasks is to enhance shareholder value. Continual increases in EPS each year will raise shareholder value through its recognition in a higher P/E ratio and usually a

Table 16–1: Constant Return on Equity vs. EPS Growth

Year	Beginning Shareholder's Equity	Net Income	Dividends Paid	Ending Shareholders' Equity	Rate of Return on Beginning Equity (%)	Dividend Payout %	EPS	Growth in EPS (%)
19X6	$250,000	$50,000	$12,500	$287,500	20	25	$5.00	—
19X7	287,500	57,500	14,375	330,625	20	25	5.75	15
19X8	330,625	66,125	16,531	380,219	20	25	6.61	15
19X9	380,219	76,044	19,011	437,252	20	25	7.60	15
20X1	437,252	87,450	21,863	502,839	20	25	8.75	15
20X2	502,839	100,568	25,142	578,265	20	25	10.06	15
20X3	578,265	115,653	28,913	665,005	20	25	11.57	15

Table 16–2: Per Share—Return on Equity vs. Growth Rate

Year	1	2	3	4	5	6	7
Book value, beginning	$25.00	$28.75	$33.06	$38.02	$43.72	$50.28	$57.82
Earnings[a]	5.00	5.75	6.61	7.60	8.75	10.06	11.57
Dividends[b]	1.25	1.44	1.65	1.90	2.19	2.52	2.89
Retained earnings	3.75	4.31	4.96	5.70	6.56	7.54	8.68
Book value, ending	$28.75	$33.06	$38.02	$43.72	$50.28	$57.82	$66.50
Increase in EPS:							
Amount		$ .75	.86	.99	1.15	1.31	1.51
Percent		15	15	15	15	15	15
Increase in dividends:							
Amount		$ .19	.21	.25	.29	.33	.37
Percent		15	15	15	15	15	15

[a] At 20% on beginning equity
[b] At 25% on payout ratio

rising dividend payment. Moreover, the growth in EPS is one of the measures of management as viewed by the financial community, including financial analysts. Given the importance of EPS, the controller should keep in mind that the earnings per share will increase as a result of any of these actions:

- The plow-back of some shares of earnings, even as long as the rate of return on equity remains just constant—as illustrated by the calculations in Tables 16–1 and 16–2. (A growth in EPS does not necessarily mean that the management is achieving a higher rate of return on equity.)
- An actual increase in the rate of return earned on shareholders' equity.
- Repurchase of common shares as long as the earned rate of return on equity does not decrease.
- Use of prudent borrowing (i.e., financial leverage).
- Acquisition of a company whose stock is selling at a lower P/E than the acquiring company:
- Sales of shares of common stock above the book value of existing shares, assuming that the return on equity is maintained.

Financial planning should keep all the alternatives in mind. However, of all of these actions, the one that is most likely to be sustainable and translatable into a healthy growth in EPS is a constant, or increasing, return on shareholders' equity.

The management of shareholders' equity must always keep debt relationships in mind when planning future financing, whether the financing be debt or equity. There are two principal ratios used by rating agencies and the financial marketplace in judging the debt worthiness (or value of the equity) of an enterprise:

1. *Ratio of long-term debt to equity*—This compares the investment of the long-term creditors to that of the owners. Generally, a ratio of greater than 1

is an indication of excessive debt. However, the ratio should be compared to others in the industry. The ratio is calculated as follows:

$$\text{long-term debt to equity} = \frac{\text{long-term debt}}{\text{shareholders' equity}}$$

2. *Ratio of long-term debt to total capitalization*—A ratio of greater than 50% reflects excessive use of debt. Again, comparisons should be made with industry averages. The ratio is calculated as follows:

$$\text{long-term debt to total capitalization} = \frac{\text{long-term debt}}{\text{total capitalization (including long-term debt)}}$$

COST OF CAPITAL

Investors are willing to place funds at risk in the expectation of recovering such capital and making a reasonable return. Some individuals or companies might prefer to invest in an almost risk-free security, such as U.S. government bonds; others will assume greater risks but will expect a correspondingly higher rate of return. Cost of capital, then, may be defined as that rate of return that must be paid to investors to induce them to supply the necessary funds. Thus, the cost of a bond would be represented by the interest payments plus the recovery of the bond purchase price, perhaps plus some capital gains. The cost of common shares issued would be represented by the dividend paid plus the appreciation in the value of the stock. Capital will flow to those markets where investors expect to receive a rate of return consistent with their assessment of the financial and other risks, and a rate that is competitive with alternative investments.

Knowledge of the cost of capital is important for two reasons. First, the controller must know the cost of capital and offer securities that provide a competitive rate in order to attract the required funds to the business. Second, in making investment decisions, such as for plant and equipment, the controller must secure a return that is at least as high as the cost of capital. Otherwise, there is no reason to make an investment that yields only the cost or less. Therefore, the cost of capital theoretically sets the floor as the minimum rate of return before any investment should even be considered.

Determining the cost of capital is easy in concept, although in actual practice a great deal of judgment is required. The steps in the process are:

- Select the appropriate capital structure for the enterprise (i.e., the relative proportion of long-term debt to shareholders' equity).
- Determine for each segment of the capital structure the appropriate rate of return to the investor and the after-tax rate to the entity.
- Calculate the cost of capital by applying the appropriate rate to each weighted segment.

A sample corporate cost of capital is summarized in Table 16–3.

The principal element in calculating the cost of equity capital is the market price of the stock in relation to earnings. In the example in Table 16–3, the expected earnings as perceived by the marketplace was $5.50 per share and the price was $36.42. Therefore, the cost of equity capital was:

$$\frac{\$5.50}{\$36.42} = 15.1\%$$

Since management must be concerned with future capital costs more or less related to the period over which the investment must be recovered, the probable future costs estimated over perhaps five years should be the ones applied; this will involve financial judgment. The rates for securities can be determined from new issues, adjusted for probable trends.

DIVIDEND POLICY

Dividend policy is a factor to be considered in the management of shareholders' equity in that: (1) cash dividends paid are the largest recurring charge against retained earnings for most U.S. corporations; (2) the amount of dividends paid, which reduces the amount of equity remaining, will have an impact on the amount of long-term debt that can be prudently issued in view of the long-term debt to equity ratio that usually governs finance; (3) dividend payout is an influence on the reception of new stock issues; and (4) dividend policy is an element in most loan and credit agreements, with restrictions on how much may be paid.

A certain company may not pay cash dividends on the basis that it can earn a higher return on reinvested earnings than can a shareholder by directly investing in new purchases of stock. This is not always true, so the issue is whether or not paying a dividend will increase the long-term return to the shareholder. The firm should consider the type of investor attracted to the stock and the expectation of the investors. In general, the ability to invest all the earnings at an acceptable rate of return is not a convincing reason to avoid paying a dividend. After all, a dividend is here and now, and future growth is more problematic. Probably, other

Table 16–3: Sample Corporate Cost of Capital

	Capitalization		Cost	
Segment	Amount	Percent	Amount	Percent
Senior debt	$100,000	24.40	$8,970	8.97
Equity capital	310,000	75.60	46,800	15.10[a]
Total	$410,000	100.00	$55,770	
Weighted rate				13.60%

[a] Derived from the expected earnings per share divided by the share price

than in the case of a highly speculative situation or a company in severe financial difficulty, some dividend should be paid. This decision, however, is highly judgmental.

Dividend payments are determined by a number of influences including:

- Need for additional capital for expansion or other reasons.
- Cash flow of the enterprise.
- Industry practice.
- Shareholders' expectations.

The amount to be paid is calculated either by the dividend payout ratio or as a percentage of beginning net worth each year. The most common practice is to measure dividends as a percentage of earnings. The payout ratio is calculated as follows:

$$\text{payout ratio} = \frac{\text{annual dividends paid to common shareholders}}{\text{annual earnings available for common shareholders}}$$
$$\text{(after preferred dividends)}$$

Another way of calculating dividends, although less common than the payout method, is as a percentage of beginning net worth. The calculation is as follows:

$$\text{dividend payment ratio} = \frac{\text{annual dividends paid to common shareholders}}{\text{beginning common shareholder book value}}$$

Dividend paying practices send a message to the financial community, and investors and analysts accept the pattern as an indication of future payments. Hence, when a dividend payment rate is set, a dividend reduction should be avoided if at all possible. Dividend payments may follow any one of the following patterns:

- A constant or regular quarterly payment
- A constant pattern with regularly recurring increases
- A constant pattern with irregular increases
- A constant pattern with periodic extra increases so as to avoid committing to regular increases

In planning, any erratic pattern should be avoided.

LONG-TERM EQUITY PLANNING

For those companies with a practical financial planning system, the long-term planning sequence might be something like this.

1. The company financial management determines an acceptable capital structure and gets the agreement of management and the board of directors.
2. As part of the long-range financial plan, the amount of funds required in excess of those available is determined, by year, in an approximate amount.
3. Based on the needs over several years, the desired capital structure, the relative cost of each segment of capital (debt or equity), the cost of each debt issue, and any constraints imposed by credit agreements, or the judgment of management, the long-term fund requirements are allocated between long-term debt and equity.

Ordinarily the needs of additional equity capital are known some time in advance, and planning to take advantage of propitious market conditions and under generally acceptable terms results in a competitive cost of capital.

Now, let us provide some illustrations of these points. Assume that the CFO's recommendation has been approved by both the controller and company management and that the capital structure is as shown in Table 16–4.

Moreover, at the end of the current year the capital structure is expected to be as shown in Table 16–5.

In the process of completing the strategic planning cycle and the related long-range financial plan, the required long-term funds, without designation as to type or source, are estimated to be $67 million in three years. This program for substantial growth is reflected in Table 16–6. Furthermore, after a slight hesitation in plan years 4 and 5, management thinks the cycle will be repeated.

There are a number of observations regarding the preceding funding plans, particularly in regard to the cost of equity, the separation between actual and budgeted debt/equity levels, and the need for different types of funding in the future. The observations are as follows:

- *General*—Since the cost of equity capital is highest, and issuance of new equity tends to dilute earnings, equity capital should generally be used sparingly—only to maintain the borrowing base and reach and remain at the desired capital structure.
- *Current year*—At the end of the current year, equity will provide only 68.5% of capital (Table 16–7), as compared to management's target of 80% and a minimally acceptable level of 75%. Obviously, the debt share of capitalization is too high.

Table 16–4: Proposed Capital Structure

Segment	Preferred Structure	Minimally Acceptable Structure
Long-term debt	20.0%	25.0%
Shareholders' equity	80.0%	75.0%
Total	100.0%	100.0%

Table 16–5: Projected Capital Structure

Long-term debt	31.5%
Shareholders' equity	68.5%
Total	100.0%

- *Plan year 19X5*—Given the start of an acceleration in annual earnings, management decides to hold the dividend payout ratio to 20%, and to borrow under the term loan agreement (interest rate of 15%) the needed $8 million. The equity share of capitalization, even so, will increase from 68.5% to 72%.

- *Plan year 19X6*—With $28 million in new funds required, the company decides, in view of the heavy investment in fixed assets and a lower borrowing rate available, to issue a new mortgage bond. Some of the funds will be "taken down" or received in this plan year and the balance in the next year. Despite the high level of borrowing, the equity share remains at 72%. The management decides it can "live with" such a level—for a temporary period, given the high volume of income.

- *Plan year 19X7*—The balance of the new mortgage bond proceeds covers the requirements with no reduction in the equity share of capitalization.

- *Plan year 19X8*—With the net income level now at a level of $70 million, and a proposal by an insurance company to provide new funds through a new mortgage bond, management decides to (a) accept this new loan of $58 million and (b) pay off the more expensive term loan. Given the continued high level of earnings, equity capital at year-end will provide 76% of the capitalization. This is within the minimally acceptable standard used by the company.

Table 16–6: Long-Term Fund Requirements

Item	Current Year (Estimated)	Plan Year 1	2	3	4	5	Total
Funds Required							
Working Capital	$25	$30	$36	$42	$55	$30	$193
Long-term debt repayment	12	12	12	12	12	15	63
Fixed assets	15	14	40	50	15	40	159
Dividends	8	9	10	12	14	15	60
Total	$60	$65	$98	$116	$96	$100	$475
Internally Generated Funds							
Net Income	$40	$45	$50	$60	$70	$75	$300
Depreciation	10	12	20	25	28	31	16
Total	$50	$57	$70	$85	$98	$106	$416
Funds Required (Excess)	$10	$8	$28	$31	$(2)	$(6)	$59
Cumulative funds required (net)	$10	$8	$36	$67	$65	$59	

Table 16–7: Long-Term Fund Allocation ($ in millions)

Year/Item	Beginning Balance	Net Income	Dividends	New Equity Offering	Ending Balance	Year-end % of Capitalization
Shareholders' Equity						
Current year	$260	$40	$8		$292	
Plan years						68.5%
19X5	292	45	9		328	72.0
19X6	328	50	10		368	72.0
19X7	368	60	12		416	72.0
19X8	416	70	14		472	76.0
19X9	472	75	15	$50	582	81.0
Contingency years						
20X0	582	80	16		646	80.0
20X1	646	85	17		714	83.0
Long-term Debt						
Current-year, estimate						
Term Loan	$100	$10	$—	$90		
Mortgage bond, present	46	2	=	44		
	146	12	=	134	31.5	
Plan Years						
19X5						
Term Loan	$90	$10	$8	$88		
Mortgage bond, present	44	2	=	42		
	134	12	8	139	28.0	
19X6						
Term Loan	$88	$10	$—	$78		
Mortgage bond, present	42	2		40		
Mortgage bond, new	=	=	28	28		
	130	12	28	146	28.0	
19X7						
Term Loan	$78	$10	$—	$68		
Mortgage bond, present	40	2		38		
Mortgage bond, new	28		31	59		
	146	12	31	165	28.0	
19X8						
Term Loan	$68	$68		$—		
Mortgage bond, present	38	2		36		
Mortgage bond, new	59	=	58	117		
	165	70	58	153	24.0	
19X9						
Mortgage bond, present	36	13		23		
Mortgage bond, new	117	2	=	115		
	153	15		138	19.0	
Contingency years						
20X0						
Mortgage bond, present	23	13	—	10		
Mortgage bond, new	115	10	—	105		
Debenture, new			50	50		
	138	23	50	165	20.0	

(continues)

Table 16–7: (continued)

Year/Item	Beginning Balance	Net Income	Dividends	New Equity Offering	Ending Balance	Year-end % of Capitalization
20X1						
Mortgage bond, present	10	10		—		
Mortgage bond, new	105	10		95		
Debenture	50	=		50		
	$165	$20		$145	17.0	

- *Plan year 19X9*—In this last year of the 5-year long-range plan, management believes the growth cycle is ready to start again. Without going through the complete long-range planning cycle again, it asks the financial vice president to estimate fund requirements for two more years—the "contingency" years. This quick review discloses that another $50 million will be needed in 20X0, with possibly a limited amount required also in 20X1. Accordingly, to raise the equity capitalization to the desired 80% level and to provide the needed equity base for expansion in future years, it plans for an issue of $50 million in equity funds.

The management and board of directors feel comfortable with the equity base; in the event of a downturn in business for a limited period, and yet being in a position to borrow additionally if this becomes necessary. The summary of the planned debt reduction, new indebtedness to be incurred, shareholders' equity, and capitalization percentages is given in Table 16–8.

Table 16–8: Summary of Planned Changes in Capital Structure ($ in millions)

Item	Interest Rate	Begin. Balance Amount	%	19X5	19X6	19X7	19X8	19X9	Ending Balance Amount	%
Long-term Debt										
Term loan	15%	$ 90		$(10)	$(10)	$(10)	$(68)		$—	—
Mortgage bond	14	44		(2)	(2)	(2)	(2)	$(13)	23	
Mortgage bond	12	—		—	28	—	—	(2)	26	
Mortgage bond	11.5	=		=	=	31	58	=	89	
Total		134	31.5	(4)	16	19	(12)	(15)	138	19.0
Shareholders' Equity										
Beginning balance		292							292	
Net income		—		45	50	60	70	75	300	
Dividends		—		(9)	(10)	(12)	(14)	(15)	(60)	
Net issue		=		=	=	=	=	50	50	
Subtotal		292	68.5	36	40	48	56	110	582	81.0
Total		$426	100	$32	$56	$67	$44	$95	$720	100

In terms of management of shareholders' equity, the emphasis should be on planning, especially long-term planning so as to achieve the proper capital structure and use it as the basis for prudent borrowing. Additionally, the many other aspects already discussed need to be reviewed, and policies and procedures developed or continued that will enhance the shareholders' value. The portion of the annual plan related to equity changes should be similar to that found in Table 16–9.

REPURCHASING COMMON SHARES

Conceptually, a company is enfranchised to invest capital in the production of goods or services. Hence it should not knowingly invest in projects that will not provide a sufficiently high rate of return to adequately compensate the investors for the risk assumed. In other words, the enterprise should not invest simply because funds are available. Business management should identify sufficiently profitable projects that are consistent with corporate strategy, determine the capital required, and make the investment. Shareholders might interpret the repurchase of common stock as the lack of available investment opportunities. To some, the repurchase of company stock is not an "investment" but a return of capital. It is "disfinancing."

Some legitimate reasons for the repurchase of common stock are:

- Shares may be needed for stock options or employee stock purchase plans, but the management does not wish to increase the total shares outstanding.
- Shares are required in the exercise of outstanding warrants or for the conversion of outstanding convertibles, without issuing "new" shares.
- Shares are needed for a corporate acquisition.

Table 16–9: Annual Budget for Shareholders' Equity

Month	Beginning Balance	Estimated Net Income	Dividend Payments	Purchase of Treasury Shares	Estimated Dividend Reinvestments	Estimated Options Exercised	Ending Balance
January	$158,500	$ 2,650		$1,000			$160,150
February	160,150	2,410		1,000		$ 500	162,060
March	162,060	2,790	$1,720		$80		163,210
April	163,210	2,840					166,050
May	166,050	2,620		1,200		500	167,970
June	167,970	2,530	1,620		100		168,980
July	168,980	2,600		1,000			170,580
August	170,580	2,860				500	173,940
September	173,940	2,820	1,620		100		175,240
October	175,240	2,770		1,000			177,010
November	177,010	2,710				700	180,420
December	180,420	2,800	1,520		100		181,800
Total	$158,500	$32,400	$6,480	$5,200	$380	$2,200	$181,800

Some guidelines in deciding to repurchase shares are:

- If a company is excessively leveraged, it might do well to use cash to pay down existing long-term debt to reach the capital structure goal it envisages and not repurchase common shares.
- The management should examine its cash requirements for a reasonable time into the future, including fixed assets requirements, working capital needs, and other investment options, before it concludes that excess cash is available and that the equity capital genuinely is in excess of the apparent long-term demands.
- The cash dividend policy should be examined to see that it helps increase the market price of the stock.
- Only after such a review should the management decide to dispose of "excess equity" by purchasing company stock.

Given these conditions, timing may be important. Thus if the market price of the stock is below book value, the purchase of shares in fact increases the book value of the remaining shares. It might be prudent to purchase shares below book value rather than at a price that dilutes the shareholder equity.

CAPITAL STOCK RECORDS

An administrative concern in the management of shareholders' equity relates to the maintenance of capital stock records. In the larger companies in stock ledgers and transfer records are kept by the transfer agent. The information relative to payment of dividends on outstanding shares, for example, is secured from this source. Often the database is contained on computer files, and any number of sortings can produce relevant data regarding ownership, such as by geographical dispersion, the history and timing of purchases, market price activity, and the nature of the owners (e.g., individuals or institutions). Under these circumstances a ledger control account for each class of stock is all that is maintained by the company.

If a company has its own transfer department, then a separate ledger account must be maintained for each stockholder regarding each class of stock. The ledger must contain information such as the stockholder's name and address, the date of changes in holdings, the certificate numbers issued and surrendered, the number of shares in each transaction, and the total numbers of shares held. Optionally the record may include a history of dividend payments. The stock ledgers should be supported by registration and transfer records that give the details of each transaction.

The company's management has an interest in monitoring, perhaps monthly, large holdings and the changes therein. Such a review may provide signals about possible takeover attempts. For this purpose, as well as for soliciting proxies, the services of outside consultants that specialize in such matters may be used.

17

OPERATIONAL ACCOUNTING

In this chapter, we focus on how to upgrade the accounting function so that it runs as a world-class department should. We do this by first defining the jobs of everyone in the department, followed by the creation of a very specific work schedule and staff meetings to follow up on particularly difficult problems. Then we move on to the proper treatment of accounting errors and how to avoid them, followed by a lengthy discussion of how to use best practices to improve operations. We also review the pluses and minuses associated with outsourcing selected functions within the department. Finally, we explore the specialized area of managing the accounting department in an explosive growth environment. By following these guidelines, a controller can create a confident accounting department that is thoroughly capable of quickly and accurately processing all assigned tasks.

CREATE DEPARTMENTAL JOB DESCRIPTIONS

The first step in running an accounting department is to determine who is responsible for each task. Without it, there is no way to control the flow of activities, or to know who to talk to about fixing problems. The typical departmental structure is for there to be one or more assistant controllers who are responsible for a selected set of functional areas, such as accounts payable and accounts receivable, or cost accounting and the general ledger. Below these personnel are a number of accountants and clerks. The organizational structure is similar to the one shown in Figure 17–1.

Once the controller has determined the reporting relationships of the accounting group, it is time to define the exact job description for each position. These

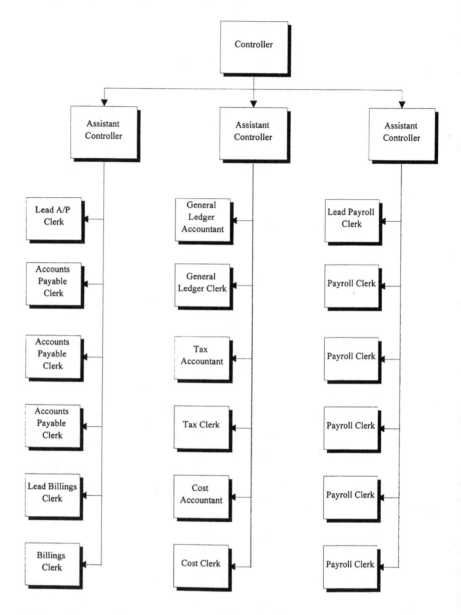

Figure 17–1: Accounting Department Organizational Structure

should be set up in a standard format by job title, not by individual, since the descriptions must otherwise be constantly restructured as employees come and go, or are promoted within the department.

After each job description is created, the controller should review it in detail with each person whose job it describes, since there may be missing line items that the controller has overlooked. Once it has been finalized, each employee should be given his or her own copy, and the controller or one of the assistant controllers should go over it with him or her at each performance review to ensure that all tasks are being completed and that the description is still accurate.

CREATE A DEPARTMENTAL TRAINING PROGRAM

Once the controller has decided which employees are supposed to complete which tasks, it is time to see if they are capable of doing so. The best method is a combination of sitting with them to see how they complete work and reviewing their error rates and time needed for completed work. It takes time to form an accurate opinion of the abilities of each person, so a controller should assume that at least a month, and probably longer, will pass before he or she has become knowledgeable in this area. Once the controller has completed this initial review, the next step is to create a matrix of training programs needed to bring the accounting staff up to an expert level in all assigned areas of responsibility.

This matrix is an extremely important tool, for it precisely delineates the training requirements for each person, as well as when the controller expects training to be completed. An example of such a training matrix is shown in Figure 17–2. It lists the names of accounting employees across the top of the report and the names of training modules down the left side. The training grid has a shaded area for those training classes that have not yet been completed, with a due date inside it. For those training classes that an employee *has* completed, the shading is removed and the completion date is listed. For cases where the employee is not required to complete a class, there is no shading or due date.

An important point in regard to the use of a training program is that the required classes be specifically targeted at the current or prospective job functions of each person. It is useless to force an employee to train for a skill that the person cannot use, since the skill is soon forgotten, and the employee's time has been wasted. Similarly, if the controller expects an employee to take on a new job function in the near future, be sure to assign the training *immediately* prior to the assumption of the associated new job functions, so that the employee has no chance to forget what he or she has learned.

Training is made easier if there are pre-packaged training programs available, either within the company or through an outside service, that meet the needs of the controller's training program. Since training for accountants frequently involves the company's accounting software, much of this training may be through seminars offered by the software provider. The other most common area of training for accountants is in specialized accounting topics, perhaps involving changes in FASB rulings. For training updates in this area, it is best to arrange for seminar notifications from the local CPA organization, or from the Institute of Management Accountants. If the staff needs to learn more about PC-based software packages, such as Excel, Word, or PowerPoint, there are usually many training organizations available in urban areas that provide this service. Main-

Training Program for Accounting Department

[Correct score of at least 80% required to pass training]
[Shaded areas indicate required classes and due dates]

Training Description	Anderson, B. (Assistant Controller)	Draston, Q. (Cost Accountant)	Dudley, F. (Accounts Payable)	Ephraim, J. (Accounts Receivable)	Jones, J. (General Ledger)
Accounting Software Training:					
A/P - Entering a credit	July-01		July-01		
A/P - Entering an invoice	July-01		July-01		
A/P - Entering an invoice	July-01		August-01		
A/P - Matching documentation	July-01		August-01		
A/R - Applying cash	August-01			July-01	
A/R - Creating a credit	August-01			July-01	
A/R - Creating an invoice	August-01			August-01	
A/R - Deleting an invoice	August-01			August-01	
G/L - Alter report format	May-01				July-01
G/L - Create chart of accounts	May-01				August-01
G/L - Enter a journal entry	May-01	July-01			September-01
G/L - Enter the budget	May-01				October-01
Accounting Seminars:					
Acquisitions seminar	September-01				
Archiving	April-01				November-01
Bank reconciliations	October-01				
Closing the books	November-01				December-01
Consolidations	December-01				December-01
Cost accounting, activity-based	March-01	August-01			
Cost accounting, direct	March-01	August-01			
Cost accounting, job cost	March-01	September-01			
Cost accounting, process	March-01	September-01			
Foreign currency translation	January-02				
Incorporation documentation	February-02				
Outsourcing	March-02				
Payroll taxes	April-02				
Personal property taxes	May-02		September-01		
Sales taxes	June-02		October-01		
Target costing	March-01	October-01			
PC Software Training:					
Beginning Access			June-01		March-01
Intermediate Access	June-01	October-01			
Advanced Access	July-02	November-01			
Beginning Excel			May-01	April-01	July-01
Intermediate Excel	April-01	December-01		May-01	August-01
Advanced Excel	August-02	December-01			September-01
Beginning Word				August-01	February-01
Intermediate Word	March-01			September-01	
Advanced Word				October-01	

Figure 17–2: Sample Employee Training Matrix

taining this list of possible training classes is an important part of the controller's training responsibilities.

Training is an area to which the typical controller assigns a low priority, because the benefit may not be immediately obvious, and employees usually do not push for it either. However, given the long-term benefit of having a highly trained and competent staff, the controller should schedule some time once a month, on a recurring basis, to meet with the accounting staff and go over their training accomplishments from the last month, as well as their goals for the next month. Only by ingraining training into the fabric of the department in this manner can the controller be assured that the staff will follow a consistent and targeted training program.

CLEAR OUT EXCESS DOCUMENTATION

For a new controller who is trying to attain control over an accounting department it can seem overwhelming — piles of documentation related to taxes, billings, supplier invoices, cash receipts, and on and on. There seems no end to the paperwork, and nowhere to start. To avoid this problem, one of the very first acts of any controller should be to clear as much paperwork out of the department's confines as possible. This means going through every filing cabinet, every drawer, and every box, and determining the age and value of the papers contained inside. The main point is to get extra copies and information not currently needed off the premises, so that the controller can clearly see the tasks that still need to be done. This does *not* mean throwing out any documents. The objective is strictly to move out the documentation, not get rid of it permanently. Instead, the controller should box all the unneeded items, carefully label the boxes, and create an index that lists what is in every box, so that the accounting staff can easily find it again.

DOCUMENT ALL MAJOR PROCESSES

Though the controller has now determined the skill levels of the accounting staff and organized them along functional lines, he or she still has no knowledge of how the department operates. We solve this problem by undertaking an in-depth review and documentation of all processes.

The best way to begin a process review is to sit with the most knowledgeable person who is involved with each function and document every step of the process in great detail. The documentation should itemize the exact file locations used, both in the computer and in filing cabinets, as well as the precise keystrokes needed to complete each step. The reason for this level of detail is that the written procedure will probably be incorporated by the controller into a departmental procedures manual that will be used by new recruits who must learn the system "from scratch." After the first draft is complete, the controller should review it with the most knowledgeable staff person, and perhaps also distribute it through the department, with a request to highlight errors and then return the corrected document.

Once the initial process documentation is complete, the controller should review the workloads required to complete each process with either the assistant controllers or the most experienced staff people available, with a particular emphasis on peak work periods of the month, additional staffing requirements, particular areas in which errors are endemic, and changes that will smooth the flow of work. Of particular interest is the concept of process centering, which means that one can eliminate much of the move and queue time inherent in most processes by centralizing as much of the work as possible with one person, rather than only allowing one person to complete a small task out of the entire process, with many other people completing their small, specialized tasks later in the process flow. For example, the accounts payable process can switch to process centering by having a single person conduct all documentation matching, supplier contacts, research, and data entry, rather than keeping these functions separated among different specialists.

SCHEDULE THE DEPARTMENT

Once the controller has outlined each person's job and has identified the major processes, it is time to create a schedule of activities for each position. This should be a simple calendar, such as the one shown in Figure 17–3, that lists the major activities that each person is to complete on a given date. Each person should have a different calendar that matches his or her job responsibilities. For the controller to maintain good control of daily activities, this person should have a master calendar that notes all the activities of all personnel, which he or she can then use to walk through the department each day to ensure that tasks are being completed on time. There may be a few positions, such as the accounts payable clerical positions, where the job does not vary much per day so a calendar is not necessary.

Activity calendars of this sort will likely require correction at least once a month, so it is best to hold brief staff meetings at the end of the previous month to go over these changes and to hand out new activity calendars. It is also useful to supplement these schedules with a vacation calendar, perhaps of the erasable white board variety, that is posted in a visible spot in the department where employees can list their approved days off. This is a very useful tool for the controller, since this clarifies those days on which backup support may be needed in order to complete assigned tasks.

CORRECT THE UNDERLYING CAUSES OF ERRORS

Depending on the level of experience, training, and procedural accuracy in an accounting department, it is possible that the accounting staff spends up to 50%

Sunday	Monday	Tuesday	Wednesday	Thursday	Friday	Saturday
1	2 Month-end close Weekly statistics	3 Issue flash report	4 Department meeting	5 Collections review Check run	6 Financials due Executive committee	7
8	9 Weekly statistics	10 Quarterly staff review	11 Department meeting Target cost review	12 Collections review Check run	13 Executive committee	14
15	16 Weekly statistics	17	18 Department meeting ABC review	19 Collections review Check run	20 Executive committee	21
22	23 Weekly statistics	24 Inventory review	25 Department meeting Job cost review	26 Collections review Check run	27 Executive committee	28
29	30 Weekly statistics Pre-close meeting	31 Review accruals				

Figure 17–3: Activity Calendar for the Controller

of its time just correcting errors from earlier transactions. For example, a fixed asset may have been recorded in the fixed asset register with an incorrect depreciation period, or an expense was charged to the wrong account number, or a customer was billed twice, or a supplier was paid twice. All of these transactions must be corrected, and each one may take hours to fix properly. Furthermore, because the adjustments are exceptions to the normal routine that someone (such as an auditor) may not understand when he or she reviews it at some point in the future, one must also fully document the reasons why the corrections have been made, which takes up still more time. Finally, if the corrections are large enough, they may even have a material impact on the financial statements, which results in additional explanation as footnotes in the statements. This also takes time, not to mention being an embarrassment to the accounting department. Unless the controller takes steps to correct the core reasons why these errors continue to arise, the accounting department will never have a chance to work its way out from under the workload related to error correction.

When correcting errors, a controller should follow a specific set of steps that greatly assist in focusing attention on those errors that arise most frequently. The first step is to keep a log of all errors found. This log should include the nature of the error, when it occurred, who caused the error, and the underlying reason for the problem. An example of this log is shown in Figure 17–4. Compiling this log can take some work, since the accounting staff may hide its errors from the controller and fix the problems without publicizing their mistakes. To find these errors, the controller must create error-spotting systems, such as a monthly review of all credits issued to customers, all journal entries, and all unvouchered accounts payable, which are the most common locations for error corrections. Then the controller researches each item found and inserts it into the log. The next step is to create a Pareto analysis (i.e., 20% of the problems cause 80% of the total errors) that groups the errors by quantity of occurrences, so that the controller can see which problems arise the most frequently. At this point, one can target those errors causing the bulk of the problems, outline a correction plan, and implement it, which will rapidly reduce the incidence of errors. This should be one of the key functions of the controller, since it has such a major operational impact on the efficiency of the accounting department.

An additional column that could be added to the example is one for the size of the error, in case the controller wants to focus on fixing problems of great magnitude, rather than those with the highest incidence of occurrence.

The reason for the "Date Error Occurred" column in the example is that the controller may have already fixed a problem that has only now been discovered. For example, if the error is dated three months previously, but the controller fixed the underlying problem the week before, then it can be safely ignored. However, if the problem occurred in just the past few days, then the underlying problem is clearly still an issue and requires further action.

It is also important to create a feedback loop to the accounting staff regarding the elimination of errors, because this system will have a major negative impact

Date Error Found	Date Error Occurred	Person Causing Error	Error Type	Cause of Error
06/11/01	03/04/01	Smith, J.	Incorrect pricing	Due to special deal by salesperson.
06/10/01	06/09/01	Novak, K.	Incorrect supplier cost	Due to incorrect accounts payable entry, shifting dollar amount by one decimal.
06/10/01	05/31/01	Orson, P.	Incorrect payroll accrual	Due to not using standard journal entry calculation to compile month-end expense.
06/09/01	06/09/01	Dudley, F.	Incorrect property tax accrual	Did not include cost of assets at secondary location.
06/09/01	06/01/01	Johnson, A.	Incorrect pricing	Due to customer service overriding standard price in computer.
06/08/01	02/28/01	Smith, J.	Incorrect cash book balance	Did not complete bank reconciliation last month.
06/08/01	01/13/01	Johnson, A.	Incorrect supplier cost	Due to incorrect accounts payable entry, shifting dollar amount by one decimal.
06/08/01	05/15/01	Anderson, L.	Tape inventory too high	Due to unit of measure change by engineering that switched tape quantity in inches to quantity in rolls.

Figure 17–4: Example of an Accounting Error Log

on staff morale if it is not presented to them properly. To use a real-life example, a general manager created this technique to spot every conceivable problem in a company and used it to target employees for firing, rather than focusing on the problems that the system had highlighted. As a result, employee morale disintegrated, many staff left the company, and those remaining decided not to inform the general manager of any new problems, since they eventually received the blame for the problems. A vastly better approach is to inform the accounting staff of what the process is designed to do, and keep them informed during every phase of the system installation. Also, the staff should be included in the decision-making for resolving errors, which also gives rise to more fruitful ideas than any controller could originate alone.

USE OF BEST PRACTICES

Even after documenting the accounting department's work flow, positioning employees in the correct jobs, and setting them up for the appropriate training programs, there is no assurance that the department will operate in a sufficiently effective manner. The controller may compare the work done by his or her accounting staff, and find that it falls well behind the efficiency level of the accounting department of a competing company. The reason for the difference may be that the competition is using best practices to improve its operations. A best practice is any operational improvement that allows the accounting staff to generate more work with an equal or less amount of effort. There is a constant stream of innovation coming out of companies all over the world, so there is no end to the number of best practices one can implement. The main problem is finding them. One of the best sources is *Management Accounting* magazine (Institute of Management Accountants) which contains stories submitted by the accounting staffs of many organizations, revealing precisely how they improved their operations. Another source is *Accounting Best Practices* (John Wiley & Sons, Inc. 1999), which lists and explains a large number of best practices, including implementation issues, control problems, and related costs.

Once a controller has discovered a best practice that may fit into his or her organization, it is very important to research the issue thoroughly to ensure that the following points have been covered prior to commencing with an implementation:

- *Cost-benefit analysis.* A best practice may seem extraordinarily "sexy" in concept, but the controller must always ensure that the cost of installing it does not exceed the savings from using it. For example, a document imaging system may eliminate virtually all the paperwork from an accounting department, but the only identifiable savings from doing so may be the storage costs that are perhaps a few hundred dollars per month or year.
- *Control issues.* A new best practice improvement may result in a major reduction in the volume of work, but it may also eliminate a key control point in the old system that is being replaced. If so, there is now a control risk that may result in a loss that greatly exceeds the potential savings from using the best practice. For example, if procurement cards are used to replace the bulk of a company's small purchases, this will avoid the use of purchase order authorizations, thereby allowing procurement card users to abuse small purchases, knowing that no one is reviewing what they buy.
- *Capacity.* If a controller is contemplating a mammoth project that will vastly improve the efficiency of the accounting department, it would be useful to first determine the capacity of the department to perform the installation, since it must find the time amongst its other work to complete the project. It is unrealistic to assume that the existing staff, which is usually overworked, can also complete additional work related to best practice installations. Accordingly, it

is frequently necessary to schedule additional help, either from other departments or consultants, who can assist with or even manage the work.

- *Murphy's Law.* Always expect that something will go wrong with the installation of any best practice, and be prepared for the worst possible case. For example, if switching to an automated vacation accrual tracking system that lists accruals on employee pay stubs, what must be done if some of the accruals are incorrect? The controller should prepare a plan for this contingency, and expect to use it.

- *Time requirements.* The longer an installation project runs, the worse its chances of succeeding, since there will inevitably be other work that will take priority, the spirits of the implementation team will drop, and it will be more difficult to continue to obtain both funding and the support of senior management.

- *Track record.* If the controller has a poor track record for installing best practices in the past, for whatever reason, it will be very difficult to convince the staff to participate in yet another project with any degree of enthusiasm. In such cases, it is best to start with an extremely small project that can be completed in the shortest possible time period, in order to build up the trust of the department.

- *Personnel issues.* If a proposed best practice will require the approval or participation of someone who does not have a good record for assisting in previous implementations, then the controller must fix the problem with this person, either through replacement, presenting a convincing argument, or shifting responsibility to a different person, before even beginning to think about any other implementation-related issues. Without total personnel support, a best practice cannot be installed.

- *Support by top management.* If a best practice can be installed without any involvement from other departments, then the chance of success is much higher than if another department must be brought into the process, since this other group may have an entirely different agenda and does not want to cooperate. Given the level of difficulty when other departments are involved, the controller should always be sure that the top management group has fully bought into the best practice concept and will be fully supportive if other departments cause difficulties.

If the controller has reviewed the preceding items and finds no roadblocks that could seriously interfere with implementation efforts, it is time to determine which best practices to install first. The key issue here is to not immediately go after the one item with the biggest potential payback, because it may also be the most difficult or expensive one to implement. Instead, the controller should focus on creating an accounting organization that is used to always working on the implementation and maintenance of just a few best practices at a time, so that there is a tradition of improvement woven into the fabric of the department.

OUTSOURCING SELECTED ACCOUNTING FUNCTIONS

Once the controller has straightened out the accounting process flow, eliminated recurring errors, and installed best practices, it may become evident that the department is spending too much of its resources on those accounting activities that do not create value for the company. For example, there may be a large workforce of hourly personnel that requires a numerous in-house payroll staff and lots of management attention, whereas the main value driver from the accounting perspective is generating cost accounting reports for the management team regarding the margins being earned on company products. In a situation such as this, the controller may want to review the cost-benefit of shifting some of the less important accounting functions to a supplier, who will run them on behalf of the controller.

All of the accounting functions can be outsourced, but the most common one by far is payroll. Such major suppliers as ADP, Paychex, and Ceridian perform the payroll processing for tens of thousands of companies. The reason why this function is commonly outsourced is that it is a combination of being a non-value added activity and one that can result in significant government fines if tax payments are not made by specified dates. Thus, with lots of downside risk and no upside potential for doing the job better, many controllers elect to hand this painful chore to a supplier. Other accounting functions are not so clear-cut, however. Smaller firms can have a supplier process their billings and accounts payable off-site, while outside bookkeepers can process the month-end close for a very small company. There are also a few cases where a supplier will take over the entire accounting department, such as Arther Andersen, which handles all of the accounting tasks for the United Kingdom drilling and piping divisions of Conoco. However, there are also good reasons for treading carefully in these non-payroll areas, because the cost of using a supplier may greatly exceed the cost of performing the same tasks in-house. Also, the company and its supplier can develop strained relations if the outsourcing deal does not work out well, and the controller may be constantly bogged down in contract revisions, when he or she thought there would be more time available for other activities. Given the number of issues surrounding the use of outsourcing, the following is a list of accounting functions that can be outsourced:

- *Bank reconciliations.*
- *Check printing.*
- *Collections.*
- *Internal auditing.*
- *Payroll.*
- *Period closings.*
- *Tax form preparation.*
- *Transaction processing.*

If a controller decides to proceed with outsourcing an accounting function, there are several contractual issues to consider. In the case of payroll processing, the main variable is the price of the service, which is divided into a variable fee per person, plus a fixed monthly charge. Both fees are negotiable, though other terms cannot be varied much. The outsourcing of tax form preparation can be negotiated on the price of the service provided, as well as the specific people used by the supplier to complete the work. A controller can usually specify that the same group of people work on all tax forms, so that there is a base of experience and consistency. The main focus of collections outsourcing is the price, which can be either a fixed fee per invoice collected or more commonly a percentage of the dollars collected. Giving a supplier a higher volume of collections work can be used as leverage to reduce the per-invoice cost to the company. From a contractual standpoint, internal auditing is similar to tax form preparation in that the primary items for negotiation are the hourly rate and the personnel to be used. Another issue is what type of internal auditing methodology will be used, which can be specified by the controller. The contract for transaction processing requires the largest amount of negotiation. The single largest issue here is to avoid add-on fees (which tend to be very high) by rolling as many tasks into the monthly baseline fee as possible. Also, if company personnel are being transferred to the supplier, be sure to specify the minimum period for which they will be retained, or the severance pay they will receive. In addition, determine the minimum period over which key personnel will be retained on the company's account before they can be moved to other supplier work sites—this keeps experienced personnel working on company business for as long as possible. Finally, be sure to retain approval control over any efficiencies the supplier wants to implement, since these may change the flow of information to other parts of the company, and may have political consequences. Given the number of negotiable items, it is apparent that a controller must be prepared to negotiate transaction outsourcing at some length in order to arrive at an advantageous contract with a supplier.

When outsourcing accounting functions, there are a few transitional issues to be aware of so that the shift to a supplier is as painless as possible. First, no matter what function is given to a supplier, there must be a functional coordinator who is in charge of the move, so that there is a single responsible person who can monitor the process. This person anticipates problems, deals with supplier and personnel issues, and tracks the progress of the transition against a time and activities budget. If payroll is being outsourced, then the key issue is the timing of the transition, for it is easiest for the supplier if it takes place on January 1 of the new year, when the year-to-date records for all employees are reset to zero. Otherwise, the supplier cannot guarantee that the information that will appear on each employee's annual W-2 form will be correct. Also, a payroll supplier offers a number of add-on services, such as check stuffing, direct deposit, and automatic vacation accruals; however, it is best to transition to the most basic functions first to ensure that they work properly, and then incrementally add on the other options later. If the controller is shifting the preparation of financial statements to a supplier, then the main issue is to verify with the supplier the individual accounts that will roll up into separate line items on the financial statements, and to monitor this information for several months to ensure that the correct roll-up is occurring. When outsourcing the internal audit function, there are several extra steps to complete. Since the auditors will be meeting with many employees throughout the company, it is important to screen them for a minimum level of experience, then walk them through all relevant policies and procedures, train them in the use of the in-house auditing procedures (if they are to be used), negotiate the details of the audit plan for the upcoming year, and set up a monitoring plan to ensure that the audits are being conducted to the controller's satisfaction. Tax form preparation is much easier to begin, since the controller only has to authorize the auditing firm to begin work, which it can then do based on the audit work papers it has already prepared; however, if the tax work is to be done by a different supplier, then the controller must send written permission to the auditing firm for it to copy all relevant audit work papers and send them to the tax preparation firm. Finally, the transition of transaction processing is the most difficult task of all. This involves transferring the accounting staff to the supplier, training any additional staff or supplier managers, either shifting the company's accounting database and application programs to the supplier's location or shifting the database to the supplier's software, and testing to make sure that the data has been successfully moved. The transition for transaction processing can be so complicated that a controller should assign one or more senior staff members to the oversight of this process.

Another part of outsourcing is maintaining proper control over the suppliers who are now running parts of the accounting department. A key issue is to keep the outsourcing of the internal audit function away from any suppliers who are handling other parts of the accounting department; otherwise, the supplier's auditors will be reviewing their own activities, which is a poor way to control the department. Another good control is to set up separate general ledger accounts for each supplier who is handling accounting department functions, summarize all their billed expenses through these accounts, and compare the expenses to the contractual amounts that were originally agreed upon. Also, the controller should consider building bonus and penalty clauses into the contract with each supplier, so that they have an incentive to complete required work both accurately and on time. Finally, there should be a periodic review meeting with supplier management, preferably quarterly, to go over problems that have arisen since the last meeting and how to resolve them. By keeping the lines of communication open between the controller and suppliers, most problems can be quickly resolved.

Setting up adequate controls over suppliers of accounting functions is not enough, however. The controller must be able to measure their performance to ensure that preagreed standards are being attained, which may result in bonus payments or penalties, depending on the outcome. In the case of collections, the controller's main concern is the ability of the supplier to collect the highest possible proportion of overdue accounts receivable. Accordingly, the best measure is the percentage of collected funds from the dollars of billings that were assigned to the supplier. If there is a supplier who is creating financial statements for the controller, then the two main concerns are accuracy and timeliness. Accordingly, the controller should measure the accuracy of all accruals made, the number of material irregularities that must be adjusted in later financial statements, and the time required to issue the statements. If internal auditing is outsourced, then the controller should be most concerned with the ability of the supplier to complete a high percentage of the audits that were originally agreed upon. Another good measure is the average cost per audit. If payroll is being outsourced, then appropriate measures are the timeliness of the supplier in paying payroll taxes to the government, the average transaction cost per employee paid, and the number of payroll payments sent by the supplier to the wrong company locations. If there is a supplier handling tax form preparation, then the controller certainly wants to know about any tax penalties paid that are due to incorrect or late tax filings. Finally, if the controller outsources transaction processing, then several measures should be used. The most important is the average cost per transaction, which should be compared to the cost prior to using the supplier, to ensure that costs are in line with expectations. Another is the supplier's error rate in completing transactions, though this is a difficult one to measure (since the supplier can easily cover up any errors). A major measurement from the perspective of the rest of the company is the supplier's timeliness in completing transactions, especially when this involves the processing and payment of employee expense reports. Finally, if the supplier is responsible for accounts payable, then a significant measure is ensuring that 100% of all possible early payment discounts have been taken. A controller should consider the above measures to be nothing more than the bare minimum set of measures to use when dealing with suppliers, and should add as many as necessary to adequately track their performance.

A final issue is the management of outsourced functions. Though suppliers are technically responsible for their output, the controller is held responsible for all aspects of his or her department by senior management, and so must stay in close touch with the activities of all suppliers. To do this, there must still be tight management control of the outsourced functions from within the company. This means that the controller should assign one or more assistant controllers the task of supervising all suppliers. These people should receive extra help from the company's legal counsel or purchasing staff in the matter of negotiating and reviewing contracts. Their typical job descriptions will be to negotiate supplier contracts, authorize payments to suppliers, measure suppliers' performance, monitor supplier service levels and discuss any changes needed to improve them, review and approve all supplier outputs, such as financial statements or completed tax forms, and manage the transfer of functions to the suppliers. These are significant changes from the typical role of accounting managers, who tend to specialize in particular accounting areas, so some extra management training may be necessary for these employees before they are fully equipped to take on the task of managing the suppliers to whom accounting functions have been outsourced.

18

CLOSING PROCEDURES

Management must be provided with summarized information for the various operating periods—by month, quarter, and year. Management decisions to a large extent are based on past performance, trends, and actual results relative to potential or plan; thus, the more current the information, the better the chances for taking effective and prompt action. Management's primary information interests are sales volume, operating margins, net profits, financial position, and a selection of key statistical data (e.g., business booked, current ratio, inventory and receivables turnover, etc.). In addition, the controller must decide on the dates of the fiscal year end, the number of interim reporting periods, comparisons to be made, and how to prepare period-end reports as rapidly as possible.

SELECTING THE FISCAL YEAR

The controller must establish a fiscal year (if the company is new), or consider whether the present basis is the most suitable. The most common accounting year in use is the calendar year, which ends on December 31. The natural business year is the period of 12 consecutive months that ends when the business activities have reached the lowest point in their annual cycle. Generally at this time the inventories are the lowest, the peak volume of sales has passed, the receivables are declining and borrowing and other liabilities are at a minimum or are being reduced. Each business usually has a natural business year, and it frequently does not coincide with the calendar year. The advantages of adopting a natural business year lie in facilitating certain operations essential to the conduct of the business.

- *Taking inventory*—Smaller stocks mean that the count can be taken, checked, and summarized more easily. The smaller scope of the job also allows a smaller margin of error in valuing the inventory.
- *Preparing more accurate financial statements*—Financial statements are always a combination of facts and opinions. With smaller inventories and receivables, there are fewer estimates or arbitrary provisions. Valuation reserves, such as for receivables and inventory, are lower because of such lower valuations.
- *Securing credit*—Bankers or creditors prefer statements at the end of a natural year because they may better appraise the business. Also, it is to the advantage of the company if the financial statements show its most liquid condition.
- *Completing the annual audit*—Auditors can give more attention to a client who's fiscal year end does not fall into the audit "crunch time" immediately following the calendar year-end. Some auditors offer fee discounts to clients with non-calendar year ends, to encourage them to stay away from the auditor's busiest time of the year.

It is a relatively simple matter to determine the natural business year of a corporation. The controller should tabulate the monthly data to determine what month has the lowest activity or minimum investment in such matters as the value of production, inventory, sales, receivables, and payables. This may be done by listing the dollar values for each item for each month of the year; the trend over several years may be checked in order to avoid any anomalies occurring within one year.

For existing corporations desiring to change their fiscal year, it is important to obtain approval from the IRS to effect the desired change. Normally, permission is granted when it is based on sound reasons. Similar permission may be required from state or other authorities, or a notification of the change or special reporting may be all that is needed—for example, to the SEC. In establishing a new corporation, the desired fiscal year is simply written into the by-laws.

SELECTING INTERIM REPORTING PERIODS

Most companies use the calendar month as a basis for summarizing and reporting operating results within the fiscal year. The advantages of this approach are that industry statistics usually use this method, billings are frequently monthly, and relations with customers and vendors are likely to involve the calendar month as a basis of calculation. The disadvantage is that monthly revenues and expenses are not comparable due to the different number of days in each month.

An alternative is the 13-month calendar, which consists of 13 months of 28 days each, accounting for 364 days. The extra day is not in any month, nor is any leap day. This system avoids the problem of comparing months of different lengths. However, under this scheme when monthly or period statements are prepared for stockholders or the government, adjustments must be made to conform to the calendar periods, requiring extra effort and cost. Also, it results in one added closing per year. Finally, monthly fixed charges, such as rent payments, only occur twelve times per year, so one period does not receive fixed charges, resulting in artificially high earnings in that period.

NEED FOR PROMPT REPORTING

The reports of the controller are a driving force in the guidance of business policy and in cost and revenue control. If reports are tardy, not only is management left without the facts it needs—resulting in problems going unaddressed—but also the cost of preparing the reports is wasted.

It may take several days to close a period, but various subsystems will close and have information available prior to the final period close. If it is judged final and not subject to adjustments, then this subsystem information can be released to management as "flash reports." Typical flash reports can be for sales (in dollars or units), inventory (split into raw materials, work in process, and finished goods), receivables (split into aging categories), and total disbursements for payroll and payables.

QUICK CLOSE

In most companies, information can be available within the first few days after the end of the period. Computers can speed up the process of delivering information to management, but the processes being automated are frequently in need of overhaul as well. In fact, without a careful review of the underlying systems, new computer automation may speed up a process that is not even needed. This section contains a number of process improvement steps to follow in order to cull unnecessary items from the closing process and thereby make computer processing of the remaining steps more efficient.

Quality is a key component of the fast close. Why should the controller consider quality in the closing process? Manufacturing operations have so far been the primary focus of quality improvement efforts. Recently, the same improvement techniques have been used by controllers to improve their operations and control their headcount. It has been estimated that a good "quality" program can reduce closing activities by 25% to 40%. That is the estimated amount of effort required by accountants to correct errors, eliminate roadblocks, and ensure the accuracy of their data.

A quality manufactured product is one that meets the customer's specifications and is delivered on time and at the right price. How can that definition be applied to the accounting closing process? To answer that question, we must look at each part of the definition in detail:

Who is the customer? The customer is whoever uses the output from the process. Therefore, the customer is any user of the financial statement, usually lenders, investors, and management.

What is the customer's product specification? The specification of this set of customers is to receive financial information that is accurate. The definition of the word "accurate" is crucial, for perfect accuracy is expensive in manpower and time requirements. However, if "accuracy" is defined as "information that will not lead to incorrect decisions by the customer," then the controller can cut both the manpower and time required to issue the financials by using selected estimates for the financials, and adjusting the estimates after the period close.

When is delivery required? The optimum delivery time should be at midnight on the last day of the accounting period. This may seem impossible, but the goal should be set; if the current time requirement is eighteen days, then work to shave a day off the process, and continue to close in on an instantaneous close as an ongoing process.

What is the right price? Closing the period does not add any value to the product received by the company's final customer, so the effort going into it should be considered a non-value-added activity. Consequently, the goal should be to close the period at minimal cost, preferably using zero manpower and assets. Again, this goal may seem impossible, but the ongoing process of reducing costs must be established.

Thus, we now have a definition for a quality close of an accounting period: The product of the accounting close must provide information to lenders, investors, and management that will not lead to incorrect decisions by those users. The information must be provided immediately after the close of the accounting period at minimal cost to the company.

The definition sounds impossible. Let's look at ways to make it possible. The following set of sequential steps, when repeated continually, will help the controller gradually reduce the time required to produce financial statements. We emphasize that this process should be repeated continually, for additional processing improvements can always be found; in addition, new technological developments will shrink the processing effort even further, and must be incorporated into the process as they are perfected. For example, using electronic data interchange for receiving accounts payable will eventually allow the controller to close the accounts payable subsystem immediately following the end of the accounting period, with no time lag whatsoever.

1. *Clear out the junk.* The process is similar to cleaning out your garage. The first step is throwing out the trash so you can have a better look at what is left. In this case, try the following:
   - Eliminate items that require multiple approvals; one should be enough.
   - Eliminate items that must be filed multiple times (e.g., alphabetically, numerically, by state, etc.); one should be enough.

- Clean the accounting area; if it is inundated in paper, then either file the paper or (even better) review its usefulness and then (perhaps) throw it away.

2. *Document the process.* Do not implement solutions without first reviewing the process in detail. Here are several ways to document the process—you should use *all* of these techniques before continuing.

- *Create a flowchart.* This is a quick review of how the process flows. There are few symbols to remember; just list the process sequentially. In addition, list the time required to perform each step, including the time required to go from step to step. A flowchart is shown in Figure 18–1.

- *Create a functional flowchart.* This shows how a process moves between departments or personnel within departments, and is very useful in pin-

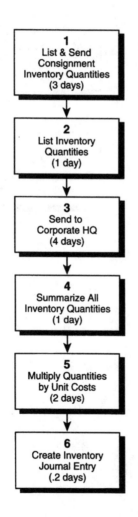

Figure 18–1: Flowchart

pointing where time accrues during the process. A functional flowchart is shown in Figure 18–2.

- *Create a geographic flowchart.* This shows where paper travels during a process, and allows the controller to determine where wasteful movement occurs. A geographic flowchart is shown in Figure 18–3. The flowchart indicates that the controller should swap the locations of the receivables clerk and the cost accountant in order to reduce the receivables clerk's travel time to the fax, copier, and storage room.

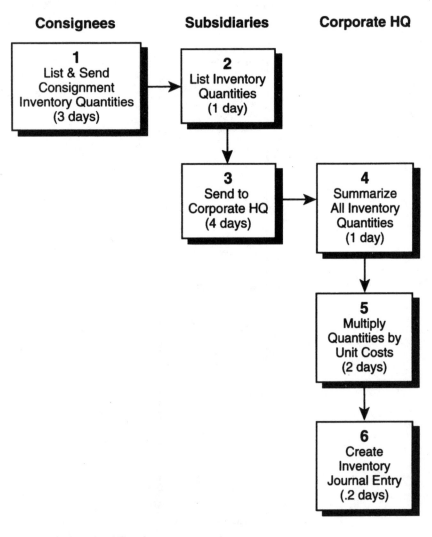

Figure 18–2: Functional Flowchart

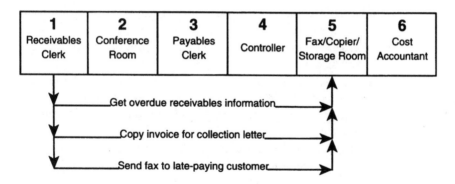

1	2	3	4	5	6
Receivables Clerk	Conference Room	Payables Clerk	Controller	Fax/Copier/ Storage Room	Cost Accountant

Get overdue receivables information

Copy invoice for collection letter

Send fax to late-paying customer

Figure 18–3: Geographic Flowchart (Credit Collection Process)

3. *Eliminate duplication.* Duplication typically occurs in two places during the closing process. First, information compiled at a subsidiary location is cross-checked at the consolidating location. Second, a subordinate's work is reviewed by a supervisor. Using the flowcharts developed during the preceding stage, highlight duplications and eliminate them. Elimination is not easy if the cross-checking is done to fix numerous mistakes. The process must first be made idiot-proof so that errors cannot be made. For example, staff can receive better training, and tasks can be either automated or simplified. In addition, information received from subsidiaries can be quickly checked for significant variances, with small errors being reviewed after the close and adjusted, if necessary, in the following accounting period.

4. *Defer routine work.* Take note of those items being performed during the closing process that are unrelated to it and can be deferred until a later date. For example, performing account analysis on janitorial supplies is not crucial, and can wait until the financial statements have been issued.

5. *Automate standard items.* Prepare certain accounting entries on a standard basis and adjust periodically as in the case of depreciation and insurance. Please note that this is a common area for errors, because standard entries eventually change, and the changes are frequently missed. To avoid mistakes from occurring, the underlying documents that show change dates should be attached to the journal entry documents. For example, a lease payment amount changes once a year. Rather than file the change schedule separately, either attach it to the journal entry or conspicuously note the change date on the journal entry form, and cross-reference the source document.

6. *Set investigation levels.* If variances are minor, then their impact on the accuracy of the financials will be minimal. Investigation can safely be done after the financials have been issued, with any adjustments appearing in the financial statements for the following period.

7. *Move activities into the previous month.* Many tasks associated with the closing can be performed prior to the end of the period. For example:

- *Prepare forms in advance*—If journal entries or other reports are included in the closing process, then complete as much information as possible in advance, such as descriptions, account names, plan or budget data, and prior period figures.
- *Anticipate problems*—Be aware of areas where problems may develop and do as much analysis and reconciling as possible prior to closing. This could be the case where intercompany transactions are extensive and reconciliations may be difficult.
- *Develop distributions*—Create as many allocation bases as possible before the end of the period. Allocation bases and certain ratios for distribution of costs may be determined in advance.

8. *Reduce cycle time.* Cycle time is the total time required to complete a process. Frequently, the actual value-added time is minimal, whereas the wait time between tasks constitutes the bulk of the process time. Target the longest wait times and take steps to reduce them.

9. *Automate manual processes.* After reviewing cycle times, select the manual processes that take large amounts of time, and automate them. For example, taking inventory and extending unit costs to derive a total inventory valuation is extremely time-consuming. However, with an on-line perpetual inventory (see Chapter 13, Inventory) and automatic collection of unit costs through the accounts payable system, this activity can be reduced to a few keystrokes on a computer.

10. *Replace serial activities with parallel activities.* Based on the flowcharts developed earlier, identify steps that are currently performed in sequence, but which could be performed in parallel; and then convert to parallel processing. For example, when the information on a report is needed by three people in order to generate their closing reports, don't wait for them to pass it along from one person to the next. Instead, give copies to all three so that they can process the information in parallel.

11. *Rearrange work space.* After the closing process has been cleaned up and the paper flow made more efficient, the controller should review the work space. If the work area can be rearranged to reduce paper movement to a minimum and cut the level of nearby traffic (thereby reducing interruptions), then moving the staff is justified. This is also a good time to review the location of the nearest copiers and fax machines to see if moving or adding such equipment would reduce unnecessary travel time. Copier, fax machine, and fax/modem card prices continue to drop, thereby possibly justifying the purchase of basic units to service small groups of staff (and fax/modem cards for *all* staff personal computers).

12. *Train the staff.* The accounting staff must be well-trained in the closing procedures. Cross-training the staff will minimize the problems of peak loads, trouble spots, and absenteeism. The training should include indoctrination in the closing schedule. The schedule should include:

- Tasks to be accomplished.
- Responsibilities for recording, preparing, analyzing, or transmitting information.
- Exact times (day and hour) by which each task must be completed.
- Specific cutoff dates by subsystem.
- Periods to be reported.
- Number of weeks to be included in each month or quarter.
- The day of the week on which the period closes.

Reviews with all managers must be held before the schedule is finalized to ensure that everyone fully understands the closing process and can execute it. Any period-specific trouble spots (such as scheduled vacations) should be analyzed and solved at this time.

13. *Do it again.* This improvement process must be repeated again and again in order to continually shrink the processing time. There are several reasons for this: first, bureaucracy tends to creep into a process via extra filing requirements, added steps, and additional approvals. Bureaucracy must be guarded against by constant review of the process. Second, the competition is always refining its processes. If competitors continue to cut their costs and cycle times while your company does not, then they will eventually gain an advantage through reduced overhead costs. Finally, staff morale is good whenever you attend to their needs. If the process review is always ongoing, then the staff will feel that they are important, and will both perform better and support the continuing improvements.

In addition, interview your customers periodically to see if portions of their needed information can be sent to them prior to the issuance of completed financials, if they need additional information, or if there is information they no longer need. Finally, read the literature for ideas; there are many publications to help controllers improve the quality of their closing procedures.

For a fast closing to be successful, a well-coordinated organization, teamwork, and good leadership are required. The controller must lead the process of constantly reducing the time and effort required to achieve a quality closing.

The following miscellaneous items should be considered by the controller when devising the closing process:

- *Create a chart of accounts*—Develop a practical and uniform chart of accounts. This should include a proper grouping of accounts to ensure uniformity in reporting, both between segments of the business and from period to period.
- *Set up report due dates*—Establish a firm schedule of management report due dates from which to determine the cutoff of various types of transactions and the recording of accruals if applicable.

- *Control output*—Control the release of information so that premature or incomplete data are not given to management. Otherwise, an excessive amount of time may be required to correct inaccurate information. Also, management may make decisions based on inaccurate information.
- *Use exception reporting*—Where possible, use exception reporting to save management time. Certain variance levels can be reported, below which there is no impact and therefore need not be reported.
- *Create branch schedules*—Realistic cutoff dates must be established for branches, overseas operations, and remote locations. It is very important that the corporate controller has clearly assigned the accounting responsibility for every operation of the business, thereby ensuring that there are no gaps in recording and no duplications. Use modems to transfer information directly to the headquarters computer to avoid data rekeying. The data format is important, since the corporate computer may not be able to read the transmitted information. A good "low tech" approach is to fax the information to corporate headquarters or to deliver the information on a diskette by overnight mail.

19

PERFORMANCE MEASUREMENTS AND TRENDS

If the controller is to give quality information to management, then the ability to look objectively at the business is crucial. The controller must be familiar with its strengths and weaknesses, and must understand the interrelationships of the functions of the organization. An important part of this knowledge revolves around the information provided by those ratios that describe the condition of the business, as well as the trends of key operating statistics.

Performance measures are used by the board of directors and management to judge and correct the performance of the company. Bank lending officers use financial ratios to determine how much funding the company is qualified to receive. Investors, suppliers, and securities analysts use the information to evaluate the creditworthiness and valuation of the company.

The use of a *few* sound relationships is recommended, rather than deluging top management with many ratios and trends. However, the controller should maintain a chart book that is exhaustive in its scope, to better explain to management the background and reasons for the conditions. In general, emphasis should be on *detailed analysis* by the controller and on *simplicity* in what is presented to management.

The performance measures that we describe in this chapter tend to reflect patterns that are indicative of stages in a company's growth. These stages can be either startup, rapid growth, maturity, and decline—ratios will vary considerably depending on the company's stage in this cycle. Thus, the relative "health" of a company's ratios may depend somewhat on the company's cycle and not on the performance of the management team.

Performance Measurements

Some of the more commonly used performance measures are discussed in this section. Not all of them will apply to every company, but if the controller selects those most applicable to his or her company, then they will yield a good view of the firm's financial and operating performance. When a comparison is made of selected ratios of the company with those of particular competitors, much of the database can be secured from the annual report to shareholders or the SEC 10K report, if the measurement is against a public company. Industry averages may also prove useful. Figures for this type of comparison can be secured from a number of sources, including *Almanac of Business and Industrial Financial Ratios, Dun & Bradstreet's Key Business Ratios,* Federal Trade Commission *Quarterly Reports,* SEC publications, and industry association releases. The performance measures follow.

Profitability Measures

These measures relate several profit factors to a significant base.

- *Percent return on net sales*—This indicates what share of the sales dollar is translated into profit. Industry averages are available from the FTC and SEC for comparison purposes.
- *Ratio of gross profit to net sales*—This is a key ratio; changes in the volume of sales, manufacturing costs, and the mixture of products sold will affect this ratio. A low margin may be evidence of intense price competition, poor pricing policies, or insufficient volume to cover fixed manufacturing costs.
- *Percent operating margin as related to sales*—This measures profitability unmarred by changes in income tax rate or other income and expense.
- *Percent return on assets employed*—This measures how management has utilized the company's assets to produce a profit, and is considered by many to be the premier measure of a company's performance. It has several components. As noted in Figure 19–1, improvements in the ratio can occur either by improving earnings or by reducing the asset base, which includes both fixed assets and working capital.
- *Percent return on shareholder equity*—This is the other major measure of corporate performance. It reflects not only operating efficiency but also the impact of debt leverage, so that management is incented to use debt instead of capital as a source of operating funds.
- *Market value added*—This is a measure of wealth creation. It takes a firm's total market capitalization and subtracts from it the company's capital from debt and equity offerings, bank loans, and retained earnings. Any excess amount indicates that the company has created more wealth than it has used.
- *Economic value added*—This is a company's after-tax net operating profit for the year, minus its cost of capital for that year. Any excess amount indicates that the company has created more wealth than it has used.

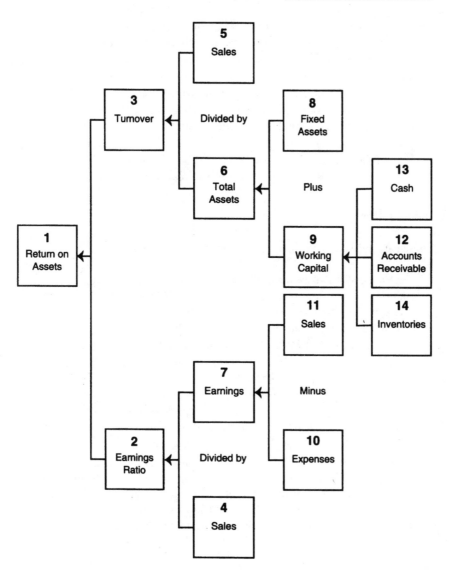

Figure 19–1: Components of Measurement of Percent Return on Assets Employed

- *Percent return on total capital employed*—This measure does not distinguish between debt and capital.

Measures of Growth

This information provides methods to determine a company's growth.

- *Percent increase in sales*—This measure can be compared to the size of the market to determine if the company has changed its percentage share of the market. It can also be reviewed for sales changes based on volume or price increases.

- *Percent increase in net income*—This measure is heavily used, but does not account for asset or equity usage; nor does it consider the impact of long-term R&D or other capital investment decisions.

- *Percent increase in earnings per share*—This measure indicates the avoidance of stock dilution, the use of debt, the use of retained earnings, or the acquisition of a company with a lower price/earnings ratio.

Liquidity Measures

These data measure the firm's ability to meet short-term obligations.

- *Current ratio*—This is one of the most widely used ratios, particularly among credit people, to assess liquidity. It is calculated by dividing the total current assets by the total current liabilities. A ratio of 2 to 1 has long been considered as reflecting a satisfactory condition. When evaluating this ratio, the turnover rate of receivables and inventory should also be considered, since low turnover rates actually contribute to an enhanced current ratio.

- *Quick ratio*—This is a supplement to the current ratio. It is defined as the relationship of cash, receivables, and investments to the current liabilities. This ratio excludes inventory on the assumption that inventory takes time to liquidate, and is not indicative of the ability of the firm to meet its current obligations. A ratio of 1 to 1 is considered acceptable.

- *Positive (Negative) Working Capital*—This is not a ratio. Companies are now striving to achieve negative turnover in order to release cash for other purposes, such as capital investments, stock buyouts, and acquisitions. Negative working capital is achieved by increasing the number of receivables and inventory turns, while keeping or lengthening payables turnover.

Debt Measures

The debt indicators measure the firm's ability to retain and pay for debt.

- *Ratio of long-term debt to shareholders' equity*—This relationship is an expression of the company's capitalization. Investors and bankers compare this ratio to acceptable norms for the industry. An excessive amount of long-term debt as related to net worth—for example, over 80%—raises questions of solvency in adverse times and usually heightens the cost of debt financing.

- *Number of times fixed charges are earned*—This ratio is used to indicate the margin of safety for the creditor. It is determined by dividing the net profit after taxes by the interest on fixed indebtedness, including discount amortization.

Activity Measures

The controller can measure the firm's ability to convert assets into sales or cash:

- *Receivables turnover*—This ratio is calculated by dividing net credit sales by the receivables at the end of the period. A proper turnover rate will depend on the industry's standard collection terms. For example, freight companies collect within ten days, whereas credit card companies collect within thirty days. Lengthening turnover may be caused by overextension of credit, ineffective collection policies, too liberal a credit policy, or ineffective credit investigation.
- *Inventory turnover*—This ratio reveals how many times during the period the inventories are sold. It is calculated by dividing the cost of goods sold by the average inventory. Investigation into a poor turnover rate is necessary, because it can be caused by lowered prices, slow-moving inventory, obsolete inventory, incorrect cost extensions, and so on.
- *Payables turnover*—This ratio reveals how rapidly the firm is paying its obligations. It can indicate that payables are being stretched too far, or that apparently all discounts are being taken.

Operating Measures

By use of these ratios, the controller can express a relationship between items on the income statement and/or balance sheet:

- *Ratio of operating expenses to nets sales*—This is a widely used device for internal management purposes. The review can be made by examining individual types of expenses, groups of expenses, or total functional expense in relation to net sales. The resulting percentages indicate in part the ability of management to adjust expenses to varying sales volume.
- *Ratio of sales returns and allowances to gross sales*—This reflects a cause of change in gross margin through reducing the sales income. It is an indication of the pressure on the sales force for price concessions and a weather vane of customer satisfaction. An increase in this ratio also indicates higher freight costs because of returns and increased expenses for adjusting and handling such matters.
- *Ratio of purchase discounts to purchases*—This ratio measures the efficiency of the accounting department in taking all available discounts. It can also be a sign of financial distress, when a company cannot meet its obligations in a timely manner and cannot take early payment discounts.

- *Ratio of repairs and maintenance to fixed assets*—This ratio is a valuable guide for checking maintenance policy. In periods of low profits, some managements defer maintenance, allowing the equipment to go into a state of disrepair, in an effort to continue reporting profits. This policy tends to increase long-term maintenance expenses and probably property losses.

- *Ratio of depreciation to fixed assets*—This ratio is a rough check on the adequacy of the depreciation policy. It furnishes a simple means of comparison with other companies. Differences in accounting policy, maintenance policy, and the share of fixed assets owned have their effect on the ratio.

- *Ratio of fixed assets to shareholders' equity*—This relationship indicates if shareholders are contributing towards working capital, if the ratio of fixed assets to equity is less than one. An excessively high fixed assets ratio may indicate an overinvestment in fixed assets, depending on the industry.

Cash Flow Measures

Another category of ratios gaining in popularity is cash flow ratios. Increasing use of this group began especially after the Financial Accounting Standards Board (FASB) required the preparation of a statement of cash flows—the successor statement to the statement of sources and uses of cash.

Cash flow ratios may be classified in two groupings: (1) sufficiency ratios and (2) efficiency ratios. The former category describes the adequacy of the cash flows in meeting the needs of the entity. However, the efficiency ratio indicates how well a company generates cash relative to selected measures. Of course, the ratios can be compared to other companies and to successive years in the same entity.

The *sufficiency ratios* are outlined in Table 19–1. Keep in mind, concerning these ratios, that:

Table 19–1: Sufficiency Ratios

Ratio	*Derivation*
Cash flow adequacy	$\dfrac{\text{Cash from operations}}{\text{Long-term debt paid} + \text{funds from assets purchased} + \text{dividends paid}}$
Long-term debt repayment	$\dfrac{\text{Long-term debt payments}}{\text{Cash from operations}}$
Dividend payout	$\dfrac{\text{Dividends}}{\text{Cash from operations}}$
Reinvestment	$\dfrac{\text{Purchase of assets}}{\text{Cash from operations}}$
Debt coverage	$\dfrac{\text{Total debt}}{\text{Cash from operations}}$
Depreciation–amortization relationship	$\dfrac{\text{Depreciation} + \text{amortization}}{\text{Cash from operations}}$

- The *cash flow adequacy ratio* measures the ability of the entity to generate sufficient cash to pay its debts, reinvest in its operations, and pay dividends to the owners. A value in excess of 1 over a period of years reflects an ability to satisfactorily cover these principal cash requirements.
- The next three ratios of *long-term debt repayment, dividend payout,* and *reinvestment* reflect the sufficiency of cash to meet each of these purposes. When added, and expressed as a ratio, a percentage of the resulting number shows the share of cash required for these three purposes combined, without the need to borrow or use other sources of funds.
- The *debt coverage ratio* reflects how many years, at the current level of cash generation, are needed to retire all existing debt.
- The *depreciation–amortization relationship* reflects how much of the cash flow from operations is due to the impact of the depreciation and amortization charges, and the ability of the entity to maintain its asset base.

The three *efficiency ratios* growing in use are shown in Table 19–2. The cash efficiency ratios reflect the effectiveness or efficiency by which cash is generated from either operations or assets. Specifically:

- The *cash flow to sales ratio* reflects the percentage of each sales dollar realized as cash.
- The *operations index* reflects the ratio of cash generated to the income from continuing operations.
- The *cash flow return on assets* reflects the relative amount of cash which the assets (or assets employed) are able to generate.

Other Nonfinancial Measures

- *Sales per employee*—Some companies measure efficiency in terms of sales per employee. This measure can be artificially enhanced by employing contract labor.
- *New products developed*—This measure gauges the firm's ability to bring new products to market. It is best measured by calculating the percentage of

Table 19–2: Efficiency Ratios

Ratio	Derivation
Cash flow to sales	$\dfrac{\text{Cash flow from operations}}{\text{Sales}}$
Operations index	$\dfrac{\text{Cash flow from operations}}{\text{Income from continuing operations}}$
Cash flow return on assets	$\dfrac{\text{Cash flow from operations}}{\text{Total assets}}$

sales that are taken up by new products, and can also be divided into sales due to significant product enhancements, as well as entirely new products, and old products sold into new markets.

- *Make-up of work force*—Minority hiring is a considerable concern to many companies; it can be measured not only in aggregate, but also for the direct labor, professional staff, and management segments of the work force.

TRENDS

The controller is often so deeply engrossed in current problems that he or she fails to watch trends. It is occasionally no small source of amazement to find some very revealing figures with little expenditure of effort, through the use of trend analysis. Trend fluctuations should also be investigated in detail, so that the precise reason for change is examined, and corrective action taken if necessary. Of course, it is easiest to keep historical records of all of the statistics and ratios mentioned earlier in this chapter; however, at a minimum, the controller should review the following trends:

- *Trend of sales volume*—Trends here should be examined by territory and for each product.
- *Trend of gross margins*—The margins by product and volume should be investigated, so that the controller knows the source of the firm's contribution margin.
- *Trend of pricing*—The controller should be aware of changes in pricing, and track the sensitivity of sales volume to pricing changes.
- *Trend of product returns*—Sudden changes in product returns can signal a quality problem in the product, or that the distribution "pipeline" is filled, and the company is forcing too much product onto its distributors.
- *Trend of cost of distribution channels*—The controller should periodically analyze the cost of various methods of selling (through distributors, direct sales, catalogs, and so on) versus the margin earned through each method of sale.
- *Trend of sales quotas*—Some sales managers predict higher sales without budgeting for increased sales staffs to bring in the business. The controller can discover such a problem by reviewing the trend in quotas per salesperson.
- *Trend of cost of sales calls*—The controller should see if the 80/20 rule applies to his company: Do 20% of the customers account for 80% of the business? If so, the controller can analyze the cost of servicing smaller accounts, and recommend dropping certain accounts to improve the company's profitability.
- *Trend of cost of freight*—The company may extend into new geographical areas without considering the cost of shipping product into those areas. A review of the freight cost as a percentage of sales will spotlight this problem.

- *Trend of amount of utilized storage space*—This can be a major item, for it can highlight a myriad of smaller problems, such as obsolete inventory, returned goods, scrapped parts, and excess finished goods.
- *Trend of utilized plant capacity*—This is a good indicator of the need for starting a second shift, for overtime pay, for increased maintenance costs, and for more facilities.
- *Trend of direct labor rates*—This trend can tell the controller if rates are too low compared to the local market rate (perhaps resulting in a disgruntled work force), or that, during a layoff period, the average labor rate is rising because the lower-paid, lower-level people have been laid off.
- *Trend of the accuracy of inventory, bill of material, and labor routing information*—These three items are all required at levels of 98% accuracy or above in order to operate a material requirements planning (MRP) system. Accurate bills of material are required for a just-in-time (JIT) system.
- *Trend of ratio of overhead to production labor*—A company's overhead can balloon rapidly, and this is a primary means of detecting such a trend.
- *Trend of return on shareholders' equity and return on assets*—A significant decline in these measures signals reduced cash flow, more difficult borrowing covenants, and many other problems, such as reduced margins and increased expenses.

INTERRELATIONSHIP OF RATIOS

The controller will find that focusing on a "problem" ratio and fixing the underlying issues can create problems with other related ratios. For example, a company's debt covenant may specify a current ratio of 2 to 1. If the ratio is 1.5 to 1, then the controller can borrow money and retain the cash to improve the current ratio. However, the controller's action could worsen the company's ratio of long-term debt to shareholder's equity. Table 19–3 shows examples of the impact on related ratios of efforts by management to alter ten key ratios.

IMPACT OF EDI ON PERFORMANCE° MEASURES

The advent of electronic data interchange (EDI) may have a significant impact on the acceptability of certain ratios. If a company were to use EDI for all transactions, then the turnover of inventories, receivables, and payables would greatly accelerate, resulting in minimal amounts of all three items on the balance sheet. As a result, the following ratios that include inventories, receivables, and/or payables would be highly skewed:

- Current ratio
- Quick ratio

Table 19–3: Interrelationship of Ratio Changes

A change in this ratio...	Affects these ratios
Current ratio	Management improves the ratio by borrowing money and retaining the cash; the *ratio of long-term debt to shareholders' equity* worsens because debt has increased.
Ratio of long-term debt to shareholders' equity	Management improves the ratio by liquidating short-term investments to pay down the long-term debt; the *current ratio* worsens because investments have been reduced.
Ratio of net sales to receivables	Management improves the ratio by factoring receivables; the *ratio of net profits to net sales* worsens because there is a service charge associated with factoring the receivables.
Turnover of inventories	Management improves the ratio by selling off inventories; the *ratio of gross profit to net sales* worsens because management must pay premium prices to buy raw materials on short notice and ship it to the company by express freight.
Ratio of net sales to working capital	Management improves the ratio by extending payables; the *ratio of gross profit to net sales* worsens because suppliers will not ship additional raw materials, so management must pay premium prices to buy raw materials on short notice and ship it to the company by express freight.
Ratio of repairs and maintenance to fixed assets	Management improves the ratio by cutting the amount of maintenance work on equipment; *the ratio of net income to net sales* worsens because production capacity drops when equipment breaks down.
Number of times fixed charges are earned	Management improves the ratio by using cash on hand to pay down debt; the *current ratio* worsens because the cash is used.
Ratio of gross profit to net sales	Management improves the ratio by increasing prices; the *ratio of net income to net sales* worsens because fewer people buy the product at the higher price.
Ratio of operating expenses to net sales	Management improves the ratio by reducing the accounting department's payroll; the *ratio of gross profit to net sales* worsens because there is no cost accountant to review increased product costs.
Ratio of net income to net sales	Management improves the ratio by selling manufacturing equipment and recording a gain on the sale; *the ratio of gross profit to net sales* worsens because production capacity is reduced, and production must be given to subcontractors at a higher cost.

- Ratio of net sales to receivables
- Average collection period
- Turnover of inventories
- Turnover of current assets
- Ratio of net sales to working capital

The changes imposed by EDI may render industry comparisons useless, since ratio results will vary so widely between EDI and non-EDI firms, unless an entire industry converts to EDI at the same time, allowing all companies to report the new ratio levels.

JIT Ratios

The controller needs to use a different set of ratios when evaluating the performance of a just-in-time (JIT) manufacturing system. A JIT system operates on the principal that the facility should only receive enough supplier components to build parts, produce only enough parts to build the desired number of products, and only produce enough products to meet demand. In order to produce with the exact number of required components from suppliers, the components must be delivered to the company on time, in the right quantities, and with perfect quality (no defective components). In order to produce only enough parts to build the desired number of products, setup times must be minimized, work-in-process (WIP) must be drastically reduced, and scrap must be carefully tracked. In short, the controller must devise data collection procedures for information that does not appear on the balance sheet or income statement. The only ratio related to JIT that can be derived from the balance sheet is inventory turnover.

Appropriate JIT measurements are shown in Table 19–4. Consider, about these measurements, that:

- The *on-time part delivery* measure should be tracked by supplier. The performance measure should then be graphed on a trend line and shared with the supplier, so that worsening trends can be discussed and corrected. The definition of "on time" will vary by company, since some must have the product within a specified hour, while others can wait a day or more. Also, exces-

Table 19–4: Ratios Used to Measure Performance in a JIT Environment

Ratio	Derivation
On-time part delivery	$\dfrac{\text{Number of parts delivered on time}}{\text{Number of parts ordered for delivery date}}$
Part delivery in correct quantities	$\dfrac{\text{Quantity of parts delivered}}{\text{Quantity of parts ordered}}$
Quality of delivered parts	$\dfrac{(\text{Total number of parts}) - (\text{Number of effective parts})}{\text{Total number of parts}}$
Average setup time	Time from end of previous production run to start of next production run
Inventory turnover	$\dfrac{\text{Cost of goods sold}}{\text{Average inventory}}$
Amount of scrap	$\dfrac{\text{Dollar value of scrap}}{\text{Dollar value of production}}$

sively early deliveries should not be considered "on time," for the company must then store the materials longer than it should.

- The *part delivery in correct quantities* measure should be tracked by supplier. Again, the measure should be graphed on a trend line, and the information shared with the supplier. Excessive amounts of delivered quantities should be considered incorrect quantities, since the company must then store and track the excess items.

- The *quality of delivered parts* measure should be tracked by supplier. Again, the measure should be graphed on a trend line, and the information shared with the supplier. The allowable tolerance limits used to define an item as being "within specifications" should be continually narrowed as the more generous tolerance goals are attained by the supplier, so that quality levels constantly improve.

- The *average setup time* measure should be tracked by machine, and plotted on a trend line. Management should closely follow the setup times of machines that cause bottlenecks, and prioritize setup reduction analyses on those machines.

- The *inventory turnover* measure should be broken down into raw materials, work in process, and finished goods, so that slow turnover areas can be more easily highlighted.

- The *scrap* measure should be broken down into many categories, such as losses due to obsolescence, damage caused by material movement, and pilferage. Using such a detailed analysis, management can quickly focus on the most significant scrap problems.

20

FINANCIAL ANALYSIS

In this chapter, we will explore a number of additional analysis techniques that will give a controller a much more comprehensive set of tools for evaluating a company's various financial illnesses. Also, many sections contain sample management reports that list not only the financial analysis, but also the controller's written evaluation, which is usually the most read and influential of all the information released by the accounting department.

ANALYZING FINANCIAL STATEMENTS

When the controller issues financial statements, the management team will probably not have the time or the financial skill to review them in enough detail to obtain sufficient knowledge about corrective actions to be taken. It is the job of the controller to provide additional information about the financial statements that reveals trends, risks, and opportunities for improvement.

The layout of the typical financial statement shows the current month's performance as well as that of the previous month, plus year-to-date information. Unfortunately, this does not include a sufficient volume of information for management to ascertain any trends in activity or profitability. An additional report is needed to present such information to management. An example of this is shown in Figure 20–1, where we itemize both the balance sheet and income statement for every month of the year. By using this format, managers can quickly scan through the information and determine trends in the major categories. However, this is not a format supported by the typical accounting system, so the controller may have to authorize custom programming to create the report, or else manually transfer the information into an electronic spreadsheet, which runs the risk of including typographical errors. If there are key line items in this full-year format that are of particular importance to management, then the controller can convert them into a graphical presentation, which is easier to read. An example of graphical layouts, using the information from Figure 20–1, is shown in Figure 20–2. These include separate graphs for the cash balance, revenue, and net profit.

In addition to trend information, the controller must provide the management team with information about the financial risks to which the company is currently subject. This can include an analysis of how closely the company is coming to minimum loan covenants, since dropping below them would give lenders the option to call their loans. Another good measure is a company's debt to equity ratio, since a high ratio is indicative of an excessive degree of leverage that may be difficult to work off. A related measure is the number of times the interest expense is covered by current earnings, since dropping below a ratio of 1:1 would mean that a company cannot pay for, and therefore will probably default on, its debts. Other useful risk measures are the current and quick ratios, because they compare the amount of a company's current assets to its current liabilities. If the ratio is near or below 1:1, a company may have difficulty paying its liabilities. These ratios are noted in Figure 20–3, which uses the same full-year format used earlier in Figure 20–1, and clearly shows any positive or negative trends. It is very useful to include the formulas for each ratio in this analysis (as is demonstrated in the example), since management can then see for itself exactly how the numbers come together to form each ratio.

The statistics report in Figure 20–3 reveals a great deal of information about a company. In the example, we see a company that is heavily burdened by debt, and which achieves a miniscule return on assets and net profit. However, its sales have surged as the year has progressed, which has slightly increased its profitability. Also, it has gradually reduced its investment in working capital, which has allowed it to pay off a modest amount of debt. However, there is still far too much interest expense, and a lender must wonder how long the company can continue to take funds from working capital to pay off its debt, especially since there is more than twice as much debt as working capital. Finally, the lender must be waiving all covenant requirements, since the company is unable to meet any of them. In short, the ratio analysis reveals a company trying to pull itself out from under a monstrous load of debt with only the slightest of profit margins, but using its assets wisely to improve its financial position toward the end of the year.

Also included in the second half of the example in Figure 20–3 is a listing of ratios that show developing changes in the financial condition of the company. These are useful leading indicators of potential problems that the management team should address as soon as possible. For example, the amount of sales per employee signals a change in the efficiency of the company in generating sales. The same measure is later applied to gross margins and net margins. Also, an increase in the annualized rate of employee turnover will possibly result in a later drop in the efficiency of the company, since new employees must go through a

Balance Sheet by Month

	Jan	Feb	Mar	Apr	May	Jun	Jul	Aug	Sep	Oct	Nov	Dec
ASSETS												
Cash	-227,181	-525,509	-494,706	-438,354	-157,490	-156,705	-156,044	-155,979	-155,519	-155,266	-155,154	-155,084
Accounts receivable	2,197,873	2,450,378	2,042,165	3,035,957	2,997,925	2,983,026	2,970,431	2,969,194	2,960,432	2,955,618	2,953,493	2,952,163
Inventories	2,007,041	2,273,238	2,418,776	2,715,241	2,587,566	2,574,708	2,563,838	2,562,770	2,555,207	2,551,052	2,549,217	2,548,069
Total current assets	3,977,733	4,198,107	3,966,235	5,312,844	5,428,000	5,401,029	5,378,225	5,375,985	5,360,120	5,351,405	5,347,556	5,345,148
Net P & E	5,240,995	5,091,069	5,004,064	4,949,893	4,873,264	4,796,635	4,720,006	4,643,377	4,566,748	4,490,119	4,413,490	4,336,861
Other assets	97,042	97,042	97,042	35,113	45,676	52,019	48,442	49,503	50,026	51,247	52,068	53,006
Total assets	9,315,770	9,386,218	9,067,341	10,297,850	10,346,940	10,249,683	10,146,673	10,068,865	9,976,894	9,892,771	9,813,114	9,735,015
LIABILITIES												
Accounts payable	1,151,944	1,862,154	1,671,275	2,575,146	2,585,191	2,675,719	2,682,612	2,739,248	2,747,322	2,787,249	2,816,385	2,841,512
Accrued liabilities	470,605	277,914	273,981	244,332	330,597	342,169	343,050	350,293	351,325	356,431	360,157	363,370
Total current liabilities	1,622,549	2,140,068	1,945,256	2,819,478	2,915,789	3,017,894	3,025,668	3,089,547	3,098,654	3,143,687	3,176,548	3,204,889
Long-term debt	7,572,513	7,138,983	7,004,849	7,347,400	7,289,850	7,091,621	6,967,058	6,811,315	6,696,395	6,552,842	6,425,603	6,304,912
Stockholder's equity												
Common stock	15,000	15,000	15,000	15,000	15,000							
Retained earnings	105,708	92,167	102,236	115,972	126,302	140,168	153,947	168,003	181,845	196,242	210,963	225,214
Total stockholder's equity	120,708	107,167	117,236	130,972	141,302	140,168	153,947	168,003	181,845	196,242	210,963	225,214
Total liabilities & equity	9,315,770	9,386,218	9,067,341	10,297,850	10,346,940	10,249,683	10,146,673	10,068,865	9,976,894	9,892,771	9,813,114	9,735,015

Income Statement by Month

	Jan	Feb	Mar	Apr	May	Jun	Jul	Aug	Sep	Oct	Nov	Dec
Revenue	1,502,978	1,497,352	1,432,057	1,700,024	1,776,442	1,809,052	1,825,056	1,840,723	1,872,154	1,895,003	1,913,457	1,925,665
Cost of sales												
Materials	762,010	759,157	619,133	869,053	902,280	917,189	925,303	933,247	949,182	960,767	970,123	976,312
Labor	263,835	225,446	201,941	240,561	238,054	236,986	239,082	241,135	245,252	248,245	250,663	252,262
Factory Overhead	462,194	445,763	490,262	467,053	519,050	528,243	532,916	537,491	546,669	553,341	558,729	562,294
Gross margin	14,939	66,986	120,721	123,357	117,058	126,634	127,754	128,851	131,051	132,650	133,942	134,797
S, G & A	90,553	89,554	103,940	100,463	99,841	103,524	104,789	105,423	107,982	108,654	109,408	111,045
Operating income	-75,614	-22,568	16,781	22,894	17,217	23,110	22,965	23,428	23,069	23,996	24,534	23,752
Tax benefit (expense)	-30,246	-9,027	6,712	9,158	6,887	9,244	9,186	9,371	9,228	9,598	9,814	9,501
Net income (loss)	-45,368	-13,541	10,069	13,736	10,330	13,866	13,779	14,057	13,841	14,398	14,720	14,251

Figure 20-1: Full-Year Presentation of Financial Results

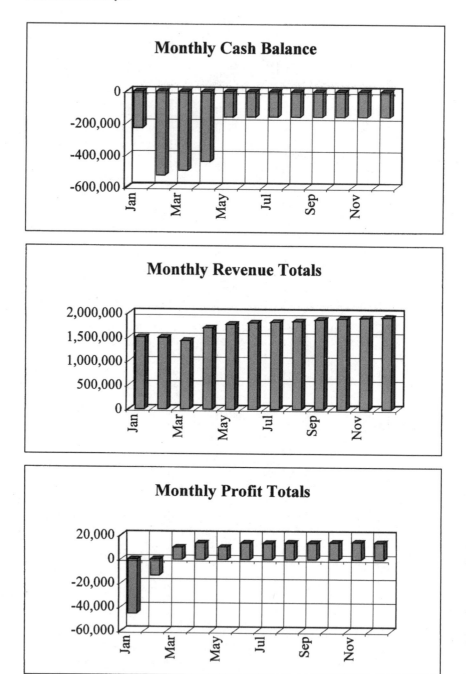

Figure 20–2: Graphical Presentation of Financial Trends

Statistics

	Jan	Feb	Mar	Apr	May	Jun	Jul	Aug	Sep	Oct	Nov	Dec
Loan Covenants (required):												
Quick ratio (1.0:1)	1.2	0.9	1.0	0.7	0.7	0.7	0.7	0.6	0.6	0.6	0.6	0.6
Current ratio (1.5:1)	2.5	2.0	2.0	1.9	1.9	1.8	1.8	1.7	1.7	1.7	1.7	1.7
Debt/Equity (1:1)	62.7	66.6	59.8	56.1	51.6	50.6	45.3	40.5	36.8	33.4	30.5	28.0
Times Interest Earned (2:1)	−0.8	−0.3	0.2	0.2	0.2	0.3	0.3	0.3	0.3	0.3	0.3	0.3
Financial Risk Measures:												
Inventory turnover	8.9	7.6	6.5	7.0	7.7	7.8	7.9	8.0	8.2	8.3	8.4	8.4
Accounts receivable turnover	8.2	7.3	8.4	6.7	7.1	7.3	7.4	7.4	7.6	7.7	7.8	7.8
Employee turnover (annualized)	14%	16%	21%	27%	23%	24%	21%	19%	18%	21%	23%	25%
No. of employees	160.0	163.0	165.0	168.0	172.0	184.0	188.0	191.0	199.0	203.0	204.0	206.0
Revenue per employee	$112,723	$110,235	$104,150	$121,430	$123,938	$117,982	$116,493	$115,648	$112,894	$112,020	$112,556	$112,175
Total working capital (000s)	$3,053	$2,861	$2,790	$3,176	$3,000	$2,882	$2,852	$2,793	$2,768	$2,719	$2,686	$2,659
Return on assets (annualized)	−5.8%	−1.7%	1.3%	1.6%	1.2%	1.6%	1.6%	1.7%	1.7%	1.7%	1.8%	1.8%
Gross margin percentage	1.0%	4.5%	8.4%	7.3%	6.6%	7.0%	7.0%	7.0%	7.0%	7.0%	7.0%	7.0%
Net profit percentage	−3.0%	−0.9%	0.7%	0.8%	0.6%	0.8%	0.8%	0.8%	0.7%	0.8%	0.8%	0.7%

Measurement Descriptions:

Quick ratio	(Cash + Accounts Receivable)/(Current Liabilities)
Current ratio	(Current Assets)/(Current Liabilities)
Debt/Equity	(Short Term Debt + Long Term Debt)/(Total Stockholder's Equity)
Times Interest Earned	(Net Profit Before Interest Expense)/(Interest Expense)
Inventory turnover	(Cost of Goods Sold* 12)/(Inventory)
Accounts receivable turnover	(Revenue* 12)/(Accounts Receivable)
Employee turnover (annualized)	(Total Departed Employees)/(Total Employees at Beginning of Year) * 12)
No. of employees	Total Full Time Equivalents
Revenue per employee	(Monthly Revenue * 12)/(No. of Employees)
Total working capital	(Accounts Receivable + Inventory − Accounts Payable)
Return on assets (annualized)	(Net Profit/Total Assets) * 12
Gross margin percentage	(Gross Margin)/(Revenue)
Net profit percentage	(Net Profit)/(Revenue)

Figure 20–3: Full-Year Presentation of Risk and Financial Ratios

learning curve before they can become as productive as the employees they replaced. The exact measures used will vary by business, since each one operates in a different environment, and therefore requires different leading indicators of its financial activity.

Once a controller has assembled all this information, the management team should have sufficient information available to form conclusions regarding the financial condition of the company, its prospects in the near term (based on current trends), and what actions to take to improve the business. However, this information is still largely numerical, which may not be the best way to present information to the management team. Accordingly, the controller should attach a written executive summary to the financial statement package that itemizes the main issues. In order to lend some organization to this presentation, it is best to set up standard categories in which the controller can insert information, such as the main line items in the balance sheet and income statement, plus information about loans, capital expenditures, and working capital.

DIRECTING MANAGEMENT PERFORMANCE

In this section, we review the types of performance that management wants to achieve, the performance measures that a controller can use to ensure that the management team is pursuing those targets, and their impact on manager performance.

There are three standard approaches to growing a company. Each one requires a different set of performance measures to ensure that managers are targeting the correct activities that will contribute to the appropriate growth strategy. The controller must determine which strategy is being followed and tailor a performance measurement system to it. If the controller uses the wrong measures, then the management team may be driven by the measures to alter their behavior away from the target strategy, which is likely if large performance bonuses are tied to the measures; thus, the controller's choice of measurements can have a powerful impact on a company's ability to achieve its designated growth strategy. The three types of growth strategies are

1. growth by acquisition,
2. growth by product development, and
3. growth by territorial expansion.

While the controller is assembling the set of measurements for the management team, it is extremely important to also consider the impact these measures will have on the managers and to plan accordingly. For example, if the key performance measure for a general manager is corporate net profit, this person can artificially increase the profit by ratcheting up production, which increases the level of inventory and capitalizes more overhead costs, which in turn reduces the cost of goods sold and increases profits. Unfortunately, this strategy also greatly increases the company's investment in inventory, which the general manager may not care about if he or she has just received a large performance bonus based on the surge in profits. The best way for a controller to avoid such a problem is to create countervailing performance measures that require managers to not only keep profits high, but also to keep asset usage low. Such measures are as follows:

- The change in working capital in real dollars, or the rate of working capital turnover.
- The change in fixed assets in real dollars, or the rate of fixed asset turnover.
- The return on assets.

Any of these measures will keep managers from altering the true intention of performance measurements.

ANALYZING WORKING CAPITAL

A company can experience excellent profitability and still go bankrupt for lack of cash. This is most commonly caused by increases in accounts receivable and inventory, or a decline in accounts payable. The first two are the primary operating investments that a company must make in order to support sales to customers, while the last is a key source of funding for operations. The management team can be taken by surprise by sudden shifts in these cash flows unless the controller keeps a watchful eye on the company's investment in working capital and relays reports on changes.

The main tasks for the controller are to not only track the dollar amount of working capital, but also to conduct a sufficiently detailed investigation into the causes of variations to write a detailed analysis of any problems, along with recommendations for changes. In order to conduct such an in-depth analysis, it is first necessary to understand the reasons (listed below) why there are changes in working capital.

- *Accounts Receivable—Poor collection efforts.* The investment in accounts receivable will rise if the collections staff does not actively investigate all overdue invoices, contact customers regarding the reasons, and correct any problems that are preventing the customers from paying. This may also require the use of dunning letters or even lawsuits to collect the funds.
- *Accounts Receivable—Poor credit setting standards.* The investment in accounts receivable will rise if the finance department is issuing excessively high credit levels to customers who do not have the financial capacity to pay for such large purchases (or at least not for a long time). A secondary problem may be that the sales staff is selling to new customers in advance of their having been approved for credit, and is then using the customer purchase orders as a tool for pressuring the finance staff into granting excessively high levels of credit. The best way to avoid this difficulty is to set new customer

credit standards in advance, as well as to regularly review credit ratings for old customers.

- *Accounts Receivable—Delivery problems.* The investment in accounts receivable will increase if there are delivery problems to the customer, such as incorrect products or quantities, as well as product quality issues or damage due to incorrect packaging or shipping. In all these cases, customers will refuse to pay for billed amounts. The only way to resolve these issues is for the collections staff to investigate each one, collect evidence from the customers, and issue them credits, which is a very time-consuming process. To correct these problems, the controller must collect the error information forwarded by the collections staff, and meet with the related departments (e.g., warehouse, production, engineering, and quality) on a regular basis to determine and implement corrective actions, based on this information.

- *Accounts Receivable—Billing problems.* The investment in accounts receivable will increase if there are problems with the invoices sent to customers, such as an address that routes it to the wrong customer location, incorrect unit pricing, missing customer purchase order numbers, or any other incorrect or missing information. As was the case with delivery problems in the preceding point, the collections staff must research these problems with the customer; but in this case, a new invoice is sometimes issued, which requires extra transit and processing time, and so greatly lengthens the interval before the customer pays for each invoice. To avoid these problems, the controller should actively investigate all billing problems uncovered by the collections staff, correct them, and watch for any repeat incidents that will need additional corrective action.

- *Inventory—Excessive purchasing.* The investment in inventory will increase if the purchasing staff buys an excessive quantity of parts. This is a common problem when the purchasing department is focusing on being efficient by reducing the number of purchase orders, which results in buying many months' supply of parts. It is also caused by the use of economic order quantities, which generally results in large-quantity purchases. This approach also keeps the purchasing staff from absorbing blame for running out of parts, since they always keep too much on hand. A better approach is to use just-in-time purchasing techniques or a material requirements planning (MRP) system without economic order quantities that details the precise part quantities needed. It is also helpful to avoid any purchasing department ranking systems that alter purchasing behavior in the direction of buying too much inventory.

- *Inventory—Excessive quantities forecasted.* The investment in finished goods inventory will increase if the sales and marketing staff forecasts an excessive amount of unit sales, because the production department will build to this forecast, which will result in a major increase in finished goods inventory. The best way to mitigate this problem is to keep very close track of unit sales, perhaps as frequently as on a weekly basis, and notify the management group as soon as it appears that sales forecasts will not be matched by actual sales.

However, this is a difficult issue for products with strongly seasonal sales, since nearly all product sales may occur in such a short time frame that there is no way to modify the production schedule. In such cases, it may be best to use a substantial markdown of the inventory in order to clear it from stock; otherwise, there may be a risk of product obsolescence.

- *Inventory—Excessive quantities produced.* The finished goods and work-in-process inventory investment will increase if the production department runs excessively long production runs. This is a common situation, since the production department wants to create as much product as possible before it tears down an equipment setup that may have taken hours to complete. To avoid this situation, the controller can suggest measuring the production department on the leanness of its work-in-process inventories or switching to just-in-time production cells that use kanban pull systems.

- *Inventory—Premature engineering changes.* The raw materials inventory investment will increase if the engineering staff institutes an engineering change order on a product that requires the replacement of existing component parts with different parts. If there are quantities of the old part in stock at the time of the changeover, and if those parts cannot be used on other products, then they will automatically become obsolete. The best way to avoid this problem is to set up a procedure that requires the engineering staff to check on existing part quantities prior to implementing an engineering change order, as well as involving the purchasing staff, so they will know when to stop buying the parts that are to be eliminated.

- *Inventory—Distribution issues.* The work-in-process and finished goods inventory investment will increase if there are problems with the distribution system. For example, if the company has decided to add several new warehouses to improve the delivery time to customers, then each one requires an investment in inventory. Also, if the company shifts its work-in-process to a different location for final assembly, there may be a large buffer stock of inventory at that location, which is used to keep the assembly operation running in case deliveries do not arrive on time. This problem can also arise if the production department is producing on a different schedule from the one used by the assembly department. These problems are best resolved by closely reviewing the cost-benefit analysis for each additional warehouse, as well as by more closely meshing the production operation and any downstream departments that rely on its output, perhaps by using a kanban pull system.

- *Accounts Payable—Use of early payment discounts.* The funding available from accounts payable will decline if the controller elects to take all early payment discounts that are allowed by suppliers. Though this is for a good cause, and will result in reduced expenses on the items purchased for which deductions are being taken, it also means that the company will have a smaller float on the money being loaned to it by suppliers. One way to mitigate this issue is to determine the corporate cost of capital and make sure that all discounts taken will result in savings exceeding that cost.

- *Accounts Payable—Changes in supplier payment terms.* The funding available from accounts payable will decline if suppliers reduce their days of payment terms. This happens either when the purchasing staff negotiates better prices in exchange for a reduction in payment terms, or because the company's payments have previously been so overdue that the credit departments of suppliers are forced to cut back on their terms. If the cause is related to a price reduction negotiated by the purchasing department, then the controller should review the pricing change to verify that the savings from the cost reduction exceeds the added funding cost resulting from a more rapid payment to the supplier.

- *Accounts Payable—Changes to new suppliers.* The funding available from accounts payable will also decline if the purchasing staff switches to new suppliers who have shorter payment terms than the ones they are replacing. There may be good reasons for the switch, such as lower prices, better product quality, or more reliable delivery service. Once again, the controller should compare the savings from using the new supplier to the cost of losing supplier funding. Since the purchasing staff usually does not change suppliers without good reason, there is not normally a good alternative to using a new supplier.

- *Accounts Payable—Paying suppliers too early.* The funding available from accounts payable will decline if there is a problem in the accounting department that results in early payments to suppliers. This may be caused by poor training of the accounting staff, pressure from suppliers for early payment, or else payment procedures that result in very infrequent check runs, so that the accounting staff feels obligated to make some early payments, rather than waiting several weeks for the next check run. This area is entirely within the controller's area of responsibility, and so can be quickly influenced by procedural or training improvements. If there is pressure from other departments to make early payments to suppliers, the controller should obtain high-level management support of a policy that suppliers will not be paid early.

Given the large number of possible reasons why a company's working capital investment is increasing, and the number of departments that could be involved in the increase, it is evident that the controller should conduct more than a superficial investigation of causes, so that an explanation can accompany the working capital report to management that clearly defines the issues and recommends solutions. Otherwise, management will only know that there is a problem, but not how to fix it. An example of a working capital trend line report is shown in Figure 20–4 that includes both a graphical representation of a company's working capital investment and a further breakdown of the components of the total. In addition, the analysis in Figure 20–5 contains a sample set of controller's notes to management that itemize the precise problems that have caused the changes in working capital, and which include specific recommendations for modifications. This type of format is necessary for management to fully understand the reasons for changes in working capital, as well as the ramifications of what will happen if the problems are not fixed.

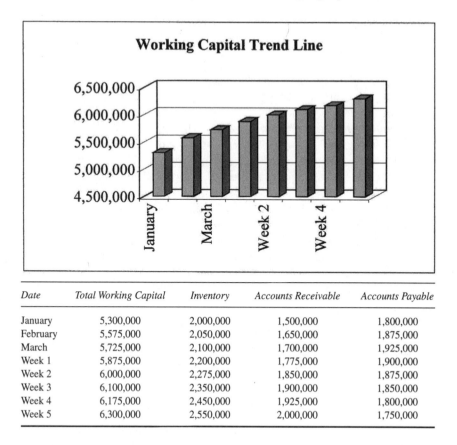

Date	Total Working Capital	Inventory	Accounts Receivable	Accounts Payable
January	5,300,000	2,000,000	1,500,000	1,800,000
February	5,575,000	2,050,000	1,650,000	1,875,000
March	5,725,000	2,100,000	1,700,000	1,925,000
Week 1	5,875,000	2,200,000	1,775,000	1,900,000
Week 2	6,000,000	2,275,000	1,850,000	1,875,000
Week 3	6,100,000	2,350,000	1,900,000	1,850,000
Week 4	6,175,000	2,450,000	1,925,000	1,800,000
Week 5	6,300,000	2,550,000	2,000,000	1,750,000

Figure 20–4: Sample Working Capital Analysis

Note that the layout of the working capital analysis in Figure 20–4 lists the month-end working capital for each of the past three months, as well as for the five weeks of the current month. This gives the controller a good feel for how the working capital investment has been tracking over the short term. In some situations, it may also be necessary to add prior-year figures, which yields a longer trend line. This later approach is most useful for companies with very slow growth rates, since current operating conditions will be very comparable to those of previous years.

ANALYZING CAPITAL INVESTMENTS

The controller is frequently called on to pass judgment on the acceptability of new capital projects. There are several steps to follow in doing so, which are outlined in this section.

The company's working capital investment has increased by $1,200,000 in the past three months. This is due to several factors, one of which is the conversion to a new motor for the Roto-Wash clothes washer before the old stock had been fully depleted. The inventory investment in the old motors is $250,000. Also, the production department made an excessively long production run on the Roto-Wash, resulting in an excess finished goods inventory of $300,000. Further, our accounts receivable from CAS (Central Appliance Stores) are overdue by $500,000, which was caused by the pre-placement of a $500,000 customer order prior to approval by the credit department, with override approval by the executive committee. Finally, the controller chose to take early payment discounts that resulted in a net decrease in accounts payable of $50,000. Since the company has now used up its entire line of credit, and has no spare cash, we recommend the following actions to reduce the company's investment in working capital:

- Reverse the engineering change order for Roto-Wash motors until the old stock has been depleted, which should be three months, based on current sales levels, and which is subject to the following item.
- Stop production of the Roto-Wash for two months, which will allow demand to catch up with current finished goods inventory stocks.
- Put an immediate credit hold on Credit Appliance Stores until its $500,000 overdue invoice is paid, followed by the imposition of a revised $100,000 credit limit.
- Stop taking early payment discounts of all kinds until the working capital investment allows enough excess cash flow to begin taking them again.

Figure 20–5: Sample Controller's Notes on the Preceding Working Capital Analysis

First, when a controller receives a request for capital expenditure, he or she must determine if it is for a profit-making venture, or for some other purpose. For example, it may be for the construction of handicapped access to various parts of the building, or the installation of legally required scrubbers in the factory smokestacks. If it is for such items as these, the controller has no further work to do, since the expenditures are required by law. The only influence the controller may have over such projects is to recommend slight variations in the timing of the expenditures, in case they will have an adverse impact on cash flows, or else to request an investigation into less expensive alternatives.

Year	Description	Cash Inflow (+) or Outflow (−)	Value Present Value Factor	Present Value of Line Item	Cumulative Net Present Value
0	Machine purchase	$–250,000	0	$–250,000	$–250,000
1	Working capital	–100,000	.8929	–89,290	–339,290
1	Revenue	+350,000	.8929	+312,515	–26,775
1	Reduction in taxes due to depreciation	+10,000	.8929	+8,929	–17,846
2	Maintenance costs	–20,000	.7972	–15,944	–33,790
2	Revenue	+350,000	.7972	+279,020	+245,230
2	Reduction in taxes due to depreciation	+10,000	.7972	+7,972	+253,202
3	Revenue	+350,000	.7118	+249,130	+502,332
3	Reduction in taxes due to depreciation	+10,000	.7118	+7,118	+509,450
4	Maintenance costs	–20,000	.6355	–12,710	+496,740
4	Revenue	+350,000	.6355	+222,425	+719,165
4	Reduction in taxes due to depreciation	+10,000	.6355	+6,355	+725,520
5	Revenue	+350,000	.5674	+198,590	+924,110
5	Reduction in taxes due to depreciation	+10,000	.5674	+5,674	+929,784
6	Maintenance costs	–20,000	.5066	–10,132	+919,652
6	Revenue	+350,000	.5066	+177,310	+1,096,962
6	Reduction in taxes due to depreciation	+10,000	.5066	+5,066	+1,102,028
7	Revenue	+350,000	.4523	+158,305	+1,260,333
7	Reduction in taxes due to depreciation	+10,000	.4523	+4,523	+1,264,856
7	Working capital recovery	+100,000	.4523	+45,230	+1,310,086
7	Machine salvage value	+75,000	.4523	+33,923	**$1,344,009**

Note: All revenue line items are net of income taxes paid.
Note: The present value factor is based on a discount rate of 12%.
Note: The reduction in taxes due to depreciation expense is based on a depreciable asset value of $175,000, straight-line depreciation for seven years, and an incremental corporate tax rate of 40%.[1]

Figure 20–6: A Sample Cash Flow Analysis for a Capital Expenditure

If the project under review is intended for profitable activities, then the controller should use the net present value calculation to evaluate it. This method summarizes all positive and negative cash flows related to a project by period and then discounts the cash flows based on a discount rate, which yields a positive or negative cash flow. This information is summarized in a cash flow report similar to the one shown in Figure 20–5. The cash flow summary should include the initial expenditure for the project, plus any additional payments for maintenance, personal property taxes, and income taxes. Offsetting these cash outflows will be the annual cash inflow from profits related to the project, plus the cash from the sale of the equipment at the end of the project. Also, an early cash outflow will be the working capital required to support sales from the project, which will include incremental increases in accounts receivable and inventory. The cash flow analysis should also include the cash inflow at the end of the project, when the working capital investment is no longer needed. Finally, the depreciation expense from the purchased equipment is a non-cash expenditure but can be used to reduce the amount of income taxes paid, which *is* a cash outflow, and so must be included in the analysis.

In the example, there is a set of discounting factors listed in the "Present Value Factor" column. These are from a present value table (available in most accounting textbooks and on many electronic calculators) and are used to reduce the value of a future cash flow by the discount rate, which is 12% in the example. Near-term cash flows are discounted less, while those far out in the future are discounted the most. This discount rate is derived by calculating the company's cost of capital, which is its weighted average cost of debt and equity, and is described further in Chapter 16. Since the discount rate is a company's cost of funds, the cash flows from any new project must be discounted at this rate to see if there is any positive cash flow after the cost of capital has been subtracted from them. If the resulting cash flow is positive, then the project is generating more cash than is required by the initial investment. If it is negative, then the cash flows generated by a project are less than its cost, and a controller should advise management not to invest in it.

Another way to evaluate a capital expenditure is to calculate its payback period. This tells management how long it will take for a project to earn back its initial investment, and is a useful way to determine a project's risk—if it pays back quickly, then it has a low risk, with the reverse for a project that takes many years to pay back. The calculation is simply the average annual cash flow, divided into the initial investment. The trouble with this calculation is that it ignores the time value of money by not discounting cash flows and it also does not give management any idea of a project's return on investment—just its ability to pay back the original investment. Consequently, this is generally considered an inferior analysis tool and should only be reported to management alongside a more sophisticated measure, such as a project's net present value.

When a controller is asked to pass judgment on many projects, perhaps during the budgeting process, a key issue is the amount of funds available for them. For example, if twenty projects all have positive cash flows, but there is only enough funding for ten, then the controller should recommend only those with the highest net present values, since they will generate the greatest cash flow to the company. Then, if the company is able to procure additional funding, the lesser projects can also be implemented, though the controller should re-evaluate those projects based on the incremental funding used to pay for them. For example, if a company has a cost of capital of 12%, but it can only find financing for additional projects at a rate of 15%, then this incremental rate of 15% must be used to discount the additional projects, since projects that could only generate a positive cash flow at the lower rate of return will otherwise not provide enough cash for the company to pay for its newly obtained debt.

ANALYZING CAPACITY UTILIZATION

It is widely accepted that the controller is responsible for the capital budgeting process. However, buying an asset is really only one piece of the total capital budgeting process, for it also includes determining the timing of when new equipment is needed, as well as when existing assets should be sold off. These two extra items can be readily reviewed by the controller through the technique of capacity utilization.

Capacity utilization involves clustering all major machinery into groups of work centers (at least on paper), and then comparing the capacity of each work center to its amount of actual usage. This reveals those work centers that continually do not use all their available capacity, as well as those that are constantly bumping up against their maximum run rates. In the first case, the controller can recommend eliminating equipment (which may result in significant cash inflows from sale of the equipment), while the later case is a clear sign that additional equipment should be purchased. An example of such an analysis is shown in Figure 20–6, where we list the monthly utilization for a set of work centers over the last four months. The individual utilization for each machine within each work center is also revealed, so that one can see which ones are poorly utilized (possibly due to equipment down time). The example is based on a work week of 168 hours, which assumes a full rate of operation, seven days a week and twenty-four hours per day. A 168-hour week is the only way to review capacity utilization, since a company that operates on a forty-hour week may think that it has maximized the use of its machinery *during that period,* but actually still has the option to run it during other shifts as well. Thus, though it may appear unpalatable to the management team, the controller should always point out that equipment can be run during other shifts, rather than incurring the added capital expense of new equipment to be run only during the first shift.

A key factor when determining capacity utilization percentages is calculating the point at which the equipment has reached its theoretical capacity level. There are very few situations where any type of equipment can run for 168 consecutive hours without some kind of maintenance or down time for operator breaks. Accordingly, the controller must look at actual experience to see what the highest level of utilization has been on each type of equipment; when the capacity utilization of an entire work center reaches that level, it is time to purchase new equipment—*not* when management is vainly waiting for actual utilization to reach the theoretical 168 hours-per-week level.

Another issue regarding the analysis of capacity utilization is seasonality. It is possible that there are a few peak periods during the year when all equipment is

Description	Machine Age	January	February	March	April
Band Saw	—	**43%**	**45%**	**35%**	**35%**
Saw #1	1995	50%	45%	50%	40%
Saw #2	1999	60%	60%	35%	40%
Saw #3	1985	20%	30%	20%	25%
Table Saw	—	**80%**	**80%**	**86%**	**82%**
Saw #1	2000	80%	90%	88%	80%
Saw #2	2000	75%	84%	86%	90%
Saw #3	1998	85%	67%	85%	75%
Power Sander	—	**75%**	**90%**	**84%**	**90%**
Sander #1	1997	80%	90%	85%	92%
Sander #2	1996	70%	95%	85%	90%
Sander #3	1999	75%	85%	82%	88%

Figure 20–7: Capacity Utilization Report

being used to its utmost, but which is not readily apparent at other times of the year when business is slow. If this is the case, the controller should modify the capacity utilization report so that it shows utilization for the entire year, and perhaps for the preceding year as well, so that there is a factual justification for eliminating equipment.

If there is a case where equipment must be eliminated, the controller may be in a good position to recommend which specific items to sell. This is done by including the age of each machine in the capacity utilization report. For example, the preceding utilization report shows there is excess capacity in the band saw department. The controller can quickly skim through the list of equipment on the report and see that the third band saw is ten years older than any other one in the work center. On the assumption that the oldest machines require the most maintenance, it is obvious that this is the machine to be sold.

A final issue regarding capacity utilization is the controller's recommendation regarding what size equipment to purchase, if a work center is reaching its maximum level of utilization with the existing machinery. This is partially a question for the engineering and production staffs to answer, since they will know what equipment will fit in the remaining floor space, as well as what types of new equipment run the most efficiently. However, the controller can make some meaningful input in the area of how much extra capacity is needed by taking the sales forecast and translating it into future capacity requirements by work center, and then subtracting out the existing capacity to determine the additional amount that is needed in the short run. The resulting answer may be shortsighted, since it does not focus any further into the future than the range of the furthest sales forecast. However, it is a factually based analysis that may keep the management team from buying equipment that has a larger production capacity than is strictly necessary.

The simple analyses noted in this section will assist a company in finding the precise mix of equipment that it currently needs to operate its production facility at the highest reasonable rate of utilization, which keeps a company's capital investment at a minimum.

ANALYZING FINANCING OPTIONS

The controller is sometimes called on to give recommendations regarding the types of financing that a company should use, especially when there is no chief financial officer to fill this function. This is a key issue, because each type of financing carries with it certain unique risks and benefits that other members of the management team may not be aware of, and which can have a significant impact on a company's financial risk and return on equity.

There are two basic types of funding. One is debt, which is an agreement to pay interest on a loaned sum, that must eventually be returned to the creditor. It may also be collateralized against certain company assets in the event of default. Some variations on this concept are the balloon payment loan, which requires minimal periodic payments and a large final payment; the lease, which is a loan targeted at a specific asset and under which the creditor may continue to own the asset; and preferred stock, which is a crossover instrument that requires period interest payments, but has no provision for paying back the initial principal payment. A variation on the loan from a lender is a bond issuance, in which a company issues debt directly to individual investors, and which results in similar costs and terms as a bank loan, though the costs tend to be somewhat lower. The interest rate on all these types of debt will be lower if there is associated collateral, since the lender has minimized its risk by having the option to sell company assets to pay itself back. However, the interest rate can be extremely high if there is no collateral, since the lender has a much higher degree of non-payment risk. Also, if the form of debt is a lease, there are so many variables involved in the determination of lease rates (current and ending asset valuations, maintenance and tax costs, and interest rates) that a company can end up paying a very high interest rate unless it is extremely careful in analyzing all components of each lease deal. Thus, the cost of this option can vary considerably with the terms of the debt.

The other type of funding is equity. This is the payment made by an owner to purchase common stock. The company need not pay back the owner, nor is there any stated interest rate. However, a company should never think that this is "free money." Quite the contrary—since owners have no collateral in the business, they expect outsized returns in exchange for their investments. Accordingly, the company must either issue board-authorized dividends or else increase the company valuation to such an extent that owners can sell their shares for a substantial profit. There is also a major risk to management in issuing common stock, because owners control the Board of Directors, which in turn can hire or fire the management group. Some variations on the equity concept are preferred stock, since it involves the non-redeemable purchase of preferred stock, and stock rights, which are rights for current stockholders to purchase additional shares in proportion to their current holdings. Finally, there are warrants, which are rights to buy common stock at attractive prices, and which are attached to debt instruments, such as bonds, to make the purchase of the debt instruments more attractive.

A variation on both the debt and equity concepts is the convertible security, which is a debt instrument that the holder can convert over to equity at a fixed price. This is an attractive option if the actual share price is much higher than the fixed price at which a lender is allowed to purchase stock—the difference between the two prices is a pure profit to the lender when converting from debt to equity.

When considering which of these options to recommend, the controller must understand the cost and risk of each type of funding. Except for the most highly leveraged situations, the incremental cost of debt is always less than the cost of equity. This is because interest payments to lenders are tax deductible, which substantially reduces its cost, whereas dividend payments to the holders of common stock are not. In addition, lenders take no ownership interest in a company, so there is no risk that they will unseat the management group, which is not at all the case if the company sells common stock. However, there is a risk in procuring too much debt, since the amount of interest payments can eat up all excess cash flow, which can force a company into bankruptcy if cash flow declines for any reason whatever, such as during a business downturn. Accordingly, lenders frequently insist that a company not exceed a specified debt/equity ratio, which forces a company to obtain some equity from investors at regular intervals. Also, lenders can require onerous loan covenants that require a company to obtain lender approval for special activities, such as the sale or purchase of assets, or special distributions to shareholders; these covenants are essentially designed to ensure that the lenders are paid back, and not that the company will use the funds most effectively, so there is some conflict in how the loaned money will be used.

The advantages and disadvantages of each type of debt and equity are itemized in Figure 20–7, which is reprinted with permission from the author's *The Controller's Guide to Financial Analysis* (John Wiley & Sons, Inc. 2000).

When choosing financing options from among the list shown in Figure 20–7, the controller should remember that the correct option will vary over time, since the correct mix of debt and equity, with their associated levels of cost and risk, will vary from year to year in response to changes in the organization's cash flow, the willingness of lenders to provide more debt, and stated changes in the targeted rate of return to shareholders. Consequently, the correct type of financing must be constantly re-evaluated based on changing circumstances.

CREATING FORECASTS

The national and international economies are subject to variations in the level of activity that are altered by outside influences, such as floods, earthquakes, or

Financing Option	Advantages	Disadvantages
Leasing	Good for replacement of assets that wear out quickly; the sale-and-leaseback option makes available a large amount of cash.	Can be very expensive unless all components of the transaction are carefully evaluated and negotiated.
Loans	Least expensive form of funding.	May require assets as loan collateral, as well as loan covenants, some control over operations, and first call on the results of asset sales in the event of a liquidation.
Common stock	Can raise substantial amounts of funds, and there is no need to pay back the capital.	Shareholder expectations for returns are very high, and it also gives them the ability to oust the Board of Directors and (indirectly) the management team if their performance expectations are not met. Also, dividend payments are not tax deductible.
Convertible securities	Can avoid paying off bond debt, as well as reducing interest payments and improving the debt/equity ratio.	Reduces the earnings per share and weakens the control of current share-holders, but only if conversion to shares occurs.
Preferred stock	Can avoid paying back the principal.	The interest expense is not tax deductible.
Stock rights	Simple way to raise funds from existing shareholders.	Will not necessarily retain ownership interests in the same proportions prior to the stock rights offering.
Warrants	Can reduce bond interest rates.	Dilutes earnings per share and may weaken owner control of the company.

Figure 20–7: Summary of Financing Option Advantages and Disadvantages

wars, or by internal factors, such as changes in interest rates, tariffs, or commodity prices. Given the average severity of each decline in the economy, as well as its relative frequency, a controller should be aware of the key indicators of a decline, so that he or she can pass this information along to the management team, which can use it to prepare for the changing business environment; These preparations can include a cutback in credit to suppliers, reduced inventory investment, or a reduction in capital spending. This is also a good warning for the sales department, which can use it to scale back its sales forecasts, which in turn has an impact on the amount of production being scheduled for completion.

There are several external sources of information about business forecasts. These include several departments of the federal government, such as the Federal Reserve Board and the Commerce Department, as well as the economists for a number of large regional or national banks and brokerages. However, their estimates tend to be for the entire economy, rather than for smaller segments in which individual businesses are ensconced. This can make a significant difference, for a company in the push lawn mower manufacturing business may find that its business actually increases during lean times, as people look for less expensive ways to mow their lawns. Consequently, there is a substantial need for business forecasts that are more precisely tailored to the needs of the individual business. A company can obtain this from an independent economic forecasting firm (of which there are many), but these services tend to be very expensive and so are limited to the use of larger and wealthier companies.

A different approach is for a controller to assemble a small list of leading indicators, and to track and include them in ongoing management status reports, so that company management can reach its own conclusions regarding the business conditions in the specific market in which a company operates. A leading indicator is any measure that tends to change in advance of an actual change in the economy, and so is a way to forecast future events. An example of a leading indicator is the number of new housing permits, which tend to decline well in advance of a slowdown in the economy. A single leading indicator is not sufficient in most cases, since it may suddenly vary based on one-time or extraneous variables that give a false reading to those who are relying on it to judge the business forecast. Consequently, a better approach is to use a number of leading indicators, so that a few odd variations in measurements will be more than compensated for by the overall impact of changes in all the variables.

The main problem for the controller is deciding on which leading indicators to use. These should be factors that have a clear impact on the specific market that is under analysis, and which have an equally clear and understandable reason for signaling a change in the market. A bad example of this is the much-cited correlation between the height of women's skirts and the rise and fall of the stock market, which is a patently absurd leading indicator, but which has also been supported in fact by a number of changes in the stock market. A better example of a leading indicator is the price of resin in the plastic injection molding industry. Because it is the prime component of most plastic products, a substantial increase in the price of resin is sure to spark an increase in plastic products, which in turn gives an incentive to consumers to shift their purchases to other non-plastic products; this makes the price of resin a predictable and understandable reason for a future change in the business cycle of the plastic injection molding industry.

Once the controller has decided on somewhere between five and ten of these leading indicators, they can be included in a simple report to management that reveals changes in the indicators. Managers can interpret this information for themselves and arrive at their own conclusions regarding the extent of future changes in the business cycle, as well as the timing of when those changes will occur. However, it is the controller's job to not just compile and present information, but to interpret it as well. Thus, a better approach is to provide some additional interpretive analysis to management. The controller can do this by researching industry statistics for the last few decades (probably available through the national industry trade organization), which will reveal the timing and size of business cycle changes following changes in the leading indicators. The controller can manually determine the average time intervals between the two occurrences, as well as how closely the size of business cycle changes correspond to the size of changes in the leading indicator. When performing this chore, the controller should strongly weight the analysis in favor of the relationships revealed between the business cycle and leading indicators over just the last few business cycles, because the relationship may have changed over time, and will certainly continue to do so in the future. The resulting analysis will be extremely rough, but it will be more accurate than the analysis that any other member of the management team could provide—after all, the controller's specialty is financial analysis, which makes anyone in this position better qualified to conduct a business cycle forecast than people in other management positions.

IMPROVING SHAREHOLDER VALUE

The controller can recommend several changes that will improve the value of shareholder earnings, most of which are not immediately obvious to the other members of the management team. The reason for this is that other factors also have a great impact on shareholder value besides net profit. What are all the issues that give a share of common stock its value?

The minimum value of a share of common stock is its share of a corporation's liquidation value, which is the surplus of any assets remaining after they have been used to pay off liabilities, divided by the number of outstanding shares. However, this is only the minimum price. The actual valuation can be stratospherically higher for several reasons. One is that a stock purchaser is willing to pay more for a share due to expectations for profits in the near future—this has been the cause of astronomical share prices for a number of Internet-based firms. Another reason is a company's cash horde, patents, or properties that a potential acquirer can use to realize additional value. And, yes, it is based on current reported profits and cash flows. However, only the last items have any lasting value in the long run. For example, shareholders will not continue to bid up the shares of speculative Internet stocks year after year, unless they finally show a profit to realize some of their potential. Similarly, the perceived value of a company's patents or properties may vary over time and should not be thought of as a good store of value unless they can be increased with more patents or properties. This leaves us with net profits and cash flows. Of the two, reported net profits can be suspect, since they are subject to some variation by management in the form of reserves or accruals taken, modifications to accounting policies, and other non-cash variations that can have a substantial impact on actual profitability. Whenever management engages in these accounting games, it must eventually "pay the piper" and recognize gains or losses that it has previously hidden in the financial statements. This sort of gyration in reported earnings can have a major impact on the share price, since investors will be confused regarding the actual profitability of the company. However, there is nothing especially difficult to understand about a company's reported cash flows. They are clearly stated in a separate report in the financial statements, allowing any reasonably well-informed person to rapidly discern any problems that a company is having, or where it is using its money. If investors use cash flow as their primary source of information in determining a share price, then the controller can focus on some clear and simple recommendations to the management team—work toward the minimal cash investment required to secure the maximum cash outflow from the organization. Thus, a company's ability to generate an increasing stream of positive cash flows is the primary determinant of shareholder value. This must be tempered by shareholder expectations of the ability of the company to continue to generate the same or greater cash flows into the future, however, which is based upon its ability to maintain or replace patents, stave off competitors, and continually churn out a string of new products.

So how can the controller use financial analysis to improve shareholder value? We will begin with the income statement and work our way through the balance sheet, pointing out a number of approaches for improving cash flows in several areas.

A key area for the controller to review is the price of each product sold. Though management may think that this is driven by nothing but the list price, the controller has access to more information about the true cost of each product sold, such as discounts granted for volume purchases, bad debts for specific customers, product returns, and quality costs, that can drive down the actual product price to a much lower level. When these extra costs accelerate, either due to product quality problems or an increasingly competitive environment, a company's gross margin will drop, which results in a worsening cash flow. Given the number of ways in which prices can be reduced, management may not know what is going on even as it sees cash flow drop, so the controller must assist in compiling and revealing the exact causes.

Material costs typically represent the largest single cost on the income statement, and yet it is one of the least analyzed areas, perhaps because there are so many components to it that most controllers do not feel that they have time to undertake a thorough analysis. However, given the extreme cash flow impact of an increase in this cost of just a few percent, the controller must undertake some kind of analysis to assist management in determining the causes of cost increases. One of the best ways is to summarize the cost of each product based on its bill of materials, which should be completed before a project reaches the production stage and be updated at regular intervals. This is not an exact representation of actual costs, since there are variances from it based on changes in pricing, quantities used, and anticipated scrap rates; nonetheless, a well written bill of materials should be a very close representation of a product's cost. If the controller can extract this information from the computer system and add the standard price, he or she can determine the direct cost (and margin) of each product. Then the list of costs can be sorted in ascending order by gross margin, such as is shown in Figure 20–8, so that management can see those products with the worst margins at the top of the report. Also noted in the same example is the addition of overhead costs that are allocated based on a simplified activity-based costing model, which uses cost pools and multiple allocation bases to determine a product's cost as precisely as possible. The example contains two gross margin percentages—one for the direct margin alone, which does not include the overhead cost, and the other for all costs. This is particularly useful if there is any doubt by management about the allocated overhead costs, since it still shows the minimum margin percentage (the direct margin), and which may also be useful for incremental pricing deals. Finally, the controller can track this information over time and plot it on a trend line (at least for the major products or product groups), so that management can see if there are increasing cost problems on certain products that require more extensive review. This approach is particularly useful if a company uses target costing to determine a product's initial cost before it is produced, since the controller can use this initial cost as a benchmark against which all subsequent bills of material can be measured.

The controller should pay close attention to direct labor costs. Even though this has been a historically shrinking component of total company costs, it still comprises a sufficiently large amount to have a significant impact on corporate cash flows if it is not managed wisely. Though the rest of the company tends to focus on the average direct labor headcount and hourly wage, the controller has access to additional information. One item is the overtime cost. If a company adds second or third shifts, or works on weekends, then the overtime premium will be significant and should be reported both in total and on a per-person basis, as well as on a trend line. Also, the controller should compare the number of direct labor full-time equivalents to the amount of product created by the production department to ensure that the per-person efficiency level is being maintained. This can drop if management is unwilling to lay off employees when sales levels decline, or when production managers are not scheduling employees for work in an efficient manner, which can result in paid downtime.

Description	Price	Material Cost	Labor Cost	Overhead Cost*	Direct Margin%	Total Margin%
Camera case	$12.00	8.00	2.75	1.00	10%	2%
Lens cover	1.50	.75	.50	.10	17%	10%
Lens cap	1.00	.45	.35	.12	20%	8%
Camera stand	14.50	6.50	5.00	1.25	21%	12%
Tripod	10.00	4.75	3.00	.85	23%	14%
Camera filter	3.75	2.00	.75	.15	27%	23%
Box case	4.50	2.00	1.00	.35	33%	26%
Box camera	28.00	12.00	5.00	2.80	39%	29%
35mm camera	37.50	11.00	5.75	2.25	55%	49%

* Overhead cost is based on an allocation from the activity-based costing system.

Figure 20–8. Sample Direct Costing Analysis of Products, Sorted by Gross Margin

Companies in many industries, such as electronics, pharmaceuticals, and biotechnology, must make a considerable investment in research and development in order to remain competitive. For the controller who is mindful of improving shareholder value through increasing cash flows, this is a difficult area in which to make recommendations—if a company cuts back too much on research, its cash flow will certainly improve in the short run, but at the expense of its long-term competitive posture in the industry. Accordingly, the controller needs to compare the current expenditure to those of competitors, as a percentage of sales, and on a historical trend line to see if current costs are out of line. The best approach of all is to team with people from other departments to conduct a continuing and long-term review of each research project to determine the expenditure needed to continue each one, as well as to evaluate its economic viability. Only through considerable detailed analysis can a controller make an informed recommendation to management in regard to changes in the research and development expense.

As described earlier in this chapter, a company's investment in working capital can have a major impact on its overall cash flows. The controller can impact this flow by regularly measuring the investment, exploring the reasons for variances, and recommending changes to the management team that will reduce the overall level of investment in this area.

A major cash outflow is for the procurement of fixed assets. The controller plays a major role in this through her control of the capital budgeting process, which involves a comparison of prospective purchases to those already approved in the annual budget, as well as through a net present value calculation (as described earlier in this chapter) that reveals if a purchase will result in a positive stream of cash flows in the future. These processes are designed to weed out all capital expenditures that will reduce a company's cash flow without creating a new stream of positive cash flows.

An area that is well within the control of either the controller or chief financial officer is adjustments to the existing mix of debt that will result in an improvement in cash flow. For example, if the mix of outstanding debt instruments includes something with a very high interest rate, it may be possible to retire that debt and replace it with a lower-cost debt that will reduce the cash outflow related to interest expense. Also, if there is an upcoming surge in cash flows related to one or more debt balloon payments, the controller can arrange for re-financing that will reduce the immediate cash outflow.

An area that definitely improves the value of each share of common stock, but which does not improve cash flow, is buying back shares, so that fewer are left outstanding. By doing so, earnings can be spread over fewer shares, which increases the price per share. For example, if a company earns $1,000,000 and has 500,000 outstanding shares, then the earnings per share are $2. However, if the company buys back half of those shares, then the earnings per share rise to $4. Though this may seem like an ideal way to increase shareholder value, it also increases the level of a company's risk. The reason is that this method uses up a large amount of cash being spun off by operations (perhaps all of it), which reduces the cash available for funding internal capital projects that will fund future growth, or for funding the working capital needed to support an increase in sales. If so, management has the alternative of incurring debt to fund its needs, but this increases the risk that the company will not be able to pay off its obligations, which can lead to bankruptcy, especially if the company is not a very profitable one or is already highly leveraged. In addition, the interest expense on new debt will reduce earnings somewhat, so that the increase in earnings per share that resulted from retiring some stock will be cut back by the amount of this extra expense. The best approach for a controller when recommending this approach is to determine the amount of additional principal payments and interest costs that will be incurred when a certain number of shares are bought and retired, and to determine the point at which the company can still afford to pay back the debt even if its margins are unexpectedly reduced to a reasonably foreseeable degree. This is the maximum number of shares that should be repurchased. Any larger buyback would put the company in too great a position of financial risk to justify the increase in shareholder value.

ENDNOTES

1. Reprinted with permission. Steven Bragg, *The Controller's Guide to Financial Analysis,* (Wiley, 2000).

21

TAXES

The reporting requirements of all governmental agencies have increased significantly and have become more complex. This is particularly true of the reporting requirements for federal and state taxes. There are endless rules and regulations that are always changing to be consistent with national policy and economic objectives. It is mandatory that business develop and maintain adequate records to meet the requirements of these widely diverse patterns of federal and local tax laws. If the records and reporting systems are not properly planned, a company will be subject to considerable financial exposure. Emphasis must be placed on the proper recording of financial transactions, accuracy in preparing data for tax reports, and timely reporting to concerned taxing authorities.

Some companies follow a practice of referring federal tax matters to public accountants or tax attorneys. There are, of course, times when such assistance is desirable and necessary. However, the tendency to place such responsibility in hands outside the home organization is dangerous and carries with it certain disadvantages. Knowledge of tax laws does not in itself assure the best answer. Such information must be applied in a manner that benefits the company to the greatest possible extent. This requires an intimate knowledge of the business and its transactions—something the external tax advisor cannot gain through an occasional or annual visit. More than this, the application of the tax laws must be considered in many of the day-to-day operating decisions. In addition, the controller has as a primary function the determination of the periodic and annual earnings, and federal laws are an important factor in such determination. The controller, then, has a fundamental responsibility to be fully informed on tax matters, particularly federal income taxes, and to use this knowledge to avoid paying excess taxes.

In summary, the controller should be able to check the more important tax computations. The entire accounting staff should have a general understanding of the tax laws and should be sufficiently aware of tax implications to inquire into, and secure an answer to, the probable tax results of any given transaction.

TAX ORGANIZATION

The responsibility for the tax activities should be placed with a financial executive who understands the relationship of the accounting function to the tax laws and compliance. As the tax function affects cash flows and accounting determinations, it is a controller's function.

The increasing importance of taxes as a cost of doing business and the significant number of taxing authorities to be considered make it imperative that the administration of tax matters be regarded as a separate function in the organization. The plan of organization in most companies gives formal recognition to the tax function. In some companies with complex tax problems and worldwide business interests, management considers taxes important enough to appoint a vice-president of taxes. In other situations, a separate department is established, headed by a manager responsible for all facets of taxes. Depending on the complexity and size of the tax problems, the tax department may be organized according to the types of taxes, such as federal income taxes, state income taxes, sales taxes, property taxes, and payroll taxes.

A prime consideration in organizing and staffing a tax department is the degree of centralization concerning the administration of tax matters. This is particularly important when a company has several plants, branches, operating units, and international operations. Normally, a centralized tax organization will exercise control over all tax policies and procedures within the company. In addition, it will manage the home office tax organization and in some cases direct the day-to-day activities of the decentralized tax people. However, in any event, functional control over the field tax organization should be vested in the corporate tax manager.

There are some advantages to having local personnel handle certain tax functions because of the relationships with the local taxing authorities, as in the case of property taxes. The corporate tax manager should make periodic reviews in these instances.

The preparation of tax returns can be centralized or decentralized, depending on the circumstances and economics. If the data is in the local office, it may be advantageous to have the return prepared locally, with appropriate review by the tax manager's staff. The records to be maintained should be prescribed by the corporate tax department. Some companies, for example, have the payroll department of each entity prepare payroll tax returns, since the detail information is readily available from the payroll records. However, the tax manager will review and probably sign and file the returns.

As in any function, there are advantages to the centralization of the tax responsibilities. It is more economical, permits a higher degree of specialization, is a more efficient use of tax resources (e.g., a centralized tax library), promotes uniformity, and allows more flexibility in handling the workload. There can also be disadvantages to a centralized tax function, such as the lack of sufficient contact with local taxing authorities. In those cases where decentralization is used, the central tax department should still provide guidance, instruction, and review services.

ROLE OF THE TAX MANAGER

The functions of the tax manager will vary with the organization. However, the following list is an indication of the extent of responsibilities assigned to the tax department in a large company:

- Develop, recommend, and implement approved plans for an effective tax management program applicable to all elements of the corporation. Ensure that the company complies with all applicable laws, rules, and regulations pertaining to taxes.
- Select personnel, assign duties, and establish appropriate control over activities.
- Plan for the administration of local or branch office tax functions.
- Maintain adequate tax records, prepare forms and working papers, and establish designation of the files.
- Prepare a complex tax manual establishing procedures and responsibilities.
- Evaluate the effect of tax laws, regulations, rulings, and court cases on the company's tax liabilities and potential business activities.
- Develop policies and procedures to minimize the company's tax liability.
- Determine that the company has filed all tax returns, reports, and declarations required by law.
- Recommend action concerning all tax adjustments proposed by the various taxing authorities or by the company's independent public accountants and represent the company, or cause the company to be represented, in all negotiations affecting the company's tax liabilities.
- Initiate action to obtain IRS approval, when required, with respect to changes in accounting methods and procedures and matters pertaining to retirement or savings plans.
- Prepare and prosecute in cooperation with counsel, formal protests, claims, petitions, or court actions with respect to disputed tax matters involving the company, coordinating all such activities with other concerned functions, such as legal and accounting.
- Initiate action, when required, to obtain IRS rulings regarding the company's tax liability.
- Analyze the tax implications of proposed acquisitions to determine present or potential problems and examine tax carry-back or -forward possibilities.

- Provide information concerning federal, state, local, and foreign tax matters, based on the advice of counsel where necessary.
- Analyze the tax effect of legal documents affecting the company and render advice regarding appropriate action to minimize the company's tax liabilities with respect thereto.
- Review the annual and strategic plans to develop the tax liabilities for each period and incorporate the results into the approved plan.
- Research the foreign tax consequences of the business plan; the company is entitled to a credit against its federal income tax liability for any foreign income tax paid.

It is imperative that the tax department communicate with all units of the organization. To be effective, the tax department should be involved in management decisions on business acquisitions, pension plans and fringe benefit programs, financing agreements, establishment of foreign entities, including their location and form, contract terms related to taxes, divestitures of business units or products, location of facilities, and various kinds of business arrangements such as joint ventures or consulting agreements. Tax planning includes making all levels of management aware of the significance of tax considerations in the decision-making process. An effective tax manager will create the opportunity to present sound and creative tax ideas to members of the management team on a regular basis.

The tax manager must have an intimate knowledge of the company and its products, services, and general business operations. To achieve this, he or she must be in touch with all concerned and develop a network of communications sensitive to situations having tax implications. Success is achieved when the tax department is consulted before the fact on transactions involving tax matters.

TAX RECORDS

The tax laws are so complex, so great in number, and of such differing natures that it is not practical to know all the provisions of the laws and all the facts of the business which have a direct bearing on taxability. Consequently, the company must have the necessary records if adequate tax planning is to be completed, if management is to have a clear view of the tax situation, or if any degree of administrative control is to be successful. The penalties for oversight or incompetence are heavy.

The nature of the records will be governed by the relative complexity of the tax problem. Broadly speaking, however, certain records are needed for administrative control purposes, to support the tax returns, and to meet the specific requirements of the law. Tax records are grouped into four major classifications:

1. *Tax calendar*—A schedule that serves as a reminder regarding the due dates for filing tax returns, preparing reports, paying tax bills, hearing dates, audit

dates, assessment dates, and any other key tax event. When computerized, this schedule can automatically remind the staff of upcoming deadlines. An abbreviated tax calendar is shown in Table 21–1.

2. *Information records*—This is a summary of the tax law and related matters as they affect the business. This record is used as a reference when preparing the tax return. A sample tax information record is shown in Table 21–2. The information to be recorded about each tax includes:

- Name of the tax.
- Description of the tax.
- Basis.
- Tax rates.
- Exemptions from the tax.
- Time of the filing return.
- Return form number and name.
- Approximate time required for preparation.
- To whom the return is sent, and when.
- Source of the data for preparing the return.
- Why the company is subject to the tax.
- The tax accounting.
- The procedure, including any special instructions.
- Penalties for nonpayment.

3. *Working paper files*—These files contain the facts incident to the year-to-year returns. These operating files are of an infinite variety and are perhaps comparable to the permanent files and working paper files created in connection with an audit. Essentially, the files must contain a complete and orderly record of the following information, plus additional material that may vary by type of tax:

Table 21–1: Tax Calendar

Event	J	F	M	A	M	J	J	A	S	O	N	D
Estimated payments for the year				15		15			15			15
Mail Y/E tax packets to subs	15											
Federal use tax							31					
Federal excise quarterly return	31			30			31			31		
Federal excise monthly prepay #2	31	28	31	30	31	30	31	30	30	31	30	31
Federal excise monthly prepay #1	15	15	15	15	15	15	15	15	15	15	15	15

Table 21–2: Tax Information Record

Information Needed	Federal Income Tax
Description and type	Income
Locations covered	All except foreign legal entities
Who must file	All domestic legal entities, consolidated
Where filed (address)	IRS—Salt Lake City, Utah
Form number	1120, plus any other applicable forms
Period(s) covered	19XX
Due dates	3/15/XX (Extensions through 9/15/XX)
Rate or basis of tax	34%
Approximate amount of tax	$5,000,000
Information required	Detailed income statement, balance sheet, and comprehensive analysis of differences between book income and taxable income. Calculation of Alternative Minimum Tax (AMT).
Source of data	Books and records of the various profit centers
Account charged	Number 260
File index	Federal file #3, drawer #2
Comments	Revise scheduling for asset depreciation range and guideline depreciation

- Record of payments.
- Record of assessments.
- Reconciliation of tax data to the records.
- Copies of the return.
- Refund record, including basis.
- Correspondence on the tax.

4. *Supporting ledgers*—These are the accounting records maintained by the accounting department. The tax manager should be closely involved in the construction of a chart of accounts that records information needed to file tax returns, in order to avoid the laborious manual compilation of information.

TAX VERSUS BOOK ACCOUNTING

The principal source of information required for federal income tax returns is the regular accounting records of the company. However, although tax accounting and book accounting are generally the same, there are three important respects in which they differ:

1. *Income and expenses specifically excluded for tax purposes*—Examples include the tax-exempt income from government bonds or contributions in excess of the allowable maximum. These data are not difficult to account for; they appear on the reconciliation, and that usually ends the matter.

2. *Differences resulting from the recognition of the time when losses or income may be recognized*—The reserve positions and related charge-offs are

included in this group. Supplementary worksheets are sufficient records for this information, and separate ledgers need not be maintained.

3. *Differences in cost bases*—This general category includes differences in depreciation rates and bases, treatment of maintenance and repair costs, and inventory valuation. Major information recording problems can arise in relation to different cost bases. It is necessary to determine whether a separate series of supplementary accounts need to be maintained. For example, where substantially different depreciation bases and rates are used, separate ledgers may be required.

An important schedule for the controller's review is the reconciliation of net income contained in the federal income tax return. This schedule reveals the major differing points between tax and book accounting.

The controller and tax manager are faced with the problem of how these differences should be treated in the records. It is obviously necessary to maintain a running record of these differences and to reconcile book and tax figures if a company is to secure full tax benefits. The maintenance of such records is essential to ensure that the company will not overlook a tax deduction to which it could properly be entitled in a subsequent year. However, it does not follow that a completely independent set of books need be maintained for tax purposes.

PROPER CLASSIFICATION OF ACCOUNTS

When designing the accounting records and account structure or chart of accounts, the controller should be aware of and consider the accounting data required for the preparation of tax returns. If provision is made in the establishment of the accounting records, it can facilitate the tax work and protect the interests of the company from a tax viewpoint.

It is desirable to include in the account structure the capability for detailed analysis of various items such as repairs and maintenance, so it can be readily demonstrated that additions to a plant have not been expensed. Also, where practical, a segregation of nontaxable income or nonallowable deductions should be made in the accounts. Such an account structure will save valuable time in making costly analyses at critical times and make less likely the possibility of not including those items in the tax return.

22

SELECTING A FINANCIAL INFORMATION SYSTEM

The controller is primarily responsible for seeing that the financial information system meets the needs of those who receive and use its output—management, shareholders, creditors, suppliers, customers, government agencies, and stock exchanges as well as the general public.

This chapter contains a proven approach to selecting and implementing an automated financial information system (FIS). It includes an overview of reasons why financial system software should be purchased instead of developed in-house, an explanation of how to thoroughly define systems requirements, an approach to preparing a Request for Proposal (RFP), and ways to evaluate software, hardware, and the vendors who sell it. Selection and implementation of an FIS are extremely important to an organization's financial operation. As a result, the organization must be willing either to devote a substantial amount of time and effort to these activities or to hire outside consultants to assist in the process.

For the purposes of this chapter, it is assumed that the selection process includes both computer hardware and software. Many selecting organizations already have computer hardware in place. However, where possible, it is recommended that an organization select software that best meets its needs without being constrained by the hardware currently in place.

REASONS TO PURCHASE SOFTWARE

In general, it is recommended that software packages be purchased, instead of developed in-house, to meet the needs of an organization's financial operations.

The reasons include:

- *Implementation Speed.* Packaged software generally can be implemented much more quickly than software developed in-house.
- *Fewer Software Problems.* Packaged software normally already has been thoroughly tested and debugged before it is sold.
- *Lower Overall Cost.* The total cost of packaged software tends to be significantly less than the cost of software developed in-house.
- *Software Vendor Assistance.* Most software vendors, especially those in the midrange (microcomputer) and mainframe market, provide ongoing support and maintenance for their software.
- *Package Enhancements.* To maintain market position and sales, software vendors generally provide enhanced functionality and new modules.
- *Documentation.* Most software packages come with a variety of manuals, including user, technical, and operations.
- *Training.* The vast majority of software vendors provide a variety of training classes for users and technical personnel.
- *Research and Development.* Software vendors are in the business of selling system solutions. To maintain (and improve) a competitive market position, they must invest a substantial amount of money in research and development.
- *Information Systems Support.* In general, it is much easier to locate personnel who are familiar with packaged software and can support it than to find good support for in-house systems.
- *The User Group.* Packaged software vendors tend to support and encourage user groups. Participation in these groups can be an effective means of identifying ways in which to use the system more efficiently.

DEFINING SYSTEMS REQUIREMENTS

Before software is selected, the specific requirements need to be precisely defined. The application areas typically included in an FIS are: budgeting, purchasing, accounts payable and check reconciliation, general ledger, accounts receivable and revenue accounting, fixed assets, cost accounting, inventory, and order entry and billing.

If application requirements are not thoroughly defined and documented, the software selected probably will not meet the organization's needs. It will be useful to develop a Systems Requirements Definition (SRD) document that:

- Serves as the basis for the Request for Proposal (RFP).
- Communicates the organization's requirements to the vendors.
- Helps the selected software meet the organization's current and future needs.

- Enhances the organization's understanding of each application area (e.g., accounts payable and accounts receivable) and how automation can assist in improving access to information in that area.
- Prioritizes the application areas to be automated.
- Matches requirements against the software's capabilities to determine where it is deficient, and where modifications must be developed.

There are a number of approaches that may be used to develop FIS requirements. These approaches include questionnaires, executive interviews, document reviews, and outside sources.

Questionnaires

Questionnaires may be used to develop a general understanding of an organization, its objectives, and the environment in which it operates. They also may be used to define major financially oriented tasks, analyze transactions, determine major systems interfaces, and assist with the development of FIS requirements.

The questionnaire should not be so long that it discourages completion. Alternatively, it should not be so brief that it does not identify specific requirements. Figure 22–1 illustrates the types of questions that can appear in the questionnaire.

Executive Interviews

The purposes of conducting executive interviews include:

- Developing an overall understanding of the organization—its strategies, environment, and objectives.
- Defining the executive's information needs.
- Determining the executive's opinions on the current system.
- Identifying the organization's goals, objectives, and critical success factors.
- Identifying the executive's system expectations.
- Predicting growth areas or new needs that must be planned for by IS.
- Improving the executive's buy in to the selection process.

Executive interviews should not be designed to elicit detailed information on systems specifications. Rather, they should help elicit general information needs and the strategic goals and objectives of the organization.

It is important that the information and reporting needs of executives be emphasized and identified early in the selection process. Too frequently, only the needs of staff and middle management are incorporated. The resulting FIS frequently does not provide executives with the reports necessary for effectively managing the application areas.

QUESTIONNAIRE TO DEFINE FIS APPLICATION REQUIREMENTS

1. For what functions are you responsible?

_____

_____

2. What are the primary goals of your job?

_____

_____

3. With what other departments do you interface?

_____

_____

4. What major tasks do you perform?

_____

_____

5. What reports do you prepare? (Please attach a sample of each report.)

_____

_____

6. What forms do you use? (Please attach a sample of each form.)

_____

_____

7. Where do these forms originate?

_____

_____

8. Where do these forms go when you complete them?

_____

_____

9. What financial information do you receive from other departments?

_____

_____

10. What changes do you predict will occur in your job over the next one to three years?

_____

_____

11. What additional information could you use?

_____

_____

12. What automated system do you currently utilize?

_____

_____

Figure 22–1: Sample Questionnaire for Defining Application Requirements

Document Reviews

Another way to develop systems requirements is to review input forms and reports. Doing so provides the organization with a listing of its current data elements and helps to define the minimum reporting requirements of the proposed FIS.

Outside Sources

Another source of requirements that should be included in an SRD is the environment in which the financial organization exists. Economic trends, changes in laws and practices, and revisions to governmental regulations may all affect the reporting requirements of an FIS and, therefore, should be reviewed.

There is a cost involved in collecting systems requirements. As a result, an organization should not spend an excessive amount of time documenting them, because it may never get to the point of selecting software.

Vendor Demonstrations

A final source of requirements is through software vendor demonstrations. These demonstrations can provide organizations with new information about system features.

EXISTING SYSTEM DOCUMENTATION

After the questionnaires and executive interviews have been completed and the other sources of information reviewed, it is critical that the existing manual and/or automated financial systems be documented. Included in this documentation should be the following factors:

- The key objectives of the system (for example, to maintain the general ledger and produce financial reports)
- Who supports the system
- The major system inputs, edits, controls, and outputs (reports)
- All system interfaces and special features
- The volume of transactions processed by the system
- The approximate costs of operating the system.

In addition, if the system is automated, it is important to note the hardware platform on which it operates, the language in which it is written, its age, and the approximate amount invested in the system.

JOINT SESSIONS

An effective and efficient means of ensuring a thorough system requirements survey is by conducting joint sessions with the employees who will be using and supporting the system. The benefits of conducting joint sessions include development of a more complete SRD and an improved user "buy in." The steps required to conduct a joint session include:

- Prepare "straw man" requirements for each application. These requirements generally are based on research previously conducted by the organization, information obtained from software vendors or computer-related literature, or IS consultants.
- Distribute the requirements document to the employees interested in or affected by the specific application.
- Conduct a joint session for each application area. During these sessions, which generally are facilitated by a selection team member or a consultant, the participants are asked to:
  — Prioritize each requirement (state whether the requirement is required, desired, optional, or not applicable).
  — Identify additional requirements.

After the current financial systems are documented and the joint sessions conducted, it is then time to finalize the SRD. The purpose of the SRD, which will become part of the RFP, is to communicate to software vendors the organization's systems requirements and allow the vendors to identify software products that can meet those requirements. The SRD should be divided by application area (general ledger and accounts payable). The application area should be further divided into the following topics: general systems narrative, processing requirements, inquiry requirements, reporting requirements, and data requirements.

The requirements should be stated as a single sentence. Table 22–1 gives a very abbreviated example of these factors for an accounts receivable system.

PREPARING THE REQUEST FOR PROPOSAL

An RFP is used to effectively communicate the FIS's requirements to software and/or hardware vendors. It is prepared after the SRD and serves the following purposes:

- Communicates the organization's systems requirements to vendors and facilitates a uniform response to those requirements.
- Requests specific commitments from vendors, such as the system's functionality, the level of support and documentation provided, the costs, and contractual arrangements.

Table 22-1: Accounts Receivable System Requirements

Accounts Receivable System Narrative

The accounts receivable system should be designed to handle all of the organization's receivables and collection requirements. The system must interface both with the order entry system to obtain billing information and with the general ledger system to post billings, cash receipts, and bad-debt journal entries.

Processing Requirements

The accounts receivable system should be able to perform the following functions:

❏ Post to different revenue accounts depending on the type of service performed.

❏ Enter non-accounting data to the master file on-line.

❏ Disallow the deletion of data with an account balance greater than zero.

❏ Interface with the order entry/billing system.

Inquiry Requirements

The accounts receivable system should include the following inquiry features and capabilities:

❏ On-line review of billing and payment history

❏ Inquiry as to the status of a bill using a variety of data elements including:

• Customer name
• Customer number
• Invoice number

Reporting Requirements

The accounts receivable system should produce the following reports:

❏ *Accounts receivable aging report*—a report indicating the amount of time an accounts receivable balance has been outstanding.

Frequency: weekly and on demand

❏ *Cash receipts register*—a register containing information on:

• Date of receipt
• Check number
• Customer name and number
• Dollar amount
• Invoice number applied to
• General ledger account posted to

Frequency: daily and on demand

Data Requirements

The Customer Master File should contain the following data elements:

• Customer Name—60 alpha/numeric characters
• Customer Number—20 alpha/numeric characters
• Customer Address I
   — Street—60 alpha/numeric characters
   — City—20 alpha characters
   — State—20 alpha characters
• Customer Address 2
   — Street—60 alpha/numeric characters
   — City—20 alpha/numeric characters
   — State—2 alpha characters
• Customer Contact I
   — Name—40 alpha/numeric characters
   — Phone number—9 numeric characters
   — Street—60 alpha/numeric characters
   — City—20 alpha characters
   — State—2 alpha characters

System requirements documents may be from 5 to well over 100 pages per application, depending on the number and the level of detail desired. Be careful not to overdefine the requirements or make the SRD so general that it allows all software packages to meet its needs.

After completing the SRD, the prioritization of the applications should be performed. It is vital for an organization to clearly define each application in the order of importance, to help it evaluate the completed FRP and identify the factors upon which the software selection will be decided. Factors to consider when assigning priorities of applications to be automated include:

• The impact of the system on the organization and its customers.
• The costs and benefits of the system.
• The demand for the system.
• The dependence of the system on other systems.

- Serves as a tool for effectively comparing vendors. The RFP should be designed in a way that allows the selecting government organization to easily compare the proposals of various vendors.

Depending on the organization's situation, RFPs may be prepared for software, hardware, or both. However, no matter what the organization selects, the RFP must be well structured and precise in order to elicit a clear and concise response from vendors. A vague and poorly organized RFP is likely to result in proposals that are too general and difficult to compare and are lacking details in many areas. Table 22–2 shows a typical contents page for an RFP.

Cover Letter

The cover letter notifies the hardware and/or software vendor that the organization is requesting a proposal for specific applications and/or hardware. In addition, the cover letter should contain the following information: important deadlines (such as the date of the bidders conference and when the proposal is due) and the projected installation and implementation dates; the overall objective of the RFP; the individual within the organization to contact with questions; and the format and content of the RFP.

General Information/Proposal Guidelines

The general information/proposal guidelines section contains information on how the proposal is to be completed, how the selection process will be conducted, and the importance of a concise and timely response. Also included in this section is whether site visits will be made by the organization, a statement that the cost of preparing the proposal is entirely the vendor's responsibility, that the organization reserves the right to reject any and all proposals, and that the confidentiality of the material contained in the RFP is assured.

Background Material

The background material includes information about the organization that is of interest to the vendor. Generally included in this section is a description of the

Table 22–2: RFP Table of Contents

Request for Proposal Table of Contents
I.   Cover Letter
II.   General Information/Proposal Guidelines
III. Background Material
IV. Vendor Questionnaire
V.   Vendor Cost Summary
VI. System Requirements

organization's different business functions currently being performed and by which departments; volume statistics (e.g., the number of payroll and accounts payable checks issued per month and the number of general ledger transactions); the current hardware, financial system software and modules, and operating system, if any; and the hours of operation. This information is very useful for vendors when preparing their proposals.

Vendor Questionnaire

The vendor questionnaire asks a variety of questions on the vendor's background, clients, training, and growth; systems reliability, security, and performance; how modifications are handled; how reports are produced; acceptance testing and implementation schedule; data control; staffing; R&D expenditures; documentation; and hardware proposed, if any. The answers to these questions will assist the organization with determining the final vendor. This section must be extremely well-constructed and the questions concisely formulated (See Table 22–3 for examples of vendor evaluation criteria.)

Vendor Cost Summary

In the vendor cost summary, the vendor is requested to complete a cost schedule specifying the costs of the proposed FIS. Each vendor generally is asked to provide information on recurring and nonrecurring costs over a five-year period and supplemental schedules to explain the derivation of all costs and what is included

---

Table 22–3: Vendor Evaluation Criteria

Key factors to consider when evaluating vendors:

Product Support
- Location of nearest sales and support office.
- Size of the support staff at nearest service office and their qualifications.
- Availability of remote diagnostics.
- Availability of twenty-four hour support and associated cost.
- Guaranteed response time for system problems.
- Preventative maintenance approach and policies.
- Problem resolution procedures.
- Availability of installation and implementation support.
- Existence of and level of support of a user group.
- Existence of complete user and technical documentation.
- Frequency of documentation and system updates.

Reputation and Stability
- Number of years in the computer industry.
- Number of similar installations of the particular system still operating.
- Sales growth rate of applications being reviewed.
- Financial condition of the vendor and/or its parent company.
- Research and development budget and number of staff.

in such items as installation and maintenance fees. An example of a vendor cost summary schedule is shown in Figure 22–2.

System Requirements

The system requirements section sets forth the processing, inquiry, reporting, and data requirements developed during the systems requirement definition process. Each vendor is asked to complete a matrix that contains all application requirements. The vendor is asked to respond to the following categories for *each* requirement:

- Whether the current system can satisfy the requirement. The only acceptable responses are yes or no.
- Cross Reference (X-REF)—Where in the vendor's documentation is the requirement described.
- Comments—Any comments the vendor may have regarding the specific requirement.

Table 22–4 reproduces a page from an accounts payable information requirements section, together with a possible vendor response.

DISTRIBUTION OF THE REQUEST FOR PROPOSAL

Once the RFP is completed, the organization must determine the vendors to whom it will be sent. With over 50,000 software packages available, narrowing the field can be a difficult task. However, there are some basic factors to consider.

- *Geographic location.* The ability to receive timely support is extremely critical. Since many software vendors may not have offices located near the organization, this factor can be used to eliminate many vendors.
- *Hardware considerations.* Many software programs run only on certain hardware configurations (e.g., IBM or Hewlett Packard hardware only). Therefore, if the organization owns hardware or has a preference for a certain manufacturer, the software options are significantly reduced.
- *Organization size.* The size of the organization influences the size of the computer system that must be acquired. Software is generally designed to run on microcomputers, midrange systems, or mainframes. As a result, the software vendors to which the organization may send the RFP are limited.
- *Organizational preference.* Some organizations prefer to deal with firms that develop software only. Other organizations prefer to deal with turnkey vendors that supply both hardware and software. The organization's decision in this area will influence the number of vendors to which the RFP can be sent.

Vendor Cost Summary

	Year					
	1	2	3	4	5	Total

Recurring costs

Hardware
CPU lease	$	$	$	$	$	$
Terminal lease						
Printer lease						
Other lease						
CPU maintenance						
Terminal maintenance						
Printer maintenance						
Other maintenance						

Software
Software license						
Software support						
Other fees						

Supplies
Disks, tapes						
Ribbons, paper						
Other						
Total	$	$	$	$	$	$

Nonrecurring costs

Hardware
CPU purchase	$	$	$	$	$	$
Terminal purchase						
Printer purchase						
Other purchase						

Software
Software purchase						

Installation
Freight						
Cabling						
Site preparation						
Training						
Customization						
System initializing						
Installation						
Other						
Total	$	$	$	$	$	$

TOTAL	$	$	$	$	$	$

Figure 22–2: Vendor Cost Summary

Table 22–4: Completed Accounts Payable System Requirements

Requirement	Response Yes	Response No	X-REF	Comments
1. Enter invoices on-line.	X		User Manual Pg. 5–22	
2. Enter vendor credit memoranda for future payments.	X		User Manual Pg. 6–21	$5,000 additional fee
3. Write checks automatically based on invoice date and a predefined pay period (e.g., 30 days from invoice date).	X		User Manual Pg. 3–22	
4. Automatically process recurring payments.		X	User Manual Pg. 2–10	
5. Process and post manual checks to correct vendor and general ledger account.	X		User Manual Pg. 3–12	
6. Automatically interface with general ledger system.	X		User Manual Pg. 7–12	
7. Edit for duplicate invoice numbers to the same vendor.	X		User Manual Pg. 6–10	$3,000 additional fee
8. Allow for standard discount terms (e.g., 1/10 net 30).	X		User Manual Pg. 3–20	

- *Vendor characteristics.* It is frequently possible to prescreen vendors to determine if it is appropriate to send them an RFP. This can be accomplished by calling a vendor representative, reviewing vendor literature, looking at one of the many software reference manuals such as *Datapro* or *Data Decisions* or discussing vendors with organizations similar to yours. When prescreening a vendor, look at factors such as the vendor's stability and related experience, list prices, and flexibility.

Other means of identifying vendors that should receive the RFP include engaging a consultant experienced in hardware and software selections, reviewing computer-oriented magazines, contacting hardware vendors for lists of potential software suppliers, and networking with other organizations.

In general, the RFP should be sent to between five and ten vendors; any more than that, and the process becomes cumbersome; any fewer, and the choices become too limited. The vendor should be given sufficient time—3 to 6 weeks— to complete the RFP accurately and thoroughly.

REVIEW OF THE VENDOR'S COMPLETED PROPOSAL

When the proposals are returned, they should be given an initial brief review. This brief review will most likely eliminate the proposals that do not meet the organization's minimum critical needs.

In general, systems decisions should be more heavily influenced by the software, not the hardware. Therefore, the organization should first review the software proposed by the vendors. The goal of this review is to determine the two or three finalists.

There are two types of software the organization needs to evaluate: application and systems. Application software is the software that performs the functions needed by the end-user, such as generating paying invoices, preparing financial statements, and recording cash receipts. It is used to perform specific processing or computational tasks. Examples of application software include accounts payable, accounts receivable, and general ledger systems. Systems software makes it possible to utilize the application software. Included in this broad category are operating systems, database management systems, report writers, database compilers, and debugging aids. The system requirements section of the RFP is used to review the vendor's application software. As previously mentioned, each vendor is asked to respond to each requirement. The selecting organization should tabulate these responses to determine how well the vendor's software meets the organization's needs. Use the following guidelines:

1. Prepare a spreadsheet listing all of the requirements. The spreadsheet should look exactly like the information systems requirement section displayed in Table 22–4.
2. Determine the number of points a response is worth. For example, a "Yes" response may be worth 10 points to a "Required" requirement, but only 6 points on a desired feature. (A sample scoring scheme follows.)
3. Tally the vendor's responses.
4. Total the score by application area.
5. Determine the vendor's total score.

Response	Required	Desired	Optional
Yes	10	6	4
No	0	0	0

The spreadsheet should look exactly like the information systems requirement displayed in Table 22–4. The rating sheet in Table 22–5 can be effective in evaluating the vendor responses. In addition, the organization should review the following characteristics of each vendor's application software.

- *Flexibility.* Is the software very easy to modify? Will it handle the organization's needs five years from installation? Is it easy to debug?
- *Documentation.* Is it easy to use? Is it accurate and thorough? Is it regularly updated? Does it describe all error messages? Are all screen formats pre-

Table 22–5: Application Software Rating Sheet

Requirement	Required or Desired	Response Yes	No	Comments
1. Enter invoices on-line.	R			
2. Enter vendor credit memoranda on-line and apply credits to future payments.	R			
3. Write checks automatically based on invoice date and a predefined pay period (e.g., 30 days from invoice date).	R			
4. Automatically process recurring payments.	D			
5. Process and post manual checks to correct vendor and general ledger account.	R			
6. Automatically interface with general ledger system.	R			
7. Edit for duplicate invoice numbers.	R			
8. Allow for standard discount terms (e.g., 2/10 net 30).	D			

sented? Does it clearly describe recovery procedures? Are terms defined? Who maintains it?

- *Controls.* Is a clear audit trail of all transactions available? Are data validated before files are updated? Does password security exist? Are all errors flagged? Is a listing of log-on attempts provided? Are different authorization levels available? Can check digits be used? Are batch totals available?

Analyzing systems software can be more difficult than analyzing application software, because it is harder to quantify. However, the following guidelines can be useful:

- *Determine the systems software factors to be evaluated.* For example, it is likely that the selecting organization will want to review the following:
  - The operating and database management system.
  - Multi-user capabilities.
  - Programming language utilized.
  - Compilation speeds.
  - Systems utilities such as file maintenance programs, backup and restore programs, and sorting and text editors.
  - Systems support software such as file management processors, password protection, screen formatters, report writers, and print spoolers.
  - Compatibility of the system with other software products.
  - Interactive and communications capabilities.
  - Ease of operation.
- *Once the factors have been determined, prioritize and assign numeric values to them.*

- *Review the vendor's proposal and assign a score to each factor.* Assigning scores is a somewhat subjective process. However, it is important that it be performed.
- *Total the vendor's score in this section.* Table 22–6 provides an example of how systems software can be prioritized and scored.

As previously mentioned, the software decision usually takes precedence over the hardware decision. However, a thorough review of the proposed hardware is extremely important to ensure that the FIS will meet the organization's needs. The size of the proposed hardware system depends on three factors.

1. The volume statistics listed in the background section of the RFP.
2. The organization's projected growth rates.
3. The vendor's experience with similar clients.

Acquiring a system that meets the organization's current and future needs is extremely important. Either an in-house IS specialist or an experienced IS consultant must review the capabilities and flexibility of the proposed hardware configuration. Other hardware factors to review include:

- Central processing unit.
- Peripheral devices (such as disk and tape drives).
- Remote devices (such as communications support equipment).
- Environmental considerations.
- Flexibility and expandability.
- Systems reliability.

Once the hardware evaluation factors have been identified, they should be prioritized and assigned a numeric value. (This is similar to the method recommended for

Table 22–6: Scoring for Systems Software

Factor	Points Assigned	Vendor A Score
1. Operating system	18	16
2. DBMS	12	12
3. Multi-user capabilities	10	6
4. Programming language	6	6
5. Compilation speed	6	2
6. Systems utilities	8	6
7. Systems support software	10	7
8. Compatibility	8	8
9. Interactive and communications capabilities	10	9
10. Ease of operations	12	8
Total Points	100	80

reviewing systems software.) Then, each vendor's proposal should be reviewed and assigned a score on each factor. The total score on hardware is then determined.

After the hardware and software have been evaluated, the next step is to evaluate the vendor(s). Depending on the system desired, this may involve reviewing a software vendor and a hardware vendor. The primary factors to consider when evaluating a vendor are:

- Product support.
- Reputation and financial stability.
- Experience.
- Product availability and enhancements.
- Documentation.
- Training.

Once the software, hardware, and vendor have been evaluated thoroughly, the selection of the finalist vendors can occur. The finalists are then analyzed further by means of reference calls, attendance at vendor demonstrations, and site visits. Because substantial amounts of time and money are invested in reviewing the finalist vendors, it is vital that the selecting organization choose vendors who can actually provide it with an FIS that meets its needs.

REFERENCE CALLS

One of the most important aspects of the systems selection process is making reference calls to existing systems users. Reference calls are a means by which an organization can find out what a vendor may not want them to know. For example, the organization may discover that a vendor's documentation and support are not as good as its sales literature claims.

The questions asked during a reference call should be both fact- and opinion-oriented. The users should be asked to list the software implemented and their overall opinion of the software. Topics to cover when making a reference call include:

- Type of Organization
- Volume Statistics
- Software Packages Purchased
- Software Packages Implemented
- Ease of Installation
- Operating System
- Database Management System
- Hardware Installed
- Hardware Dependability

- Systems Security
- Response Time
- Quality of Reports
- Approach to System Selection
- Why Vendor(s) Were Chosen
- Ease of Operation
- Quality of Training
- Quality of Documentation
- Modifications Made
- Quality of Support
- Vendor Dependability
- Unforeseen Costs
- User Group Membership/Satisfaction
- Overall Satisfaction
- Names of Other Users

The names of other systems users are important because vendors frequently provide only the names of satisfied users. Asking a user for names of other users may lead to one who is not pleased with the system.

DEMONSTRATION

After the reference calls have been completed, the organization should consider attending vendor demonstrations to obtain additional information on the software and vendor, see how the software operates, and review the look and feel of the system, its ease of use, and the level of complexity.

Prior to attending the vendor demonstration, the organization should prepare an agenda for the vendor to follow, develop a feedback form for the attendees to rate various aspects of the software and the vendor (e.g., screen layout and ease of use), and prepare a list of questions and sample transactions for the vendor to enter into the system (e.g., matching a purchase order and invoice).

It is important to remember that the vendors obviously will be presenting their software in its best light. You must be in a position to evaluate this information.

SITE VISITS

After the reference calls have been made and demonstrations attended, the organization should arrange to see the system at a working installation, not at the vendor's headquarters. The purpose of the site visits include:

- Viewing the system in a real-life environment.
- Answering questions that may have arisen during the selection process.
- Assisting the organization in deciding whether the system will meet its current and future needs.

The site visit should take place at a user's place of business and should be on a live rather than demo system so that the vendor has no opportunity to manipulate the demonstration to its advantage. Although the majority of vendors are ethical, manipulation of potential customers is not unheard of.

The individuals present at the demonstration should include in-house IS personnel; potential system users, such as the accounts payable supervisor; and the IS consultant, if one is being used. The visit should take no more than a day to complete. The selecting team representatives should come prepared with a set of questions to ask the other organization and a feedback form on which to record ratings of the vendor.

If possible, the organization should arrange to make site visits within a two-week period to more easily compare the systems.

COST OF THE SYSTEM

The costs of purchasing hardware, software, and implementation support can be a very critical factor in a selection process and should be carefully analyzed. The vendor cost summary portion of the RFP may be used to compare the costs of proposed systems. However, other cost factors need to be clarified before comparing the total costs of the proposed systems. Consider:

- What will the proposed enhancements cost?
- How will the cost of future enhancements be determined?
- Is there an additional fee for installation?
- Is there an additional fee for training?
- How much does maintenance cost?
- Is there an additional fee for twenty-four-hour support?
- Is there a charge for system updates?
- Will the organization receive a discount if it purchases other applications?
- Does the software license allow for the use of the software at multiple sites? If not, what is the charge for the other sites?
- How much does the warranty cost and how long is it in effect?
- When does the warranty go into effect? (Ideally, the warranty should go into effect on the date the system is accepted, not on the date the system is installed.)
- Does the vendor guarantee in writing a full refund if the software does not perform as promised?
- Is the price of documentation included in the total price?

- Can the organization duplicate the documentation, or must it pay for additional copies? If so, what is the cost for additional copies?
- Is the source code (a copy of the programs) included in the system's price? If not, what is the charge for the source code?

FINAL SELECTION

Once the software, hardware, and vendor have been thoroughly reviewed and the reference calls, demonstrations, and site visits completed, the organization is in a position to select the system. If the organization has completed the steps outlined in this chapter, it should find itself with an IFS that meets current and future needs. Once the final selection has been made, the organization is in a position to begin contract negotiations.

CONTRACT NEGOTIATIONS

After the software and hardware have been selected, preparation for contract negotiations between the organization and the vendor(s) should ensue. The objectives of contract negotiations are to:

- Define the organization's expectations clearly to avoid misunderstandings.
- Define precisely what remedies are available if the vendor fails to perform as promised.
- Protect the organization against unexpected occurrences, such as the bankruptcy of the vendor.
- Ensure the best terms possible for the organization.

Negotiating a contract can be a long and costly process. When negotiating, there are several points to remember:

1. Do not accept the vendor's standard contract.
2. Negotiate with someone with the authority to bind the vendor.
3. Never accept oral promises.
4. Do not make unreasonable demands.
5. Obtain advice from a professional experienced in contract negotiations.

Four specific steps are essential for effectively negotiating a mutually beneficial contract:

1. Choose a negotiating team to represent the selecting organization, including an IS specialist, an individual who will be using the system, an attorney or

consultant with significant computer-related contract experience, and a purchasing department representative.

2. Determine the specific objectives of the negotiations and prepare a plan of action to take if the negotiations fail.

3. Review the standard contract terms offered by the vendor and identify problem areas and points that are missing.

4. Meet with the vendor to negotiate the contract.

The contract should clearly specify the costs for hardware, software, maintenance, installation support, modifications testing, and upgrades. The organization should attempt to ensure that it is protected from any price increases without its written consent. The contract should also clearly identify the terms of payment. The organization should hold back a substantial portion of the purchase price (10 to 30%) until the system is fully operational for a specified period of time and has passed all acceptance tests.

POST-IMPLEMENTATION REVIEW

After a system has been implemented, a post-implementation review (PIR) should be completed. It should have the following objectives:

- Determining if the anticipated results of the selection and implementation process have been attained.
- Comparing the original cost estimate to the actual costs.
- Identifying weaknesses in support, documentation, training, and functionality.
- Reviewing the adequacy of reports, security, and ease of use.
- Identifying additional systems enhancements that may be required.
- Reviewing the timeliness of report preparation and distribution.

The best time to perform a post-implementation review (PIR) is approximately 6 to 18 months after the system is installed. During this period, users have become familiar with the new system. This timing also allows significant system problems or issues to surface. Conducting the review earlier than six months will not allow time for people to relinquish old habits. The areas to be reviewed during the PIR include:

- How successfully the system has been implemented.
- The efficiency and effectiveness of the system.
- How well the system is being utilized.
- If system features exist that have not been implemented or used.
- If user's needs are being met.
- If the system is sufficiently secure.

The steps to be taken to perform a PIR include:

1. Reviewing the statement of requirements, RFP, and the selected vendor's proposal.
2. Interviewing key individuals from the selection committee, implementation team, IS staff, user group, and internal audit.
3. Reviewing the system's implementation, training, documentation, support, security, operations, input forms, and reports.
4. Evaluating the implementation process.
5. Formulating the findings, conclusions, and recommendations in a report.

The benefits of performing a PIR include:

- Detecting issues related to the system.
- Evaluating the effectiveness of training and determining whether additional training is required.
- Determining whether additional documentation is necessary.
- Determining whether the expected benefits have been realized.
- Preparing recommendations for improvements to the system to maximize its use.
- Providing guidance and insight for future systems implementations.

23

INFORMATION SECURITY SYSTEMS

In survey after survey, *information security*—protection against unauthorized use of computer systems—shows up as a top concern of controllers and information technology (IT) managers. While other security issues, such as physical plant security, remain the domain of corporate security officers, why does information security so often make it onto the radar screen of controllers and chief financial officers? One reason is the tremendous potential for loss of critical business data; the very data of greatest concern to financial professionals is stored in computer systems. This makes the controller or chief financial officer (CFO), as the "owner" of this data, ultimately responsible for its protection. Another reason for heightened concern is the rapidly changing nature of the information security landscape. Traditional security techniques based on controlling physical access do not translate well to distributed networked computing systems where physical access to the data repositories is largely irrelevant. Whatever the reason, controllers should expect to be confronted with decisions regarding information security. This chapter presents some essential information that will enable these decisions to be informed ones.

Often, the controller's role as decision maker is one of choosing between security alternatives—perhaps between the highly secure but expensive and disruptive option, and cheaper, more convenient alternatives. There is really no such thing as an "unbreakable" security system; the entire security profession is oriented around managing risk—reducing risk to an acceptable level. As with other forms of risk that the controller manages, some security risks should be eliminated, while others

---

This chapter was written by E. Edward Bassett III, Senior Systems Security Engineer, Denver Technological Laboratories.

are best accepted because it is too expensive or limiting to mitigate them. As an evaluator and accepter of risk, controllers should ensure they have sufficient information at their disposal to make informed risk management decisions.

DEFINING INFORMATION SECURITY

The field of information security covers all aspects of protecting computer-based processes and business information stored in computer systems and networks. This growing field has been variously called *computer security, ADP (automated data processing) security,* and *AIS (automated information system) security.* Every company defines the boundary between information security and other corporate security functions differently. In some cases, all security functions are consolidated under a common corporate security officer. Often information security is separately managed because of its "high-tech" nature.

Whatever it is called, expect information security to include a whole gamut of security measures to protect computing systems and the information they process and store. These measures generally include technical measures, such as password protection of logons, and nontechnical measures, such as configuration management policies. Physical protection of the computer systems and the rooms that house them is optionally considered part of information security or included with overall plant security. Likewise, personnel security measures for key information systems people, such as background checks, can be included in an information security program or they may be part of a general security effort.

CORPORATE SPENDING ON INFORMATION SECURITY IS INCREASING

There are several key factors that have motivated increased spending on information security in recent years. The most significant of these factors is a move toward highly networked distributed computing systems. Another important factor is the ever-increasing number of mission-critical business functions that rely on automation. Where a company of some years ago would rely on mainframe computers to handle mainly batch (or non-real-time) "back office" processing, today's organizations rely on complex networks of real-time and near-real-time computers for critical front-line functions as well.

This increased complexity and increased reliance have made information security a front-burner issue throughout IT organizations.

With this increased reliance on computers and networks for day-to-day operations, companies cannot afford the risk of lax security. Computer failures caused by teenage hackers, corporate spies, disgruntled employees, human error, or even unreliable hardware or software can cost thousands or millions of dollars per incident. The 1996 Information Week/Ernst & Young Information Security Survey found that 78% of respondents had suffered a measureable financial loss related to information security in the past two years.

Although some of this risk can be mitigated by insurance, much of the potential loss cannot, especially intangible costs such as loss of customer satisfaction and confidence if the company has unreliable or inaccurate computer records. Nearly everyone has experienced the modern-day phenomenon of calling a customer service representative and hearing the response, "I can't help you now; our computers are down." Even short disruptions of these types of systems cost money in terms of lost orders, unhappy customers, and idle front-line employees.

The solution to these types of problems—the ones that insurance alone cannot compensate—is a comprehensive information security program designed to minimize computer system disruptions while balancing cost and other operational factors.

The information security industry has responded by producing more sophisticated and more affordable security technology. The use of ultra-high-tech protection mechanisms such as the use of encryption to create protected networks within the main corporate network—known as *virtual private networks*—has become widespread just in the past two years. Other advances, such as more flexible and reliable access controls to replace clumsy passwords, are just now emerging and will likely be integrated into a large number of corporate networks in the near future.

TYPES OF SECURITY THREATS

The common view of information security is that it is focused on preventing "hacker attacks." Intrusions by teenage "whiz kids" into important government and corporate computers receives a lot of attention in the media. Computer virus "infection" is another topic that has received wide coverage in the mainstream media. Information security covers a broader range of threats than these news stories might imply.

The types of threats that information security focuses on stopping fall into two main categories: intentional and unintentional. Both types can have significant detrimental effects on computer systems, but they require different types of protections and are, therefore, considered separately.

Some examples of *intentional threats* are:

- *Unauthorized access by an outsider.* This is the classic "hacker" attack: someone outside the organization uses computer networks or dial-in lines to access a computer system for which they have no authorized access. The motivation for this type of attack can range from "intellectual curiosity" to industrial espionage. In the former case, the intruder is likely to make a big splash (so as to draw attention to their accomplishment) but do little actual damage. In the latter case, the intruder will take much more precaution to be surreptitious but will likely steal or destroy valuable business information. Recent years have seen a dramatic increase in attacks by "professional" hackers.

- *Unauthorized access by an insider.* The most common type of "intrusion" is that perpetrated by someone who already has some access to company systems: employees, vendors, or contractors. The classic example of this type of intrusion is a student entering school administration computers to change grades or account information. Another example is a disgruntled employee who destroys critical records or steals valuable intellectual property to "get back" at his or her employer. This type of attack is often overlooked, but it is the most significant threat to most systems. It is also a very difficult type of attack to prevent since the insider, by definition. requires access to the system.
- *Malicious software.* Viruses and trojan horses are the two most prevalent forms of malicious software. A *virus* is self-replicating software that spreads from computer to computer by attaching itself to other files. A *trojan horse* is software that appears to be a desirable program but actually contains some hidden malicious instructions. Either of these threats can be used in a targeted attack to damage specific computer systems. Viruses, though, are more generally spread in a nontargeted fashion. Their authors let them replicate "in the wild," spreading to any system they can. Malicious software can perform very serious destruction or, in the case of some viruses, merely annoy users.

Some examples of *unintentional threats* are

- *Hardware or software failure.* Unreliable hardware or software can cause system outages or corrupted data. Outright failures are always easy to detect and, if proper preparations are made, can be relatively easy to recover from. Data corruption is a much more subtle problem that can be difficult to detect.
- *Human error.* For critical business systems that rely on the accuracy of information, errors made during data entry can propagate and affect key business decisions. Errors in customer records, for example, can cause significant expense in correcting them as well as creating customer dissatisfaction.

BASIC SECURITY PRINCIPLES

Goals and Objectives

The goal of information security is to protect systems and data in three ways:

1. *Confidentiality.* Information that represents trade secrets, intellectual property, personal information, or other sensitive data must be protected so that only authorized people can read or copy it. In addition to the obvious category of proprietary information, many companies also must protect private customer information, such as credit card numbers, that they are entrusted with.
2. *Integrity.* Information that is relied upon to make business decisions must be accurate. Protecting the integrity of data involves controlling both who can

enter and change data and how they can change it. For example, an accounting clerk might be allowed to change data in the current quarter, but changes to previous quarters might require a second person's authority.

3. *Availability.* Systems that provide critical business functions must be available when they are needed. This is an especially critical factor for real-time or near-real-time systems that are used in front-line operations and production systems. Back-office systems can often tolerate a longer period of unavailability, but even these systems can generally not be "down" for longer than a day or so without causing considerable disruption and expense.

The security measures that are employed to achieve these three protection goals can be selected based on their benefit to the organization. Cost-benefit analysis can be applied to determine when the cost of securing a system is less than the risk of loss.

A Risk-Driven Security Approach

As was mentioned, there is no such thing as perfect security and no such thing as an unlimited security budget. To make the most effective use of limited dollars, many organizations use a risk-driven approach to select the optimal mix of security features. This approach involves analyzing security risks using qualitative or quantitative approaches to determine where the highest potential of loss exists. Security measures can then be applied to these high-risk areas. The goal of this approach is to avoid buying security for the sake of security (or because of some unbased fear).

There are a variety of security risk analysis tools available to assist in this process. Although they vary in detail, they generally use quantitative methods to calculate "annual loss expectancies" that are essentially the annual probability of a loss multiplied by the value of an asset being protected. Security measures can then be applied that reduce the probability of loss for the assets that have the most "exposure."

As an alternative to this quantitative technique, many security practitioners use qualitative techniques to identify the most significant risks based on an analysis of the threats and vulnerabilities of a system. Figure 23–1 shows a typical risk analysis process that is used to assess risk and select countermeasures (safeguards) for an information system.

COMPONENTS OF AN EFFECTIVE SECURITY PROGRAM

An information security program includes several functions performed by participants from many organizational elements. Figure 23–2 depicts the basic information security functions (boxes in the center of the exhibit) and shows their interactions with the system/software development life cycle (lower row of boxes).

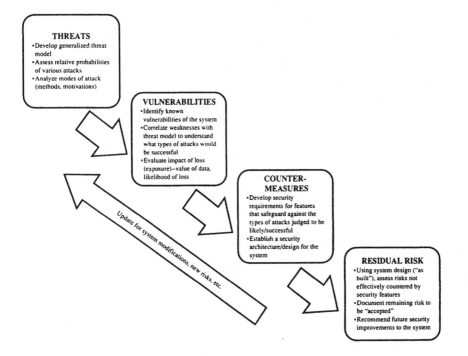

Figure 23–1: Typical Risk Analysis Process

In order to effectively document information security decisions, several key documents are required. Figure 23–3 shows an example of the document tree for an organization with a relatively formal information security program. Of particular interest to the controller will be the Organization Statement of Direction for Security, which will establish the overall goals and objectives of the information security program. Also of interest as it relates to key financial systems will be the Risk Assessment Guideline and Incident Response Plan.

The following four sections describe the main components of an information security program: security policy, security management, technical security measures, and nontechnical security measures.

Security Policy

At the top level, information security is driven by corporate policies that determine what is to be protected and what level of protection is required. In some cases, there are legal requirements for protection of information. In other cases, companies want to restrict access to information because it is proprietary or because it is critical to an important business function.

Security policy should be written so as to clearly define the categories of information and systems needing protection. Many companies have adopted a

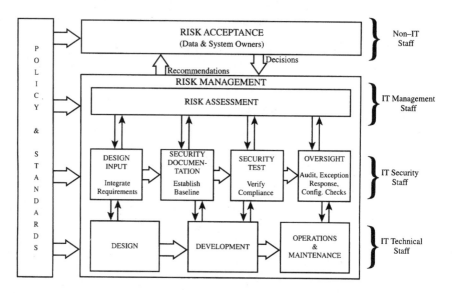

Figure 23–2.: Basic Information Security Functions

system of "levels" of data in which more important information is more tightly protected. Because protection costs money, a system of levels can ensure that the most extensive protection is reserved for only that small amount of information that is truly sensitive (e.g., trade secrets, safety-critical systems, etc.). Some typical levels of information are:

- *Restricted.* Access is controlled on a by-name basis to a select group of people. Use of this category is generally limited to the most sensitive information whose unauthorized release would cause serious loss of competitive advantage. For example, details of an upcoming product or acquisition might be protected at this level.

- *Company confidential.* Access is limited to trusted employees who have signed nondisclosure agreements. This category is often used for trade secrets or other proprietary information for which the company must enforce protection vigorously to maintain the legal status of the information as proprietary. This level of protection also provides some legal basis for action if employees violate their confidentiality agreements.

- *Internal use only.* Access is limited to employees and often contractors, vendors, and others who play an integral role in the business operations of the company. This information is to be provided only to those with a bona fide business reason to have the information. Often future planning and operations details are protected at this level, unless a higher level is warranted by the potential for loss of competitive advantage if the information is released. This level represents a "default" protection that employees will apply to company information that has not been designated as falling to another category.

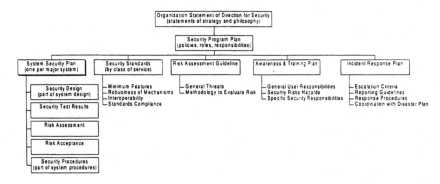

Figure 23–3: Information Security Documentation

- *Public.* This information has been approved for release to the public, generally by the public relations staff. It is given freely to customers, shareholders, and the media.

Another tool that many companies use is "classes of service" for their various systems and applications. This scheme allows various systems to be categorized based on their relative importance to day-to-day operations. It provides a basis for decisions about integrity and availability security decisions, whereas the levels of information described previously are more useful as a basis for confidentiality security decisions. Some typical classes of service are:

- *Production—mission critical.* Systems that perform mission-critical business functions will require the most rigorous security measures. Generally, their configuration is tightly controlled and monitored. Although these systems generally have a large number of users, the type of access the users have is strictly limited. A system for taking customer orders would be an example of such a system. Another candidate would be widespread services, such as E-mail, wherein failure could have pervasive impacts on business operations.

- *Production—non-mission critical.* Support systems and other less critical systems may require less strict security. However, production systems are generally held under tight configuration control.

- *Development.* Development systems are very difficult to configuration control because they are constantly changing as development progresses. However, access to these systems is generally restricted to a relatively small number of developers. It is wise to perform development on systems separate from production systems to ensure that errors in development do not propagate to production systems.

- *Experimental/prototype.* These systems generally have minimal security controls to allow maximum flexibility and speed of development. However, they should be isolated from mainstream systems for two reasons: first, to keep malfunctions in experimental systems from affecting operational systems;

second, to limit access to sensitive or proprietary software being developed in the experimental system.

Another factor that should be considered in defining an information security policy is legal "standards of care" that are required for certain types of information. Especially in industries that act as custodians for privileged personal information, such as the medical and legal professions, certain standards of care must be applied to this information. Trade secrets and other intellectual property may also require protection to maintain their legal status. Legal counsel should be consulted to determine the appropriate information security protection to be applied to information in these categories.

In addition to categories (or levels) of information sensitivity and classes of service, a company information security policy will include an overall protection philosophy, establish rules for "acceptable use" of corporate computers (for example, whether employees may use company E-mail for personal messages), and define user responsibilities. The use of a "user agreement" that users sign as a condition of access to computer systems is a recommended way of enforcing compliance with the information security policy.

Security Management

Traditionally, security functions have been centralized within an organization. Often security is separate from the normal organizational structure, reporting directly to upper management. As the "gatekeepers" of the organization, it follows that security should maintain "independence." Information security organizations, however, have found it impractical to follow this model. Often, information security requires specialized technical expertise spanning all the computer systems and applications used throughout the organization. Additionally, IT systems tend to be very fast moving, making it difficult for security to keep up unless the security staff is tightly integrated with the IT organization.

It is important to maintain the balance between integration and independence. In particular, it is important to avoid the all-too-common situation in which a new type of system is understood by only one or a few "gurus" who make, implement, and enforce their own security policies.

A successful information security program must include many security management functions to ensure that security is consistently applied and that lapses in security are identified and corrected quickly. The key functions of the security management staff are:

- *Risk management.* This is the process of assessing risk and implementing security safeguards to mitigate the risk to an acceptable level.
- *Input to system design.* Security is a critical component of most system and application designs. Although many systems come with security features, deciding how to use these features to the best advantage of the company is an important part of the system/software development process.

- *Security testing.* Security features are often subjected to rigorous tests that include both positive tests (confirm the security features work as required) and negative tests (confirm that the security mechanisms cannot be bypassed or defeated).

- *Audit/oversight.* Periodically, security features should be checked for proper configuration. Audit records should be checked to ensure security procedures are being followed. This function is often combined with other audit functions.

- *Training and user awareness.* Many security mechanisms rely on trusted employees using the correct procedures. Also, many types of security problems, from breakins to reliability problems, can be spotted by vigilant users if they know what to look for and how to respond. A formal training program for both users and system administrators is an important step to ensure security awareness in the organization is high.

- *Incident response.* Early detection and quick reaction to information security breaches is vital to limit the damage caused by the incident. Formal response procedures and a trained incident response team are being used by many companies to reduce their security-related losses.

Technical Security Measures

Technical security measures are the computer-based safeguards. They include a range of mechanisms; some are very common and are included in nearly all computer systems, others are fairly esoteric and are employed only by systems that require a high degree of protection. Some of the types of technical security measures in use today are:

- *Access controls.* Various mechanisms are used to identify users and determine their privileges. Nearly all systems and networks have some form of access control. Desktop PCs are an exception, but many newer desktop operating systems now have access controls. The most common types of access controls are:
  —*Passwords/personal identification numbers (PINs).* This is the most common form of access control. A user has a "secret" word or number that is used to gain access.
  —*Biometrics.* Physical properties, such as fingerprints, retinal patterns, or a signature, are used to identify users. This technique is generally used only for very-high-security systems.
  —*Smart cards.* Users carry a "token" that is inserted into a reader to gain access. Smart cards come in many varieties and are gaining popularity, especially for remote access to corporate networks.
  —*Certificates.* Users present digitally signed credentials to gain access. Certificates use encryption to create hard-to-forge digital "passports." They

are being deployed widely to enable Internet commerce where two parties with no prior relationship must reliably identify each other and communicate securely.

—*Dial-back modems.* Some remote access systems use special modems that call the remote user back at a predetermined number. This prevents intruders from calling in from unauthorized locations.

- *Encryption.* Both hardware-based and software-based tools are available to "scramble" data while it is being transmitted across networks or while it is stored in a computer. Encryption can be used to keep data "private" by preventing eavesdropping. It can also be used to check the integrity of data and to perform a digital "signature" analogous to a written signature that guarantees the authenticity of information.

- *Firewalls.* Many corporate systems now have connections to their vendors, suppliers, and customers that use private network connections or the Internet. Special gateways called *firewalls* are used to monitor the communications with external systems to prevent intrusion into internal systems.

- *Intrusion detection.* Many vendors make software tools that monitor network and computer system activity to detect behavior that might indicate a break-in attempt. These tools use rules, artificial intelligence, and knowledge of common intrusion techniques to spot suspicious activity and sound an alarm.

- *Audit.* Most systems have a feature to keep tamper-resistant records of system activity. These "audit trails" can be used to detect unauthorized activity and catch the perpetrator.

- *Virus detection.* Tools that monitor desktop systems for infection by known viruses are widely deployed. These tools scan files to find viral "signatures." Most also allow the user the option of cleaning their system to remove the virus.

- *Backup.* Most systems include a tool for creating copies of the data on the system. These backup copies are often stored on magnetic tape or on large archive servers. Backups are important for rapid recovery from system failure or data corruption. Backups represent a very low cost way of mitigating the damage that might be caused by a wide range of threats.

- *Uninterruptible power supply.* Special power supplies that allow graceful system shutdown in case of a power failure allow files to be saved and prevent the data corruption that is common if systems are allowed to "crash." Some high-reliability systems use alternative power sources, such as generators, to allow continued operation even if commercial power is lost for an extended period.

Most systems use a mixture of various technical security measures as well as the nontechnical measures described in the next section. Technical security measures provide very robust, reliable security because computer hardware or software is being used to enforce the security. Technical measures also tend to be more expensive to implement than nontechnical measures.

Nontechnical Security Measures

Nontechnical security measures are those safeguards that primarily rely on some action by human users to protect the system. The most common nontechnical measure is a "security procedure." This is some step-by-step process that users must follow to prevent security breaches. Some examples of nontechnical security measures are:

- *Software use policy.* Many companies restrict users from installing software that is not authorized by the company. This is a good method of keeping malicious software such as viruses and trojan horses off company computers. It is also a good way to avoid software licensing violations.
- *Incident response procedures.* Rapid detection and decisive response to intrusions and other unauthorized use are important to limit or prevent losses due to security breaches.
- *Acceptable use policy.* A policy that defines how employees are allowed to use company systems is valuable to prevent overuse of resources and to limit potential liability for actions that are taken with company computers.
- *Least privilege.* Employee privileges are generally limited to only those privileges needed to do their job. Also, certain privileges are often identified as mutually exclusive, meaning the same employee cannot perform both functions. This technique is especially useful in financial systems where a system of checks and balances requires two or more individuals to perform certain functions.
- *Physical protection of computer resources.* Nearly all technical security measures can be bypassed if an intruder has physical access to the computer system. Security measures such as guards, door locks, desktop and notebook computer locks, and intruder alarms are valuable to prevent someone from simply stealing the computer hardware and the data along with it.
- *Desktop computer security.* Most desktop computers have few technical security features. End users must follow specific procedures to ensure their desktop computers are properly secured. These procedures can include not storing passwords on the local disk, making backups of important files, and frequent file saving to prevent data corruption due to power loss.
- *Employee security.* Background checks, drug screening, and other safeguards are used to determine and monitor the trustworthiness of key IT personnel.
- *Insurance coverage.* Some types of security-related loss can be recovered by having proper insurance coverage.
- *Disaster recovery.* Rapid system recovery in case of a major disaster is critical to limiting the financial loss due to these events. Most computer systems should be covered by a disaster recovery plan that will restore the system within a time frame dictated by the type of processing the system performs. Although disasters happen very infrequently, they can occur at any time. Peri-

odic testing of the disaster recovery plan is essential to a successful recovery in case of a real disaster.

Nontechnical security measures, by definition, are not enforced by an automated mechanism. In general, this makes nontechnical measures less robust than comparable technical measures. However, they can be relatively inexpensive and quick to implement. Nontechnical measures are often used as a stopgap while technical measures are being developed.

ENTERPRISE SECURITY STRATEGIES

Client Server Systems

The move to more distributed client server systems has brought new information security challenges. Mainframe systems generally have a unified set of security mechanisms that interoperate to provide flexible, robust protection of the information on the mainframe. Obtaining this same level of protection in a client server environment requires the careful coordination of security features on several systems and in several software packages. In a typical client server system, security features of the server operating system, database management system, application software, client operating system, and interconnecting network must all be designed to apply a consistent security policy.

Several security solutions designed to provide end-to-end enterprise security are emerging. These solutions involve the establishment of a security infrastructure that is used to protect many different applications. Kerberos and the Distributed Computing Environment (DCE) are examples of these types of security solutions.

Networks and the Internet

The percentage of company networks connected to the Internet has risen dramatically in the past few years. The addition of Internet connectivity to corporate networks has added a new security exposure to sensitive and mission-critical internal systems. Specialized security products have been developed to prevent unauthorized entry into corporate systems. The most common solution is a "firewall"—a specialized security gateway designed to limit the access that outsiders have to internal systems.

Because Internet connectivity also provides an inexpensive option for remote access by branch offices and telecommuters, many companies also utilize remote access products that allow remote users to access internal systems securely. These products provide features to reliably identify the remote user as well as a capability to encrypt, or "scramble," the transmissions to preclude eavesdropping. The use of encryption to create a private link across a public network such as the Internet is known as "virtual private networking." This can be a very efficient way of connecting remote employees by using low-cost public networks.

Interconnected Customer and Vendor Systems

Internetworking technology has made it possible to share information with suppliers, customers, and partners quickly and efficiently using electronic data interchange (EDI). The information security challenge is to create these interconnections in a way that permits the free exchange of some information but does not expose other information that is not being shared. Encryption techniques—in particular, public key certificates and digital signatures—are emerging that will allow these interconnections to be protected. This technology is replacing the need for mutual trust between the owners of the interconnected systems.

Controller's Role in Information Security

The controller's role in information security includes several areas:

- Establishing top-level information protection goals for the information and business processes he/she controls.
- Monitoring compliance to security standards and policies, perhaps as part of the overall audit function.
- Assessing risk to mission-critical systems and balancing the cost of risk mitigation against the potential for financial loss due to security breaches.
- Participating in the investigation of security incidents, including the evaluation of the loss or impact of an incident.

24

PROJECT RISK MANAGEMENT

The controller's division is not immune from the business pressures that are causing organizations to undertake numerous performance improvement projects. These projects may take a variety of forms: reengineering, systems enhancement, and reorganization, to name a few. In addition to these potential changes, the controller's division frequently lends its expertise to other projects within the company through a variety of roles, such as providing financial analysis and participating on project teams. Unfortunately, in many companies, management is frequently disappointed with project results because these results often fall far below original expectations. Although the reasons for these failures vary, there is one common denominator: earlier in the life of the project, these reasons were *risks* to the project.

Over the past few years, many organizations have concentrated on building the specialized skills and defined methods that are necessary to effectively manage projects. In their processes and procedures for project management, it is common for companies to carefully track and manage the issues that have begun to negatively impact the project. However, it is important that these processes and procedures be augmented by an effective process for identifying and addressing project risks *before* these risks become issues. Most of the issues that arise on projects could have been foreseen and probably were anticipated by one or more people close to the project. Fully leveraging this early foresight offers the project team a variety of options. For example, priorities or schedules may be changed, key decisions may be escalated to higher levels of management, activities may be

This chapter was authored by Sara Moulton-Reger, Principal, IBM Consulting Group, Denver, Colorado.

added or enhanced, and additional (or different) resources may be obtained. For these reasons, it is valuable to include an approach for managing project risks in the overall project management process.

Project risk management is a method for addressing project risks in a proactive manner. In addition to reducing the overall risk of projects, project risk management benefits projects in other ways, by, for example:

- Ensuring that project plans are realistic, with corresponding improvements in the overall business case and definition of project net benefits.
- Enhancing management's understanding of the project's implications during the early stages of the project, which can reduce unwelcome surprises and perhaps even lead to an appropriate "no go" decision before significant resources are wasted.
- Providing the opportunity to identify and consider a broader range of options than may be possible when the risk has become an issue, which can conserve resources.
- Allowing more time to be made available to address the risks in a careful and well-planned manner.

This chapter describes a framework that companies can use to identify and manage project risks at the earliest possible stage in the life of a project.

PROJECT RISK CATEGORIES

Before beginning the process of managing project risk, it is important to understand the distinction between issues and risks:

- *Issue:* A current problem that is negatively impacting a project.
- *Risk:* A possible occurrence that would expose a project to potential failure in some or all respects.

In some instances, a risk is an issue that will happen in the future. However, not all project risks become issues.

In addition to understanding the distinction between issues and risks, categorizing project risks can be valuable in assisting a project team to identify and consider the potential risks the project may face. Four categories of common project risks are project management risks, technical risks, human risks, and business risks.

1. *Project management risks.* Potential for unmet requirements in areas such as project management capabilities, project planning, and resource requirements. Some examples of project management risks include:
   - Inadequate project management processes, procedures, or skills

- Incomplete planning assumptions
- Overly aggressive time, budget, or benefits estimates
- Inadequate project resource commitments (e.g., departmental representation, participation of individuals with key knowledge or skills, percentage of time, or dates of availability)
- Resource coordination difficulties (e.g., geographical distances)
- Failure to coordinate intraproject linkages and relationships

2. *Technical risks.* Potential for unmet requirements in terms of project designs, delivery schedules, information availability, and the like. Some examples of technical risks include:
   - Inadequate definition of future state requirements
   - Designs that do not address the full scope of objectives
   - Hardware or software incompatibility
   - Design incompatibility between interdependent project components
   - Missed delivery schedules
   - Scheduling problems between interdependent project components

3. *Human risks.* Potential for various human dynamics to impede project objectives or to reduce or negate benefits. Some examples of human risks include:
   - Sponsorship that is inadequate to legitimize and sustain the project
   - Inadequate support from middle or lower levels of management
   - Differing or inadequate motivation toward the project or specific components of the project
   - Differing or unclear understanding about the project scope or impacts
   - Inadequate or ineffective communication
   - Incompatibility between the project and facets of the existing organizational culture
   - Lack of alignment between project requirements and facets of the existing management support structure (e.g., performance measurement, compensation and rewards practices, or organizational structure)
   - Ineffective anticipation and management of resistance
   - Project overload (e.g., too many projects running concurrently or too little time since another difficult project)
   - Residual issues from previous project implementations (e.g., expectations that the current project will fail because previous attempts have also failed or unresolved conflict between departments or key individuals)
   - Changes in key sponsors or project personnel during the life of the project

4. *Business risks.* Potential for occurrences external to the organization, or in other parts of the organization, that could negatively impact the project. Frequently, these risks fall outside the control of the project team. Some examples of business risks are:

- Strikes
- Competitor actions
- Legislative or regulatory changes
- Significant problems or opportunities that redirect executive attention and/or funding

These project risk categories and examples are not intended to be an exhaustive listing but rather an illustration of the various types of risks that projects face. In implementing project risk management, it may be valuable for each company to develop categories, descriptions, and examples that are specifically applicable to itself and to its project experiences.

PROJECT RISK MANAGEMENT APPROACH

Project risk management is an iterative process and should be directly tied into the process for managing and tracking issues throughout the life of the project. An effective approach for managing project risks involves steps; as noted in Figure 24–1:

1. Identify the risks that are relevant to the project.
2. Evaluate the risks to determine which risks deserve the most attention.

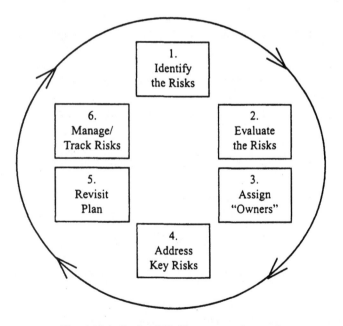

Figure 24–1: Project Risk Management Approach

3. Assign people to "own" the key risks.

4. Address the key risks through containment or contingency plans (prepared before the risk becomes an issue to the project).

5. Revisit the project plan for adjustment or enhancement if the plan has already been prepared.

6. Manage and track the risks throughout the life of the project.

Risk management is especially important during the initial stages of a project. However, it is appropriate to consider project risks at other times as well, such as:

- After achievement of key project milestones
- Before beginning new project phases
- When relevant information is received (e.g., knowledge about changes in business conditions, announcement of organizational changes, or announcement of or discussion about changes in a project sponsor or project member)

If a project is underway and its risks have not been identified and evaluated, it is advisable to begin the risk management process without delay.

Identify the Relevant Risks

When identifying risks, it is valuable to brainstorm and consider a wide variety of potential negative impacts to the project. The best approach to identifying risks depends on the size and importance of a project. In some cases, facilitated sessions are warranted. In other cases, it may be appropriate to seek input in writing. However, in all circumstances, it is beneficial to seek contribution from a variety of sources. Key contributors to this process may include project sponsors, project team members, and people with related expertise or experiences.

In preparing to identify project risks, a few prerequisites are necessary:

- The project objectives must be clear.
- Proposed targets for schedule, budget, and resource requirements need to be understood.
- Other relevant information should be understood, such as:
  — Implementation history for similar projects.
  — Planning assumptions.
  — Dependencies with related projects and/or other parts of the business.
  — Project organization, and roles and responsibilities.[1]

After these prerequisites have been met, the first activity in the project risk management process is to develop a list of relevant project risks. Depending on the nature and size of the project, a variety of methods exist for developing this list, such as ad hoc requests or surveys. If the project warrants a facilitated session, it is helpful to collect a draft list of risks prior to holding the session. Once the essence of each risk has been identified, risk statements should be developed. Examples of risk statements for each category of risk are:

- *Project management risk.* "There is a risk that key individuals will be pulled from the project too soon to complete some of the reporting refinements."
- *Technical risk.* "There is a risk that the pricing module will be delayed and that this delay will impede the ability to begin the new marketing programs as scheduled."
- *Human risk.* "There is a risk that users will reject report formats and schedules."
- *Business risk.* "There is a risk that funding may be jeopardized by problems in manufacturing."

During this first step, it may be valuable to use the risk categories to prompt the contributors to consider additional areas. Also, it may be helpful to encourage contributors to review the inputs of others. However, it is important to note that the objective of this step is to create a list of *relevant* risks that should be tracked and managed. When the contributors believe that the list contains these relevant risks, it is time to move on to the next step in the process.[2]

Evaluate the Risks

The second step involves evaluating the risks in preparation for taking appropriate actions. Depending on the nature of the project and the culture of the organization, this step may involve the entire project team or may be designated to specific sponsors and project team personnel only.

There are several ways to evaluate the list of project risks. Some ways are:

- By the probability of occurrence
- By the potential for negative impact to the project, in terms of:
  — Unmet project objectives
  — Missed schedules
  — Budget overruns
- By the degree to which the project team is able to control the risk or take action to reduce the probability and/or impact of that risk

The first step in evaluating project risks involves determining which risks warrant the most attention. This step involves analyzing each risk on two dimensions. The first dimension is the probability of that risk occurring. The second dimension is the potential for negative impact if the risk were to become an issue. These two dimensions can be plotted onto a matrix to determine the over-all severity of each risk, as shown in Figure 24–2.

The second evaluation step involves identifying the appropriate manner in which to address the risks, which is the subject of Step 4 in the project risk management process. The severity of each risk is an important element in making this evaluation. The second element involves the degree to which action can be taken on that risk. Although the project team may not have direct control over the risk, it is often possible for tasks to be undertaken that will reduce the probability of occurrence and/or decrease the negative impact if the risk becomes an issue. For some risks, however, there are no actions that are appropriate prior to the occurrence of the issue. An example of a nonactionable risk may be the risk of losing resources and momentum due to the possibility of a strike. In this case, the potential for a strike may be out of the control of the project team, and it is likely that no direct actions are appropriate unless the strike does occur.

In identifying the appropriate manner in which to address the risks, another matrix may be valuable. This matrix evaluates risk severity against the degree to which action may be taken (see Figure 24–3).

Containment plans include actions that *will* be taken and consequently need to be included in the overall project plan. Contingency plans are preparations for actions to be taken in the event that a key nonactionable risk becomes an issue. The tracking list is a mechanism to document the identified risks for monitoring and future consideration. The actions identified through the use of this matrix guide the actions to be taken in Step 4 of the project risk management approach.

Assign Risk Owners

By this step in the risk management process, the key risks for the project are known and understood, so it is an opportunity to assign a person to "own" each

Probability of Occurrence		Potential Negative Impact	
	Low	**Medium**	**High**
High	Medium Severity	High Severity	Very High Severity
Medium	Low Severity	Medium Severity	High Severity
Low	Low Severity	Low Severity	Medium Severity

Figure 24–2: Degree of Risk Severity

		Actionable	Not Actionable
Degree of Risk Severity	Very High	Containment Plan	Contingency Plan
	High	Containment Plan	Contingency Plan
	Medium	Tracking List or Containment Plan	Tracking List or Contingency Plan
	Low	Tracking List	Tracking List

Figure 24–3: Risk Management Actions

key risk. This helps to ensure that the key risks are managed and tracked adequately. For very high and high severity risks, risk owners are necessary. Also, depending on the importance of the project, it may be valuable to assign owners to risks that are moderately severe.

Risk owners are accountable for:

- Preparing the containment or contingency plans
- Monitoring changes in the probability and/or impact of the risk and notifying the project manager and team of any significant changes
- Taking the lead in initiating and managing the containment or contingency plans, as appropriate

The risk owner may look to others for assistance with these activities, especially if it is deemed appropriate for one individual to own several risks.

Address Key Risks

At this point in the process, the actions appropriate for each risk begin. The risk management actions matrix from Step 2 showed three types of actions for the project team to undertake:

1. *Containment plans.* These plans involve specific actions that *will* be taken to:
   - Reduce the probability of the risk turning into an issue
   - Reduce the negative impact to the project if the risk becomes an issue
   Containment plans might include the following types of actions:

- Negotiating firm commitments for individuals with critical knowledge or expertise
- Involving additional (or different) people in important roles, activities, or pivotal decisions
- Lengthening schedules for certain activities
- Obtaining additional budget and/or time to expand the scope to address important linkages between project components or among related projects
- Narrowing the project scope to make the project more manageable
- Enhancing communication activities
- Adding education and follow-up support mechanisms to existing plans for training (e.g., mentoring, "chalk talks," or single subject short courses).

2. *Contingency plans.* These plans involve preparation for actions to be taken in the event that a nonactionable risk becomes an issue. Contingency plans might include the following types of actions:
   - Identifying and preparing backup resources for critical activities or areas.
   - Distinguishing between vital project components that need to be continued and components that could be delayed with the least overall impact to the project.
   - Purchasing insurance.

3. *Tracking list.* This list is a mechanism to ensure that the identified project risks are retained and tracked as the project moves forward. Although no immediate action may be warranted, periodic review of the risks on the tracking list will assist the project team in "keeping their eyes on the horizon." The frequency of reviewing the list depends on the project, but it is valuable to specify the dates for these reviews in the project plan to ensure that they are not overlooked.

Revisit the Project Plan

Many project plans are prepared before the project risk management process has begun. If this is the case, it is important to revisit the original project plan after the containment and contingency plans have been prepared. A common problem that has been traced to many project failures stems from project plans that were unrealistic given the conditions. The information available at this point in the risk management process allows the original plan to be evaluated carefully for additional actions and trade-offs that will make the plan more achievable.

Manage and Track the Risks

As the project progresses, the risks that have been identified need to be:

- Managed carefully in the case of risks for which containment plans were created

- Monitored closely for indications of changes in probability and/or impact in the case of risks for which contingency plans were created
- Tracked for changes in probability and/or impact in the case of the remaining risks. If changes in the probability and/or impact of these risks increase the severity of the risk, containment or contingency plans should be created using the same criteria employed earlier in the process.

It is best to include steps to review and oversee the project risk management activities in the project plan. The frequency of these steps depends on the nature of the project. Projects that represent major change for the organization (e.g., involve significant disruption to present processes or power bases within the organization or require cross-functional cooperation to a greater extent than normal) will benefit from fairly frequent and close review of the identified risks.

ENDNOTES

1. Ensuring clarity around the project objectives and needed resources is an extremely important ingredient to project success. Many organizations initiate projects before the project vision and its business case have been established. Projects that begin in this manner may run the biggest risk of failure.
2. It is not uncommon to encounter "naysayers" who will voice negative views about a project and its potential for success. Project risk management can be a way to assure these people that their views have been captured and will be tracked throughout the project, which may help to diffuse the potential for conflict.

25

SYSTEMS PERFORMANCE MANAGEMENT

WHY MANAGEMENT OF PERFORMANCE IS IMPORTANT TO THE CONTROLLER

It is important, as a key member of your organization's management team, that the controller understand the components of performance and how they affect companies. Systems performance can affect all aspects of an organization's operations. However, it is not always obvious how your company is being adversely affected by bad systems performance. This chapter will help you identify the components of performance, the presence of performance problems, and the adverse effects of such problems on your business. The chapter will also explain the terminology and associated methodologies that are necessary to help you to control and manage your company's systems performance.

Performance Management

Performance management is the ongoing process of ensuring a business' work is done on time and within budget. As part of that process, performance management takes into account that business volume, needs, and available resources may vary from one time to another. A good performance management program

---

This chapter was written by Alan R. Arnold, a manager in the IT Management Consulting group at Ernst & Young's Irvine, California, office.

helps a company prevent surprises by providing criteria for estimating in advance what resources are needed and then periodically giving you updated information to ensure that you do not exceed your estimate. Performance management is a continuous process and not something you do only as a reaction to performance problems. It is important that someone within the organization be focussed on performance management issues.

Performance management is an important element in managing any business' data-processing resources. It maintains business efficiency, provides a smooth transition when business conditions change, increases user satisfaction, improves change management, and provides rapid response time.

As the controller, it is usually not within the scope of your day-to-day responsibilities to directly manage performance issues. However, it is important to realize that you must set, or help the information systems department set, the organization's performance objectives, which must be managed.

Performance Problems

Performance problems affecting your organization occur in a number of different ways. For example, there may be a user or group of users who consistently experience *wait time* between each key stroke. This wait time could be translated as lost productivity. If your company has hundreds, or even thousands, of users, this little problem of poor response time just became an exponential problem of thousands of lost hours of productivity. Continuing this example, what if while your user was waiting on the system, he or she in turn had a customer waiting for a response on an inquiry. The time the customer spends waiting could lead to low customer satisfaction with your company. How many times have you called a customer service agent for a company and been asked to please be patient while the person waited for the system. It is almost an acceptable excuse, like being late for a meeting in Los Angeles because of traffic. As competition continues to strive for better customer service and responsiveness, this excuse will continue to be less and less acceptable.

Understand the Business Requirements of the Organization

Besides the customer satisfaction issue, there is also a productivity issue involved with this second scenario. The company could probably hire fewer customer service agents if the existing agents were more productive, which could be helped by a more efficient response time.

DEFINE YOUR ORGANIZATION'S PERFORMANCE METHODOLOGY

As the controller, you have to assess your own performance situation and help your information systems department develop a performance plan by which you can judge how well your system is meeting your organization's needs. The organization must do more than monitor performance, it must manage it. The objectives managed must be set by the senior business managers within the information systems group.

What is Performance?

The question, "What is performance?" can be answered several different ways. Performance means different things to different people and may mean something different to a single person at different times. It is hard to pin down "good" performance for a single system because performance varies in a nonlinear fashion as the system load increases; that is, performance can get very bad, very rapidly.

The most concrete, practical answer to the question is that a system's performance is based upon a system's productivity and speed. Furthermore, criteria such as response time, throughput, batch work, capacity, and resource use must all be included. To get good performance, a company must make the most of each of the following criteria, each of which requires a different definition of performance.

Performance Criteria

Minimizing Response Time. On many systems, interactive response is typically the primary criterion for defining and measuring performance. The system must respond fast enough that users do not perceive delays. Because of this requirement, it is important that the highest priority be assigned to highly visible interactive functions, such as customer service.

Maximizing Throughput. A system must respond fast enough for each user to complete a specific amount of work in a certain period. For example, a customer service agent working telephones does not want customers to experience long waits while the system is verifying their customer information. A system can be configured (most of the time) to ensure that every transaction gets into the system and starts working immediately, even though interactive work already in progress is using the available central processing unit (CPU) and storage. In some cases, the definition of performance is maximizing throughput.

Maximizing Batch Work. Most companies have an end-of-day processing requirement (as, for example, an insurance company will run their file updates and policy-generating jobs), and their primary performance concern might be maximizing the batch work. The time necessary for batch jobs to run is often directly proportionate to the amount of interactive work that preceded it. This is especially true when the interactive work being done during the day becomes the input to the batch processing done at night.

You will normally become concerned with the management of batch work only when it is not finishing in its allotted time. For example, you would have a problem if your end-of-day batch cycle takes ten hours to finish and you have only four hours to run it. The extra six hours may affect your interactive availability window or not allow your company to finish its backups, which are also usually run in the evenings.

Ensuring Adequate Capacity.   An insurance company, for example, can expect that, on unpredictable occasions (such as after earthquakes and hurricanes), its system must handle unusually high claims-processing loads and still maintain an adequate level of throughput and a satisfactory response time. To prepare for acceptable performance in the aftermath of disasters, the insurance company must give its system more resources than it needs for its regular workload. In such cases, the definition of performance is adequate capacity and preparation at all times. By helping your organization prepare for unexpected high-capacity periods, you can ensure that the company will be able to handle the workload.

Maximizing Resource Use.   Some systems stay busy at all times and use all resources to their fullest to maximize the use of expensive computer hardware components. Such demands probably are not a problem if the workload is consistent from one day to the next and if all users are satisfied. However, if the workload grows or the processing varies from day to day, continually operating on the edge is a dangerous proposition.

For example, when data is not in main storage, the processor (the most expensive component of any system) may have to wait for the data to be brought in from disk (the least expensive component). In this situation, the system makes run-time adjustments to move data quickly in and out of main storage to keep the processor working as close to capacity as possible.

THE SIX ESSENTIAL STEPS: A PERFORMANCE METHODOLOGY

Every organization should develop a standard performance methodology that will be used to manage performance and performance expectations. In Figure 25–1, we are showing the six steps that make up a good performance methodology. As an executive, it is critical that you be involved with steps one and six. In these steps, you help define and interpret the results of the performance data. The following discussion defines the six steps.

Understand the Business Requirements

You must understand the business requirements the system is meant to address. Besides these requirements, no doubt your system's operation must stay within

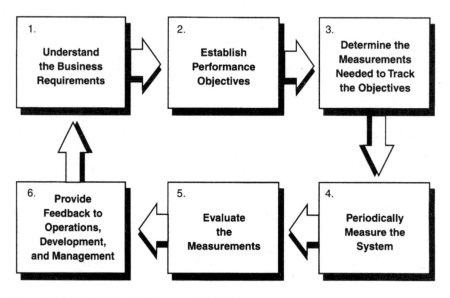

Figure 25–1: Steps in Good Performance Methodology

certain constraints, such as budget limitations. These business requirements and constraints have a direct relationship with system requirements. Any change to the requirements will have an impact on information system requirements. You need to understand the business requirements to establish system performance objectives and to understand your options for meeting those objectives.

Establish the Performance Objectives

Setting objectives for your organization establishes (or defines) a set of goals and expectations for measuring system performance. The objectives should focus on a particular issue. A typical performance objective may define average or maximum response times or transaction throughput rates. For example, if your users are getting five-second response times and you want subsecond response times, your performance objective would be subsecond response time.

It is extremely important that you establish these objectives in writing. When a performance objective is defined, it should be as specific as possible. It is also important that these decisions be made by a team that includes the information systems organization and key users as well as you, the controller.

Performance objectives for an organization become moving targets unless you have agreement from everyone involved. You do not want your organization to start out trying to get better interactive response time and end up on some different, endless performance tangent in which nothing seems to get accomplished. You will avoid this situation by getting agreement to a documented set of performance objectives. Once your organization has identified performance objectives, it is well on its way to solutions.

Determine the Performance Measurements Needed

After you have set your objectives, determine how you are going to collect performance data to track the objectives. There is a direct relationship between your performance objectives and the way your company will collect performance data. Your information systems data collection options are going to be determined by the platform your company is using and by the performance tools installed.

Measure the System Periodically

You need to measure the way your system is performing. A simple set of graphs showing systems resource usage and workload will help you track your progress. Based on your organization's defined objectives, you can find out how often you will need to see measurements. Measurements can be as simple as a print screen produced by an operator once an hour or as detailed as a performance monitor run by your performance analyst, with specific collection periods.

Evaluate the Measurements

The evaluation of the performance measurements is the analysis part of the performance methodology. The analysis work is based on the type of data collected and the volume of data collected. This work must be done by a trained performance expert who is familiar with your company's computer platform. The majority of large companies have a performance analyst who can perform this work. Smaller companies usually need to hire a consultant to help with this part of the performance methodology. Performance data should be kept for an extended period of time so that long-term performance analysis, referred to as *trending analysis,* can be done.

Obtain Feedback and Make Key Decisions

When the analysis work is completed, it is vital to use the findings to make decisions that will improve the organization's performance. Documentation of the decisions is key to this step. It is critical that your technical staff, or consultant, present the analysis data in a manner with which you are comfortable. If you are delivered a stack of detailed reports that you cannot understand, return them to the source and ask for a translation in a format that you can understand.

In this final step of the performance methodology cycle, decisions that may require financial expenditures need to be based on facts. There is no room for misinterpretation of the data. Large decisions, such as a decision to buy new hardware to fix performance problems, should usually be verified by more than one source. It is important that the decisions be based on the performance facts and be consistent with the organization's strategic goals, and not be based on some group's alternative political agendas.

Once you finish the performance methodology cycle, you sometimes discover that your objective in step one was not the correct objective. You have to redefine the objective and repeat the performance methodology cycle. It is not uncommon to repeat this cycle many times, depending on what is uncovered during the analysis step.

For example, you may decide that once you have better interactive performance, you need to work on the performance of your batch jobs. Once you get batch and interactive under control, you may decide to work on your remote users. Therefore, you may have to repeat your six performance steps often until all of your organization's performance objectives are satisfied.

THE PERFORMANCE DETAILS

The Components of Performance

A computer system's performance is made up of different components. Although you are more than likely not managing these detailed systems components, it is important for you to understand each of these components and what part they play in the performance equation. Most organizations have an analyst or team of analysts who focus specifically on performance issues.

All user requests, both interactive and batch, use system resources. Interactive requests require CPU time, main storage space, and usually disk input/output (I/O) resources. In addition, some communications line time and I/O processor resources are necessary to enter the request and to communicate the results back to the user. For batch processing, you can consider a request to be the time between successive reads of a primary input file. These requests also require CPU time, main storage space, and disk I/O resources.

With this view of what makes up interactive and batch work, you can consider all work on the system as comprising multiple transactions. The total time each transaction takes to complete consists of blocks of time spent waiting for or using a specific system resource. Because the system generally services multiple transactions concurrently, a transaction often spends time waiting for an unavailable system resource. Such resources include communications line resources, processor resources, disk access, and memory.

You can think of these components as services that a transaction needs to do the requested work on the system. You can appreciate the many factors that influence transaction response time if you consider the components as servers and realize that contention exists for the services because of multiple concurrent transactions. Transaction response time depends on how long it takes to acquire and use each server. This amount of time, in turn, depends on how many servers there are, how fast each server is, the arrival rate for the server, and how the requests are selected for the service. Each performance component has its own characteristics in connection with these factors. Let's look at some of the details of these components.

Line Component. Communications requires special performance considerations. Line speed, communications I/O processor utilization, device-controller and line utilization, and line errors all affect how much time is necessary for a transaction to get through the line component.

Processor (CPU) Component. All users of a system compete for CPU time. The system grants CPU time in a priority sequence. Once the system gives the CPU resource to a transaction, no other transaction may share that CPU resource until the transaction waits on another resource. This is a simplistic overview of how a transaction requests the CPU resource. Most systems work differently; thus, if you wish to understand exactly how a system allocates CPU resources, you will have to talk to the information systems professionals at your organization.

Disk Component. When a transaction needs access to a disk, several considerations come into play. The time to process a disk request depends on disk I/O processor usage, drive usage, type of operation, arm contention, disk protection schemes (Mirroring, RAID, etc.), file placement, and cache hit ratios.

Memory Component. A transaction requires memory to contain the necessary programs and data for the CPU to work with. If these requirements are in main memory, the memory server does not delay the transaction. However, a transaction that needs memory has to wait while the system allocates memory and brings the objects into memory from disk. Different computer systems use their own methods to optimize moving objects between memory and the CPU. These techniques are beyond the scope of this chapter.

THE FLOW OF PERFORMANCE INFORMATION WITHIN THE ORGANIZATION

The flow of performance information within the organization is important. The larger the organization, the more formal the performance information communication process must be. Figure 25–2 shows an example of a performance information flow for an organization.

In Exhibit 25–2, we are showing a group called performance management. This group is where the performance expert(s) are located within the management information systems (MIS) department. All performance information for the organization flows through this group. The end-user groups communicate all performance issues directly to the performance management group. In turn, the performance management group returns trending/capacity information, perfor-

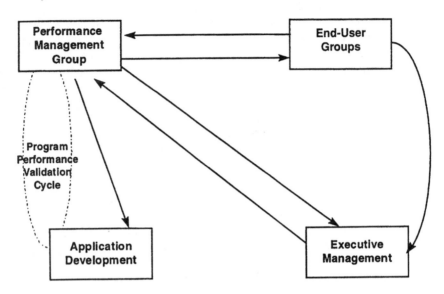

Figure 25–2: Flow of Performance Information Within the Organization

mance problem statistics, and problem determination information back to this user group.

If your company has an application development group, it is important that programs being placed into your company's production environment meet certain minimum performance objectives. For example, a performance problem may result when an application program is changed. If a customer service program is producing subsecond response time, and a change to the program creates five-second response time, your programmer has just created a new application performance problem.

Your performance management group can avoid these kinds of application performance problems by benchmarking before and after performance of applications. It is also a good idea for the performance management group to be proactive about performance management, to set minimum guidelines for application performance for the organization, and to educate the application development staff on optimized programming methods.

The executive management group must set the corporate performance objectives and supply business growth estimates so that the performance management group can ensure sufficient capacity for the systems to handle the company's growth. As part of the capacity planning for the organization, the executive management group must work closely with the end-user groups to understand, or drive, their growth plans for the future. In turn, it is important for the performance management group to validate all modeling and trending information and report this information back to executive management. This performance information must be presented in a manner that is understood by executive management, which usually means graphs and summarized performance numbers should be used.

Be Careful in the Translation of Performance Data from the Tech to the Executive

It is extremely important that the actual performance data of a system be presented accurately to the executive management of an organization. All information that is subjective in nature should be fully explained to management. Performance analysts sometimes make assumptions based on their own personal understanding of an organization and not on the true organizational objectives. We have also seen performance management groups that chose to interpret the results of performance tests to help justify their own political agenda. For example, a group may prefer a certain operating system, software package, or hardware platform that can be justified in performance benchmarking. All performance data should be explained in a clear and concise manner. If executives do not understand what is being presented to them, the analysis is not effective for making critical organizational decisions.

Managing Expectation

One last point about the flow of performance information within your organization: It is important that performance expectation get managed correctly. As performance information is communicated between the groups of your organization, it is important to keep the information focused for the group that is going to use it. Technical groups, based on our experience, will sometimes set a higher level of expectation than is realistic. User groups are especially susceptible to being "oversold" on a project's or projects' results. Executive management must understand enough of the details to help set the expectation level of the managers within the user groups of the organization.

26

SOFTWARE PACKAGE INTEGRATION

Software package integration projects (e.g., the implementation of an accounting or human resources system) differ from custom-built projects in that the application to be integrated is already coded, operational, and, in most cases, marketplace-tested. Once the software package is selected, only the steps to integrate it into the organization remain. The execution of these steps can result in a successful project or in a project that fails miserably.

Many organizations find it difficult to structure, plan, and budget for an integration project and then meet those estimates with a successfully executed integration effort (i.e., one that results in an application system that meets user and organizational requirements). System implementation projects typically do not fail because of technical problems; rather, they fail because of a lack of management. Controllers and chief financial officers (CFOs) frequently are responsible for the successful implementation of a variety of systems, therefore it is particularly important for them to make certain that the appropriate techniques are used and the appropriate steps are taken to better ensure the success of the project.

The focus of this chapter is twofold. Presented first are four management techniques that if employed early on and throughout an integration project, will help to better ensure the success of the project. Following these techniques, the specific steps of an integration project are outlined. Note that each project is different and thus calls for an individual evaluation and subsequent identification of the management techniques and integration steps best suited to handle the unique characteristics and issues of the project. If done, however, the project will have a greater probability of absorbing surprises during the integration and concluding

This chapter was written by Sandra Borchardt, Senior Manager, Ernst & Young LLP, Boston, MA.

in a manner that results in a cost-effective system that meets the goals and requirements that justified the project in the first place.

Management Techniques for Software Package Integration

Integrating software into an organization successfully depends on many factors including effective project leadership, a clear understanding of the project, and organizational commitment and adaptability. In addition to these factors, certain project management techniques can be used to increase the chance of success of the project by overcoming common stumbling blocks. Four specific management techniques are presented on the following pages: project management, risk management, change management, and quality management (see Figure 26–1).

PROJECT MANAGEMENT

Project management is the process by which a project is planned, executed, and completed. The objective of project management is to conduct the project in a systematic and organized fashion in order to reduce uncertainty and encourage productivity.

Project management is made difficult by the very nature of projects. The communication process is at best inexact, causing potential misunderstandings of the project scope, requirements, and expectations. Changes in the regulatory environment or in the business itself may change the goals of the project or even ren-

Figure 26–1: Management Techniques for Software Integration

der the project unnecessary. A project estimate is just that—a best guess at how long it will take to complete the project; how many resources, when, and with what skill set, will be needed; and what costs will be incurred. Quality deliverables may take more time than expected to complete. To obtain high productivity, project team members must be led, motivated, counseled, and apprised of their performance. To combat these difficulties, however, certain project management techniques can be used. Project planning, although an estimate at best, can provide the initial focus and step-by-step guide for the project. Project tracking can then be used to monitor actual progress against plan, identifying exceptions early and allowing for replanning based on these experiences.

Managing Projects

Project management begins at the start of a project and continues until its completion. Project management techniques are project-tested and have been used successfully to integrate software packages into organizations. Some common project management techniques include the following:

- *Planning.* The planning process begins by identifying and confirming the business problem to be solved.
- *Estimating.* The estimating process builds on the information developed during the planning process. Plans are detailed to achieve the project objectives within the terms defined in the project scope.
- *Defining Deliverables.* After the planning process has outlined the types of deliverables required by the project, this process customizes these deliverables for the project situation.
- *Monitoring.* The monitoring process is an ongoing process that measures actual progress against planned progress and identifies those areas requiring corrective action or adjustments to the plan.
- *Managing Risk.* The risk management process consists of early identification and control of project risks through the use of tools and techniques for identifying project risks, assessing their criticality, and developing and implementing strategies to manage these project risks. (Risk management will be discussed in more detail later in this chapter.)
- *Managing Change.* In the context of project management, change management has two important meanings:
    1. *A technique that targets the human factor affected by the project*—This type of change management identifies resistance to the changes brought on by the project, works to understand the nature of the resistance, and implements change management strategies to overcome the resistance.
    2. *A mechanism through which project changes can be requested, tracked, investigated, and rejected or approved*—A change of this nature is an

addition to, deletion from, or modification of a system during its design, development, or implementation.

- *Managing Quality.* The quality management process consists of the use of tools and techniques to build quality into a project.

Project management tools support project management techniques throughout the life of the project. Some of the more common project management tools include:

- *Scope Document.* The project scope document identifies what will be accomplished by the project and what will not. It contains the definition of the project, its boundaries, and its completion criteria. Other information about the project, such as the budget, time frames, and resource requirements, may be included in the scope document.
- *Work Plan.* The project work plan is a detailed, step-by-step plan that clearly defines what work needs to be done, how long it will take, who will do it, and when it will be completed. The project work plan provides a tool against which actual progress can be measured. Figure 26–2 provides a sample page of a detailed project plan. Figure 26–3 presents a high level plan in a PERT chart format.
- *Status Reports.* Status reports identify accomplishments, work-in-progress, issues, and tasks that, when compared to the project plan, are overdue. Status reports should be frequently and regularly produced by project team members. These reports communicate progress against plan and outstanding issues.
- *Issue Log.* Issues identified during the project (e.g., on status reports) are captured, reported, and tracked using an issue log. Issues are matters that require decisions to be made by project team members or other organizational representatives. Issues may impact project progress and must be analyzed in a timely manner.
- *Project Meetings.* Frequent and regular project meetings with project team members, and separate meetings with project sponsors, provide a forum for discussing progress to date, outstanding issues, and follow-up items. Presentations of status reports and issue logs can be used to guide these meetings. Project meetings are an excellent communication tool and also serve to evaluate progress against plan.
- *Change Requests.* Change requests are the formal documentation of an addition to, deletion from, or modification of a system during its design, development, or implementation. Change requests allow for the proper tracking of changes and their resulting rejection or approval.
- *Project Documentation.* Project documentation organizes the project management information used to manage the project. Project documentation contains the project scope, project organization, detailed project plans, standards and procedures, project deliverables, and all project authorizations and related correspondence.

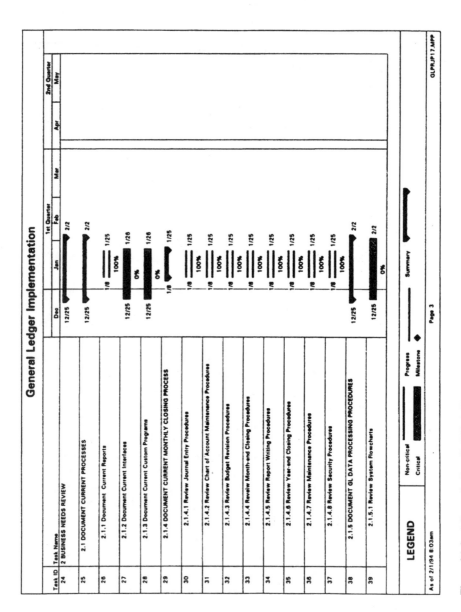

Figure 26–2: A Page of a Detailed Work Plan

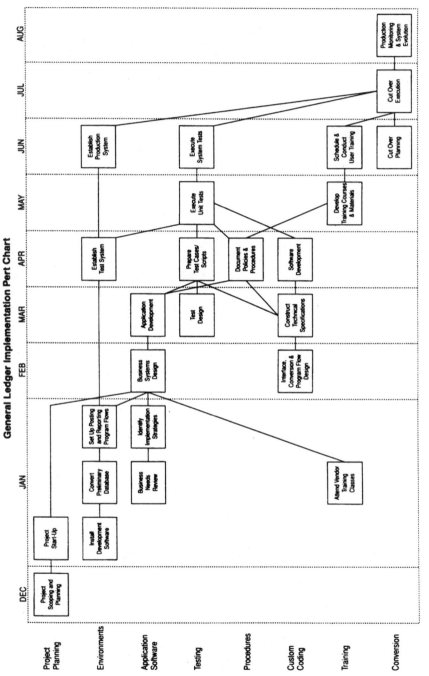

Figure 26-3: A PERT Chart Representation of a Project Work Plan

RISK MANAGEMENT

Risk in a software integration project is the probability that the project will not finish on time or within budget, or, upon completion, that the system will not function as expected. Other risks include the possibility that the application will not integrate with the hardware or other applications systems, will not meet technical performance expectations, or will fail to provide the expected benefits. Risk management is the early identification and control of these and other project risks through the use of tools and techniques for identifying project risks, assessing their criticality, and developing and implementing strategies to manage these project risks (see Figure 26–4).

Identifying Risks

The risk identification process should begin early in an implementation project and be reviewed and adjusted throughout the project. Early identification allows for a broader choice of options to deal with the risk. Detailed questionnaires of typical project risks are often used to perform the initial and follow-up risk identification. These questionnaires cover topics ranging from project size to project structure and technology.

Examples of risks related to the size of the project include: the number of hours estimated to complete the project, the project time frame (estimated over calendar months or years), the size of the project team, the number of interfacing systems, and the number of entities within the organization involved in the project. The greater the magnitude of any of these project size indicators, the greater the risk of the project.

Risks related to project structure include

Figure 26–4: The Risk Management Process

- How well defined are the scope, deliverables, benefits, and requirements of the project?
- Does the project team include knowledgeable application, technology, and business area specialists?
- Does the project have an organizational sponsor and the support of management and users?
- How extensively will the system change current work flows, policies, procedures, and organizational structure?

A well-defined project, when staffed with a knowledgeable project team, supported by the organization, and expected to have little impact on current operations, is a much less risky project than any of the alternatives.

Assessing Risks

Once potential project risks have been identified, these risks must be assessed as to their criticality. Different projects may identify similar risks; however, the magnitude of these risks is project specific. For example, the risks identified for the following two projects are:

Project I. Implementation of an automated system to replace manual processes.

Project II. Implementation of additional automated features to enhance already automated processes.

The types of risks these two projects may encounter include:

- *Timing.*
- *User Acceptance.*

In this example, Project I is much riskier than Project II. Timing is less of an issue in Project II, because changes to processes would be less drastic than in Project 1. Further, contingency plans would more likely be in place and experienced in Project II as a result of the current automation, whereas these would need to be developed as part of the integration of the new system in Project I.

User acceptance would also be less of a risk in Project II because the users are experienced and comfortable with automation; thus, changes in their current processes, work flows, and job descriptions would most likely be less severe.

Risk identification and assessment should involve all levels of the project team, including the project sponsor, project management, and user and technical representatives. Reconciling these different perceptions of risk will enable all parties to come to the same understanding of the risks of the project. With this basis, these project representatives can then reduce risk by revising the assumptions on which the project is based, or accept risk by agreeing that the result is in line with the organization's goals.

Managing Risks

Although most of the recommended approaches to risk management focus on specific aspects of the project (e.g., size, structure, or technology), there are some general strategies to manage a project's overall risk, as follows:

- Understand and document expectations and what will be done during the project.
- Assign appropriately trained staff to the project, including industry, application, and technology specialists.
- Partition the work into manageable segments.
- Reduce the dependency of the project on other development efforts.
- Involve users in the project.
- Prepare the organization for changes that will occur as a result of the system's implementation.

Specific risk management strategies relate to the specific risks identified. For example, risks associated with a lengthy implementation time frame include the following:

- Team members may leave the project and other personnel inexperienced in the specifics of the project may be assigned to replace them.
- Team members' motivation and sense of urgency are hard to maintain on a long project, and a potential result may be lower levels of productivity.
- A change in the organization's business could cause a change in user requirements.
- A change in the organization's executive levels could lead to revised priorities.

Strategies for managing these risks include:

- Partition work into subprojects that build on one another and show results frequently.
- Identify clear milestones and deliverables throughout the project.
- Recognize individual needs of team members and provide work variety accordingly.
- Use application development tools (e.g., Computer-Aided Software Engineering (CASE) tools) to enhance productivity, thereby reducing the time needed to complete specific tasks. Note that this strategy may mean introducing new technology, which may increase risk in that area.

- Reduce project scope to reduce the amount of work to be done, which in turn will reduce the overall project time frame.

When developing strategies to manage risk, examine the relationships and dependencies among risk factors. In some cases, a strategy to reduce risk in one area actually increases risk in another. For example, a decision to reduce the risk of a lengthy project by increasing team size may increase the risk of ineffective team coordination and communication.

QUALITY MANAGEMENT

Quality management is the use of tools and techniques to build quality into a project. Through the use of quality management techniques, projects should better meet expectations, requirements, budget estimates, and planned time frames.

Quality assurance is the set of actions performed to bring about quality in a project. Quality control checks for and corrects exceptions in completed work products or projects. The difference between the two is that quality assurance techniques are preventative measures whereas quality control techniques are after-the-fact quality measures.

It has been proven that preventative measures are much more cost-effective than inspection-based measures. However, it is important to note that quality control can be used to monitor the quality assurance program, indicating how closely the project is meeting expectations and requirements, and in what areas improvements are needed to provide a better quality product.

Managing Quality

The quality management process is based on building quality strategies into the project, beginning at the start of the project. Each of the quality management strategies illustrated in Figure 26–5 is discussed below:

- *Exceed Expectations.* Every project team member—in fact, the project as a whole—should strive to exceed the expectations of the organization, project management, and users.
- *Do It Right the First Time.*
- *Follow an Implementation Methodology.*
- *Use Project Planning and Tracking Techniques.* A detailed plan constructed by knowledgeable and experienced project management will clearly define what work needs to be done, how long it will take, who will do it, and when it will be completed.
- *Measure Quality.* Although many quality indicators are not easily measured, certain indicators, such as project costs, time frames, and results, can be mea-

Figure 26–5: Quality Management Strategies

sured against initial cost and time-frame estimates and user requirements, respectively.

- *Conduct Training.* Training project team members is essential for a quality project, especially if team members have never before been involved in a software integration project.

- *Conduct Testing.* A formal, rigorous test of the system prior to placing the system into production is essential to the quality of the project for several reasons. Testing new custom programs ensures that the code executes without error and meets all requirements documented in the technical specifications. Unit testing the software modules ensures that each module executes as expected, without error. Integration testing of the entire system ensures that all modules interact with each other as expected and without error. Acceptance testing ensures that the system accomplishes the user requirements in a manner acceptable to the user community.

- *Conduct Reviews.* The earlier an exception from expected results is identified, the broader the options for handling the exception. Among the several types of reviews recommended for integration projects are:

  — *Project Team Review.* Project management reviews work products to ensure consistency across the project, to ensure completeness of individual pieces of the project and to provide the final, comprehensive review of a deliverable before it goes to the organization for approval.

  — *Organizational Review.* Organization management and users review the work products to ensure that expectations and requirements are met, to allow for feedback of concerns or suggestions, to communicate project information and status, and to involve responsible executives in the major organizational and operational decisions related to the project.

Reviews can be executed by reading the deliverable and meeting with appropriate project team members to question points and provide feedback. Reviews can also be executed through the use of formal presentations, where the project team member(s) responsible for the deliverable presents the ideas and conclusions to an audience of reviewers. This type of structured presentation provides immediate feedback and a forum for working through revisions to the deliverable.

INTEGRATION STEPS

This section deals with the specific steps necessary to integrate software. In some cases, certain steps may not apply. For example, one integration step pertains to hardware/software installation. If in fact the software to be integrated will operate on hardware already installed and operational in the organization, the step of hardware installation is not applicable to this particular integration project. Thus, when beginning an integration project, all integration steps should be reviewed and elaborated as to their specific role in the project under consideration.

Project Organization

Project organization is a critical aspect of the project planning process. Before the project can get underway, it is necessary to identify the major project roles and the responsibilities that accompany those roles. Individuals must then be selected to fill the roles, based on their skills and experience in solving similar problems.

The organization for a specific project depends on the nature of the project: the software package being installed, the particular project responsibilities of the organization, the vendor, and other project characteristics. However, certain roles are common to every project. The following paragraphs discuss these roles and Figure 26–6 shows how they fit into a sample project organization.

- *Project Sponsors.* Have the ultimate authority over and responsibility for the project. The sponsors are executives who have a vested interest in the results of the project, fund the project, resolve conflict over policy or objectives, and provide high-level direction.
- *Resource Coordinators.* Hold management level roles in the organization and are in some way, shape, or form affected by the project. Resource coordinators provide support to the project by providing staffing for project tasks and subject matter expertise for the organizational functions for which they are responsible.

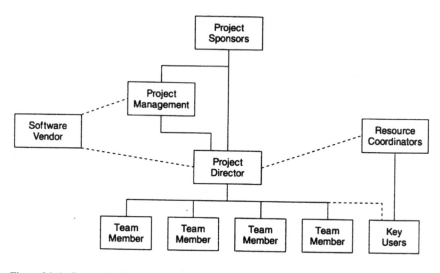

Figure 26–6: Sample Project Organization

- *Project Managers.* Have a direct responsibility or stake in the results of the project. Project management is not only responsible for approving the work of the project team throughout the entire project but also ensuring that the information system that results from the project will meet the requirements and be properly integrated into the organization.
- *Project Director.* Has primary management responsibility for the entire project, including administration, planning and scheduling, issue resolution, and technical leadership.
- *Project Team.* Is made up of various individuals with different skill sets which in combination provides the overall talent necessary to successfully integrate the application into the organization. System analysts, designers, programmers, documentation specialists, and trainers are all important members of the project team. Project team members may represent all areas of the organization affected by the integration effort, including user and technical organizations. Although a core project team will support the integration effort from start to finish, other project team members may be brought in (e.g., for system acceptance testing) as specialized talent is needed.
- *Key Users.* May not support the project directly as project team members but are important to involve in the integration project for two reasons. User involvement is essential to ensure that the new application is designed and integrated in a manner that satisfies user requirements and that the transition to the new system is straightforward (because the users have been involved and have a stake in the effort). Key users can supplement the project team on an as-needed basis to assist with the design of the application as well as any decision making regarding functionality. Key users should be kept informed

throughout the project as to project status and key decisions and be involved in the project as much as their schedules permit.

- *Software Package Vendor.* Is primarily responsible for the delivery and installation of the basic software package. In addition, the software vendor or an independent consultant may participate in validation and system testing, provide user and operations training, and assist in conversion activities. Software vendors are frequently responsible for customizing the software packages. The exact nature of the vendor's and consultant's responsibilities on an engagement should be clearly defined in a contract. A more comprehensive list of services most often provided by vendors or independent consultants can be found in Figure 26–7.

Project Management

As discussed earlier in this chapter, the objective of project management is to plan and control the integration project from initiation to conclusion with high levels of productivity and quality and low levels of uncertainty. And again, project management begins at the start of a project and continues throughout the project until its completion.

The role of a project director is one of a leader and a process manager. As a leader, the project director is responsible for managing and communicating a clear vision of the project objectives, and motivating the project team to achieve

Figure 26–7: A List of Vendor/Consultant Integration Services

them. As a process manager, the project director must ensure that the right timing, resources, and sequencing of work efforts are applied to create the project deliverables within a given time frame and budget.

Project management activities can be grouped into six major processes as depicted in Figure 26–8.

1. *Structuring the Project.* The focus of this project management process is to document the objectives of the project, secure project sponsorship, define the project approach, and estimate the project in terms of effort, duration, and cost. These tasks are conducted initially at the start of the project but are also revisited throughout the project as the project evolves and changes.

2. *Planning the Project.* Tasks in the planning process include developing a detailed work plan including a budget and resource assignments; defining a plan to manage risk, quality, issues, and scope; and gaining approval from project sponsors and executive management on the project plans.

3. *Assessing Change.* In the context of project management, change management has two important meanings:
   a. A technique that targets the human factors affected by the project, and
   b. A mechanism through which project changes can be requested, tracked, investigated, and rejected or approved.

4. *Reporting Project Status.* These reports identify the status of a project or a part of a project at a certain point in time. Status reports should be fre-

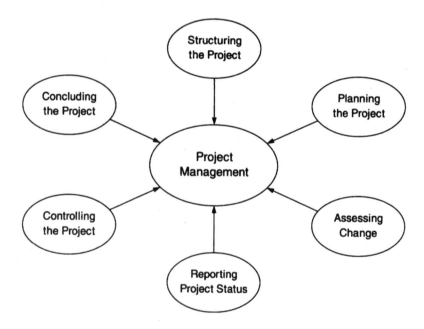

Figure 26–8: Project Management Processes

quently (e.g., weekly) communicated to project management, project sponsors, the user community, and other interested parties. This project management process occurs on a regular basis throughout the project.

5. *Controlling the Project.* During the execution of the project, it is the responsibility of the project director to compare actual progress to planned progress, evaluate the results of this comparison to determine project status, and recommend or take appropriate actions based on the results of the evaluation. This process occurs on a regular basis throughout the project.

6. *Concluding the Project.* This process normally occurs in the final stage of a project. It takes place once project management and sponsorship have agreed that the project has satisfied its completion criteria as defined at the start of the project.

Project Planning

Project planning is one of the first steps of any integration project. Tasks included in project planning are: documenting the scope of the effort, assessing project risks, evaluating change management challenges, identifying a quality management program, and constructing a detailed work plan. Each of these deliverables were discussed in earlier sections of this chapter.

Project Start-Up

Tasks in the project start-up step include: identifying the project team members who will satisfy the resource requirements identified in the plan; establishing the project environment (e.g., desks, telephones, supplies, computer equipment, system access); briefing the project team, user community, and other interested parties on the project goals, approach, and schedule; and establishing the project control system (e.g., documentation standards, issue capture and control mechanisms, time reporting, filing).

Project Meetings

Although at first glance, this step would appear to be more logically combined with a task of another step in the integration project instead of its own step, it is broken out due to the number of hours associated with preparing for, attending, and documenting project meetings. The project meetings covered under this step include:

- *Project Team Meetings.* Conducted by the project director on a frequent basis (usually weekly), these meetings facilitate communication regarding progress to date on assigned tasks, outstanding issues, and follow-up items.

- *Project Management Meetings.* Conducted by the project director, these meetings can occur less frequently than team meetings. They serve to keep project management up to date on the project status and major project issues.

- *Senior Executive Meetings.* Conducted on a more infrequent basis or on an as needed basis, these meetings serve as a communication tool for appropriate senior executives in the organization. These meetings are conducted by the project director or a member of the project management team.

- *Resource Coordinator Meetings.* As noted previously, resource coordinators are organizational representatives affected by the integration project but do not participate directly on the project team. Resource coordinators usually support the project team in one of two ways: by providing additional resources to assist in accomplishing project tasks, and/or by supplementing project team knowledge with their expertise of their organizational function.

- *User Meetings.* Users who are not part of the project team must be kept up to date regarding the project. This communication begins at the start of the project often via a formal meeting at which the project objectives, approach, and schedule are presented. Throughout the project, user involvement is critical not only in designing and integrating an application that meets their needs, but also in facilitating the change process so that once the application is available for everyday use, the users feel comfortable and confident with the new application.

- *Organizational Meetings.* Any major integration project will be of interest to the organization as a whole. Communication via a formal meeting to organizational representatives (or the entire organization) will provide the organization with real information regarding the project rather than allowing informal communication, which could misstate elements of the project.

Business Needs Review

The results of the Business Needs Review step form the foundation for the new application. It is critical to the success of the integration project to review the business requirements to confirm or redefine the application needs. To accomplish this, key members of the project team gather and finalize data about the information requirements of the business areas with appropriate business managers and staff. As the result of these interviews, project team members document, at a high level, current business inputs and outputs, processes, manual work flows, and controls. These interviews will also provide the project team with the necessary information to develop high-level information models. Additionally, high-level specifications for key interfaces as well as data, operational, and technical requirements will be reviewed. Lastly, a current systems reports and forms binder is constructed as part of this step.

The deliverables of this step include a requirements document and documentation of the current processes. Figure 26–9 provides an example of documentation for one of the current system processes: a high-level interface chart.

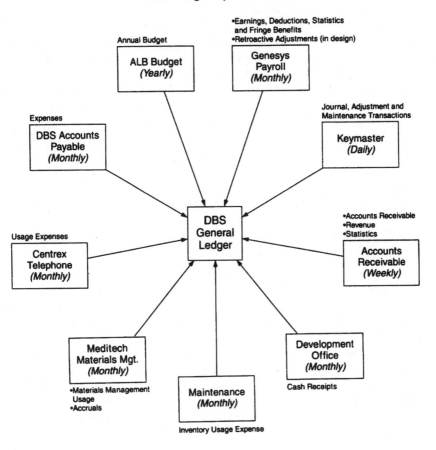

Figure 26–9: Interface Chart

Hardware/Software Installation

At the very least, a software integration project requires that the software to be integrated must be installed on the organization's information systems. It is often the case, however, that new hardware and/or system software (i.e., software necessary to operate the hardware and application software together) is required and must be installed as well. This step of the project represents these installations as well as testing of the installation to ensure that the new software and hardware are operational. Information systems representatives usually participate in the hardware and software installation, but information systems and user representatives both should participate in the execution of the installation test scripts. Testing the installation not only helps ensure a proper and complete installation of the software and hardware but also provides additional training for information systems personnel and the users regarding application functionality as well as system construction and operation.

Hardware and software vendors usually provide additional assistance during this step of the integration project. Vendors may provide on-site assistance with the installation as well as supply and help execute test scripts to ensure a complete installation. Alternatively, instead of providing on-site assistance, software vendors may provide a tape with instructions for loading the software and executing test scripts. Installation support is also available via a "1–800" phone number which accesses the vendor's help desks. It is important to understand exactly what type of installation assistance will be provided by the vendor's contract terms prior to signing the contract for the purchase or lease of hardware and software. Prior to executing the contract, compare the installation services offered with the capabilities and comfort of your own information systems staff and construct an installation support agreement that is satisfactory to all parties.

Business Systems Design

In this step, the application is designed from the end user's perspective. Project team analysts design application parameters, tables, and files as well as the policies and procedures necessary to support the business. Reports and forms for each module of the application are also designed.

At this point in the project, project team members should have a fairly good understanding of the new system functionality based on the vendor training provided in the *Project Startup* step. Matching the new application's functionality to the requirements identified in the *Business Needs Review* step will often highlight deficiencies in functionality that must be addressed. Decisions as to how to handle these gaps must be made. Several alternatives for handling gaps are available and are discussed below.

- *Customize the Application.* This alternative requires design, implementation, and testing of application customizations that will overcome gaps in required application functionality. It should be noted that customizations increase the complexity and length of the project, usually significantly. Additionally, customizations can invalidate the software warranty and make the application of upgrades extremely difficult. Therefore, any customizations should be carefully reviewed and every attempt made to avoid customizations for these very reasons.

- *Create a Work-Around.* Instead of specifying a customization to the application, this alternative suggests the development of a process in or around the application that will handle the requirement.

- *Reject the Requirement.* In many cases the requirement driving the gap in functionality is desired but is not critical to the application's success in solving the business need. In these cases, it is recommended to integrate the application as is, operate the application at least six months, and then determine if the functionality is required. If the functionality is determined necessary, then the organization can begin the process of specifying the functionality design and contracting with the vendor to customize the application to include the functionality.

No matter which alternative is determined to be the most optimal for handling each gap in functionality, the results of this task must be incorporated into the project work plan.

Another task included in this step is process assessment and redesign. In the past, organizations have integrated new applications to solve their business needs with little or no attention paid to the processes existing before and after the integration of the new application. This particular task suggests that the current business processes should be reviewed and nonvalue or redundant processes eliminated. Then, based on the functionality of the new application, the current processes should be redesigned to take advantage of the new application. The deliverable for this particular step is a design of new work flows which maximizes the benefits of the new application.

Last, strategies for future steps in the integration project are defined at a high level. Strategy statements for data conversion, testing, training, and operations are developed as part of this step. For example, a strategy statement for data conversion would include a high-level discussion of the following aspects of conversion: the scope and pace of the effort; data conversion techniques; the approach for data reconciliation, maintenance, and synchronization; the plan for data security; and a contingency strategy for production cut-over.

Deliverables for this step include:

- A brief description of what data will be loaded in the parameters, tables, and files of the new application; where the data will come from; resource requirements; and time frame necessary to complete the data loading.
- An outline of the procedure manuals proposed for the project, a design of the structure of these manuals, identification of the resource requirements, and the time frame necessary to complete the documentation effort.
- A design of new reports and forms required by the new application.
- A gap analysis report with recommendations of how functionality gaps will be handled by the project.
- A design of the processes surrounding the new application.
- High-level strategy statements for key steps of the integration project: data conversion, testing, training, operations, and so on. Table 26–1 provides an example of one such strategy statement.

Interface and Program Flow Design

This step defines a specific approach for developing automated interfaces to and/or from the new application. Also, as part of this step, technical design of program flows and the nightly batch processing are completed, if necessary. Each will be discussed separately.

When investigating which interfaces might be appropriate for the new application, apply the following tests:

- If the new application replaces a previously automated system, any established automated interfaces to/from the to-be-replaced application are prime candidates for replacement (and probably should be replaced).
- If data needed for input into the new application is available from a report generated by an automated system, an interface is quite feasible from the source system.
- If data needed for input into the new application is available on another automated system, an automated interface should be evaluated.
- If data which is expected to be in the new system is needed in a downstream system, an automated interface from the new application to the downstream system should be investigated.

Many system integration projects limit the number of interfaces to be implemented to only those that replace a previously automated interface. This is done for several reasons, but primarily to limit the scope of the project and by doing so, better ensure project success (by meeting aggressive deadlines and conservative budget estimates). Interfaces, because they usually result in custom coding, add significant time and resource needs to the integration project for design, coding, testing, and so on. Further, interfaces identified but not implemented during the initial integration of the application can always be implemented once the application is up and running.

As part of designing the interfaces, their relationship to how the application operates must also be determined. For example, if a daily interface from an accounts receivable package to a new general ledger application is proposed, and if the accounts receivable transactions are posted in the general ledger application once received, a potential program flow scenario might be to execute the interface (which loads the transactions into the general ledger) then execute the general ledger posting program. Each interface must be reviewed individually as to where it fits in relation to the new application's program flows, resulting in a new flow design.

Further, applications may provide for many different program scenarios which also must be designed in this step. For example, suppose that the expectations for the new general ledger application include nightly posting (five days per week), weekly reporting, and on the last working day of the month, posting of all allocations of overhead and monthly interfaces and the generation of the monthly reports. Thus, the program flow on Monday through Thursday (except at the end of the month) would include posting but would not include reporting, allocations, or interfaces. The program flow on Fridays (except at the end of the month) would include posting and weekly reporting but not allocations, interfaces, or

Table 26–1: Sample Training Strategy

Two types of general ledger training efforts will be undertaken during this project: 1) training the implementation team and 2) training end users.

The implementation team consists of those users who will assist in the definition of how the upgraded software will be implemented for the organization and in the execution of this design. Depending on their role in the implementation, implementation team members will attend vendor training courses on the general ledger and/or both report writers. We will also provide internal training to project team members who did not attend the vendor sessions. We envision that this internal training will occur at various times during the implementation on an as-needed basis.

End user training will be scheduled for late June/early July as we hope to time the training of users with their actual use of the system for the July close. At this point in the project we think that an off-site training session would be beneficial for end users for several reasons:

- Motivation—Getting away from the office for a day and spending the day in a pleasant training facility will have a motivational impact for learning the new features and functionality and for focusing on how to apply these features to their own environment.

- Positive PR for the upgrade—A day away from the office in a pleasant facility with professional trainers will definitely boost goodwill toward the system.

- Focus—A day away from the office will allow the end users to focus entirely on the subject matter at hand: learning the new general ledger.

- Training Expertise—Professional trainers will set scripts and exercises that will not only cover the necessary material completely but will reinforce how to use the general ledger through exercises and question and answer periods.

Since we have developed internal training classes, we will need to evaluate whether or not the offsite training will be handled by the organization at its training center or by the vendor at its training location.

In either case, we envision end user training to consist of a one-day session which will cover the following topics: basic journal processing, special journal processing, maintenance, and error correction. We plan to include organization specific information into the training session, such as how to number journal batches, how to use source code, how to code intercompany journals, and so on.

We also plan to develop reporting and budget training courses for use initially to train implementation team members. These courses then would be offered to a subset of end users; those users who will be actively involved with report writing and/or budgeting for the department.

Once live on the upgraded general ledger, each operating area will be responsible for training new employees or retraining current employees on the use of the general ledger.

---

monthly reporting. Saturday and Sunday cycles would not include posting, reporting, allocations, or interfaces. On the last day of the month, all monthly cycles would be executed (including posting of the allocations and interfaces). A monthly schedule for this example is illustrated in Figure 26–10. It is easy to see that determining daily, weekly, monthly, and so on, program flows is not straightforward and must be carefully planned. Also allow for a process to insert ad hoc programs into an established program flow as needed (for example, if the weekly reporting programs need to be executed midweek).

The deliverables for this step of the integration project include functional specifications for all automated interfaces, interface reports, and program flows.

June						
SUNDAY	MONDAY	TUESDAY	WEDNESDAY	THURSDAY	FRIDAY	SATURDAY
			1 Posting	2 Posting	3 Posting, Weekly Reporting	4
5	6 Posting	7 Posting	8 Posting	9 Posting	10 Posting, Weekly Reporting	11
12	13 Posting	14 Posting	15 Posting	16 Posting	17 Posting, Weekly Reporting	18
19	20 Posting	21 Posting	22 Posting	23 Posting	24 Posting, Weekly Reporting	25
26	27 Posting	28 Posting	29 Posting	30 Allocations Overhead Posting Monthly Reports		

Figure 26–10.: A Sample Monthly Processing Schedule

Data Conversion Design

This step defines a specific approach for converting necessary data from each to-be-replaced source system to the appropriate destination database. Two types of approaches are most often used in data conversions:

1. Automated—This approach transfers data automatically from the source system to the new application's database(s) while providing an audit trail of the process.
2. Manual—This approach is used when an automated approach is not practical and consists of manual procedures for loading the application database(s).

Most data conversions consist of both of these approaches. An automated approach is ideal for converting a source database that is very similar to a destination database. For example, most general ledgers store account balances. If a general ledger is being replaced and the chart of accounts for the most part remains the same, an automated program to convert the chart of accounts and account balances to the new application may be beneficial. When deciding on a data conversion approach, factors such as the amount of time it would take to manually convert a database versus the amount of time it would take to design, code, and test an automated conversion program must be weighed. Factors that can complicate automated conversions include combining data from multiple sources where data records are not a one-to-one match, where the data cannot be sorted in the same manner, or where data elements were used inconsistently between and within each system.

Prior to conversion, using either approach, it is recommended that the organization make a concentrated effort to review, correct, or delete the information to be converted so that the database which is ultimately converted is accurate, complete, and timely. A software integration project is a perfect opportunity to clean up current information and establish an accurate, complete, and timely database on the new system.

A third conversion option exists: not to convert. Some situations warrant the completion of open transactions on the current system while executing all new transactions on the new system. For example, it might be more cost beneficial to complete the open purchase orders on the current accounts payable system rather than converting them to the new system. Reasons for doing this include the complexity of converting one system's transaction records to another system's format; many times this conversion is not straightforward. Also, the new system numbering scheme usually differs from that of the old system, yet all vendor correspondence regarding the old system's purchase order will include the old system's purchase order number. This approach, however, has its costs, including maintaining the old system and staff to operate it, sorting invoices and check requests between old system transactions and new system transactions, and responding to inquiries, some regarding old system transactions and some regarding new system transactions. At some point, it becomes more cost beneficial to convert the remaining transactions off of the old system and phase that old system out. Usually this conversion can be accomplished manually due to the small number of transactions remaining on the old system.

The deliverables of this step of the integration project include:

- An overall design document which discusses the approaches, strategies, resource requirements, timing, and contingency plans to be used to establish the databases in the new application system.
- A functional specification for each automated data conversion being considered, including the approach, strategy, and overall discussion of the particular data conversion; mapping of the source system file layout to the new application system file layout; timing considerations; resource requirements; security needs; reconciliation processes; contingency plans; and documentation strategy to satisfy internal/external audit requirements. This functional specification will be used by programmers to develop the conversion programs.
- A functional specification for each automated download being considered. Again, these automated downloads would consist of source system data formatted onto an input document representing the input screen of the new appli-

cation. Included in this specification are the approach, strategy, and overall discussion of the file download; mapping of source system data records to positions on the input document; plans for reviewing, confirming, and completing the input documents; resource requirements; prioritization schemes; documentation control processes; contingency plans; and documentation strategy to satisfy internal/external audit requirements. This function specification will be used by programmers to develop the programs to create the input sheets.

Test Design

During this step, high-level plans for unit, integration, and acceptance testing of the application software components are developed. Test plans defined the approach, controls, objectives, conditions, and test scripts for conducting software testing. The three primary objectives of testing are:

1. Prove that the application system addresses the business problem and satisfies the user's requirements.
2. Uncover application system defects.
3. Help ensure quality throughout the project.

Several types of tests are planned for in this step and include:

- *Unit Tests.* The most basic level of testing to verify that the software code works according to its specifications and to validate program logic. Unit tests are independent tests of application functionality and include tests of the baseline software, interfaces, conversion programs, and any other customizations. The objective of these tests is to ensure that each function of the application independently operates as expected. Typically, the test team is responsible for executing unit tests.
- *Integration Tests.* The testing of combinations of individually unit-tested pieces of code as they are united into a complete unit (i.e., testing of the application as a whole). Whereas unit testing ensures that each application function can operate independently, integration testing ensures that all functions, interacting together in a simulated live environment, operate as expected. Often the information systems staff that will be responsible for the application once it is in production will participate to simulate the true live environment. The test team, in this test, usually functions as the user would in the live environment.
- *System Tests.* Many types of tests can be conducted as part of system tests including: usability tests, final requirements tests, volume and stress tests, performance tests, security and control tests, recovery tests, documentation and procedures tests, and multi-site tests. Although all of these tests are important,

a focus on volume, stress, and performance tests is critical to ensure that the application will function as expected under typical operating conditions.

- *Acceptance Tests.* These tests demonstrate that the application meets the original business objectives and satisfy user and information systems requirements. If the user is not involved in the execution of unit and/or integration tests, acceptance testing is a must. Acceptance tests are executed by the user so that the user can confirm (and feel comfortable) that the application will function as expected under normal operating conditions. Usually a subset of the integrated tests are used in the acceptance test with the focus on simulating a typical day, month-end, and year-end situation. At the end of these tests, users often sign-off on the results of the tests and their acceptance of the application. It is important to note that some training of the user must take place prior to their involvement in acceptance testing so that they know how to conduct the tests. Even with training, users participating in the acceptance test may need assistance executing the tests. It is also recommended that user application training occur prior to acceptance testing so that the user, with a minimum amount of training on how to conduct acceptance tests, is able to independently execute the tests.
- *Bench Tests.* Another type of test conducted as part of an integration project and related to custom code development. Bench testing is the first of all tests conducted and is performed by the programmer to ensure that the custom code developed meets the requirements identified in the functional and technical specifications. Custom code is developed for interfaces and conversion programs, for example, and thus bench testing is an integral part of the development of that code. Bench testing will be discussed in more detail in the Software Development section of this chapter.

A test plan or design consists of several components: an overall test strategy; the test control system; and test objectives, conditions, and scripts. Each is discussed below.

- *Test Strategy.* This strategy discusses the overall plan for accomplishing testing during the integration project. A test strategy identifies which tests will be conducted, by whom, and in what time frames. The strategy also defines the scope and approach for each of the tests to be executed.
- *Test Control System.* This system was developed to document and control when tests will be executed and by whom, what tests are complete, what tests have yet to be executed, and what tests did not complete as expected and require follow-up. Typical output of a test control system is a schedule of tests by day and responsibility, a log of all tests and their status, and a log of all tests needing follow-up (usually called an issues log). The issues log indicates the specific test that did not execute as expected, who was responsible for executing the test, who is responsible for following up and resolving the issue, priority of the issue, current status of the issue, resolution of the issue,

and date resolved. The issue log is used to manage incomplete tests and their timely resolution.

- *Test Objectives, Conditions, and Scripts.* Once the test strategy is understood, the detailed tests can be documented. Detailed tests consist of three major elements: objectives, conditions, and scripts as presented in Table 26–2. Test objectives are the overall statement as to the goal of the test.

Training Design

During this step, detailed training programs for users and information systems support staff are developed. Included in the training material are participant training manuals, training presentation materials, and hands-on exercises. Prior to developing the training materials, the types of training classes necessary and their content must be identified. To do this, the training audience and their skill set must be evaluated. Often the vendor provides training and materials; however, vendor training is usually generic and not customized for the organization's needs. Customized training that reflects the system use expected on a day-to-day basis is much more beneficial and easier to understand by the user. It is more difficult to learn a system whose examples reflect a car dealership and translate that use into a manufacturing organization than it is to learn a new system using everyday examples of the transactions currently processed in the manufacturing organization. However, vendor training materials are a great basis for building training programs customized for the organization.

Identifying who will conduct the training is another task covered by this step in the integration project. Again, the vendor usually is able to supply a trainer for a cost (vendor training can be contracted for when the software is purchased/leased). However, it is important to develop trainers internally not only to provide ongoing training to new users or update classes for current users, but also to eliminate the dependency and cost of resorting to vendor training once the system is operational.

A train-the-trainer program can be used to train a number of employees to become trainers on the software functionality. A train-the-trainer program is one where a knowledgeable project team member or vendor representative trains a group of users, identified as potential trainers, on how to conduct training classes on software functionality. These new trainers then team teach with the vendor or project team trainer until they feel comfortable taking on the class themselves. The project team trainer or vendor then reviews and supports the trainers until the new trainers are experienced enough to handle classes on their own. Formal surveys of attendees can also diagnose trainer issues as well as content, format, and other issues and are recommended for all training classes.

Other tasks included in this step are identifying responsibility for and scheduling of the training sessions, preparing the appropriate hardware and facilities in which to conduct the training, identifying the database requirements necessary for execution of the training courses, and preparing the system database so that training exercises can be completed in class.

Table 26–2: Sample Test Objective, Conditions, and Script

Unit Test Script
Accounts Payable—Invoice Entry

Case Number: AP01

Test Objective:	To unit test the invoice function using all invoice types in the organization.		Forms/Reports Used:	Vendor Invoice
Test Cycle:	1		Report(s) Produced:	Transaction Schedule
Test Schedule Date:	6/4/94			Transaction Log

Condition #	Condition Description	Activities	Expected Results	Verified By	Date	Issue #
I. AP01.01	Complete Match: Invoice total matches P.O. and Receiver.	Process the invoices, using the Invoice Entry Procedure and the invoice(s) marked to be used for this condition.	Invoice is able to be entered in summary due to complete match.	B. Scott	6/4/94	None
I. AP01.03	Incomplete Match: Invoice total does not match P.O. and Receiver but within tolerance.	Process the invoices, using the Invoice Entry Procedure and the invoice(s) marked to be used for this condition.	Invoice is within tolerance and is able to be input in detail.	B. Scott	6/4/94	9
I. AP01.06	Enter an invoice a second time.	Process the invoices, using the Invoice Entry Procedure and the invoice(s) marked to be used for this condition.	System replies "already on file" for duplicate invoice.	B. Scott	6/4/94	None
I. AP01.57	Process a standing order invoice.	Process the invoices, using the Invoice Entry Procedure and the invoice(s) marked to be used for this condition.	Standing order invoice is able to be processed. Adjusted standing order balance correct.	B. Scott	6/4/94	11

Software Development

All custom software (i.e., interfaces, conversion programs, and application customizations) is coded and bench tested as part of this step. (Bench testing, as described in the *Test Design* step, is the testing conducted by the programmer to ensure that the program code executes without error and meets the requirements identified in the functional specification.) This step includes preparing a technical specification from the functional specification developed in the *Business Systems Design, Interface and Program Flow Design* and *Data Conversion Design* steps. A technical specification, usually developed by a technical analyst, is a more detailed specification as to how the program modules will be designed, coded, and linked to accomplish the functionality documented in the functional specification. Often a pseudo coding language is used in the technical specification; this language is easily translated into program code by a programmer. The technical specification also addresses requirements for the construction and bench test environment and the development and testing of common models and program skeletons. These components are then used to develop the specific software.

As previously discussed, the vendor can be used to develop much of the custom software components. Areas requiring the organization's involvement include programming to provide the vendor with interface or conversion data directly from the organization's source systems. The vendor then takes the data and restructures it into a format that is acceptable to the new application. The vendor can also provide an output interface in a format readable by the organization's destination systems, however the organization may need to develop programs that reformat the data into files that can be accepted by the destination system.

Application Development

This step of work includes loading the application software per the specifications developed during the *Business System Design* step. Tasks include loading set-up parameters, tables, files, screens, and reports. Note that in some cases, application files may be loaded automatically by the conversion programs designed in the *Data Conversion Design* step and constructed in the *Software Development* step.

If certain large files are not able to be loaded automatically, as discussed in the *Data Conversion Design* step, this step, *Application Development,* is where the data input sheets would be completed, reviewed, and manually keyed into the new system. Note that file building of this nature may not be trivial. For example, if the application to be integrated is a purchasing and/or accounts payable application, building the vendor file manually is not simple, especially if the current vendor file maintains information on thousands of vendors (as most do). Be sure to plan plenty of time to gather and validate all the necessary file information as well as the time necessary to input the required number of files. If time constraints do exist, one approach can be used to build a very usable if not complete file. Using the vendor file as an example, sort all the vendors maintained in the current system in terms of purchase volume, current activity, and/or dollar volume. Use this ranking criteria to prioritize the vendors whose profiles are to be completed first. That way if only half of the vendor file is built by the time the system is operational, at least the half that is built may represent 80% or so of the purchases. Then as new vendors are needed, the remaining vendor files can be built as part of daily operations.

Procedure Development

User manuals required to implement and operate the new application are completed in this step. These manuals are developed according to outlines generated and approved during the Business Systems Design step. Procedures cover areas such as user procedures, data center operations, help desk, data security and control, disaster recovery, and application maintenance.

The procedures documented in this step can range from abbreviated desktop user procedures (see Figure 26–11 for an example)—which focus only on how to operate the system—to full-blown policy and procedure manuals—which cover not only the procedures necessary to operate the system, but also the work-flow procedures required in and around the system and the organizational policy statements regarding the particular transaction being documented. At the start of the project, a procedure strategy should be developed to identify the type, content, and scope of the procedures to be documented as part of the integration effort. This strategy can then guide the outlines developed in the Business Systems Design step as well as the final procedures documented in this step.

Whatever strategy is implemented for procedure documentation, two types of documents will assist in the development of procedures: vendor procedure manuals and current organizational policy and procedure manuals. Vendor documentation provides a sound basis for the development of the procedures for operating the system. Similar to the comments regarding the use of vendor training only, system usage procedures should be customized using organizational examples.

Current organizational policy and procedure manuals provide a sound basis for developing procedure manuals that cover not only system usage but the other workflow procedures to be used with the new system, as well as company policy statements regarding the transactions involved. Note that organizational policy for certain transactions may not change as the result of integrating the new system; however, in many cases, workflows will. The current documentation can assist in the design and format of the new policy and procedure manual (or improvements to it) as well as provide a checklist to ensure that the new policy and procedure manual is complete (as compared with the topics discussed in the current manual).

H1.4 DELETING AN ENTIRE JOURNAL ENTRY

The DELETE JOURNALS (JRNLDEL) screen is used to delete both the header and detail lines from the system without having to delete each item individually. To delete both header and detail journal records from the system, select the DELETE JOURNALS screen as follows:

STEP 1: Place an X to the left of the JRNLDEL DELETE JOURNALS transaction on the JOURNAL MENU screen.
Press ENTER.
The Delete Journals screen (H1.4) will appear on the terminal.

```
OGLDDJRO               FINANCIAL MANAGEMENT SYSTEM
JRNLDEL                      DELETE JOURNALS                          STEP

ORG ID:  ORG NAME:
JRNL ID:  DESCRIPTION:

LN $ T/   EFFEC E/JOURNAL   D/C                          No    Reversal
NO # T    DATE H/SOURCE     G   CONTROL TOTAL    XLAT SJE STA  ERR  OOB  DATE
                                         000                   00/00/00

DELETE?(Y/N):             LINE NQ:
NEXT FUNCTION: JRNLDEL    NEXT KEY:
DC800003 ORGANIZATION NOT DEFINED
```

STEP 2: Type in the journal key to identify the journal entry.
Press ENTER
Remember, the journal key is made up of five items:
- ORG ID
- JRNL ID
- S/#
- T/T
- EFFEC DATE

The system will display the Expanded Journal Header information associated with the journal key. Detail line item information will not be displayed. Also notice a DELETE? (Y/N) prompt at the bottom of the screen. The cursor will appear to the right of the prompt. Verify that the appropriate journal is displayed.

STEP 3: If this is the journal to be deleted, replace the N with a Y at the DELETE? (Y/N) field.
Press ENTER.
The system will respond with the message RECORD DELETED.
If the wrong journal has been selected, do not replace the N at the DELETE? (Y/N) field and press ENTER.

STEP 4: To return to Journal Menu.
Press CLEAR

Figure 26–11: Sample Desktop Procedure

Test Execution

Project team members, users, and information systems representatives will execute the tests developed in the *Test Design* step to help ensure that the system meets its specified functional performance and service level objectives. Test execution consists of following the instructions contained in the test scripts and comparing actual results with expected results (also documented in the test scripts). If the actual result does not match the expected result, the outcome is documented on an issue log (see Table 26–3 for a sample issue log).

Issues arising as a result of differences between actual results and the acceptance criteria will be analyzed and corrective action taken. Usually issues fall into one of four categories:

1. *Software Bug.* Issues of this type are those where the software functions incorrectly.
2. *Expected Is Incorrect.* Issues of this type are those where the software does not act as expected. This does not mean that the software is functioning incorrectly; in fact, it most probably is functioning as expected from the vendor point of view but maybe not how the organization expected it to function.
3. *Script Is Incorrect.* Issues of this type result from errors in the test script. In other words, the actual results of the test were correct based on the way the test script was written.
4. *Script Was Executed Incorrectly.* Issues of this type result from errors in executing the test script (i.e., incorrect keystroke).

Note that in executing tests, unit tests should be executed and all issues resolved and retested prior to beginning the integration tests. In turn, the integration tests should be completed prior to conducting the systems tests, and the same for acceptance testing. Internal and external auditors should be notified at the start of test execution so that they can plan to observe the tests or review the documentation, if necessary, during the test effort. Test scripts, control documentation, and test results should be accumulated, filed, and stored in case internal or external auditors need to review the tests at a later date.

On completion of testing, user and management acceptance of the new application system will be obtained before proceeding with the integration project.

Training Execution

This step consists of executing the training designed in the *Training Design* step. Training execution should be conducted early enough at the end of the integration project so that the training is complete prior to going live; however, training should not be conducted too early so users forget the training or so the training is not reinforced as the result of operating the new system.

Table 26–3: Sample Issues Log

Issue	Function	Test Cycle	Test Run	Test Case #	Test Cond. #	Tester Name	Software Function	Issue Description
1.	Purchasing	1	1	ACQ1–11	All	E. Smith	2.10.3.11.8	Detail Purchase Order not organization's form
2.	Purchasing	1	1	ACQ5 ACQ7	All	E. Smith	2.10.3.1	Cannot print summary purchase order
3.	Purchasing	1	1	ACQ2	All	E. Smith	None	Requisitions need to be modified to match actual test case
4.	Purchasing	1	1	ACQ7	All	E. Smith	None	Requisitions need to be modified to match actual test case
5.	Inventory	1	1	INV1– INV2	1.INV1.04 1.INV2.04	T. Jones	2.9.5.2	A/xxxxxx -Alternate Reference Number search not working in test environment.
6.	Purchasing	1	1	ACQ1–11	All	E. Smith	2.10.8.2	Message displayed "**Warning**" Primary vendor: (blank) when pulled up catalog item w/o vendor in catalog
7.	Inventory	1	1	INV1– INV5	All	T. Jones	None	Need a report that shows quantity on-hand, by location, by item number, but not by vendor
8.	Inventory	1	1	INV1– INV5	All	T. Jones	None	Need a report that shows vendor packaging units, and Location and Issue packaging units on same report
9.	Accounts Payable	1	1	APO1	.03 and .57	B. Scott	4.1.1.1	Vendor address differed from PO address
10.	Accounts Payable	1	1	APO1	44.52a.52b	B. Scott	2.10.3.1	Could not print a summary PO; see Issue #2 above
11.	Accounts Payable	1	1	APO1	57	B. Scott	None	The vendor was a discount vendor; another procedure would have been used.

Training courses may need to be held more than once for the same or a subset of a previously trained audience, to reinforce the concepts or to allow the audience to pick up additional knowledge not clearly understood the first time around. Providing a training database and requiring all trainees to spend a certain amount of self-study time to reinforce the concepts taught in a training session also provide another avenue for additional training. Note that training examples should be available in the training database to assist the trainees in their self-studies.

Lastly, training does not end when the system becomes operational. Within the first month or two on the new system, a refresher training course will help to fill in the gaps not understood in the pretraining or not used or reinforced in day-to-day use of the system. Also, training for new hires must be considered. Will it be the responsibility of the organizational area to train their new users? Or will the organization sponsor training courses organization-wide on the new application at frequent intervals? If the organizational area is responsible, it is important that training be conducted by someone who is entirely comfortable with the material and who has the resources to teach it effectively. Similarly, a seasoned trainer who is knowledgeable about how the organization uses the new application should be used to provide the organizational-wide training. Finally, training materials must be reviewed and updated as the organization expands or revises its use of the application through live operations.

Cut-Over Planning

Cut-over planning includes the establishment of the production environment and development of the plan for the transition to the new user and information systems organizations. During this step, all procedure manuals and training programs are finalized to reflect any timing changes. The old system and its operating documentation is phased out and final system documentation is assembled and distributed (unless the old system is planned to continue to operate for some time; see the conversion discussion regarding the no-conversion approach in the *Data Conversion Design* step). In this step, the maintenance and testing environment will be established (so that new software releases or updates can be tested before installing them into the production environment) and a process for monitoring new system performance will be planned.

A detailed cut-over schedule is developed as part of this step. Included in the schedule are what activities regarding establishing operations on the new application will be executed each day during the cut-over period. For example, if the application to be integrated is an inventory application, activities such as conducting a final physical inventory and loading beginning inventory balances into the new system must be scheduled and staffed appropriately. Also, a plan is documented for how inventory transactions that need to continue during this "time-out" for physical inventory taking will be accomplished. Further, on what day all inventory receipts will begin to be input into the new system and how the purchase orders for these receipts will be convened to the new system must be planned for and scheduled.

A detailed schedule of at least the first month of operations is also constructed during this step and includes activities such as the reports to be printed each day, what batch processing will occur each evening, when the application will be available to the user on weekdays and on weekends, etc. Tasks like bow to handle employees that do not use the new forms must be identified, documented as to what response will be given, and responsibility for handling this situation assigned. Lastly, organization-wide communication of the new system must be delivered to let the entire organization know what will be happening and when. This organization-wide communication can be executed via a variety of means including meetings, newsletter articles, and memos.

Cut-Over Executive and Production Support

This step covers the actual execution of the cut-over plan as well as production support and fine tuning during the initial months of the new system (especially the first period-end close). If the cut-over plan is well thought-out and documented, execution of the plan becomes straightforward. That is not to say that the cut-over does not have to be managed. In fact, it must be managed closely because many cut-over tasks are dependent on other tasks; failure to execute properly and completely any of the cut-over tasks may have severe ramifications to subsequent tasks and thus to the transition of operations to the new application. Further, not all events can be planned. In fact, most transitions to a new application do not go without a hitch. But those projects that develop a detailed, well thought-out cut-over plan are more likely to successfully mitigate any unplanned problems than those projects that cut-over without a plan.

The project is not over once the cut-over plan has been executed. Much is learned in the first few days and weeks of operating the new system. Procedures, work flows, and training must be reviewed and adjusted for aspects of the application not considered during the integration project. Further, system tuning (i.e., making the system operate more efficiently from a technical standpoint) is often conducted during the first few months of an operational application. Lastly, until the application system is put through its daily, weekly, monthly, quarterly, and year-end paces at least once, these initial period-end processes may be bumpy at best.

27

SHARED SERVICES TODAY AND TOMORROW

In recent years, multinationals worked furiously to refocus on core competencies by divesting non-core businesses and streamlining or outsourcing support functions. Lean corporate structures evolved to represent the only proven approach to providing superior returns to investors. In this dynamic environment, Shared Services has emerged as a key strategic direction for organizing infrastructure processes. In fact, the trend led Gartner Group to predict that, "Shared Services structures will become, by (the year) 2000, the primary organization method for delivering highly repetitive, low-value business and IT functions to the enterprise in more than 50 percent of large corporations to reduce costs and improve efficiency."[1]

Herein, we examine some of the key developments in the Shared Services arena. The findings here derive from experiences on a wide range of Shared Services projects and an increasing volume of public discussion on the topic. Additional insights come from the recently completed Deloitte Consulting Shared Services Market Survey, conducted by International Data Corporation (IDC). The survey consisted of in-depth interviews with Shared Services leaders at more than 50 Fortune 500 companies or international equivalent.

Shared Services represents different things to different people. Interpretations of the concept have ranged from identifiable organizational structures to ad-hoc teams for "problem solving." Most observers believe Shared Services has reversed the decentralization of the late 1980s and early 1990s. However, Shared Services does not promise to be an "end-game" optimal solution. Unlike its predecessors, centralization and decentralization, Shared Services should be viewed in the context of the modern kinetic enterprise where the ability to change and adapt to the ever-changing environment is key to continued success.

Tracing the history of today's business environment, many researchers note that companies are slow to embrace change. For most of this century, enterprises organized along the centralized business model that Alfred Sloan created for General Motors in the early 1900s.[2] In the 1970s and 1980s, companies recognized the need to improve responsiveness to diverging customer requirements and decentralized operations to streamline market agility. Indeed, most leading strategic enterprise models, such as Michael Porter's, emphasized the importance of understanding local business environments and customers. However, the move to decentralized operations produced local bureaucracies. In other words, on a smaller scale, business units recreated "corporate" with duplicate tasks and activities. Executive management recognizes that cross-organizational standardization has become all but impossible, and that enterprise-wide initiatives may be hindered by decentralization. The struggle to integrate competing objectives—accelerating decision making via decentralized operations while streamlining organization-wide headcount—prompted the emergence of Shared Services.

WHAT IS SHARED SERVICES?

Traditionally, people described Shared Services as an organization approach to process high volume, low value-added, transaction-based activities within a single internal entity. The focus on low value-added activities prompted Shared Services pioneers to focus on physical and organizational consolidation to achieve cost savings. In reality, four elements comprise a successful Shared Services design:

- Technology
- Process
- Organization
- Location

The appropriate emphasis on each of the four elements varies by company. In general, common technology and processes dominate most design decisions, particularly given the rigidly declining cost of technology solutions to enable a virtual organization.

WHAT DRIVES SHARED SERVICES INITIATIVES?

Historically, potential cost drove companies to adopt Shared Services. However, market trends (e.g., continuous mergers and acquisitions, globalization, Internet, etc.) expanded the focus to include business agility and increased customer focus, as shown in Figure 27–1. Observers may find it ironic that compa-

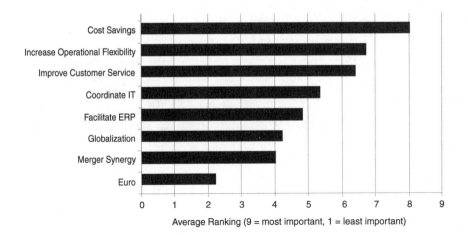

Average Ranking (9 = most important, 1 = least important)

Figure 27–1: Average Ranking of Business Drivers

nies abandon decentralization for the same reason that they embraced it—to be closer to the customer and react faster to market opportunities. However, today, understanding the customer is not synonymous to physical closeness. This trend toward increased business flexibility reflects the vital need for today's companies to be "kenetic"—that is, reacting to market events and customer demand instantly. Our recent survey of global companies operating Shared Services confirms the change in priorities.

REALIZING THE BENEFITS

The increasing popularity of Shared Services is not surprising. Regardless of the business imperatives that drive Shared Services, properly executed Shared Services initiatives consistently generate a significant return on investment (see Figure 27–2). Survey participants reported an average (return on investment) ROI of approximately 27%. Respondents also pointed to less tangible benefits, such as increased customer satisfaction and improved service levels and process cycle times.

Obviously, reducing employee headcount contributes significantly to the reported ROIs. Beyond the ROI benefit, today's constraint market for skilled employees encourages companies to re-deployed skilled resources to more mission-critical activities.

Companies understand the efficiencies gained from standardizing and reengineering processes and implementing common systems via Shared Services can reduce labor requirements. In fact, 60% of survey participants reported headcount reductions in excess of 20%, as seen in Figure 27–3.

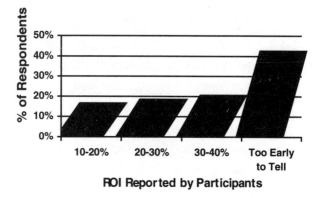

Figure 27–2: ROI from Shared Services Implementation

WHAT IS THE SCOPE OF SHARED SERVICES?

A quick review of existing Shared Services initiatives confirms that finance has led the way. This is logical considering the traditional fiduciary role of finance to champion cost reduction and profit improvement. Additionally, finance needs have driven the development of robust software applications to support transaction processing and analysis, many of which have grown into full-fledged (ERP) solutions. Another key factor in proliferation of Finance Shared Services has been its functional ability to measure performance and develop a sound business case to back initiatives. "You can't manage what you don't measure," exclaimed a CFO survey participant. Finally, Shared Services emphasizes the value of continuous improvement, often driven by metrics performance.

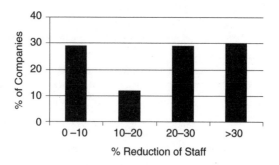

Figure 27–3: Reductions in Headcount

The implementation of sophisticated new systems in other functional areas such as human resources broadened the scope of Shared Services, but finance continues to lead. Survey results (see Figure 27–4) confirmed that financial processes overwhelmingly lead Shared Services, representing six of the top ten spots on the list of most common Shared Services processes.

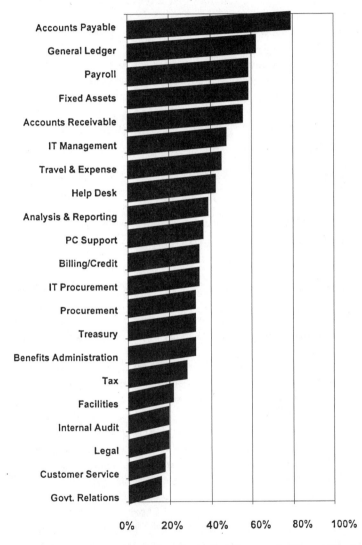

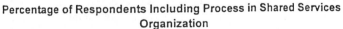

Percentage of Respondents Including Process in Shared Services Organization

Figure 27–4: Top Shared Services Processes

Experience indicates that processes tend to fall into one of five broad process bands: (1) order to cash, (2) procurement to payment, (3) recording to reporting, (4) employee services, and (5) information technology management. Notably absent from this list are processes most companies consider core, such as manufacturing, product design and development, and marketing and sales. This reflects the traditional definition of Shared Services, which states that Shared Services should focus on those activities that support, rather than replace, a company's core business operations.

Note that some of the most common processes to include in Shared Services are not low-visibility, back-office tasks. For example, accounts receivable deals with customers, accounts payable interacts with suppliers, and payroll and benefits administration interface with employees. As Shared Services organizations mature, companies add more processes to the center, including those that are less transaction-intensive. Companies derive value by adding processes to Shared Services when a potential for cost savings exists, when standardizing the process is beneficial to the organization, or when a principal process objective is improved customer service.

An interesting example of innovative Shared Services is the pilot joint venture undertaken by Ford, DaimlerChrysler, and Exel Logistics Americas last year. The overall goals of the program were to reduce costs and improve service by blending the automakers' distribution networks. More specifically, the joint venture reduced duplicate miles for dedicated carriers servicing for both manufacturers.[3]

GEOGRAPHIES OF SHARED SERVICES ARE EXPANDING AS WELL

The first wave of Shared Services focused primarily on North America and more specifically the United States. This was largely due to the uniformity of language, regulations, and business culture across the region. The U.S. is also home to a number of the largest industrial companies that emphasize new computing and communications technologies where Shared Services is likely to generate quick benefits.

While the Shared Services movement started in North America, the gap in maturity between North America and Europe has largely disappeared. A recent estimate indicated that by the year 2000, over 20,000 Shared Services sites will exist throughout Europe. Our survey confirms executives on both sides of the Atlantic cited virtually the same business drivers, implementation strategies, and ongoing management concerns around Shared Services. Some regional differences did exist. For example, Europeans placed a greater emphasis on local government, tax incentives, and workers' language capabilities when selecting a site.

The greater emphasis on these considerations helps explain why more European respondents established greenfield sites in countries such as Ireland and the Netherlands, where government incentives and multi-lingual residents are abundant. Finally, Europeans developed Shared Services to transform their organizations from country-specific businesses to pan-European, with common processes across the region.

Today, a third wave of Shared Services developments continues evolving in Asia and South America. As local trade organizations expand and countries become increasingly open, many multinationals wish to transplant Shared Services success in new territory. Ironically, Florida has become a preferred location for Latin American Shared Services. A recent publication cited 300 multinational companies that locate Latin American operations in South Florida.[4] However, as labor markets and regulations equalize, an increased number of centers will be established locally, to take advantage of the lower cost of local labor and the value of proximity to address regional cultural differences.

Shared Services from an industry standpoint probably began in manufacturing. A few characteristics help explain this trend. First, large manufacturing companies have the global scale to justify Shared Services. Also, waves of mergers and acquisitions continually change the corporate faces of many well-known companies, to include a number of loosely aligned business units. Finally, the first ERP solutions with sophisticated finance and HR modules focused on the manufacturing industry. Given the close alignment of Shared Services and technology, Shared Services naturally evolved.

Shared Services continues growing in consumer business and pharmaceutical companies. Some argue that the concept has always existed in utilities, although with a different name. In the health care industry giants like Kaiser Permanente have reduced cost structures by successfully embracing Shared Services. The massive mergers in financial services have sped the transition to Shared Services.

Shared Services concepts now appear in environments not typically associated with new reorganization/reengineering trends, such as the back offices of investment banks and brokerages. While these companies have always operated in an environment with little differences between external and internal customers, there is increased emphasis on service level agreements and pricing mechanisms, topics associated with Shared Services.[5]

When it comes to implementing Shared Services, one size does not fit all. As mentioned earlier, implementing Shared Services typically entails choosing and migrating from one or more of four major strategic dimensions, as shown in Figure 27–5.

These can be addressed in varying order based on management preference, and can be selected in sequence or in bundles. When discussing implementation approaches, survey participants generally chose a strategy of implementing systems and/or process standardization prior to organization and location consolidation. Smaller companies demonstrated a general tendency to consolidate organization and location first, while larger companies tended to prioritize common systems.

Perhaps the most significant findings have been the sheer diversity of implementation strategies companies deployed. Any company considering Shared Services must determine a unique migration strategy. For example, companies may logically standardize systems as a first step if they have many disparate systems. Alternatively, it might be better for the new Shared Services organization to break from the existing corporate culture by consolidating location and organiza-

Figure 27–5: Implementation Dimensions

tion, thereby deferring common systems. The strategy for Shared Services must align with the company's overall approach for implementing change, with large projects evaluated and prioritized according to corporate strategy. By definition, the solution will be unique.

While Shared Services initiatives from the early 1990s, such as General Electric, Mobile, American Express, and AlliedSignal, captured the headlines, new Shared Services initiatives are hardly newsworthy. While most companies recognize benefits and successes, the ride has proven to be more difficult than initially anticipated.

In 1991, Larry Bossidy joined AlliedSignal and planned to quickly implement Shared Services. With clear opportunities to simplify back-office operations of independent disintegrated business units, Bossidy championed the initiative. Since 1994, AlliedSignal Business Services have consolidated 75 business functions under a single organizational umbrella, providing processing for 77,000 employees and 325 facilities worldwide. While AlliedSignal estimates annual savings to exceed $70 million, the initiative is hardly over. "The implementation of this stuff is not at all easy," says Daniel G. Henderson, vice president and general manager of AlliedSignal Business Services.[6]

Indeed, the findings indicate that implementing Shared Services has proven a difficult and challenging endeavor. Survey participants were asked to share their experiences and a majority admitted that they underestimated the implementation difficulties, as can be seen in Figure 27–6.

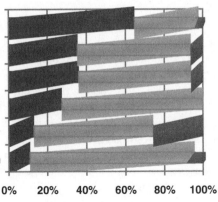

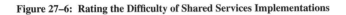

Change Leadership

Employee Transition

Implementation Timing

Implementation Approach

Implementation Partner

Physical Consolidation

0%   20%   40%   60%   80%   100%

Frequency of Responses

▌Underestimated ▌About Right ▌Overestimated

Figure 27–6: Rating the Difficulty of Shared Services Implementations

CHANGE LEADERSHIP IS WHAT SHARED SERVICES PROJECTS ARE ABOUT

The key challenges in most Shared Services implementations revolve around people. More than 60% of survey respondents underestimated the impact of change management on the implementation, while 35% underestimated the complexity of the employee transition.

Companies emphasized that success depends on devoting significant time and effort to people-related issues. Strong executive support throughout the project, continuous communication, and training for both Shared Services and business unit employees are critical to a successful project.

Unless properly managed, employees may view Shared Services as a traumatic experience. It is always a significant change. Frequently, these projects have a primary objective of headcount reduction. Establishing a greenfield location requires employees to move to a new location, and while such moves are not particularly unusual, employee retention incentives are often overlooked, especially at below-manager levels. Given the relative low pay of many operations staff, job switching becomes an attractive option. Unless properly managed, service levels will plummet. Companies that ignore these concerns clearly deliver reduced benefits and increased risk.

Rather than operating as a stealth project, Shared Services needs to be championed—and supported—by a senior executive. This sets the tone of the change process for the entire organization. Clear direction from the top removes the uncertainty of the transition for employees affected by the change.

Another critical success factor is concise communications to describe the transition to Shared Services and the company impact. From the start, employees will ask, "why are we changing?" and will be reluctant to relinquish control of the processes that have long been a part of daily routines. Managers must act as ambassadors to sell the benefits of the Shared Services model.

Physical consolidation is another important characteristic of Shared Services that companies underestimate. While customer service and technology objectives dominate today's Shared Services strategies, immediate savings from consolidating to lower cost locations captured the attention of many large companies initially launching Shared Service in the late 1980s.

General Electric was a Shared Services pioneer. In 1984, General Electric created a new centralized accounting function called Financial Services Organization (FSO) to manage financial processes for over 200,000 employees. Its initial structure involved the creation of three Shared Services centers in Schenectady, New York, Bridgeport, Connecticut, and Ft. Myers, Florida. While GE's innovative management approaches established Shared Services as a celebrated success, a significant portion of the initial cost savings from Shared Services resulted through the gradual consolidation of FSO's operations to Ft. Myers, which was a lower-cost location.[7]

Even today, relocation to cheaper operating sites continues to be a driving factor in business cases for Shared Services. For example in 1997, Deloitte & Touche LLP decided to implement Shared Services to manage its own infrastructure processes, such as time & expense, payroll, and accounts payable. The initiative included process consolidation from over 110 offices throughout North America, with 30% to 40% of projected benefits resulting from the lower cost of living at the new operating site.

Experience and research confirm that site selection significantly impacts the success of Shared Services. The two location alternatives are to use an existing company site (i.e., a "brownfield") or an entirely new site (i.e., a "greenfield"). Two-thirds of survey participants chose to co-locate Shared Services with existing facilities. However, companies choosing greenfield locations were more likely to view the implementations as extremely successful or very successful.

Greenfield sites are more common for companies that emphasize cost reduction as the primary driver for Shared Services. The apparently greater success of greenfield sites is likely related to the fresh start offered by a new location. The Shared Services leader can develop a new organizational structure, hiring policies, and incentive and compensation programs. In a customer-focused organization these factors contribute to a new culture that is difficult to achieve in a brownfield location. A less publicized reality related to setting up a new site is that staff reduction is less painful, since many existing employees choose not to relocate.

Brownfields have advocates as well. An existing site may already have the necessary infrastructure to enable accelerated implementation. The Shared

Services team can leverage existing resources and knowledge of the local market. When Deloitte & Touche LLP made its decision to relocate, the proximity to a data center with experienced IT practitioners and appropriate networking connectivity was a key consideration criteria. Such constraints, however, will become less important in the "bend-width-reach" era of virtual computing.

To summarize, it is difficult to rank benefits for two approaches. Choosing a greenfield commits a company to a Shared Services initiative and generally prompts more implementation persistence. However, the associated risk with brownfields is a lot less, since no long-term lease or heavy infrastructure investments are required.

DO YOUR HOMEWORK—MEASURE PERFORMANCE

Before launching on any journey as complex and challenging as Shared Services, it is absolutely necessary to develop a workplan vision to measure progress and deliver results on targeted dates. Survey results confirm that most successful implementations start with a detailed business case. In fact, of the companies that rated implementations extremely successful, 80% used a detailed business case—not only to justify the project in the first place, but to guide its success as the project unfolded.

Performance measurement is the heart of Shared Services. Using metrics to manage business performance is difficult, but those who master it reap the rewards. Most companies struggle to implement the right performance measures that reflect improved process performance and tie Shared Services performance to organizational goals.

Experience suggests that simplicity is key to establishing effective performance measurement programs. It is relatively easy to design a very complex metrics structure, but maintaining it is too difficult. For example, while the industry is overpopulated with sample metrics across functions, it is quite the reverse in terms of actual data tracked. Successful Shared Services have found the right middle ground by choosing a measurement system that is not a burden to maintain and comprehensive enough to communicate to stakeholders.

Further, survey findings (see Figure 27–7) emphasized the link between metrics and success. Ninety percent of extremely and very successful companies stated that performance metrics were very important to success. But performance measures are not only a vital management tool used to achieve success. They can also serve as a powerful advocate to *communicate* success. As one respondent said: "Performance metrics are critical! We can't live without them. When someone asks, `Why do you say you're the lower cost provider?' I can say, `Let me show you the three benchmark studies that I've done.' When asked, `Why do you think your level of service is better than the outsource provider?' I've got five years worth of customer satisfaction data."

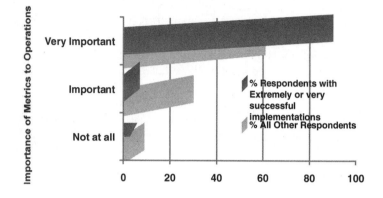

Figure 27–7: Linkage Between Metrics and Success

OUTSOURCING ALTERNATIVE

Some view Business Process Outsourcing (BPO) as an external alternative to Shared Services. Clearly outsourcing is a key element of Shared Services. Essentially, strategic direction is the same—a company is trying to separate select business processes and run them more efficiently by introducing a customer-provider relationship. In the case of Shared Services, since the provider is internal, this relationship may be less rigidly defined. Some advocate Shared Services to use almost the same rigor in developing Service Level Agreements (SLAs) and managing customer relationships as if it were a third party. However, many organizations have found that maintaining such formality may outweigh resulting benefits.

Outsourcing might be a more viable option to consider *after* Shared Services is operational and the data exists to support objective decision making. Companies with more mature Shared Services organizations are more likely to outsource business processes than companies that recently implemented Shared Services. In the survey, 69% of the companies that outsourced business processes had Shared Services organizations that were at least three years old. Fifty-eight percent of survey respondents were either currently outsourcing a business process or planned to consider outsourcing in the near future. In this context, the list of the most commonly outsourced processes closely resembles the list of processes that are typically implemented in Shared Services, as shown in Figure 27–8.

The close linkage between Shared Services and outsourcing is further demonstrated by the recent efforts of some companies to expand service offerings to external customers, effectively becoming outsourcers themselves. For example, after Tenneco significantly downsized, its Tenneco Business Services (TBS) unit had extra capacity. Having already achieved significant success in decreasing internal operating costs, the company began looking to offer services to outside customers.[8] Shell Services is another such example. With approximately 5,000

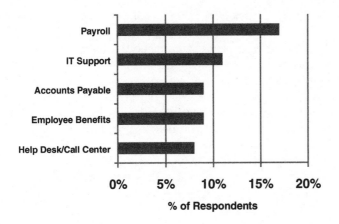

Figure 27–8: Top Five Outsourced Processes

employees this organization spans an array of competencies, including human resources, finance, procurement, and other administrative services. Shell Services, headquartered in Houston, operates as a service company, and accounts for some $1 billion in revenues. While this structure has helped Shell Oil pare costs by 30% to 40%, the company also offers its services to non- Shell customers.[9] It is important to note that both of these companies invested significantly to build external business with mixed results to date.

CHANGING FACE OF SHARED SERVICES

Over the past 15 years, Shared Services has had many faces and continues to change. At the beginning, the concept of combining non-core business process into a single location in an inexpensive location comprised all of the Shared Services universe. In today's turbulent market, companies seek new ways to extend Shared Services. We have already seen a significant expansion in the services offered by Shared Services organizations. As enterprises consider and implement e-business infrastructures, many view Shared Services as the logical structure to organize and facilitate a common e-business strategy. In the spirit of the "act now" philosophy that most e-commerce proponents recommend, most companies launched multiple, disintegrated initiatives. Deploying Shared Services concepts will encourage common approaches and improve resource leverage, both concepts championed by Shared Services.

Revolutionary leaps in technology change how we communicate and work, rendering physical location and distances less important. Shared Services benefited from the first evolution in technology that enabled consolidation of remote activities and staff. As technology and underlying behavior evolve, virtual organizations will become increasingly common.

Companies embrace Shared Services for its ability to change while maintaining its core premise, to provide services more efficiently. As Shared Services evolves to become a vital link between customers, vendors, and business units, flexibility and expertise will be even more important. After all, in an ideal world, non-core processes that do not require unique customer service would be outsourced to specialized providers who would have optimal resources to support varying requirements. In such a world, Shared Services would streamline to assume only monitoring, control, and risk assurance roles for outsourced processes. However, Shared Services will continue to fulfill the more dynamic roles of both facilitating and managing processes, which require a broad understanding of the overall organization and business strategy. These trends will be further magnified by the increased emphasis on partnerships and alliances that will reshape competitive landscapes.

ENDNOTES

1. B. McNee, T. Austin, J. Baylock, M. Blechar, B. Burton, D. Cappuccio, J. Fenn, C. Germann, C. Goodhue, E. Keller, B. Keyworth, F. Magee, J. Pucciarelli, G. Rahaelian, F. Schlier, I. Stenmark, R. Terdiman, M. West, S. Winkler, A. Cushman, Gartner Group, *Industry Trends and Directions* (March 28, 1997).
2. JoAnn Greco, *Designing for the 21st century,* Journal of Business Strategy v19n6, November/December 1998.
3. Jim Thomas, *Ford and DaimlerChrysler: Expanding the Notion of Shared Services into Their Logistics Operations. Share and Share Alike,* Logistics Management & Distribution Report v38n3 (March 1999), pp. 44–48.
4. Alexis Muellner, *S. Florida benefits from firms' shared services,* (multinational companies make South Florida the home of their Latin American operations), South Florida Business Journal, 19, 49, 12(2) (July 23, 1999).
5. Jeremy Smith, *Shared Services in the Financial Industry: Emerging Practices and Issues, External affairs, (outsourcing),* Banker, 149, 877, 68(2) (March, 1999).
6. Tom Field, *Share & Share Alike,* CIO Magazine (May 15, 1997).
7. Robert Frigo and Robert Janson, *GE Business Services: GE's Financial Services Operation Achieves Quality Results Through "Work-out" Process,* National Productivity Review v13n1 (Winter 1993/1994), pp. 53–61.
8. Emily Plishner, *Tenneco's New Business,* Journal of Business Strategy v17n6 (November/December 1996), pp. 14–19; *The Future Is Now for Shared Services,* Journal of Business Strategy, v19n6 (November/December 1998), p. 37.
9. Samuel Greengard, *FAIR SHARE, (shared services in corporations),* Industry Week, 248, 6, 42(1) (March 15, 1999).

28

INFORMATION SYSTEMS SECURITY

It is estimated that computer fraud costs American organizations between $300 million and $5 billion per year. To reduce your organization's susceptibility to fraud, a well-planned and implemented approach to information systems (IS) security is required.

Information systems security can be defined as the protection of information assets—your hardware, software, and associated data—from unauthorized or intentional disclosure, modification, or destruction. Also included under the IS security umbrella are the steps necessary to control access to system resources and ways in which to respond to unauthorized and/or unintentional access to systems. Information systems security should be designed to ensure the integrity, confidentiality and accessibility, where authorized, to the organization's information assets.

TYPES OF THREATS

There are a wide variety of threats to information systems security. Basically, these threats can be summarized into the following categories:

- *International mischief.* Caused by theft, intentional destruction of data and other IS assets, and hackers (individuals who obtain unauthorized access to a computer).
- *Lack of an effective IS security policy.* Such as the failure to perform regular system back-ups (saving your computer's software and data on tape or disk) or allowing system users to share their passwords.

- *Human accidents and errors.* Such as spilling coffee on a computer keyboard or tripping into a disk drive and causing loss of data. (Information systems security can't cure human accidents and errors. However, it can reduce the risk of and loss from them by limiting access to IS assets.)
- *Power supply threats.* Sudden lapses or surges of power that cause the loss or scrambling of data.
- *Natural disasters.* Earthquakes, fires, floods, and tornadoes fall into this category.
- *Network access.* Unauthorized access to your voice or data network.
- *Viruses.* Malicious (in general) programs that attack legitimate programs and destroy data or computer codes (e.g., the Michelangelo virus).
- *Data diddling.* The unauthorized alteration of data as it is entered into a computer or the changing of data stored in the computer (e.g., changing students' grades, eliminating speeding tickets, reducing amounts owed the organization, and transferring money from one account to another).

What can an organization do to protect against these numerous threats? The next section discusses a number of proven measures that can be utilized to protect the organization's IS assets.

PROTECTING INFORMATION SYSTEMS ASSETS

Given the large investment in and dependence on IS assets, it makes economic and business sense to protect them. Described below are some of the key means by which an organization can help ensure the integrity, assessability, and confidentiality of its IS resources.

Physical Security

There are a large number of physical measures an organization can implement to improve the security surrounding its systems:

- *Physical access controls.* By restricting access to IS assets, an organization can reduce the opportunity for unauthorized use and malicious harm to its computers. The computer room should be located away from public areas and protected by a security system (e.g., a key-card or combination lock).
- *Fire suppression control system.* The computer room should be protected by a fire suppression system (e.g., an automatic water or Halon system). Also, the room should have fire extinguishers and be kept as clean as possible to reduce the opportunity for fires to spread.
- *Water detection and control system.* Each year, a significant amount of water damage is incurred in computer rooms. The main causes of water damage

includes burst pipes, leaking air conditioning systems, and roof leaks. To reduce the opportunity for water damage, organizations should periodically review their plumbing, air conditioning systems, and roof. Also, the computer room should be equipped with a water detection system and plastic covers for the computer equipment in the event of a leak.

- *Power supply monitoring systems.* To protect against power fluctuations and outages, organizations should strongly consider investing in an Uninterruptible Power Supply (UPS) system. UPS systems filter power supply fluctuations and ensure a constant power supply to computers. Also, if there is a power outage or blackout they can provide power for a limited period of time. This power can allow the organization to safely shut down its computers without the loss of data.

- *Offsite storage of backup tapes and disks.* One of the easiest ways in which an organization can protect its IS assets is to store copies of all of its software off-site in a protected environment. The software to be stored off-site should include copies of the operating system and other system software, application software (e.g., the general ledger), and all data, including master files and transaction details.

Technical Security Measures

There are a number of technologically based security measures an organization can implement to improve the security surrounding its IS assets. These measures include:

- *Encryption.* The scrambling of data, based on a mathematical algorithm, that makes it unreadable to those without a key. Encryption can be an effective security measure for organizations that transmit data between different locations.

- *Callback devices (also known as port protection devices).* A relatively effective means of controlling telephone access to an organization's computers. After calling into a system, a user must supply an identification code and password for authentication by the device. The device then disconnects the user and calls the user's preauthorized telephone number to verify the identity of the user.

- *Password.* A sequence of alphabetic and/or numeric characters which must be entered at the beginning of a computer session to verify the user's identity and obtain access to the system. Passwords can be an effective means of limiting access to a system, especially if they are frequently changed (e.g., every 60 days), random (e.g., not a person's last name or birthdate), and are not shared with others.

- *Access control software (ACS).* Mainly available for mainframe and large midrange (minicomputer) systems, this can be a valuable security measure. ACS provides an additional layer of security on top of the application and operating system security. It also provides the ability to limit access to designated employees, monitor user violations (e.g., unauthorized attempts to access the payroll system), and report security breaches.

- *Biometric devices.* Instruments that perform mathematical analysis of biological characteristics. Today, there are wide variety of these types of devices including:
  — Voice recognition and verification systems.
  — Signature dynamics verification systems.
  — Retinal pattern verification systems.
  — Hard print geometry verification systems.
  — Fingerprint identification.

Biometric systems have been in use for some time now. Before selecting one of these systems, the organization should consider (1) the cost versus the benefits of the systems. Biometric devices can be very expensive; (2) The error rate should be very low. This means the system must be able to spot counterfeits while making allowances for normal variations (e.g., a blister on the hand or a cold); (3) The time required to enroll people into the system.

End User Computer Security

Microcomputer and local area networks (LANS) are becoming increasingly popular. As their popularity grows, so do the associated security risks. Unfortunately, most organizations tend to focus on mainframe security and fail to recognize the importance of microcomputer and LAN security. To increase the security surrounding these systems, a number of steps can be taken:

- *Security agreements.* Ensure that all personnel sign an agreement stating they will not:
  — Share their password.
  — Upload or download any software or data to the organization's computers unless instructed to do so.
  — Pirate (make illegal copies of) the organization's software.
- *Physical security.* Verify that the organization's microcomputers and LANs are appropriately located (e.g., in a separate computer room) and protected from power fluctuations, fire and water damage.
- *Data security.* Ensure that the software and the data on microcomputers and LANs are backed up on a frequent (e.g., daily) basis and the backup tapes or disks are stored off-site.

Employee Security

There are a number of key measures an organization can take to limit its exposure to IS security risks. These measures include:

- *Performing background checks.* Prior to hiring an employee, an organization should perform a thorough background check. The check should include an analysis of the prospective employee's educational and work history.
- *Analyzing employees' security posture.* The security posture of all employees should be investigated on an annual basis. This investigation should determine whether the employees' legal or credit position has changed.
- *Obtaining security agreement signatures.* All employees should be required to sign a security agreement.
- *Communicating with the personnel department.* The personnel department should immediately formally notify the IS department of all personnel changes (e.g., employees who are leaving the organization or whose responsibilities have changed). Doing so can help guard against unauthorized access to the system by former or transferred employees.

Insurance Coverage

Organizations should maintain sufficient insurance to reduce the exposure to losses from flood, fire, theft, and other types of disaster. The types of insurance coverage that should be maintained include computer equipment and facilities, media reconstruction, business interruption, and errors and omissions by employees.

Disaster Recovery Planning

Disaster recovery planning, also referred to as contingency planning or business resumption planning, is one of the most important aspects of IS security. A disaster recovery plan (DRP) is an organized and documented approach to responding to a disaster. A proven approach to developing and maintaining a DRP is outlined below.

- *Phase I—Assess the situation.* During this phase, the organization determines the types of risks to which it is vulnerable (e.g., fires, tornadoes, or earthquakes) and the potential impact of these risks.
- *Phase II—Analyze recovery strategies.* The key steps to be completed during this phase include determining the IS resources currently in place and then analyzing the alternatives for recovery. These alternatives can include:
  - *Constructing a backup site.* This involves building a data center in a location sufficiently far from the main data center so it is not subject to the same disasters.
  - *Utilizing a service bureau.* This option involves using the computer resources of a third party immediately after the disaster.
  - *Sharing computer facilities.* Under this option, the organization shares the computer systems and software of another organization for a limited period of time.

— *Obtaining hot or cold site facilities from a vendor.* This option involves contracting for the use of a computer facility while the organization's own data center is being restored. A cold site is a "computer-ready" room in which an organization can move its existing or replacement computer. A hot site is a fully operational facility with a computer and network already in place.

- *Phase III—Develop the DRP.* During this phase, the organization develops its DRP. The plan should include the following areas:
  - An overview of the plan (e.g., the purpose of the plan, recovery, and restoration strategies, key recovery activities, and how the plan will be maintained and tested.
  - *Emergency procedures.* The procedures to be taken to safeguard human life, limit damage to the data center, and minimize loss of data.
  - *Response action plan.* The steps needed to respond to a disaster (e.g., how to assess the damage, notification procedures, and recovery team members and responsibilities).
  - *Recovery operations.* A description of the major recovery tasks (e.g., the recovery logistics, off-site storage, and operating system, network, data, and personnel plans).
  - *Restoration plan.* An approach to restoring the data center (e.g., the construction and site preparation schedule, and hardware/software and telecommunication acquisition plans.
- *Plan testing and review strategy.* An approach to ensuring the DRP is properly tested on a periodic basis.
- *DRP maintenance.* An organized approach to maintaining, updating, and storing the plan.
- *Phase IV—Test and maintain the DRP.* The objectives of this plan include:
  - Thoroughly testing the DRP to ensure that if a disaster were to occur, the organization could recover from it on a timely and efficient manner.
  - Developing an approach to maintaining the plan on a regular basis.

CONTROLLER'S ROLE

The controller and/or chief financial officer should play a key role in implementing and ensuring employee adherence to security policies. These individuals should be leaders in implementing security policies and monitoring compliance to them. Specifically, they should:

- Communicate security policies to all employees within their span of control. This can be achieved by developing a security awareness program, requiring employees to sign security agreements, and providing security training.
- Ensure employees understand security risks.

- Assess risk on a periodic basis.
- Verify that all IS assets are inventoried.
- Ensure that backups are regularly made and stored off-site.
- Review the disaster recovery plan on a regular (e.g., annual) basis and ensure it is tested annually.
- Verify that access authorizations are appropriate.
- Investigate security violations.
- Ensure that dismissed or transferred employees are removed from the system.
- Communicate a positive attitude toward security.
- Instigate periodical and independent audits or reviews of the organization's computer security.

The controller can delegate some of these functions to a security officer or other appropriate employee. However, he or she ultimately should be responsible for ensuring that these tasks are completed.

29

CHANGE MANAGEMENT

Most companies are undergoing significant change. Much of this change is dictated by business environments because companies must respond to competitor's improvements. The need to change has not escaped the controller's department. It is now very common for the controller to have several significant initiatives underway simultaneously, such as the implementation of a new financial system, a new chart of accounts, and new accounting-related processes. Information technology is quite frequently an area in which organizations make changes to enhance their competitive position in today's volatile business environment.

Frequently, companies are disappointed with the results of their projects. In fact, research has shown that the large majority (over 90 percent) of major projects fail to achieve their objectives on time and within budget. Some projects fail because they are abandoned before they can be installed. However, even if the project is completed, unless the original schedule and budget are achieved the benefits expected from it will have eroded—perhaps seriously.

Why do major projects fail to achieve their full potential so frequently? Interestingly, most of the time, the identified solution is adequate for addressing the problem or opportunity that exists. Consequently, a search for a better solution is not likely to improve the outcome. Instead, most failures are directly attributable to the implementation of the solution.

Most major projects involve changes to technology and business processes. These changes will affect the way people do their work—what they will do and how they will do it. Implementing a new financial system, for example, may require people to use new equipment, understand and navigate new software

---

This chapter was written by Sara Moulton-Reger, Senior Manager, IBM, Denver, Colorado.

packages, handle transactions in a different way, and use new types of information or report formats. In implementing such a project, careful consideration is typically given to the technology hardware platform, data and reporting requirements, interfaces, and the like. Although a high degree of care is devoted to these types of technical requirements, typically less than 5 percent of effort on projects is devoted to managing the effects these technical changes will have on people.

As human beings, we know that transition is uncomfortable. For organizations, it is extremely costly. One recent study shows that during transition, productive time is consumed by a large increase in both social gossip time and retraining requirements. This study showed that productive time during transition can be as little as 25 percent of its regular level. The data clearly show how important it is to manage transition issues so that regular productivity can be achieved as quickly as possible.

The practice of managing the human elements associated with projects is known as change management. Most companies struggle with change management; consequently, most projects fail to achieve their objectives on schedule and within the originally established budget. Although there may be some comfort in being part of the majority, a competitive opportunity exists for the companies that can increase their effectiveness in this difficult area.

IMPLEMENTATION HISTORY

Like people, organizations tend to follow the patterns they have established in the past. Consequently, a careful review of a company's implementation history is valuable for understanding the challenges posed by the current project. The most applicable patterns emerge when the current project is compared to recent projects that involved the same types of changes and/or the same groups of people.

In considering the organization's implementation history, it is important to identify facets that were effective as well as facets that were ineffective toward achieving project success. After this, the reasons behind effective and ineffective results should be explored. Both pieces of information are valuable. Overcoming past weaknesses is frequently an important key to achieving success on the current project. In addition, each organization has its own reasons for success, and these strengths should be used to fullest advantage. In considering implementation history, start by identifying the past projects that can provide valuable lessons learned for the current project. Categorize these projects by the level of success achieved. The categories may include projects where:

- Objectives were achieved on schedule and within budget.
- Objectives were achieved, but somewhat off schedule and/or over budget.
- Objectives were achieved, but significantly off schedule and/or over budget.
- Objectives were not achieved, although the project was implemented.
- Project was scrapped before installation.

After categorizing the projects, look for patterns to emerge in the way the project's implementation effort was managed. Ask the tough questions, such as:

- How realistic were the implementation budgets and schedules?
- What support, in addition to training, was given to the people who had to do their work differently as a result of the project?
- How much notice was given before the change took place?
- Were people given adequate time to learn their new activities while balancing regular work responsibilities?
- How much communication was there, and what types of communication methods appear to have been the most effective?
- In what ways were middle- and lower-level employees involved in the decision making process?
- How were people held accountable for performing the new job requirements?
- How were people rewarded for adequately performing the new job requirements?
- How effectively were the projects managed?
- How were unexpected events handled during implementation?
- How well did the organization focus on the project when day-to-day problems competed for people's attention?
- What are people's perceptions about the overall effectiveness of the organization's implementation history, and how could this perception positively or negatively affect the current project?

Although the exercise of considering past successes and failures can be difficult, and humbling, it can give the management team insight into the specific actions that should be managed for the current project to be successful. If the organization has a troubled implementation history, it is important to recognize that this can be extremely difficult to overcome. However, overcoming a troubled history is possible when the organization devotes itself to the extraordinary effort and attention to the human elements that will be necessary to overcome the deficiencies of the past.

In critically assessing their implementation histories, some companies discover that their employees have very long memories. Even problems that occurred many years ago can taint people's opinion of their organization's ability to be effective. As it assessed its implementation history, one private utility had to deal with employees recalling problems from nearly a decade earlier. To put a positive light to these long memories, the president reached back to a time when the organization was held in high respect by its employees. Members of the project team received pins that portrayed the company's logo from that positive time in its history. These pins brought prestige to the project and the members of the team. However, much more important than this symbol, the typically hands-off president stayed actively involved in project activities. This demonstration of sponsorship and support was viewed very positively as a step toward overcoming some of the company's more recent troubled implementations.

COMPETING PROJECTS

Many companies pursue a large number of initiatives at the same time. Aside from the resource drain and coordination problems that often exist, this agenda of initiatives frequently affects the same groups of people, who have little, if any, relief between project implementations. Too much change too quickly can leave people feeling shell shocked, which reduces productivity even beyond that normally expected during transition. People who feel overwhelmed are less productive, more prone to conflict, more likely to miss work, and the like. To make this concern even greater, it is important to remember that changes happening at work are only one type of change going on in a person's life at any given time. A person within the controller's office who is attempting to learn the new financial system may also be dealing with the birth of a child, an illness in the family, or a divorce.

To gain an appreciation for the total amount of change the organization is requiring of its people, it is important to take a full inventory of projects. It is not unusual for this exercise to produce an amazingly long list of projects. Then these projects may be analyzed from several perspectives.

- How well does each project support the strategic direction of the company and/or the long-term goals of the division or department? Are the strategic direction and long-term goals made clearer to the organization as these projects are rolled out?
- How well do the projects relate to and support each other? Do certain projects detract from other projects or from the goals of other departments or groups? Are there adequate connections between related projects? Are all affected groups adequately represented in the project teams or management advisory groups?
- Who are the people to be affected by each project and how significant will the impact be? What is the timing of the impact? Are there overlapping impacts and time frames that should be managed or reconsidered?
- Who will perceive that they win something as a consequence of the project? Who will perceive that they lose something?

Armed with this information, the management team needs to make the following determinations:

- What are the project priorities? What projects can be delayed or scrapped? What are realistic time frames for implementation, taking all projects and their overlapping impacts into consideration?

- How should projects with overlapping impacts or time frames be managed to help reduce the potential of overwhelming the people?
- How should project priorities and other important information such as strategic direction be communicated throughout the organization?

It is important to acknowledge that people have only a finite ability to accept change over a given period of time. When this ability is not adequately considered, the company will pay a price in lost productivity that exceeds what is necessary. One company chose to implement a fully integrated information system at the same time that its industry was deregulating and jobs were changing to accommodate the industry changes. The system changes were significant, and when added to the simultaneous job and departmental changes the effect was nearly disastrous. At one point, nearly half of the organization was involved in the Employee Assistance Program for problems such as severe stress, alcoholism, and the like. To assist with these problems, the company chose to employ change management activities in conjunction with documenting and confirming the processes required by the new system. Although the problems were smoothed out over time, the short-term situation could have been made less painful, and less costly, for the organization and its people if change management assistance had been employed before rather than after the system implementation.

DEGREE OF DISRUPTION

Most people are startled to discover that they actually do not resist change. Instead, they resist the disruption that change brings. This is an important distinction because people can resist projects that they believe in and want to see implemented. Consequently, measuring the degree of disruption is the first way to start predicting the degree of resistance expected from the project.

Measuring the degree of disruption caused by a project is not especially easy, and there are no exact quantitative means to do it. However, there are several specific questions that help to define the degree of disruption:

- How significantly will the project affect the way that people do their work?
- How easy will it be for people to understand the project and accurately predict how it will effect them?
- How much of the necessary knowledge and skills do people presently possess?
- How much will their daily routines differ after the project is implemented?
- How will the project affect the organization's power and influence structures?
- How much change has been expected of people in the past, and how willing have they been to embrace it?

In defining the degree of disruption, it is important to note that management frequently underestimates the degree of disruption a project will create in the lives of the people who are affected. For this reason, it is valuable to ask the people who will be affected for their answers to the same questions.

In defining disruption, two related considerations can be helpful. First, the organization's history with regard to change can help to define people's expectations about change. Second, organizations that have work forces who feel a high degree of time pressure may find virtually any change to be disruptive.

COST OF FAILURE

When a project fails, there are costs that will be paid by the organization. The most obvious ones include wasted time, money, and effort, and the fact that little or nothing was accomplished in addressing the problems and opportunities that launched the project. However, these costs actually may have less impact on the organization than the costs that may seem less obvious.

In addition to the financial costs associated with failure, there are others that are harder to define in financial terms. These costs include the potential for decreased morale, especially for the people who worked on the project and those who were highly committed to the project goals. Also, people may begin to doubt the organization's leadership. Ultimately, people may learn to ignore directives, believing that new projects will fail as did the ones in the past. These nonfinancial costs can have devastating effects on the ability to start and sustain projects.

The management team needs to carefully consider what would happen if the project were to fail to achieve its objectives on schedule and within budget. During this analysis it is especially important to assess the nonfinancial costs, because they can have the strongest impact on the organization. Because some projects are much more important to the organization than others, this type of analysis can help determine the projects that warrant the greatest degree of care, especially in the area of managing the people risks.

Once the costs associated with failure are considered, a very important question needs to be asked: Can the organization afford the cost of failure? If so, there may be more important initiatives that warrant increased emphasis and attention. If not, it is important to ensure that realistic schedules and budgets are produced and that significant effort is devoted to managing the human aspects of the project.

In one organization that undertook a significant reengineering initiative, the ten members of the executive staff were asked questions about the cost of failure. Then each executive was asked whether the organization could afford to fail at the effort. The results indicated that six of the executives felt that the project was mission critical and that they could not afford to fail. The other four, while believing the project was very important, felt that it was not critical to the organization. The correct answer was not as important as getting these key sponsors to agree to the criticality of the project. In this instance, these differences of opinion had begun affecting the project schedule and quality. The executives who believed that the organization could afford the project's failure were devoting inadequate resources to achieve the schedule and budget that had been approved.

Uncovering these types of differences early in the project life-cycle allows for reconciliation so that there will be minimal impacts to project objectives, schedules, and budgets.

RISKS

There are a series of elements that can help to define a project's risk from a change management perspective. Research has shown that active management of these risks is very beneficial for achieving project objectives on schedule and within budget. Applying the practices known to be associated with successful projects, as well as avoiding the mistakes others have made, can greatly enhance the potential for success on any project. The full list of these risk elements is rather lengthy, but making an effort to manage the following factors can be of great benefit:

- Adequacy of sponsorship.
- Adequacy of the motivation.
- Vision clarity.
- Degree of resistance.

Adequacy of Sponsorship

Sponsorship is the single most important change management risk factor. Without sponsorship that is adequately demonstrated, the project is virtually certain to fail to achieve its objectives on schedule and within budget. Most people within organizations know the importance of sponsorship, but it is difficult for many people to determine whether or not it will be effective.

When considering a project's sponsor, most people think of a member of top management or, perhaps, the person responsible for the day-to-day management of the project. In fact, if a project is to be successful, there must be a network of sponsors that moves down the entire management chain and it must start with the person or group of people who have the organizational power to start and stop the project. Managers and supervisors must also sponsor the project because they have direct access to the people who need to change as a result of the project's requirements. Managers and supervisors can also send strong messages about the project's importance by using managerial decisions such as promotion or advancement, compensation, and rewards to motivate people toward achievement of the project objectives.

The ultimate sponsor needs to work with his or her direct reports and other influential people within the organization to help them to understand the reasons for the project and its importance to the organization. Depending on the way the project was identified and launched, there may be the need to educate the ultimate sponsor in this important area. The ultimate sponsor also needs details about the vision. This is the first step in building the network of sponsors necessary to make the project successful.

A common misconception about sponsorship is that it can be delegated to others. Unless it is absolutely clear, and believed, that the project belongs to the person or people who have the authority to start and stop it, it is possible for people to give the project less priority and support than it needs to be successful. For this reason, sponsorship cannot be a spectator sport—it must be demonstrated by the right people to be effective. The following are some characteristics of effective sponsors:

- Effective sponsors devote adequate time and attention to communications about the project, its importance, its objectives, and its status.
- Effective sponsors make sacrifices to increase the likelihood of the project's success.
- Effective sponsors ensure that adequate resources are dedicated to the project and maintain these resources throughout the project. These resources include the time of specific key individuals from the organization, even if this choice affects other priorities.
- Effective sponsors are willing to make difficult staffing and personnel decisions, but only after they have empathetically considered the impact on the individuals and the organization. Frequently, sponsors must spend a great deal of time with specific individuals to help them to understand the importance of the project and what these people need to do—and not do—to make the project successful.

Finally, sponsors need to be aware that people listen to several things. First, they listen to what sponsors say and how they said it. Also, they listen to what the sponsors do *not* say. Finally, then listen to what the sponsors *do,* which has the strongest impact because it indicates the sponsor's true intent. In sponsoring a project, it is most important to carefully consider every action and make sure that people perceive these actions as consistent with achievement of the project objectives, schedule, and budget.

Adequacy of the Motivation

Transition is uncomfortable. In particular, transition attacks a person's feelings of confidence, competency, comfort, and control by replacing the known and familiar with the unknown and unfamiliar. It takes significant emotion and mental energy to learn new things and gain new habits. Consequently, people do not willingly initiate change if it does not appear necessary, or if the benefits do not outweigh the effort that will be required to make the transition. The more significant the transition will be, the more motivation a person will need to initiate and move through that transition.

Motivation is created by an understanding of problems that have to be addressed or opportunities that can be used advantageously. These problems or opportunities may either exist in the present or be expected in the future. For many people, problems create more motivation for change than opportunities. Also, existing conditions tend to be more motivational than anticipated conditions. However, adequate motivation can be created even for anticipated opportunities. The key to creating motivation is to focus on the reasons for making the change. In other words, what are the benefits to be gained by implementation of the project? Conversely, without implementation of the project, what would be lost? Frequently, communications about projects focus almost exclusively on details about the solution and neglect to build adequate motivation among people to make the transition to that solution.

As unusual as it sounds, to motivate people to change it is necessary to help them feel dissatisfied or uncomfortable with the way things are today. If people are comfortable with the way things are, they have little or no motivation to go through the discomfort of transition. Creating adequate motivation is a matter of helping people to see and feel how unacceptable it would be to maintain the status quo.

Building adequate motivation starts by an understanding of what the organization perceives about its current state. If people are dissatisfied with the way things are today, the necessary motivation may already exist. If, however, there are some people who are resistant to the project, a good first step in dealing with that resistance is to test their level of motivation.

Do people really understand what will happen if the project objectives are not achieved in a timely, cost-effective manner? Do people understand how they might be affected if the project were to be unsuccessful?

Do people really believe that the project will happen? What specifically can be done to overcome any skepticism that may exist?

Are people getting consistent messages from all levels of management and from different departments about the importance of the project?

Some activities that organizations have used to raise the degree of motivation toward a project include:

- Establishment of a standing agenda item for staff meetings to discuss the project status and development of periodic update packages for managers to present during these staff meetings.
- Periodic executive/top management departmental visits for question and answer sessions.
- Distribution of regular project updates to management and employees through a variety of different media, such as newsletters, memos, phone messages, and so on.
- Executive/top management one-on-one meetings with specific important, influential, and/or resistant people.

Vision Clarity

Once people are adequately motivated to achieve a project's objectives, they must see that the project's vision represents an answer to the problems or opportunities that make up their motivation. Feeling motivated to take action without knowing what to do gives people a hopeless or frustrated feeling. In essence, without a clear vision, people are being asked to move toward something that they do not understand nor believe will bring the relief they seek. In this situation most people will do nothing, but some people will take action to relieve the anxiety they feel. However, without a vision to guide them, it is very unlikely that even the people who do move forward will arrive at the desired end.

Most executives understand the need to provide a vision to their people. However, where most project visions fall short of their goal is in providing people with a clear picture of what the future will look and feel like. In other words, what will be each person's daily working conditions once that vision is fulfilled? Frequently, visions contain lofty concepts, platitudes, and politically correct language. Although few people would disagree with these visions, even fewer people know how to create and work toward them. Effective visions are built with an understanding that their purpose is to target people's actions. This requires visions to be clear and actionable.

Creating an effective vision requires time. It also must involve the sponsors of the project to a great extent to ensure that the visionaries behind the project are revealing their expectations and ideas about the future. The vision needs to answer several important questions, such as:

- What are the objectives this vision seeks to achieve?
- What are the detailed changes that will occur, and what is the timing or staging of these changes?
- What are the requirements for achieving the vision?
- What will be the daily working conditions for specific job categories after implementation of the vision? For example:
  — What equipment and procedures will people use?
  — What types of decisions will they make?
  — How will they interact with others to perform their jobs?
  — How will their performances be evaluated, compensated, and rewarded?
  — How will the departments, groups, and teams be structured?
  — What knowledge and skills will be necessary to perform the work?

Evaluating these questions in detail with the sponsors and project team is an important clarification step in any project. One project team discovered firsthand the importance of taking the time to clarify its vision in this manner. After presentation of the vision to the sponsors, it was approved. The team carefully documented its approved vision, primarily to enable its easy communication to groups that had not been involved in its development. However, when it was presented in the new written format augmented with more details, the vision was found to differ from the expectations and understanding of the sponsors. This problem was discovered and corrected quickly, and the potential for wasted effort was avoided.

After the vision is documented it must be communicated, so that people understand it and its impact. One way that organizations have used to communicate their visions is to give their employees day-in-the-life information. In other words, describe what life will be like for certain departments or jobs using fictitious newspaper articles written in the future, role plays, prototype tools, and so on. Also, recognize that communicating a vision effectively requires repetition using multiple means, because communication mechanisms are not all equally effective, nor do they all reach the intended audience with the desired message.

One final note about communicating a vision—as people begin to understand the future, they will also begin to understand the disruption it will cause. Until a vision is fairly well understood, it is common for very little resistance to be felt from the organization. However, once the vision and its corresponding disruption is understood, the organization frequently displays resistance for the first time. This can leave the sponsors and project team wondering if there is something wrong because things may have seemed relatively smooth up to that point. This is an important time to carefully distinguish between real objections based on content versus the objections that represent resistance to the disruption and manage each accordingly.

Degree of Resistance

To repeat an important concept: people do not resist change; rather they resist the disruption caused by the change. This concept is important in explaining why people will resist a change that they view positively, and perhaps even initiated themselves. For this reason, resistance must be expected and planned for because it cannot be avoided. It is also important to note that resistance is not necessarily an indication that something is wrong. Instead, it is frequently an indication that people understand what they are being asked to do and, correspondingly, what it will take for the project to be accomplished. From this perspective, resistance may be a good indication that effective communication has taken place.

Resistance has a variety of causes. Some of the most common ones are:

- Confusion about the project vision.
- Inadequate motivation.
- Unclear or inconsistent messages from sponsors and other key individuals about the importance of the project (e.g., changing or conflicting priorities).
- Poor implementation history.
- Lack of adequate time to respond to and absorb the changes.
- Organization's history of failing to deal adequately with people who ignore project directives.

It is important to create an environment in which resistance can be expressed openly without fear of retribution. Suppressed resistance will still effect the project's goals negatively but will be much more difficult to uncover and manage.

Resistance is addressed by first identifying its source. One source of resistance is lack of knowledge and skills to perform to the new expectations. This contributes to a person's feelings of inadequacy and incompetence. This type of resistance is addressed through education and training. A just in time philosophy of education and training is especially effective because it enables the person to use the knowledge and skills soon after learning them. The second source of resistance comes from a lack of willingness to perform the project's requirements. Addressing resistance from this source involves answering these questions:

- Does the person really understand the need for the change? (See *Adequacy of the motivation.*)
- Are there any inconsistencies that need to be corrected? (See *Adequacy of Sponsorship and Vision Clarity.*)
- Are there adequate rewards for performing to project requirements and consequences for neglecting or performing poorly against those same requirements?

The final step requires that specific measures to assess project progress and individual achievement of project expectations be developed. Then, achievement against those measures must be assessed periodically. This step also requires a commitment to following up with people on the results of those assessments—by giving either rewards that are valuable to them or consequences that will be motivational toward improvements in the future. This type of program can be difficult to administer because it involves having to confront nonperformance, which most people find unsettling. However, allowing people to resist a project willingly and successfully invites its failure.

INDEX